A former playing member of MCC, Richard Tomlinson read History at Cambridge before pursuing an award-winning career as an editor and writer on the staff of the *Independent* and as *Fortune* magazine's China correspondent. He is the author of *Divine Right*, a history of the House of Windsor. As a cricketer, he once played on a ground where W.G. appeared – Gravesend, not Lord's.

'Grace remains a formidable challenge for biographers, and Richard Tomlinson's exhaustively researched *Amazing Grace* gets us closer to both the man and the cricketer than before, demolishing myths in considerable style'
Huw Richards, *Guardian*, Books of the Year

'My biography of the year ... a revelatory study of the giant who remains cricket's most iconic figure'
Tom Holland, *Evening Standard*

'Richard Tomlinson's new biography of the Grand Old Man of English cricket succeeds handsomely in fleshing out the nature of W.G.'s extraordinary celebrity. He captures the essential sweetness of a man who, in semi-retirement, approached his role as the manager of Eltham Cricket Club's Second XI with Captain Mainwaring-like levels of intensity. Industrious, witty, insightful, *Amazing Grace* ought to be the standard work on W.G. for years to come'
Sam Kitchener, *Independent*

'A compelling book that uncovers a man as complex and contrary as any in Victorian society'
Michael Simkins, *Mail on Sunday*

'*Amazing Grace* is a fluently humour and sympathy, that as much pleasure' David

AMAZING GRACE

GRACE

The Man who was W.G.

RICHARD TOMLINSON

ABACUS

ABACUS

First published in Great Britain in 2015 by Little, Brown
This paperback edition published in 2016 by Abacus

1 3 5 7 9 10 8 6 4 2

A CIP catalogue record for this book
is available from the British Library.

ISBN 978-0-349-13984-5

Typeset in Bembo by M Rules
Printed and bound in Great Britain by
Clays Ltd, St Ives plc

Papers used by Abacus are from well-managed forests
and other responsible sources.

MIX
Paper from
responsible sources
FSC® C104740

Abacus
An imprint of
Little, Brown Book Group
Carmelite House
50 Victoria Embankment
London EC4Y 0DZ

An Hachette UK Company
www.hachette.co.uk

www.littlebrown.co.uk

For my parents

CONTENTS

PREFACE

Eltham, South-East London, 1914

In the spring of 1914, when he was nearly sixty-six, Dr W.G. Grace acquired a new job. 'I shall have to keep you up to the mark etc.,' he wrote, with a hint of menace, to the secretary of Eltham Cricket Club, on hearing he was to run the second eleven. 'Now re ground, it is in a bad state and will want more doing to it than last year.'

Most days W.G. wandered over to Eltham CC's Chapel Farm ground near his home in the south-east London suburbs. 'If we do not get some fine weather we shall never get the ground in decent trim,' he reported back to the club secretary. He despaired of Eltham's footballers, who had messed up the cricket outfield: 'I hope you have told them they cannot play next Saturday.' Worse, a local hockey club wanted to sublet another part of the playing area. 'The Hockey ground must not be wider than 50 yds or you will spoil the cricket centre,' W.G. warned in another scribbled note.

At last the ground was ready for Eltham Second XI's opening game of the season against Lewisham Wanderers CC. W.G.'s team won by 64 runs, with the captain (who scored 2 not out) batting down the order to assess the performance of his 'colts', a term he now used for any cricketer younger than about twenty-five.

Afterwards, whisky and soda in hand, W.G. probably made his usual early season enquiries about unpaid subscriptions. 'Very little mercy indeed should be shown to defaulters,' he advised schoolboys who were thinking of starting a cricket club.

Eltham's weekend cricketers knew that while W.G. was managing them, they needed to manage him. For the past four seasons he had been the club's oldest, keenest and, frankly, most meddlesome player, on and off the field, keeping the committee 'up to the mark' on: the state of the pavilion ('The roof really wants tarring'); an unsightly boundary hedge ('Only clipped about three parts of the way'); paying the groundsman ('Please attend to this without delay'); the following season's fixture list ('I notice you have Bexley down to play on May 16th, is this all right?'); and much else besides. 'The best way to tackle the old man is to disarm him with geniality,' Alfred Jackson, Eltham CC's club captain, advised Bryan Egerton, the secretary, after another barrage of notes from W.G.

Yet, once he turned up to play for Eltham CC, W.G. expected no special favours for all his hard work. One afternoon a passer-by strolling across a park near Woolwich spotted W.G. sitting patiently on a bench with his team-mates as he waited for his turn to bat, 'like "a wind blowing out of the past".' It was as if, in the same park almost a century later, a spectator were to see Bobby Charlton lining up for the kick-off with a pub football team.

In his day W.G. was more famous than any other celebrity in the British Empire, fêted from Toronto to Sydney. Measuring Grace's fame is an imprecise science but here are some yardsticks. A search using the term 'W.G. Grace' in the British Library's online newspaper database produces about 43,000 press articles for the period 1850–99, more than double the number for Sarah Bernhardt, hailed as 'the most famous actress the world has ever known'. In Philadelphia in 1872 the American Civil War hero (and cricket fan) General George Meade sought out the twenty-four-year-old W.G. at a banquet. Grace, not Meade, was the reason why several hundred guests paid to attend the dinner, hoping to catch a glimpse of the man the Philadelphia press described, in capitals, as 'THE CHAMPION BATSMAN OF THE WORLD'. Arriving at Adelaide in 1891 at the start of a speaking tour, the explorer Henry Morton Stanley waited on board to be greeted by his customary welcoming party. Well-wishers 'rushed' the decks of the boat but ignored Stanley in their haste to shake the hand of W.G. at the start of his second Australian cricket tour. Stanley at least had the consolation of knowing that in Australia he, like W.G., would be endorsing Goodfellow's Coca Water, a 'medicinal stimulant' to treat vomiting and alcoholism.

The cricketer who upstaged Stanley was still instantly recognisable in his mid-sixties, when he played his last-ever season at Eltham. By then Grace – who stood 6 feet 2 inches (1.88 metres) tall – had put on so much weight that he was close to 20 stone (127 kilograms). His beard was the giveaway. Now grey, a little straggly, it remained the trademark of the greatest cricketer of all time as he lumbered around the playing fields of south-east London. W.G. was unmistakable, except when people came to judge the man behind the beard.

Half a century earlier Grace posed for a publicity portrait in a photographer's studio, almost certainly for money (see page xiii). The picture was probably taken in 1866, the year W.G., still only eighteen, scored a double-century at the Oval and, during the same match, won a hurdles race at Crystal Palace; or perhaps in 1867, when he might have died from scarlet fever. This teenage wonder was poised to become the 'Leviathan', the 'greatest cricketer of his or any other age'. Yet W.G.'s posthumous fate was to be patronised and at times actively disparaged.

Born in Gloucestershire, Grace came to be seen as 'rustic', or 'of pure country strain', as the cricket broadcaster and writer John Arlott described him in 1948 on the centenary of his birth. Curiously, Grace counted no one in his family or immediate ancestry who lived off the land. His people were mostly doctors and teachers from in and around Bristol. Grace's home village of Downend was a semi-industrialised suburb of the city, while his supposedly 'West Country' accent – he pronounced 'Alfred' as 'Allfred' – was more accurately described as a Bristol dialect.

Arlott was a townsman from Basingstoke who assumed that because W.G.'s roots were in the soil, Grace's cricket must have been 'instinctive'. To be fair to Arlott, a great cricket journalist, he was only picking up a theme developed by W.G.'s first posthumous biographer Bernard Darwin. A superb writer on golf, Darwin (Eton and Oxford) initially thought W.G. 'simpleminded' and did not adjust his view significantly. From Darwin and Arlott, it was a short leap to Marylebone Cricket Club's official history, published in 1987, which concluded that Grace 'had a simple, almost puerile mind' – an astonishing verdict for MCC to pass on the club's most illustrious member.

It was all untrue. Grace had a deeply analytical, creative mind, as is instantly plain from his own writing on cricket, as distinct from the turgid, ghostwritten prose that fills out most of his two, often unreliable memoirs. It helps to think of him, just a little, as one of the great Victorian inventors. 'When you block,' he told schoolboys, 'infuse a little power into what you do, and do not be content to stop the ball by simply putting the bat in its way – anyone can do that – but try and score off it too.'

As this passage from a children's encyclopedia indicates, Grace was not merely original. His approach to cricket was consciously subversive, ignoring the coaching manual when he could find a better and quicker way to score runs, take wickets, and win. He was, quite startlingly, modern. The youth who gazed back at the photographer for his studio portrait – holding a pose that bore no resemblance to his dynamic, unorthodox batting stance – would have walked into England's one-day cricket team today.

The same teenager was conventionally described as the product of everyone else: his mother, hailed implausibly as W.G.'s formative cricket 'tutor'; his elder brother Ted (E.M.), an utterly different and inferior batsman; and even the Gloucestershire soil that nurtured him, according to the writer Neville Cardus. Yet Grace, like Bradman, was in essence a self-made genius. Apart from early coaching by his Uncle Alfred, W.G. ploughed

Self-made genius
The teenage W.G. takes time off from practice in an early publicity still. 'I had to work as hard at learning cricket as I ever worked at my profession, or anything else.' (Mildew Design Ltd/REX)

a solitary cricketing path, relying on brain power rather than 'instinct' to reach unprecedented sporting heights. As he wrote in another essay: 'Great scores at cricket, like great work of any kind are, as a rule, the result of years of careful and judicious training and not accidental occurrences.'

Grace took cricket so seriously that it is easy to accuse him of losing his sense of proportion; a batsman's innings, after all, is not a Beethoven symphony or a portrait by Rembrandt. Yet Grace's immense fame demands that he, too, is taken seriously, for his long, turbulent career raised questions at every stage about the nature of sport and its place in life.

The slim, athletic teenager who posed for the photographer grew up in a society in which sport in general, and cricket especially, straddled two contrasting cultures. On one side professional cricketers, mostly artisans and small tradesmen, earned a living in the summer by touring the country, playing beery, uncompetitive games against local teams with as many as twenty-two players to even the odds. Meanwhile, 'gentlemen' amateurs from the great public schools and the two ancient universities subscribed to a muscular Christian, Corinthian ethos where cricket was about honour and morality, not winning at any cost. To play billiards or any sport 'pre-eminently well is the life's work of a man who, in learning to do so, can hardly have continued to be a gentleman in the best sense of the word,' the novelist Anthony Trollope cautioned in a compendium of British sports and pastimes in 1868. Ever the populist, Trollope knew what his audience wanted to hear.

W.G. exploded both cultures. For him, winning was the *only* thing that mattered, even at the expense of people he liked. Today his attitude seems remarkably modern; he was indeed, arguably, the first truly modern international sports star. At the time, Grace troubled contemporaries who saw cricket as a 'manly', honourable game, because part of the thrill of watching him came from his habit of playing right up against the edge of the rules – and sometimes beyond.

One incident above all captures W.G. at his best and worst, depending on the point of view. On 29 August 1882 Grace, who was fielding, ran out the Australian batsman Sam Jones, who had wandered absent-mindedly out of his ground, thinking the ball was 'dead'. At issue was whether Grace should have warned Jones not to make the mistake again – normal etiquette in cricket – or successfully appealed for a run-out to the umpire, which he did.

But what happened next, in front of a packed Oval crowd of twenty thousand, was more significant. W.G. electrified the game, triggering several hours of unbearable excitement as the Australian Fred Spofforth produced one of the greatest spells of fast bowling to win the match and gain revenge for Grace's 'cheating'. Without Spofforth's performance, England would probably have won the game; they only needed 85 to win. The London *Sporting Times* would never have published a mock-obituary for English cricket, and, several months later in Melbourne, some ladies would not have burned a cricket bail, popped it in an urn and presented it to the visiting England captain. On this trajectory, W.G.'s 'cheating' was the flame that lit the bail and created the 'Ashes', the greatest – and often the most rancorous – of all international sporting series.

Grace presents the same dilemma for sports moralists as John McEnroe, the great American tennis player of the 1980s, who – like W.G. – protested often to umpires when line calls went against him *and* was compulsively watchable; or the champion jockey Lester Piggott, whose obsession with winning prompted repeated stewards' enquiries over his rough riding tactics and overuse of the whip.

In Grace's lifetime few critics outside Australia dared publicly accuse him of outright cheating. Instead, W.G.'s detractors focused on what seems at first glance a more straightforward issue, his 'shamateurism'. In formal terms the charge is unarguable: W.G. played more or less openly for money while claiming the status of a gentleman amateur.

Behind the charge sheet, however, Grace's financial situation was altogether less secure than the press or later biographers realised. W.G.'s wife Agnes was the daughter of a bankrupt lithographer with nine surviving siblings. His mother died literally penniless, with a net worth of £0, while his childhood cricket coach and uncle Alfred Pocock lived in later years off his Grace relatives, after being bankrupted by a lead-making venture. W.G.'s anxiety about money had a context.

Many other Victorian gentlemen amateurs were 'shamateurs'. MCC's entrepreneurial secretary Robert Fitzgerald wrote cricket books for money, forced the club to pay him a salary, and set up a private Lord's Grand Stand Company to milk revenues from the 'gate'. So Grace was not an exception. He was, though, surprisingly incompetent with money for someone constantly accused of avarice.

Unlike the Australian batting genius Don Bradman, or, from another sport, the golfer Arnold Palmer, W.G. was simply no good at business or, even at the most basic level, holding on to the cash in his pocket. He sprayed tips on children who approached him in the street, he bet on the horses and he did not trust himself to invest in the stock market.

Grace needed expert advice and the kind of personal back office that modern sports stars take for granted: at a minimum a secretary to handle his correspondence, a public relations agent to get the press off his back and a professional agent to negotiate contracts, sponsorship deals and endorsements, and advise on his all-important Twitter feed. In the nineteenth century no such job descriptions existed. W.G. was probably the first-ever sportsman to lend his image to a household product that had nothing to do with his sport – a Colman's Mustard tin. As such he broke new commercial ground, while proving comically inept at exploiting his fame. It is not even certain that Colman's ever paid him for its cleverly 'paintshopped' picture of a slimmer W.G.

The basis for W.G.'s fame can be boiled down to one astounding statistic. By the time he was twenty-seven, Grace had scored fifty first-class centuries. He performed this feat at a time when pitches were so poor, and cricket gear so flimsy, that batsmen risked their lives whenever they took guard. In one match at Lord's – a ground where he would pick stones out of the rutted pitch – W.G. scored a hundred and then saw another batsman killed by a ball that smashed his head.

Much later an ingenious cricket statistician, Irving Rosenwater, calculated that one had to add up all the hundreds scored by the next *thirteen* most successful first-class batsmen in the previous decade to match W.G.'s tally of fifty. In cricket it was not until Don Bradman in the 1930s that another batsman achieved W.G.'s towering superiority; and Bradman, unlike Grace, scored most of his runs on good pitches for batting. Even today, the young W.G. still seems the only batsman worth even discussing as comparable to 'The Don'.

In hindsight W.G.'s first-class centuries were regarded as a triumphal procession, all the way from number 1, for an 'England' team against Surrey at the Oval in 1865, to number 126, for his London County team against MCC at Crystal Palace on his fifty-sixth birthday in 1904. The only hiccups were numbers 37 and 63, which many modern cricket statisticians, with some reason, claim were scored in non first-class matches. In truth W.G.'s career almost stalled before it really began, because of the obstacle presented by MCC's refusal to elect him a member for four years after his first-class debut.

All W.G.'s frustration is summed up by one moment, shortly after midday on Monday, 25 May 1868. At Lord's the Surrey batsmen Harry Jupp and Thomas Humphrey walked out of the pavilion to open the innings against MCC in the curtain-raiser for the first-class season. Eighty miles down the train line in Swindon, W.G. walked on to the Great Western Railway Club's cricket field to take on twenty-two railwaymen in a dreary professional game.

W.G. was stranded in Swindon for two specific geographical and social reasons. In 1932 Neville Cardus declared fruitily of Grace that 'he came from out of the West Country, and though in time his empire stretched from Lord's to Melbourne, never did he forget the open air of Gloucestershire, and the flavours of his birthplace'. While W.G. loved his county, as a young man he probably cursed the day he was ever born there. Gloucestershire in the 1860s had no first-class county club, and, under cricket's strict eligibility rules at the time, W.G. could not play for another first-class county side. His only route to regular top cricket was to join MCC, but here Grace encountered another problem. As the son of a provincial doctor, W.G. came from the wrong social background in the eyes of MCC's aristocratic committee, which approved all candidates for membership. In the end W.G. forced his way into MCC because Fitzgerald wanted to fill his fine new grandstand at Lord's – as did MCC's committee, which forcibly repurchased the grandstand from Fitzgerald in 1869, the year W.G. was elected.

And then, just as Grace peaked, he began to wreck his body. By the mid-1870s he had bulked up to about 16 stone (102 kilograms). A decade later he was a bloated hulk who gasped for breath whenever he chased the ball or ran a quick single. Before he turned forty the press and fellow cricketers had nicknamed him the 'Old Man' of cricket, an impression reinforced by his grey-speckled beard. W.G.'s startling physical decline prompts an unlikely thought: he could have been so much better.

Sporting legends in disintegration inspire different reactions, from the poignancy of Muhammad Ali's struggle with crippling disease to the sense of waste surrounding George Best's alcoholism. In W.G.'s case the feeling left is of someone trying to cope with sustained, occasionally unbearable stress; 'Good old W.G.', a kind of latter-day cricketing Falstaff, seems a front to disguise more complex emotions.

As Grace ages the sightings of him at the table or in his cups become unmistakably darker. He wolfs food compulsively, working his way at one banquet through 'stewed pigeons, saddles of mutton and haunches of venison' – and that was just the start of the menu. He drinks whisky and soda in the lunch interval to fuel him through the afternoon's play. His eyes dart around the lunch table, making sure everyone has their glass full and their plate piled high, so he is not eating and drinking alone.

W.G.'s gluttony and semi-secret drinking (the Victorian temperance movement claimed him as a teetotaller) were perhaps a self-defeating attempt to cope with increasing competitive pressure, as a series of brilliant, younger batsmen challenged and then surpassed him in the 1880s and 1890s. Grace may also have been seeking release from deepening private sorrows as he grew older. He could have allowed his troubles to engulf him and so abandon the game he loved. Instead, he took the opposite road and carried on playing cricket, all the way down from his last Test match at Nottingham in 1899 – when a section of the crowd jeered him for being too fat – to his last games at Eltham in the summer of 1914. He did it because he just wanted a game of cricket; after his wife and four children, cricket was the love of his life. Once he was too old and lame to play at first-class level, he was ever available for W.G. Grace's XI (captain: W.G. Grace), Eltham CC or anyone else who would have him.

Being W.G., he could not help making a point: he showed how cricket or any sport could be a solace for the sorrows and disappointments of life. He descended with dignity into the ranks of local cricket in the years leading up to the First World War, when all around London and the Home Counties cricket, golf and tennis clubs were sprouting up to cater for a new class of weekend sportsmen (and women), who played for fun. 'It will be a jolly match, do try and come,' W.G. wheedled a friend in 1914 as he tried to 'get up' a side.

The night before this fixture Grace turned up for an MCC banquet during a match to mark the centenary of Lord's transfer to its present St John's Wood Road site. To his fellow guests' amusement, the Old Man had a sticking plaster over his right eye. He had been fielding in a game against Goldsmith's College, W.G. explained, when a ball bounced and hit him on the eyebrow. Would he be attending the next day's play at Lord's? Regrettably, no, W.G. replied. He was off to Woolwich for his 'jolly' game against the Army Ordnance Corps.

As W.G. left the banquet his fellow MCC guests were looking at a stranger. W.G. did not want to revel in past glories or
celebrate pompous anniversaries. He loved cricket so much that
he wanted to play for ever.

1

BECOMING W.G.

At the age of about ten, Gilbert Grace, as he was always known to his family, went to board at Ridgway House school in the village of Stapleton, a few miles north-east of Bristol. Ridgway House was the home of the Reverend Henry Malpas, an Oxford graduate who supplemented his income by running an 'academy' for local boys. Like his competitors in the area, Malpas offered a solid vocational education for pupils whose parents lacked the income and social status to send their sons to Eton, Harrow or one of the other public schools. Gilbert and his classmates were generally destined for the army, the navy, farming or one of the professions, and Malpas tailored his curriculum to their needs. At Ridgway House the boys studied military engineering, navigation and 'agricultural chemistry', as well as maths, classics and French. More unusually, Malpas employed a German teacher, Herr Adelbert Bertelheim. This education did not come cheap. Malpas charged an annual fee of £60 for boarding pupils, about the same as a Gloucestershire plumber or bricklayer might hope to earn in a year.

Gilbert and his younger brother Fred, who also attended Ridgway House, were set to become doctors, like their father and three elder brothers. This much is certain about Gilbert's education, which included earlier spells at Miss Trotman's school in Downend and another boys' academy in the nearby village of Winterbourne. He learned to write plain, vigorous English in a clear, legible hand, his instantly recognisable prose quite different from the flowery language later used by his ghostwriters. When a subject engaged him, Gilbert also possessed formidable powers of concentration. The proof would lie in his ability to bat for hour after hour on the lethally unpredictable pitches of the 1860s. 'Patience I found to be my greatest friend,' he recalled of these early innings, when still in his mid-teens. 'Perseverance' was another word Grace used several times to sum up his approach to batting. 'I had to work as hard at learning cricket as I ever worked at my profession, or anything else.'

It is impossible to say whether Gilbert bestowed the same attention on classwork at Malpas's academy. According to Methven Brownlee, Grace's friend and authorised biographer, Gilbert was known at Ridgway House as 'a steady working lad, accurate at mathematics, with no mischief in him, passionately fond of [collecting] eggs and snakes'. This sanitised picture provides no real guide to Gilbert's academic ability, despite one former Ridgway House teacher also saying he was good at maths. Since the teacher was David Bernard, who became Grace's brother-in-law, his testimony was not objective.

It is clear, though, that Gilbert's village school background did not automatically mean he was poorly educated. His education at Ridgway House was arguably no worse, and possibly better, than the schooling received by his later cricketing friend Lord Harris, who went to Eton and Christ Church, Oxford. By his own account, Harris did almost nothing at Eton in the 1860s except play sport: 'Very good at racquets & cricket & fencing, swimming & walking; only useful at football, & fair at fives.' Harris was so backward academically that he failed to get into Oxford, even though his admission ought to have been a for-mality. 'I rushed back to London to my father & poured out my sorrow to him, but he was as dear as possible, & told me not to let it spoil my cricket.' Thanks to a private tutor, Harris scraped into Christ Church on his second attempt, '& soon made my mark as a real good rider'.

Grace was not an intellectual in the academic sense, any more than the unscholarly Harris. Yet it was not true that 'no one ever had a more unanalytic brain', as another Old Etonian cricketer, Edward Lyttelton, remarked of the young Grace. No one ever had a more 'analytic' or inventive brain than Grace on a cricket field, as he dismantled shots in his head and devised new ways to make them more effective, or fooled yet another batsman into believing his gentle slow bowling was as innocuous as it appeared. He just did not choose to parade his knowledge and so lose his advantage over opponents.

Bernard Darwin realised from first-hand observation of Grace in later life that dismissing him as a village school dunce would not do. Some other quality was needed to explain W.G.'s ability to 'read' a game or size up an opponent: 'By instinct or genius – call it what you will – he could form a judgement of a cricketer to which all others bowed ... He had that sort of quickness of apprehension that may, without disrespect, perhaps be called cunning, and is often to be found, a little surprisingly, in those who seem at first sight simple-minded and almost rustic.'

Darwin, however, fell into another common misapprehension about Grace, based on his supposedly rural 'Gloucestershire' accent and his love of hunting and shooting. Grace's roots were far too ambiguous to be classified as either 'rustic' or urban.

Grace's father Dr Henry Grace, born in 1808, grew up in the village of Long Ashton, barely three miles from Bristol, where his mother Elizabeth, originally a lady's maid, ran a small 'dame' school for young girls. Meanwhile her husband, also called Henry, remained in service as a butler for the aristocratic Smyth family, which lived some of the time at Ashton Court outside the village. The younger Henry Grace qualified as a doctor in London, returned to Bristol and in 1831 married Martha Pocock, whose father ran a boys' 'academy' on Prospect Hill in the centre of the city. The thoroughly urban Martha Grace (as she became) had no connection at all with agriculture and probably spoke with a Bristol city accent.

Henry and Martha Grace settled in Downend, about four miles north-east of Bristol, living from about 1834 at Downend House on the main street running through the village. It was easy for later writers to be fooled by Downend's bucolic-sounding name into thinking that Grace grew up in some Gloucestershire rural idyll. W.G.'s recollection of Downend was more dismissive: 'It was a small scattered village, and tourists when they travelled that way rarely paid it the compliment of staying long in it.'

By the time he was born there in July 1848, Downend was best described as a semi-industrial suburb of Bristol. In one direction the village looked towards the surrounding country-side. In the other direction Downend faced Bristol. As well as his private practice, Henry Grace worked as a Poor Law parish medical officer for an area that stretched all the way into the city. He was also surgeon to one of the coal mines that dotted Bristol's eastern hinterland.

Downend's double identity as a suburban village places W.G. in his natural milieu. As an adult Grace seems to have felt most at home with one foot planted metaphorically in the town and the other in the countryside, for he grew up in a setting where the distinction between the two was blurred. A photograph of Grace in the 1890s in MCC's archive at Lord's (sadly too faded to publish) sums up his geographic ambivalence. He is waiting with his beloved Clifton Beagles club for the start of the hunt, and is looking down quizzically at the bloodhounds all around him. Clifton's handsome mid-Victorian buildings loom behind W.G., for this is where the hunt assembled – right in the city centre.

As a boy growing up in Downend, Gilbert would soon have become aware of why his father took any medical jobs he could find. Gilbert's father was not poor, but he was financially stretched. Dr Grace received an annual salary of about £80 as a Poor Law medical officer and, in total, probably earned at least another £200 per year in the 1850s and 1860s from private patients' fees and stipends from various posts. This was a solid income, placing Henry Grace securely in Bristol's professional class, at about the same level as his surviving sister Elizabeth's husband Walter Pigeon, who was a solicitor. Yet Dr Grace's large family drained his resources. He sent all five of his sons – Henry, Alfred, Ted, Gilbert and Fred – to private 'academies' and then to Bristol Medical School. Meanwhile his daughters – Annie, Fanny, Alice and Blanche – received the kind of village education that would allow them to marry respectably.

Henry and Martha Grace, who had no money of her own, needed every penny he could make. 'My father had to make his way in life, and was at the beck and call of every sick person within a radius of twelve miles,' Grace recalled. 'He had not an hour he could call his own. The early morning saw him riding six miles eastward; at midnight he was often six miles to the west.'

All his life W.G. fretted about money, proving a fearsomely difficult negotiator in any contractual discussions. His detractors looked at the various jackpots that came his way, notably from two Australian tours and two testimonial funds, and concluded that he was naturally avaricious. This portrayal in any case jarred with Grace's unmiserly habit of spraying half-crown tips wherever he went; he was about the softest touch for any Bristol street urchin in the 1880s and 1890s. It is more likely that his bouts of financial insecurity derived from the memory of growing up in a household that lived on an extremely tight budget.

More alarmingly, young Gilbert would have learned fairly soon that his extended clan included several bankrupts and indigents. When his maternal grandfather George Pocock died in 1843, one of Pocock's sons, also called George, took over the academy on St Michael's Hill. By 1847 the younger George had gone bust. He put the school up for sale, while a local brewer and butcher took over his debts in return for interest payments.

In 1851 George Pocock's brother Alfred, who ran a small lithography shop on Wine Street in Bristol, decided to have another go at marketing the 'charvolant', a strange kite-powered carriage invented by their late father. Alfred enlisted his sister

Rose, a talented illustrator, to draw sketches of the charvolant in motion, and her schoolmaster husband became the carriage's London sales agent. The partners failed to sell a single model, with Alfred eventually lugging his own charvolant up the hill from Bristol to Downend for Gilbert and his friends to ride around the village lanes when the wind was up.

'Uncle Pocock', as Gilbert called him, married a widow called Mary Johnson in 1857, but when she died soon afterwards, he took to spending much of the time in Downend. By the early 1860s his lithography business was down to just one disgruntled customer, a 'Mr Chick', who was fed up with Alfred's constant absences. In 1862 Alfred sold the shop to a competitor and went back into business with Rose's husband, who had abandoned schoolmastering and was now settled in Worcestershire. The two partners sunk all their savings in the Patent Blue and Black Lead Works near Kidderminster, convinced that lead-manufacturing was the next big thing. They were wrong, going bankrupt within two years of patenting their unique selling point, 'a block of black lead'. Rose Gilbert, Alfred's sister, became her family's main breadwinner, running a small 'dame' school out of their home. Alfred moved in with his Grace in-laws, drifting from one member of the family to the next as a permanent lodger who paid no rent.

Viewed through the young Gilbert Grace's eyes, it would have been natural to see his various maternal uncles as a little feckless, prone to money-making schemes that never quite materialised. His father was in a sense more troubling as a financial role model, because Henry Grace was not quite what he outwardly seemed: a pillar of the local Downend community.

Some years after setting up his practice in Downend, Dr Grace posed for a photograph (see first picture section), possibly in the drawing room of the family home. The picture speaks of a man who has arrived socially and professionally. Dr Grace holds his silk top hat in his left hand, signalling that he is a person of some substance – just the type, indeed, to appoint as a trustee for someone else's estate. Henry Grace's elderly mother took exactly this course in 1849 when she named him as a trustee for her will, in which she left about £400 in government bonds to her daughter Elizabeth. Curiously, she left nothing to Henry, her other surviving child, implying that the elder Elizabeth Grace thought her reliable doctor son could be trusted to look after himself and his growing family. If so, she misread him, for behind the façade, Dr Grace was a bit of a chancer.

In the 1840s he was the proud owner of Cock-a-Hoop, a handsome chestnut horse that he rode with South Gloucestershire's Berkeley and Beaufort hunts. Top of the market hunters like Cock-a-Hoop regularly fetched more than £50 at auction in mid-nineteenth-century Bristol, or, put another way, most of Henry's salary as Poor Law medical officer. After Cock-a-Hoop, Henry owned a series of other hunters till the end of his life, keeping his fine horses in the stable with the pony that Martha kept for her trap.

The socially ambitious Henry probably justified Cock-a-Hoop and its successors as a pardonable extravagance, because his regular outings on his hunters brought him into contact with the local South Gloucestershire landed gentry. After the Beaufort hunt Henry and the other riders were sometimes invited back to Badminton House, the seat of the Dukes of Beaufort, ten miles north-east of Downend; and, if Dr Grace were really lucky, he might exchange a few brief words with the 7th Duke, who died in 1853, or the 8th Duke, who would play a significant walk-on part in W.G.'s later life.

As a child Gilbert learned early about his father's reverence for aristocracy. One of W.G.'s first memories was of standing as a six-year-old with the rest of his family by the roadside in Stapleton while the funeral cortège of the Crimean War commander Lord Raglan, a Beaufort, passed through the village on the final leg of Raglan's long journey home to Badminton.

Yet Dr Grace had another buccaneering side, closer to the mid-Victorian sporting culture of betting booths and prizefights than the traditions of the Beaufort. In his memoir *Cricket*, W.G. told a convoluted story about his father playing for the village of

Thornbury in a game in 1852 after hearing that the Bristol team, which included his eldest son and Alfred Pocock, had bet £25 they would win the match. 'Understand now and for good, you boys,' W.G. quoted his father as saying, 'I shall not allow you in future to take part in any match which is played for money, as it is introducing a form of gambling into the game, which is wrong and must do harm to it.'

The first, manuscript draft of this story shows signs of considerable editing by W.G. and his ghostwriter Brownlee, as though Grace was unsure how to frame his father's behaviour. In the manuscript Dr Grace makes no reference to the harmful influence of gambling, and while he does offer to pay 'part of the money' if his son and Alfred Pocock's team win, he then adds in the first draft (but not the print version) that he has 'a good mind to keep it out of their allowance'. The story then proceeds in both versions in a way that suggests Dr Grace is very much on for the bet. Grace's father is furious when Bristol cannot produce the promised cash to guarantee the wager, and, along with Thornbury's captain, insists that the opposition empty their pockets of gold watches, rings and other valuables before the game can begin. Bristol lose the game, thanks to Dr Grace's dogged batting, accurate bowling and the Thornbury captain's underarm 'grubs' (daisycutters), a literally underhand manoeuvre making it almost impossible for the batsman to score. 'To say that the Bristol XI were laughed at, is to express very faintly what took place,' W.G. concludes.

Aged just four, Gilbert Grace was far too young to understand the source of the amusement, if he witnessed the game at all; it was just a piece of Grace family folklore. Yet as handed down to Gilbert, the story scarcely confirmed the impression the adult Grace later tried to create that his father was adamantly opposed to making money out of cricket.

Henry Grace soon showed his true nature by plunging into a risky cricket venture for far higher stakes than a few gold watches and diamond rings. In 1854, Dr Grace was the initiator and main promoter of a cricket match between twenty-two men from his

West Gloucestershire club and the All-England Eleven, a touring team of top professional players. In theory Henry's cricket 'speculation' (the common term for such match-making) had plenty of commercial potential. In the 1840s and early 1850s, so-called 'against-the-odds' fixtures between top professional sides like the All-England Eleven (AEE) and local Twenty-Twos reached a peak of popularity. Henry was betting that he could make a profit from ticket sales after all his costs were covered.

Yet the risks were substantial for, as Grace later put it, the AEE 'were open for engagements anywhere, as long as they obtained their price'. William Clarke, the Nottinghamshire cricketer who founded and managed AEE, typically charged local promoters a team fee of about £70, plus a share of the gate revenues and 'much hospitality', according to the mid-Victorian cricket writer James Pycroft. Henry Grace could not possibly afford this outlay, and like promoters for other against-the-odds fixtures, must have recruited fellow investors to help cover costs. One of them was certainly John Wintle, landlord of the Full Moon Hotel in the north Bristol suburb of Stokes Croft, whose field behind the pub was converted into a cricket ground.

An additional danger was the weather, for in the worst scenario promoters could find their anticipated profit literally washed away by rain. Henry Grace and his partners were lucky, because it stayed dry during the fixture's three scheduled days. Perhaps the biggest risk of all was the one that no cricket lover was yet prepared to admit. Pycroft tried hard to make against-the-odds fixtures sound exciting, but in the end fell back on the idea that such games tended 'to a healthy circulation of the life's blood of Cricket, vaccinating and inoculating every wondering rustic with the principles of the national game'.

Behind Pycroft's medical metaphor lurked the reality. Against-the-odds cricket matches were almost always one-sided contests, despite the home team's numerical advantage, with the professionals easily beating their hapless local opponents. Often the only suspense lay in seeing how long club batsmen could survive against the professional bowlers. 'To keep up one's wicket for half-an-hour, even without scoring, against the best bowling in England, was to create a reputation locally,' Grace remembered. 'To score a double figure and be praised by one of those great men, was something to boast of for a lifetime.'

Henry Grace's against-the-odds game followed the usual dull pattern, as five-year-old Gilbert watched the match from the boundary in his mother's pony-and-trap. West Gloucestershire's Twenty-Two, led by Henry Grace, lost by 149 runs. William Clarke took eleven easy wickets with his underarm spinners, even though he was ill, leaving the field at one point for a lie-down. 'No-one could look on for a quarter of an hour without seeing which way the game must go,' the *Bath Chronicle* reported. At the post-match dinner in the Full Moon Hotel, Henry Grace claimed that he had 'never been so sanguine as to entertain any idea of winning'. He added unconvincingly that the match had been organised 'from a desire to give the inhabitants of the West of England an opportunity of seeing what the game of cricket was'.

Henry did not mention anything as sordid as money, and it is impossible to determine how much, if any profit Henry and his partners made from the venture. The local newspaper report, possibly written by Henry or another speculator, referred vaguely to a healthy attendance, and based on similar fixtures, it is possible that more than a thousand spectators paid to watch the game on the first day. Henry must have avoided disaster, because he was confident enough to organise another game against AEE in Wintle's field the following summer, which West Gloucestershire lost as well. There was even talk of a third fixture in the summer of 1857, but it came to nothing. W.G.'s father then gave up his cricket 'speculations' to focus once more on his humdrum career as a provincial GP.

Except for his fleeting reference to Clarke's 'price', Grace did not mention money at all in the accounts he left of these AEE games in his ghostwritten memoirs, *Cricket* (1891) and *Cricketing Reminiscences and Personal Recollections* (1899). It is a good example of why the books are largely unreliable as guides to his early life. There are moments when Grace's distinctive, plain-speaking voice breaks through his ghostwriters' prose, especially in *Cricket*, produced in collaboration with his friend Methven Brownlee. But even then, W.G.'s memory of distant events from his childhood – some of which he did not witness – was often vague or inconsistent, as shown by his habit of telling the same anecdote in different versions between the two books.

Neither memoir reveals what must have been plain to the young Gilbert Grace by the time he reached his teens. His father's risky 'speculations' and all his hard work as a doctor had failed to make any noticeable change to the family's material situation.

This point was underlined by a series of property moves which Grace was too young to remember and later described inaccurately. In the spring of 1849 Downend House, Gilbert's first home in the centre of the village, was put up for sale at auction. Henry Grace had rented the property on short-term leases for the past fourteen years, and there is some evidence that the family's departure was forced on them by the sale. A notice in the *Bristol Mirror* announcing the auction stated baldly that the Graces' leasehold was due to expire 'at Ladyday' (25 March).

For the next eighteen months the Graces rented a house and adjoining surgery in the nearby village of Kingswood, an interlude that W.G. – still a toddler – understandably forgot when he produced his ghostwritten memoirs. The family then moved to The Chestnuts, another house in Downend, or 'The Chesnuts', as the Graces perversely misspelled it. The forgotten interlude in Kingswood only matters because it casts a slight doubt on W.G.'s claim that the move to The Chestnuts was prompted by the family's need for a larger home than Downend House.

Set back from the road leading northwards to Badminton, The Chestnuts was reached via a curving driveway, past a lodge at the front gate that served as Dr Grace's surgery. At the rear of the house were two orchards, one of which the family cut back to allow space for a cricket practice area. The house itself has since been demolished, but contemporary accounts do not suggest it was significantly larger than Downend House, if at all.

In 1899 a local antiquarian described The Chestnuts as merely 'a most compact English home'.

Whatever the truth about the Graces' move to The Chestnuts, W.G.'s father did not acquire any greater financial solidity in the final years of his life. He almost certainly rented the property on another short-term lease and would eventually die intestate in 1871. This administrative oversight did not mean Dr Grace was broke. His estate was eventually valued at 'less than £600', or perhaps twice his annual income – a reasonable legacy to pass on to Martha. On the other hand, Henry Grace – 'a good upholder of Church and State', according to his newspaper obituary – did not leave much cash in the bank. Within a week of his death Henry's family put his latest hunter up for sale to provide Martha with a little more money.

It was not inevitable that W.G. would inherit his family's general ineptitude with money. Don Bradman, who came from a poorer background than Grace, took to capitalism with such aplomb that he eventually founded his own stockbroking firm. In contrast W.G.'s self-assurance seemed to desert him as soon as he addressed his personal finances. He made cautious enquiries about stock-market tips, returned cheques for better-qualified City types to invest on his account, and worried about house prices and rents.

What the young Gilbert Grace had in common with the young Bradman was more surprising. In his 1950 autobiography Bradman recalled how as a child he improvised a solitary game of 'cricket' at the back of his home by hitting a golf ball against a brick stand using a stump as his bat. At first glance Gilbert's boyhood practice sessions in a cleared patch of orchard behind The Chestnuts look quite different. The scene is crowded with brothers and sisters, his mother and father, 'Uncle Pocock' and even the family's dogs, Don, Ponto and Noble, which retrieve the ball whenever it is hit into an adjacent quarry.

On closer inspection, Gilbert's early experience of learning to play cricket was more solitary than it seemed. He was not as isolated as Bradman, but he was almost eight years younger than his next oldest brother Ted (E.M.), while his eldest brother Henry was already a qualified doctor by the time Gilbert began practising in earnest as a small boy. According to the family's rule, the adults and the elder brothers each got fifteen minutes' batting time, while Gilbert and his younger brother Fred (born in 1850) were granted five minutes 'or more if time allowed'. It sounds like a token time slot to keep Gilbert and Fred happy as fielders for the grown-ups. When the adults departed for work, Gilbert would round up the stable lad and one or two village boys, chalk a wicket on a wall, and ask them to bowl at him. To increase the challenge of hitting the ball, he sometimes used a broom-handle instead of a bat. The similarity with Bradman's backyard sessions with a cricket stump and golf ball is unmistakable.

One can push this comparison too far. As he acknowledged, Gilbert benefited greatly from Alfred Pocock's willingness to bowl at him for hours on end: 'To my uncle great credit is due for teaching me'. Yet everything that followed Pocock's early coaching sessions suggests that like Bradman, the precociously focused Gilbert Grace was at heart a self-made genius. Pocock provided him with a platform. Gilbert did the rest.

2

THE E.M. PROBLEM

On the first page of his 1899 *Reminiscences*, Grace said he was 'born in the atmosphere of cricket'. He did not say that his family made him a cricketer. Eight years earlier, in *Cricket*, he was particularly keen to correct the impression that his mother Martha had played any part in his cricketing development. 'Rarely did we practise without my mother being present as an onlooker,' Grace recalled. 'My sisters did not play the game, as has been so often stated; but my mother and they fielded the ball if it travelled their way, and bowled a ball or two occasionally to Fred and myself when we were boys. That was the extent of their efforts.'

The classification of his mother as 'an onlooker' perhaps betrays W.G.'s impatience with the myth that arose about Martha's critical early influence as his coach. As Grace knew, Martha never played cricket and never coached him, even as a child. Grace instead singled out his indefatigable uncle Alfred Pocock as the key family member who filled this role. Yet after her death in 1884, W.G.'s busy and bossy mother loomed ever larger in the traditional narrative of Grace's cricketing life. She became the first woman to feature in the 'Births and Deaths of

Cricketers' section of *Wisden*, as the mother of W.G., E.M. (Ted) and G.F. (Fred). Yet her posthumous reputation as a fine cricket coach rests almost entirely on one dubious letter. When Gilbert was twelve, Martha reportedly wrote to the Nottinghamshire professional George Parr, who had taken over the management of the All-England Eleven following William Clarke's death in 1856. Martha supposedly recommended her third son Ted, born in 1841, to Parr as 'a splendid hitter and most excellent catcher', but added that Gilbert 'will in time be a much better player than his brother because his back stroke is sounder, and he always plays with a straight bat'.

No copy of Martha's prescient and technically knowledgeable letter to Parr has ever surfaced. Parr told the Nottinghamshire player Richard Daft, who first referred to it, that he had either lost or destroyed the letter. There the matter rested until 1919 when MCC published its quasi-official *Memorial Biography* of Grace. Sir Home Gordon, the biography's main editor, cited the letter as proof that Martha was 'to a large extent' responsible for W.G.'s cricketing 'tuition'. Gordon still did not quote the words attributed to Martha, which first appeared in 1948, when John Arlott produced a semi-dramatised radio tribute to Grace on the centenary of W.G.'s birth.

The attention paid to Martha's fictitious coaching skills obscured a more intriguing question: why was she recommending her sons to the top travelling professional team in the country? It cannot have been for the money. In the mid-1860s a typical skilled labourer or craftsman could expect to earn between £50 and £75 per year, about the same as Grace's father made from his Poor Law medical officer's job alone. Most professional cricketers came broadly from this artisan class and returned to their trades in the winter. During the summer leading players like the Sussex and Surrey bowler James Southerton, a barber, or his Sussex team-mate James Lillywhite Jr., a bricklayer, reckoned to earn match fees of just £5 per game. It was a precarious living, especially as they ran the constant risk of injury on the dreadful pitches of the day.

This was not the kind of humble, journeyman career that Henry and Martha Grace had in mind for any of their sons. They wanted to put as much distance as possible between themselves and the lower orders – in Henry's case especially, as the son of domestic servants.

Martha's approach to Parr only makes sense as an attempt to address a potentially crippling disadvantage for her two talented cricketing sons. Until 1870 Gloucestershire had no first-class county cricket club. Under the strict residency rules imposed by MCC, it was almost impossible for E.M. or W.G. to appear for one of the seven county sides that played eleven-a-side first-class cricket in the early 1860s: Nottinghamshire, Yorkshire, Surrey, Kent, Sussex and, from 1864, Lancashire and Middlesex. To do so they would have needed some close family or educational tie to one of these counties, which they conspicuously lacked.

By the time Martha wrote to Parr in late 1860 or early 1861, the public was starting to lose interest in lopsided against-the-odds cricket matches between travelling teams like AEE and local clubs. Competitive, evenly balanced eleven-a-side cricket represented the sport's future. AEE certainly offered a bigger stage for E.M. and W.G. than local Gloucestershire village cricket. Yet Martha would have much preferred to press her sons' case on Surrey, Nottinghamshire or one of the other leading county clubs.

There was an irony in E.M. and W.G.'s predicament. MCC, the governing body that imposed the eligibility rules, was also the one club that could offer them regular first-class cricket. In the early 1860s MCC had an expanding fixture list, no residency qualification, and the kind of well-heeled, superior membership to satisfy the Graces' social pretentions. Unfortunately, there was a catch. MCC, the bastion of gentlemanly, amateur cricket, was unlikely to consider the sons of a provincial doctor as suitable candidates for membership.

Since 1814, when the club moved to its present site on St John's Wood Road, MCC had pottered along at Lord's, seemingly content with a ground that was little more than an expanse of cleared meadow and a pavilion that resembled a large shack. The committee deployed a herd of sheep to 'mow' the outfield, while in the 1820s and 1830s MCC's honorary secretary Benjamin Aislabie – an enormously obese wine merchant – toddled around the ground on match days, troubling members for their sub-scriptions. When he had nothing better to do, Aislabie scribbled rude poems about his colleagues on the committee in the pocket notebook he kept in his frock-coat. Roger Kynaston, Aislabie's successor as honorary secretary, was one such target:

> 'Molly Brown & Kitty Green Jane & Kitty Norton
> Cannot get a wink of sleep for thinking of Kynaston
> They won't have Lloyd, they won't have Ward nor any
>   such old Codgers
> Not one of them is satisfied unless she has her Roger'

On Kynaston's fitful watch, the committee's grip on the club's affairs weakened to the point where MCC was sometimes unable to raise a team. One member 'found it impossible to get up an eleven' to play the Old Etonians in 1857 because he did not have enough advance warning. Kynaston gave way the following year to twenty-seven-year-old Alfred Baillie, remembered by the MCC grandee Sir Spencer Ponsonby-Fane as 'a very nice young fellow with nothing to do'. Under Baillie, MCC failed to bid for the freehold of Lord's when the ground came up for auction in 1860, allowing a property developer to acquire the land.

Yet amid this decrepitude, MCC still possessed immense residual power as both cricket's wealthiest club and its governing body. Sir Spencer Ponsonby (as he then was) and his elder brother Frederick, an equally powerful figure at Lord's, inherited vast estates in Ireland; the Earl of Verulam, MCC president in 1867, and his younger brother Robert Grimston, president in 1883, owned swathes of Hertfordshire and north London. Senior MCC members like the Grimstons and the Ponsonbys were so rich that they could afford to devote all the time they needed to see off various threats to the club in the early 1860s: from the professionals, riven by internal feuds, and, more potently, from several of the larger county clubs which resented MCC's authority. 'I suppose we shall never get to the bottom of the various schisms which created so much ill-feeling about that time, and which spoiled so many important matches,' Grace later commented, 'and I question if it be worth the trouble to try.' W.G. had a point. All MCC needed was a better secretary than Aislabie, Kynaston or Baillie.

Robert Fitzgerald, a twenty-seven-year-old MCC committee member, was already doing Baillie's job when he bumped into Henry and Martha Grace on a Canterbury street in August 1862. Baillie, exhausted by his MCC duties, was on an extended sick leave. 'Fitz', by contrast, was looking for an occupation to channel his considerable energies. The son of a landed Anglo-Irish family, Fitzgerald had studied law at Trinity College, Cambridge, where he gained a Blue as an aggressive, but not especially effective batsman. After Cambridge, he showed no interest in the Bar, preferring to use his widowed mother's London town house near Regent's Park as a bachelor base. Fitzgerald filled his time playing cricket, going to the races, picking up actresses and chasing fashionable ladies at country house parties; or, as he put it, 'penetrating into the interior life upstairs'.

Once seen, Fitzgerald was hard to forget. Lord Harris remembered him as 'the "Beau Sabreur" of the cricket field, a jolly "devil may care", bearded Irishman, with the gift of the gab, & of the pen ... ' The Graces, including ten-year-old Gilbert, had first caught sight of Fitzgerald in 1859 as spectators at two cricket matches at Badminton House, where to amuse the crowd the Beau Sabreur probably performed his party trick. Fitzgerald would get down on his knees in the outfield and scuttle through the grass, pretending to scamper after an invisible mouse.

On this Saturday in Canterbury, Fitzgerald was genuinely agitated, as he explained to the Graces. The city's annual cricket festival was due to start on Monday, but an MCC-organised 'All-England' team (different from Parr's eleven) was a player short. Could the Graces help? They certainly could. Henry Grace instantly proposed E.M., on one condition: E.M. had to play as well for MCC against Kent in the second match of the week. Fitzgerald agreed, probably after consulting Sir Spencer Ponsonby, who was also down in Canterbury.

That, at least, was one version of the story, as recounted by W.G., who at the time was in Gloucestershire. Grace told two other versions in his ghostwritten memoirs, further evidence of his tendency to get in a muddle about events in the distant past. The only certainty is that Henry Grace got his way. It was the weekend, which meant the telegram summoning E.M. to Canterbury did not reach The Chestnuts until the following Monday morning. E.M. rapidly collected his cricket kit, jumped in his mother's pony-and-trap and raced down to Bristol Temple Meads station, where he caught the train to London. By the evening he was in Canterbury, having missed the first day's play of the Kent v All-England game.

What E.M. did over the next forty-eight hours would have a critical bearing on W.G.'s early career. Short, bullish and bristling with aggression, Edward Mills Grace was remembered by *Wisden* on his death as 'perhaps the most remarkable player the game has produced' apart from W.G. This was an exaggeration. E.M. was certainly the finest close fielder in mid-Victorian cricket, crouching so near the batsman at 'point' (today's silly point) that he was sometimes warned to back off. He rarely did, refusing to flinch when the ball was hit and often pulling off improbable catches.

Yet E.M. was not remotely comparable with W.G. as a batsman, either in style or achievement. E.M. swung across the line of the ball like a baseball batter, a method that occasionally achieved sensational results. 'It has always been a mystery to me how he timed the ball so accurately,' Grace later commented about E.M.'s approach. 'Good-lengths, half-volleys, and long-hops were all the same to him. He got them on the right part of the bat, and neither bowler nor fieldsman could tell to which part of the field the ball was going.' Even so, the cricketing cliché 'look in the book' (meaning scorebook) is particularly applicable to E.M. The record shows that in a first-class career lasting more than three decades he scored just five centuries, 121 fewer than W.G.

Fitzgerald knew E.M. well enough to realise he was a liability for MCC, with his ungentlemanly 'keenness' on the field and suspected willingness to play cricket for money. E.M.'s playing ability was harder to gauge. He scored huge volumes of runs in local Bristol cricket, but in two representative games at Lord's earlier in the summer had done nothing much for two 'Gentlemen' teams. At Canterbury on Tuesday, E.M. immediately reinforced the sense that he was a chancy slogger when it was his turn to bat for All-England. To his parents' horror, E.M. swung at his first ball and hit a catch straight to a fielder on the boundary. E.M. did better in All-England's second innings, scoring a rapid 56, but Kent won easily.

It was now lunchtime on Wednesday, with the next match between Twelve Gentlemen of Kent and Twelve of MCC due to start immediately. Instead, the all-amateur Kent side objected to E.M.'s selection on the grounds that he was not an MCC member and, by implication, a professional mercenary recruited to strengthen the team. Fitzgerald refused to back down. In the end Kent grudgingly allowed E.M. to take the field as an 'emergency' replacement for MCC, even though the 'emergency' had occurred in the previous game.

Perhaps the fracas was the spur E.M. needed. He started by taking five wickets with a mixture of medium-pace round-arm bowling and slow underarm lobs (still a common style at the time). Next day E.M. scored 192 not out in an MCC total of 344, hitting the ball with such force that he broke one bat. E.M. was still not finished. He took all ten wickets in Kent's second innings, with the last man, a farmer called Streatfeild, finding an excuse to leave the ground early.

E.M. returned in triumph to Downend and shortly after MCC sent him the match ball, mounted on an ebony stand. The real prize came the following May when the Ponsonbys recommended E.M.'s election to the club. It was a formality, for no one at Lord's dared go against Sir Spencer and Frederick's wishes. E.M.'s admission still takes some explaining because according to W.G., their father never made E.M.'s election as an MCC member a condition of him coming to Canterbury.

It is possible that E.M.'s stunning performance against Kent was enough to persuade MCC's committee that he deserved membership. Yet as W.G. discovered in the coming years, mere weight of runs was not enough to secure admission to MCC if you came from the 'wrong' social background. It is more likely that the Ponsonbys wanted to kill any gossip that the club had selected E.M. as a hired gun in a strictly all-amateur fixture. In this narrative it was more embarrassing to have E.M. outside MCC than inside the club.

He was, nonetheless, still a socially inferior oddity, amid all the Old Etonians and Harrovians, Oxbridge Blues and aristocrats who filled MCC's membership ledger. Worse, from the MCC committee's perspective, E.M. proved he was a 'shamateur' only a few months after his election by joining George Parr's all-professional tour of Australia and New Zealand in the winter of 1863–4. Officially, E.M. was the team's sole amateur, but the Melbourne press reckoned E.M. 'cleared' £500 on the tour in under-the-table match fees.

E.M.'s flagrant moneymaking was bound to complicate W.G.'s efforts to join the club in the coming years. In MCC's eyes, a humble professional cricketer by definition could not be a superior gentleman amateur. W.G. did not simply have to demonstrate he was as good a cricketer – if not better – than E.M. He had to show that he was not just another 'shamateur' who, like E.M., would flout MCC's amateur code. Still just a promising young local cricketer, W.G. had good reason to curse his elder brother. For the real drama of the opening seasons of Grace's first-class career did not concern him 'wavering' between the amateur and professional roles, as MCC's official history suggests. It revolved around MCC's potential to destroy the prospects of the most talented teenager in the history of the game.

3

THE RULEBREAKER

On the morning of 14 July 1864, Gilbert Grace lugged his cricket bag into the thatched pavilion at the corner of Brighton's Royal Brunswick Ground, right on the seafront at Hove. Four days short of his sixteenth birthday, Gilbert was already around six feet in height, far taller than most of the other players getting ready for this match between the Gentlemen of Sussex and the touring South Wales Cricket Club. Yet he was clearly still just a boy, with a few wispy side-whiskers on his cheeks and a disconcertingly high-pitched voice, even though it had broken.

John Lloyd, South Wales's captain, knew the Grace family well. A well-connected lawyer from Brecon, Lloyd had played against W.G.'s brothers Henry and E.M. in the Bristol area; they in turn were regular guest players on South Wales's annual tour of London and south-east England. As he won the toss at Hove and decided to bat, Lloyd possibly felt a bit of a fool. Several days earlier, he had told Henry that he wanted to drop Gilbert for the game against Gents of Sussex.

According to Grace's recollection in Cricket, Lloyd broke the news to Henry immediately before South Wales's previous game against Gents of Surrey at the Oval. In this version, Lloyd explained he had the offer of 'a very good player' for the fixture at Hove. The South Wales captain really would have looked stupid if he had tried to drop Gilbert after the Oval match, as Grace suggested in his 1899 *Reminiscences*. By then the teenager had taken five wickets with his round–arm medium–pace bowling and scored 5 and 38: not an outstanding performance, but good enough to merit keeping his place in the team, as South Wales lost heavily.

In any case Henry objected and Lloyd backed down, a decision made easier when Lloyd discovered he was in fact a man short for the Sussex fixture. E.M., down to play at Hove, was still stranded at sea, having delayed his journey at the end of his winter tour of the Antipodes with George Parr's professional team.

To be fair to Lloyd, he had little direct knowledge of Gilbert's cricketing ability until the game at the Oval. In what passed for top cricket in the Bristol and Bath area, Gilbert had so far played two games in 1863 for local Twenty-Twos against the All-England Eleven, and once just before joining South Wales's tour in 1864 for AEE against Eighteen of Lansdown. On the last occasion, Gilbert was helping to fill AEE's depleted ranks, with most of the northern members of the team (including Parr) playing for Nottinghamshire against Yorkshire. Gilbert had showed a little potential in these games, making a top score of 32, without providing any evidence that he would soon be a far better player than E.M.

Watching Gilbert bat at the Oval, Lloyd would have noticed one critical difference between the two brothers. Unlike E.M., Gilbert had a batting technique that was grounded in coaching manual orthodoxy, playing 'through the line' of the ball with a straight bat. To this degree, Gilbert was the product of his long practice sessions with Uncle Alfred in the clearing behind The Chestnuts. 'Nothing pleased him so much as watching a correct style of play,' Grace recalled of Pocock. Yet is hard to believe that Pocock had the ability and insight to produce the teenage batting phenomenon who was about to be revealed. Sport yields many examples of mediocre players who go on to be brilliant coaches.

In football the Frenchman Arsène Wenger and the Portuguese José Mourinho are conspicuous examples. But Pocock was at an altogether lower level of achievement – a village cricketer who only took up the game in his early thirties and had little opportunity to watch top players beyond the Bristol area.

In paying tribute to Pocock, Grace opened the way for misinterpretation about the extent to which he was self-made. 'I should like to be able to say that I had no difficulty in learning, and that proficiency came to me much easier than it comes to other boys,' Grace recalled. 'The reverse is the truth. I had to work as hard at learning cricket as I ever worked at my profession, or anything else.' It sounds like he is talking about his sessions with Pocock, but this was only partially accurate. As Grace made clear, Pocock was a cricket purist who wanted him to play strokes directly from the coaching manual. Yet the teenage Grace disdained classical 'batsmanship' if he could find a more efficient way to score runs. Gilbert played with a straight bat; after that starting point, any shot was permissible if it achieved the desired outcome.

The Old Etonian amateur Charles Lyttelton, who first played with Grace in 1865, recalled with some distaste W.G.'s 'clumsy and laborious' batting style. Lyttelton's younger brother Edward, also a leading amateur cricketer, remembered W.G.'s 'digging stroke' on the off side. Grace executed his strange shot with 'an awkward heave of the shoulders as he bent right over the ball'; yet 'the force with which the ball went was astonishing, till one noticed that the movement with the upper part of the body was perfectly combined with a stamp of the right foot'. Acute observers of Grace's batting also noticed his preternatural calm: 'There were no fireworks or extravagances,' the great turn-of-the-century batsman C.B. Fry wrote. 'W.G. just stood at the crease to his full height and proceeded to lean against the ball in various directions and send it scudding along the turf between the fielders. No visible effort, no hurry; just a rough-hewn precision.'

Lloyd put Gilbert at number three in the South Wales batting order for the Sussex match, directly after himself and Charles

Calvert, the heir to a London brewing fortune. Calvert was soon out, and with the score on 19 for one, Gilbert walked out to join Lloyd in the middle.

As he adjusted to the light W.G. saw a compact little ground, made even tighter by the spectators hemmed around the boundary. He saw as well that at the southern, seafront end, the light glittered on the waves in the distance, directly behind the bowler's arm. For their part, the Sussex players might have been puzzled by Gilbert's batting stance as he took guard. It looked wrong, according to the coaching books, with his front, left foot cocked towards the bowler and his weight firmly on the back foot. Gilbert's bat reinforced this sense of latent movement, hovering above the block hole like a pendulum waiting to swing. Only his head seemed completely still, his eyes trained on the bowler who now began his run-up.

That raised front foot was a statement of intent. Gilbert was poised to move forward and drive the ball if the Sussex bowlers pitched it up. If they bowled too short, he moved back to cut with equal power. William Napper, a veteran right-arm slow bowler who led the Sussex attack, insisted that Grace should have been caught when he cut a ball straight through the hands of a fielder. As Grace drily recalled, this was the last of four boundaries he hit off successive deliveries by Napper.

Finally, he got too far on top of a cut shot and chopped the ball on to his stumps – 'to his great annoyance', the *Brighton Gazette* reported. Gilbert stomped back to the pavilion, pursued by the crowd, out for a mere 170; he had had a double-century for the taking. A few minutes later Gilbert had recovered his temper sufficiently to thank Lloyd for the souvenir bat that the South Wales captain presented to him in front of the thatched pavilion. Not to be outdone, Bridger Stent, the secretary of Sussex County Cricket Club, gave the teenager a second bat to commemorate Gilbert's innings.

Later Grace's 170 at Hove would be seen as his breakthrough, the moment when Gilbert became W.G. At the time it went largely unnoticed. Only the *Brighton Gazette* covered the game in any detail, which did not count as first-class (a status South Wales CC lacked). It took the *Sussex Advertiser* almost a week just to print the match scorecard. In London the press ignored the fixture, leaving newspapers in Bristol, Bath and Gloucester to give W.G.'s performance more than a passing mention. To show it was no fluke, W.G. scored 56 not out in South Wales's second innings, as the game petered out in a draw. Then he travelled all the way home by train for a village game near Bristol.

W.G. rejoined the South Wales team at Lord's the following Thursday for the game against MCC, the top fixture of the tour. The ground he saw as he dumped his bag in the shabby, cramped pavilion was a world away from today's sleek stadium. Fitzgerald had just persuaded the committee to renovate the pavilion, on the same site as the present one, but a picture in one of his scrapbooks taken a fortnight later shows that work had not yet begun. Crude metal sidings were tacked to the side of the pavilion, a rough wooden verandah served as a balcony and, inside, there was almost no space to change or wash. W.G. would have been warned about the dreadful Lord's pitch by Lloyd and the Sussex players. Several months earlier Bridger Stent had informed MCC that Sussex would no longer play at Lord's 'in consequence of the bad state of the wickets'. Fitzgerald had sent Stent 'an indignant but dignified reply'.

On this surface, in grey, murky weather, Grace's 50 in South Wales's first innings was an even better performance than his 170 at Hove. He scored his runs against an MCC attack led by the club's senior ground staff professional, thirty-seven-year-old Thomas Hearne, a tailor by trade who was one of the best medium-pace bowlers in England. W.G., at number four, came in with South Wales's score on 14 for two, which soon became 17 for three. He prevented a batting collapse, demonstrating his exceptional powers of concentration.

Once again the press scarcely noted W.G.'s performance in a drawn match. Nor did Fitzgerald see Grace's debut at Lord's. MCC's secretary was agreeably detained in Liverpool, playing cricket for the gentlemen's cricket club I Zingari (meaning 'the

Gypsies' in Italian) and flirting with the Earl of Sefton's younger sister Cecilia at Croxteth Hall, the earl's stately home near the city. Fitzgerald did get a good look at W.G. a week later when South Wales returned to Lord's to play I Zingari. Grace shared an opening partnership of 81 with E.M. in South Wales's first innings, and in the second innings made the team's top score of 47, as I Zingari won narrowly.

Next day, after dashing back to Bristol, W.G. was in Weston-super-Mare, playing for the Gloucestershire village of Hanham.

Still only sixteen, Grace disappeared into provincial obscurity for almost twelve months. *Wisden*, in its second year of publication, did not mention him at all in its review of the 1864 season. *John Lillywhite's Cricketers' Companion* did better, recognising W.G.'s performance at Hove as 'one of the greatest batting feats of the great batting season of 1864'. Yet in terms of his prospects, W.G. was still locked into the same career path, seemingly destined like his elder brothers to qualify as a doctor by his early twenties.

For the past two years W.G. had been studying at home under John Dann, a private tutor from Ireland who was taking an external divinity degree at Dublin University. It is not certain why Grace's father pulled W.G. and his younger brother Fred out of Ridgway House. W.G.'s removal may have been triggered by a potentially fatal bout of pneumonia when he was fourteen. The overstretched Dr Grace may also have felt he could no longer afford the Reverend Malpas's fees, which came to £120 per year for Gilbert and Fred. Most probably, W.G.'s father wanted him and eventually Fred to follow the same basic medical apprenticeship as his elder sons, with Dann filling in the academic gaps.

In their teens W.G.'s elder brothers had all watched Henry Grace at work in his surgery by the front gate to The Chestnuts. Until the 1858 Medical Act it was possible for the sons of doctors to qualify for the profession by serving formal apprenticeships under their father's instruction, with both parties' obligations spelled out in indentures dating back to medieval times. E.M.'s apprenticeship contract, signed in 1857, vaguely committed his father to teach him 'the art of a Surgeon and Apothecary' while E.M. – who eventually had eighteen children – promised not to 'commit fornication' or 'play at Cards or Dice Tables'. Dr Grace realised that this training was inadequate and E.M., like his brothers Henry and Alfred, had completed his education with a brief spell at Bristol Medical School.

As W.G. went back and forth between Dann's lessons and his father's surgery, his situation differed from his elder brothers in one critical respect. The 1858 legislation had abolished the apprenticeship system, and W.G. knew he would have to attend medical school for a minimum of thirty months to qualify as a doctor. At the end of his studies W.G. would then have to pass the physicians' and surgeons' 'licentiate' exams to practise as a GP. Compared with medical students today, W.G. did not face a particularly challenging set of academic hurdles. Yet he would take almost eleven years to qualify, raising a question about his commitment to the medical profession.

There is no evidence to support the patronising theory that W.G. was incapable of focused study and was actively averse to book-learning. The slur that Grace never read a book in his life arose from an anecdote told after his death about W.G. chastising a Gloucestershire Varsity amateur for burying his head in a Greek play while waiting to bat. As the witness to this scene made clear, W.G. was making a point about the need to concentrate on the game, not about whether books should be avoided at all times. W.G. would end his life in a house that was full of books; furthermore, he told his grandchildren that he hoped they would 'always love books', an odd remark for an alleged ignoramus to make.

The dressing room anecdote actually reveals the real reason why Grace took so long to become a doctor: cricket, not medicine, was the subject that engaged his mind. Grace's lack of vocational interest in medicine was not particularly unusual for a Victorian GP. Of his three doctoring brothers, only Henry displayed any serious commitment to medicine, delivering a lecture on public health in 1870 following an outbreak of typhoid in Kingswood. W.G. took after his brothers E.M. and Alfred (known as the 'hunting doctor') in greatly preferring a day's sport to a day cooped up in a surgery. By the spring of 1865 he was ready to quit studying and get back to the more serious business of cricket.

'Cricket in my manhood dates from the year 1865,' W.G. announced in the first draft of his 1891 memoirs. 'I hope specialists will not take exception to the heading on account of my youthfulness.' W.G. then had second thoughts for the print version, pushing his 'manhood' forward five years to 1870. Yet his original comment better reflected how he saw himself after his scores the previous summer at Hove and Lord's. 'I am justified in using it [manhood] in connection with that period of my life for I was 6 feet in height and over 11 stone in weight. The company I kept that season might also be advanced in its favour.'

As it turned out, the summer of 1865 highlighted all the obstacles that still lay between W.G. and regular first-class cricket. With no first-class county club of his own, W.G. had to wait for the game's amateur establishment to select him for one of the representative fixtures that filled out the first-class season. His chance finally came in June when Surrey CCC picked him to appear at the Oval for Gentlemen of the South against Players of the South.

This game's regional flavour indicated another problem for W.G. In the mid-1860s the professionals' boycotts of each other's 'southern' and 'northern' games were at their peak, triggered by issues as petty as a player's bowling action. W.G. was not alone in being baffled by some of the arguments. In exasperation the MCC committee decided in 1866 that it would only select professionals at Lord's 'from those who are willing to play together in a friendly manner'. Fitzgerald's lofty minute glossed over the fact that whenever a boycott was in force, MCC and Surrey had to substitute 'southern' teams for representative 'national' fixtures at Lord's and the Oval, such as Gentlemen v Players.

Even so, the Oval made a fitting stage for W.G.'s first-class debut compared with MCC's ramshackle ground at Lord's. Then as now, the Oval was a grittily urban ground, hard up against a gasworks and surrounded by streets of narrow terrace houses. Its appearance was deceptive. Surrey CCC was rich and well organised, with a large membership and an efficient paid secretary, William Burrup, who during the winter ran a stationery shop in Lambeth with his brother John, his predecessor as the club's manager. The ground, like the club, was to all intents and purposes a professional operation, with the MCC grandee Frederick Ponsonby providing gentlemanly cover as Surrey CCC's first vice-president.

W.G. failed with the bat, humiliatingly. Shortly after midday on 22 June, with the sun out and several thousand spectators watching, he swung at a ball from the Kent professional bowler George Bennett, missed, and was stumped for 0. He now gave early notice of his ability to force his way into a game, persuading his captain Edward 'Teddy' Walker, a wealthy brewer from north London, to let him have a bowl. W.G. won the game, taking thirteen wickets with his round-arm medium pace.

So much was written about W.G.'s slow bowling that it is easy to overlook the quicker style of his youth. The young Grace resembled many other mid-Victorian bowlers loosely described as medium pace, a vague definition that does not indicate the actual speed of delivery. 'While his delivery was a nice one, it was quite different to what it was in his later days,' the Essex amateur Charles Green recalled. 'It was more slinging and his pace was fast medium. He used to bowl straight on the wicket, trusting to the ground to do the rest.'

Like his contemporaries, W.G. learned to bowl at a time when it was still illegal to deliver the ball above shoulder height. MCC eventually dropped this rule in 1864, following a players' walk-out at the Oval in 1862 when the Kent bowler Ned Willsher was repeatedly no-balled by the umpire for bowling with a high shoulder action. The rule change came too late to save W.G. from an awkward round-arm action that was typical of bowlers of the day; if he had been born a decade later, the tall

Grace might have developed into one of the great early over-the-shoulder fast bowlers.

'What was I doing in the way of bowling?' W.G. asked of his early efforts to master the discipline. 'A great deal; though perhaps not giving it the thoughtful attention I bestowed on batting.' Being W.G., this meant he gave the matter a lot more thought than most bowlers. 'If you are bowling to first-class batsmen, you are more likely to get them out by trying a dodge or two than you are by bowling straight over after over,' he later advised schoolboys. 'Take stock of your enemy and endeavour to outwit him.'

The press did not notice W.G.'s tricks and 'dodges', which included a well-disguised slower delivery, as he bowled the Gentlemen of the South to victory. Instead, he got his first taste of how the newspapers, like most batsmen, would underestimate his bowling over the next four decades, while he took a further 2796 first-class wickets. Grace's 'good bowling' was 'effective', *The Era*, a London newspaper, observed coolly, but the teenager was helped by some 'wretchedly bad' batting.

In any case bowling was generally regarded as a sweaty trade for professionals like Thomas Hearne and, for that reason, less likely to impress the MCC committee. W.G. needed to make a big score, but his remaining four first-class matches in 1865 were pure frustration. He kept getting out in the thirties and forties, lending weight to the possibility that his 170 at Hove a year before had been a flash in the pan.

It was not as if W.G. had many opportunities to impress MCC's committee and persuade the club to admit him as a member, following E.M.'s election. W.G. played just five first-class games in 1865, including four for various 'Gentlemen' sides and one for an 'England' eleven against Surrey. By comparison MCC played eight first-class fixtures, including a match against Sussex at Lord's, the county having thought better of its refusal to play on MCC's dangerous pitch.

W.G.'s exclusion from cricket's top tier was underlined in early August, when the MCC establishment descended on

Canterbury for the city's annual week-long cricket festival. The 'company' on the St Lawrence Ground by the Dover Road was 'numerous and fashionable', the *Kentish Gazette* reported. Sir Brook W. Bridges MP was in evidence, with 'Lady Bridges and party'; so were Sir Courtenay and Lady Honywood and party, the Misses Dickins, Captain King and party, and for some reason the Dean of Norwich. Fitzgerald stuck a pencil cartoon in one of his scrapbooks, showing 'a catch at leg by Hon. Secretary of the Marylebone Club, Canterbury, 1865'. He leaps backwards over the boundary as the ball just evades his outstretched hand. Behind him six young women, three with babies, scramble to get out of the way. Four have already been up-ended, revealing their bloomers; another flees, clutching her baby; while another drops her parasol and cries, 'Oh save me!' It was all great fun, unless you were E.M., who managed just 31 runs from four innings during the week. Far away in Gloucestershire the ineligible W.G. took out his frustration at not being at Canterbury by scoring 80 for J.J. Smith's Twelve against the village of Knole Park.

W.G. returned to the tedium of watching his father in the surgery at The Chestnuts, interspersed by lessons with twenty-three-year-old John Dann. That winter Dann may have had an additional reason for turning up at The Chestnuts. W.G.'s elder sister Blanche, now aged nineteen, became engaged to Dann some time after 1865 and married in 1869, at the start of Dann's long career as curate and then vicar of Downend.

Blanche is the only girl identified in Brownlee's authorised biography of Grace as featuring at all in W.G.'s life before his marriage in 1873. 'Miss Blanche, in her early days, was associated with many rambles over fence and ditch, and showed that she could hold her own,' Brownlee wrote, making Blanche sound like a bit of a tomboy. Elsewhere Brownlee launched into a rhapsodical passage when W.G. finally became engaged: 'There cometh a time to us all when the dreaming of dreams gives place to the mighty longing to have a companion nearer and dearer than the friends of our youth.'

It all sounds very chaste, yet it is quite possible that the teenage Grace had one or more girlfriends. Long after Grace's death, distant hearsay evidence was produced to suggest that he was shy with girls, perhaps because of his squeaky voice. Yet the contemporary glimpses of W.G. indicate that he was no more gauche than other young Victorian men in an age when courtship rituals were naturally inhibiting. By his early twenties W.G. was certainly an accomplished dancer, as he showed on his tour of North America in 1872; it is hard to believe that he only acquired this crucial Victorian excuse for getting close to girls after his engagement the same year.

If the young W.G. was essentially unpassionate, another posthumous theory, then he was markedly different from his brothers. 'My own sweet Lee,' his eldest brother Henry gushed in a letter to his future wife Leanne, 'What can I wish you this morning more than I have wished you for many years and every day of each? . . . Oh! that I may spend every succeeding one with you my darling.'

E.M.'s decision to stay on in Australia for two months in 1864 at the end of his cricket tour was probably connected with girls as well as his stated desire to visit relatives. He still found time to sound off from Melbourne about their sister Alice's recent engagement to David Bernard, one of W.G.'s former teachers at Ridgway House. 'I really thought that Alice would have had better taste or rather as the Yankees say, look higher,' E.M. wrote home to his brother Alfred. A decade later Fred Grace – by all accounts the most handsome of the brothers – skipped the last leg of W.G.'s 1873–4 Australia tour to return to Tasmania to meet a girlfriend. Perhaps W.G. felt daunted by his brothers' pursuit of women and retreated into his shell. But it does not seem very likely.

W.G. started the 1866 season in wretched batting form. He also made a terrible mistake that the MCC committee was bound to regard with distaste.

In June W.G. replaced E.M., who was mysteriously unavailable, as captain of a Nottingham and Sheffield Colts Eighteen against an AEE team captained by George Parr. This fixture in

Sheffield could have been designed to present W.G. in the worst possible light as a candidate for MCC membership. He had no connection by birth or residence with Nottingham or Sheffield, and was stunned by his first sight of the Yorkshire city's steel mills: 'I felt as if I had got to the world's end, and a very black and sooty end it seemed!', Grace had ventured into dangerous territory for an aspiring MCC member. Nottingham and Sheffield were the strongholds of the northern professionals while Parr was the main instigator of the repeated boycotts of southern games at Lord's and the Oval.

Just by showing up, W.G. confirmed that he was willing to play for money, a cardinal offence in the eyes of the MCC committee. This may have been why E.M., as an MCC member, pulled out at the last minute; following his 'shamateur' tour to Australia, E.M. would have risked his MCC membership by playing in Sheffield. Instead he landed his younger brother in an extremely awkward spot. W.G. did his best, scoring 36 in the Colts' second innings to prevent a complete rout by the much stronger AEE team, which won easily. But his season had gone badly off track, with W.G. continuing his series of low scores in first-class cricket after his misadventure in Sheffield. By late July he had scored just 98 runs from seven first-class innings in appearances for Gentlemen of England v Oxford University, Gentlemen v Players (twice), and South v North.

W.G.'s response to the first real crisis of his cricket career was revealing; he put his inventive brain to work. 'I had been thinking hard during the season that the arrangement of the field in first-class matches was not quite what it ought to be,' he recalled. 'There was a prevailing idea at the time that as long as a bowler was straight the batsman could do nothing against him and fieldsmen were nearly all close. That idea I determined to test . . .' Grace decided to hit even a slightly overpitched delivery 'hard and high' over the top of the close-set fielders into the wide open spaces beyond. If the bowler dropped short, he would pull and cut 'hard and high' as well.

His tactic seems obvious today, and indeed there were other

batsmen in the 1860s who regularly hit the ball in the air, such as his brother E.M.; in the print version of his memoir *Cricket* (but not the original manuscript), W.G. modestly credited E.M. with pioneering this approach. However, E.M.'s tendency to lift the ball was a consequence of his free-swinging, baseball style rather than the result of careful thought. Bowlers knew they always had a chance with E.M. if they continued to bowl straight and on a good length.

By contrast, W.G. aimed at dismantling all the bowler's assumptions about how to dismiss him, because he was still driving through the line of the ball with an 'orthodox' straight bat, or cutting and pulling from an essentially correct initial position. The key was placement. Much later the Bristol cricket correspondent H.E. Roslyn, who first watched Grace around 1880, would sum up W.G.'s approach: 'He was not so intent on keeping down the ball as upon dispatching it to an unguarded part of the field. Let a bowler dispense with a long-on, and then drop the ball on the leg stump, he would draw himself up and hit it hard, often over mid-on's head. It looked risky but with him the stroke was perfectly safe.'

In his prime Grace was also utterly assured about his ability to execute such shots. Roslyn remembered an incident when W.G. came into the press tent at Clifton College after making more than half Gloucestershire's total: 'An old friend remarked "Not one of your best knocks, Doctor; the ball was in the air too much." We all sat tight expecting an explosion. But the only reply made was: "Why didn't they catch it, then?"'

W.G.'s audacity in taking this approach in 1866 was still astounding. He was proposing not just to hit his way out of a deep slump of form but to do so in a manner that was almost designed to offend the principles of elegant batsmanship that defined the gentlemen amateur. Sadly, he could hardly remember anything about his batting at the Oval on 30 and 31 July for 'England' against Surrey, except 'the shouting which followed at the end of the innings'. In a passage cut from the printed version of *Cricket*, W.G. explained with disarming candour that he had only once kept that 'mental aberration', a diary, and 'there was little in it of cricket doings'. He went on: 'A diary would have been invaluable to me today, and would have thrown light upon many matches that have become very dim to me.'

The scorebook showed that W.G. scored 224 not out in a total of 521 all out. 'He played every ball, whether to the off or to the on, with the exception of one which bumped,' recalled the cricket writer James Pycroft, who watched the innings. 'This feat seems to me one of the most remarkable of his achievements, and it was rendered the more difficult because Ben Griffith [a Surrey player] was bowling in a very wild manner.'

Pycroft spotted what others would notice in future. Unlike other batsmen, W.G. rarely left the ball without playing a shot, because he had such confidence in his ability to score runs off any delivery, however dangerous. At the end of W.G.'s great innings, 'He ran from the wicket to the pavilion but experienced great difficulty in reaching his destination as his friends and admirers mustered in great force and manifested their enthusiasm in the correct Surrey manner.'

Yet outside the Bristol area the newspapers made it sound as if any decent batsman could have played the same innings against Surrey's mediocre bowling attack. W.G.'s double-century provided 'further evidence this week of the weakness of the Surrey bowling', the *Bradford Observer* commented.

It was now Surrey's turn to bat. W.G. did not bowl, but caught the batsman Julius Caesar (from Godalming, not Rome) as the home side collapsed to 84 for eight wickets at close of play on the second day. W.G. then asked his captain Teddy Walker for permission to miss the final day to compete in a quarter-mile hurdle race at Crystal Palace Park in south London. It seems he simply could not resist a competitive challenge in any sport – and in his teens and early twenties athletics, especially hurdling, was his main game after cricket. Bristol's sports fans were accustomed to the sight of W.G., in his salmon-pink running knickerbockers, hurdling around the polar bears and lions at Clifton's Zoological Gardens, which doubled up as a venue for athletics meetings.

A month earlier W.G. had won the 200 yards hurdles and the quarter-of-a-mile flat race in a contest at the zoo.

This meeting at Crystal Palace was a far bigger event, organised by the newly formed National Olympian Association (NAO), with a crowd of around ten thousand turning up on the day. It is easy to see why W.G. wanted to compete, but even he was later astonished that Walker let him leave the Oval. Grace also remembered the race as a bit of a non-event, with only one hurdler – himself – finishing the course. It was another case of W.G. needing a diary. Reports at the time show 'W. Grace of Bristol' beating Emery (second) and Collins (third). He was not missed at the Oval, where Surrey lost by the huge margin of an innings and 296 runs.

Four weeks later W.G. returned to the Oval to appear for the Gentlemen of the South against the Players of the South. Beneath thick grey clouds, W.G. took seven wickets in the Players' first innings. The light was even worse when W.G. came out to bat with the fixed intention of hitting everything he could into the Oval's large outfield. As well as driving the bowlers over their heads, 'my height enabled me to get over those that were slightly short, and I played them hard: long-hops off the wicket I pulled to square-leg or long-on without the slightest hesitation'. He scored a chanceless 173 not out in a Gents total of 297, batting in the gloom against an attack led by Kent's Ned Willsher (fast-medium) and Sussex's James Lillywhite Jr. (slow-medium), two of the best bowlers in the country.

One perceptive (and sadly anonymous) reporter grasped that the Oval crowd had seen a batting genius in action. 'When he hit,' the *Sporting Life* commented, 'the correct timing, the judgement displayed in placing, and the clean hard form in which the ball was struck, appeared to us, and all around us, to be – combined with the defence shown – the perfection of batting.'

Now, surely, the moment had arrived for MCC to elect W.G. a member. The moment came and went.

4

JOINING THE CLUB

The MCC committee could point to one particularly troublesome member of the club to explain why they were so resistant to electing W.G. E.M. had form as a 'shamateur' and with Parr and other northern players still regularly boycotting southern games at Lord's and the Oval, the committee had no reason to look favourably on W.G.'s candidacy so soon after his professional match in Sheffield.

All the same, MCC's unbending hostility to professionalism involved a blatant double standard. Fitzgerald was keen to make money indirectly from cricket while looking down on professionals who openly earned a living from the game. In 1866, hoping to boost his income and establish his reputation as a literary wit, Fitzgerald published the bizarrely titled *Jerks in from Short Leg*. Amid a jumble of 'humorous' musings about the sport, he deplored how the professionals were turning cricket into a game of 'pounds, shillings and pence. Matches are nowadays becoming speculative, and the cricketer's hand is not more often in the pocket than his eye is on the gate.' The time had come, Fitzgerald argued, for 'the gentlemen cricketers of England to assert their position, not only as patrons of the game, but as performers'.

After his two huge centuries at the Oval in 1866, W.G. obviously fitted Fitzgerald's description. It is a sign of how much W.G. wanted *not* to be seen at Lord's as E.M.'s mercenary younger brother that he played remarkably little high-profile professional cricket in the late 1860s, despite his faux pas in Sheffield. In 1865 W.G. did not play at all for the newly formed United South of England Eleven, the professional team he would frequently lead in the 1870s. He only played once for USE in 1866, and then not again until 1868, when he appeared four times for the travelling team. During the same period USE played a total of 63 fixtures.

Grace might reasonably have asked why his relative restraint did not win him favour at Lord's. Fitzgerald's normally verbose committee minutes and other MCC records are silent on why it took the club so long to elect W.G. a member. The normal process involved two members proposing and seconding a candidate, whose credentials were then considered by the MCC committee. In the 1860s Fitzgerald went on a recruitment drive that almost doubled the club's size during the decade to about 1100 members in 1869. Fitzgerald proposed or seconded many of these candidates, who almost invariably ticked one or more of the same boxes: a spell at one of the great public schools, Oxford or Cambridge, perhaps one of the smarter regiments.

Patently, W.G. came from the wrong background. He was also attempting to gain admission to MCC at a time when the club, more than ever, seemed a refuge to its upper-class members from the social and political turmoil beyond Lord's. During the 1860s MCC figures like Sir Spencer Ponsonby, a senior courtier in the royal household, found plenty in the newspapers to keep them awake at night. Prince Albert's death in 1861 plunged Queen Victoria into such protracted mourning that she effectively went on strike. Her refusal to perform the public ceremonial duties of a monarch opened the way for England's first significant republican movement in two centuries.

The 'Cotton Famine' of the early 1860s, caused in part by the American Civil War, knocked the stuffing out of Lancashire's textile industry, turning thousands of workers out on the streets. In

1866 the collapse of Overend Gurney, a once-reputable Quaker
bank that had invested in dud railway stocks, triggered a full-scale
financial panic. The future Lord Harris, then at Eton, recalled
how his father was sucked into the banking disaster, as the director of a debt-ridden railway company: 'He had worked himself up
to such a pitch that he was actually anticipating bankruptcy and
arrest & disgrace of every kind . . . He had to economise as much
as he could, so my amusements were much restricted.'

MCC's recently improved pavilion was a reassuring retreat
from such turbulence, offering members an upper-class fantasy
of a fixed social order where the professionals, as cricketing
tradesmen, were kept firmly in their place by the gentlemen amateurs. The professionals changed separately, took lunch on their
own table, and were denoted as plain 'Willsher', 'Lillywhite'
or 'Hearne' on the match scorecard, to distinguish them from
'R.A. Fitzgerald Esq.' or 'Mr V.E. Walker'. The wonder is not
that MCC imposed its apartheid system. Far more astonishing
was that the system survived until 1962, when the Rev. D.S.
Sheppard, a future Bishop of Liverpool (and anti-apartheid cam-
paigner), and Mr E.J. Craig, a future Knightsbridge Professor of
Philosophy in the University of Cambridge, walked out of the
Lord's pavilion to open the batting for the Gentlemen in the
last-ever game against the Players.

W.G. nearly made a debut of sorts for MCC in November 1866.
In the middle of the month he spent several days in Oxford competing in the annual round of athletics meetings held by various
colleges including Merton, Exeter and Queen's. It is not clear
where Grace stayed, but one possible host was the Oxford cricket
Blue Edmund Carter, who invited W.G. to breakfast at his college during a cricket match a few months earlier. Grace entered
most of the athletics meetings as W.G. Grace of 'Bristol', but for
the Strangers One Mile Handicap organised by Merton he or
someone else put his name down as 'W.G. Grace (Marylebone
Cricket Club)'. Perhaps it was a clerical error, or perhaps W.G.
was making a sly joke about MCC's failure to elect him to the

club. As it happened, he failed to turn up for the race and so missed his unofficial debut.

The following May W.G. nearly hobbled his chances of being ready for the 1867 cricket season when he sprained his ankle while training for an athletics meeting at Clifton's Zoological Gardens. He still competed in the meeting, finishing a distant fourth in the one-mile race and joint runner-up in the 400 yards. Possibly mindful of his imminent series of cricket matches in London, W.G. decided not to risk his damaged ankle by entering the hurdles, his main event. Even so, his determination not to pull out of the meeting was characteristic. All his life W.G. played through injuries and showed little sympathy for teammates who complained of niggles and strains; the game, as far he was concerned, came first.

He was fit enough a couple of days after this athletics meeting to score 75 for an 'England' team against Middlesex at Lord's. W.G. then took plenty of wickets in his next two games, also at Lord's; at which point MCC paid him his expenses for all three fixtures.

These expenses, amounting in total to £14 2s 6d, give some indication of the financial pressure Grace must have felt to play professional cricket. At first sight the sum was a lot of money for an unemployed student, at a time when the average weekly wage of a skilled building trade worker in London was about £1 16s. Yet like other amateurs, Grace was expected to pay his hotel and transport costs from his expenses, an important point that was ignored by later critics of his 'shamateurism'. He made three return train journeys from Bristol to London while playing these matches, which would have cost him in total at least £3, even travelling third-class. Financially, W.G. was therefore slightly worse off than professionals whom MCC paid at a going rate of £5 per match, a sum that covered travel, bed and board.

In early July W.G. made his third trip back to Bristol, not realising it could have been the last journey home of his life. Several days after his return, W.G. caught scarlet fever, a highly contagious and potentially fatal disease in the 1860s. Grace's father would have known enough about the illness to isolate

W.G. from the rest of the family, perhaps by setting up a bed for him in the surgery by the front gate. He was ill for over a month, admitting 'bitter disappointment' that he had not scored enough runs earlier in the summer. Still frail, W.G. reappeared at the Oval in late August for a match between 'England' and a combined Surrey and Sussex team. He had a miserable game, injuring a finger while fielding a ball and, probably as a result, failing again when he batted. So ended the unluckiest cricket season of W.G.'s career, when he played just six first-class innings.

Grace's halting progress towards membership of MCC now became entangled in a controversy surrounding Fitzgerald's latest money-making scheme. As so often with Fitzgerald, a woman was involved.

By the autumn of 1866, Fitzgerald was thirty-two and ready (so he imagined) to settle down. He became engaged to Harriett 'Ettie' Rigby, the twenty-one-year-old daughter of a prosperous Liverpool merchant. Fitzgerald had a private income but worried that he would not be able to support Ettie in the manner her parents expected. He did not have a home of his own, perambulating between his mother's town house near Regent's Park and Aucuba Lodge, a grace-and-favour cottage owned by MCC on Elm Tree Road, at the north-west corner of Lord's.

In December 1866 Fitzgerald devised an ingenious project to put his finances on a better footing before his marriage. As Fitzgerald saw the matter, he would also help MCC to improve its dilapidated ground. He sought the committee's permission to construct a two-tier grandstand, holding about three thousand spectators, 'at his own risk and expense'. Under the deal, Fitzgerald would 'receive the profits arising from the use of such stand . . . during the pleasure of the MCC'.

Sir Spencer Ponsonby and several other committee members suspected Fitzgerald of profiteering. They authorised him to go ahead with the grandstand, 'subject to such terms as may be Sanctioned by the Committee'. Over the next month Fitzgerald fought back. He recruited a consortium of leading MCC figures to join his Lord's

Grand Stand Company as fellow directors and help him overcome the resistance of Sir Spencer and his brother Frederick. Fitzgerald's partners included two recent MCC presidents, Lord Sefton and Lord Skelmersdale, his future brother-in-law Edward Chandos Leigh (MCC president in 1887) and Harvey Fellows, the club's solicitor. The Ponsonbys and their allies now agreed to the project, with one key condition: MCC could forcibly purchase the grandstand from Fitzgerald's company at any time.

Fitzgerald's grandstand was ready for its first paying customers at the start of the 1867 season. He now set in motion his second plan to bolster his finances before his impending marriage. On 1 July Fitzgerald notified the committee 'that circumstances had rendered it necessary for him to resign his office of Hon G Secy. to the MCC, and that he would bring the subject forward at the next meeting'. It was a bluff, aimed at forcing the committee to offer him a salary.

By 15 July Fitzgerald had lined up enough supporters to get the committee to vote him an annual salary of £400 for a job that during the winter months did not involve much work. He officially turned professional, becoming plain 'secretary' rather than 'hon. secretary', while insisting floridly that 'he could never forget the invaluable assistance he had always received from the Committee and also that he trusted to merit the approbation which had been so handsomely conveyed to him by the same; his altered relationship to them would only tend to increase on his part a diligent attention to the wishes of the Committee & interests of the Club'.

Fitzgerald had two last pieces of pre-marital business. On a day off from Lord's he plonked 'Mrs Fitz (as is to be)' on a Crystal Palace Patent Weighing Chair, noting her weight (9 stone 10 lbs) in one of his cricketing scrapbooks. Next, he sent all his and Ettie's love letters to I Zingari cricket club, in accordance with the jokey rules imposed on members intending to marry by IZ's three founders, the Ponsonby brothers and John Loraine Baldwin. In return, Baldwin issued Fitzgerald with his very own IZ marriage licence.

The real marriage took place on 15 October at West Derby, near Liverpool. Fitzgerald marked the occasion by sticking a photo of 'Fitz' looking dreamy in flannels and a smoking jacket in his 'I Zingari' scrapbook, and writing 'The Unknown' beneath his picture. Ominously, Ettie's adjacent picture appeared next to a press article Fitzgerald also cut out about an 'action for divorce' between Viscount and Viscountess Dupplin.

The Fitzgeralds departed on an extended honeymoon that eventually took them to Brighton. There Fitzgerald bought a saucy postcard showing the rear view of a woman on a beach promenade as a stiff sea breeze reveals her underwear. He then altered the caption to read: 'Mrs Fitz as seen [on] A Windy Day at Brighton.'

So far Fitzgerald's grandstand had scarcely impinged on W.G. In February 1868 there was another odd slip of the pen at Oxford, when 'W.G. Grace (MCC)' entered the Strangers' Handicap Hurdles at Lincoln College's annual athletics meeting. 'MCC' lost, with Grace coming second to a student from Christ Church.

W.G. returned to Oxford a month later to compete once more as 'W.G. Grace (MCC)' in the Strangers' Quarter Mile Race at the university's main athletics meeting. This no longer seemed a clerical error. As far as Oxford University was concerned, Grace had told the organisers he was representing MCC.

Still he had to wait. All W.G.'s frustration at his continuing exclusion from the real MCC was summed up just after midday on Monday, 25 May. In brightening weather the Surrey batsmen Harry Jupp and Thomas Humphrey marched out of the Lord's pavilion to open the innings against MCC in the curtain-raiser for the first-class season. Eighty miles away in Swindon W.G. walked on to the Great Western Railway Club's playing field with his United South of England team-mates to take on twenty-two railwaymen. It is likely that W.G. and his younger brother Fred were making up the numbers in the absence of Jupp, Humphrey and several other USE regulars at Lord's.

W.G. now had just seven first-class fixtures to press his case for admission to MCC. He started by scoring 66 for an 'England' team that beat MCC at Lord's in early June. A week later he returned to Lord's and took eleven wickets for South of the Thames v North of the Thames, on a pitch that *The Sportsman* described as 'especially bumpy'. By now the public was getting fed up with both the northern professionals' repeated boycotts and MCC's resort to increasingly strange regional names for teams. Strictly speaking, Grace was ineligible for South of the Thames, as he came from North of the Avon.

Another absurdity occurred a fortnight later when Grace led Gloucestershire at Lord's against MCC & Ground. Gloucestershire's team, built around W.G., E.M. and Fred Grace, included several other players who would be regular members of the side in the 1870s when the county finally achieved first-class status. But in 1868 this game did not count as first class. Accordingly, the club selected a team that was well below first-class standard. W.G. had a mediocre game but Gloucestershire still won comfortably.

Such was the build-up to one of the greatest innings that Grace ever played. On Monday, 29 June W.G. turned up to play at Lord's for the Gentlemen against the Players on a hard, almost bare surface that the ground staff disguised by flattening the few stalks of grass across the soil. As the contemporary cricket writer Frederick Gale noted: 'The wickets reminded me of a middle aged gentleman's head of hair when, to conceal the baldness of his crown, he applies a pair of wet brushes to some favourite locks and brushes them across the top of his head. So with the wicket. The place where the ball pitched was covered with rough grass wetted and rolled down.'

Nine Gentlemen batsmen, including E.M., failed to reach double figures on this groundsman's equivalent of a comb-over. A tenth batsman, the Middlesex amateur Bransby Cooper, hung around with W.G. and scored 28. At the other end W.G. played as if he were batting on a completely different pitch. He scored an unbeaten 134 in his team's eventual total of 201 all out. W.G. performed this feat against a Players' attack led by James Lillywhite Jr. of Sussex, Ned Willsher of Kent, and the Nottinghamshire quick bowlers George Wootton and Jem Grundy. 'Mr Gilbert Grace was in terrific hitting form,' the London *Standard* reported, and was 'much cheered' by the large crowd (it did not state the number) when he returned to the pavilion. He then took ten wickets in the Players' two innings to win the match almost single-handed.

Within the cricket world W.G. was by now universally rec-ognised as the game's best batsman, possible the best there had ever been. 'A magnificent batsman, with defensive and hitting powers second to none,' *John Lillywhite's Cricketers' Companion* declared in its pen portrait of W.G. for both the 1867 and 1868 seasons. *Wisden* was slower off the mark, taking a rather grudging view of W.G.'s early batting performances, as Robert Winder has shown in his recent history of the almanack. It took till 1869 for *Wisden*'s editor W.H. Knight to do justice to W.G. by belatedly praising his two great innings at the Oval in 1866 as 'a batting feat as wonderful as it is unparalleled'.

In a just cricketing universe the MCC committee would have admitted W.G. to the club when it met on 29 June. Instead, Fitzgerald and his colleagues debated whether to instal turnstiles at Lord's, deciding to postpone the matter 'for the present'. In August W.G. was invited to play at the Canterbury festival for another South of the Thames v North of the Thames fixture. He scored a century in each innings, but it made no difference. At the age of twenty W.G. finished the 1868 season as he began it: a member of Gloucestershire CCC, which lacked first-class status, and of MCC's informal, one-man athletics section.

At the end of October W.G. registered as a student at the Bristol Royal Infirmary's medical school on St Michael's Hill, a short walk from the city centre. His enrolment implied that he would be less available for matches at Lord's in 1869, an unwelcome prospect for the directors of the Lord's Grand Stand Company.

After only two seasons the company was profitable, earning £378 from premium-priced ticket sales in 1868. Seeing the same balance sheet, the Ponsonby brothers and their allies now decided it was time for MCC to get the club's hands on the income by forcibly purchasing the grandstand. All they needed was the approval of MCC members at a special general meeting in the spring of 1869. Under the Ponsonbys' plan, MCC would then acquire the grandstand at the end of the 1869 season.

In mid-April 1869, a fortnight before the meeting, MCC's elderly treasurer Thomas Burgoyne proposed W.G.'s membership to the committee, with Fitzgerald seconding the motion. The timing was significant. With his acute sense of the balance of power at Lord's, Fitzgerald probably realised that he and his partners would lose the grandstand when the summer was over. As Frederick Ponsonby argued, it was self-evidently in MCC's interest to own such a profitable venture and the wider membership was bound to agree. Fitzgerald and his partners therefore had one last season to extract as much profit as possible from the grandstand. In commercial terms it made no sense to exclude W.G. as a non-MCC member from about half the first-class fixtures at Lord's in 1869. Grace's election had suddenly become an urgent business matter.

More puzzling was why Fitzgerald only seconded W.G.'s candidacy, leaving Burgoyne to put forward the proposal. The most likely reason was Fitzgerald's sense of his own unpopularity within the club because of the grandstand furore. Burgoyne, a genial retired solicitor, was the kind of ideal committee member who made no enemies, and so a perfect front man for a delicate mission.

W.G. had to wait two weeks for the committee to consider his candidacy. While they deliberated, he let off steam by entering a steeplechase in south-west London at Richmond Cricket Club's annual athletics meeting. W.G. surged ahead of the pack until he reached the water jump, where he tripped and fell flat into the muddy water – 'right into the middle of it', the *Morning Post* reported gleefully. Drenched and furious, W.G. surged out of the water but it was too late: just for once, he finished runner-up.

*

On the evening of 5 May MCC members gathered in the Lord's pavilion to consider whether the club should buy back the grandstand. Harvey Fellows, MCC's solicitor, pleaded on behalf of the directors for a delay because 'the Proprietors had only held the Stand for the short space of two years'. Frederick Ponsonby, whose father had been Lord Lieutenant of Ireland during the Great Famine, likened Fellows to 'a Tipperary tenant, who took to a holding on certain terms, and then preferred to hold the property without the terms ... ' Fitzgerald indignantly denied there was any conflict of interest between his position as MCC secretary and his role as the company's chief executive.

He knew the game was up. On a show of hands, the meeting authorised the buyback, with peace between the two factions superficially restored at the club's annual dinner a few hours later. Frederick Ponsonby proposed a triple toast to the MCC secretary: one for Fitzgerald, one for Mrs Fitzgerald, and one for their new-born son Gerald Fitzgerald. 'The Secretary, somewhat overcome, was understood to say that he was deeply sensible of the kind feeling expressed towards him by the members,' Fitzgerald minuted theatrically.

Frederick Ponsonby and his allies now confronted the same question that had exercised Fitzgerald: why own a grandstand while excluding the game's most exciting player from MCC? On 6 May 1869, almost five years after his first-class debut, 'W.G. Grace of Downend' was finally elected a member of the club.

There was an odd footnote to this saga. In 1869 a scribbled note by Burgoyne or Fitzgerald recorded that E.M. had 'retired' his membership. E.M. did not publicly explain why he resigned from MCC, so one can only guess his reasons. Now settled in the Gloucestershire village of Thornbury, E.M. was married with a growing family and a surgery to run on Castle Street. He perhaps decided that he was too busy to play for MCC; perhaps, too, E.M. felt that getting along with the likes of the Ponsonby brothers was more than he could bear.

5

THE AGENT FROM MELBOURNE

When he joined MCC, W.G. entered an intense, five-year period that saw him transformed from a provincial hero to the world's first international sporting superstar. In 1869 a trawl of the British Library's online newspaper database produces 527 references to Grace, but the Bristol and Bath press accounted for more than half the stories that mentioned him. His fame spread nationally and internationally over the next few years for one prime reason: runs. In his early twenties W.G. produced centuries at a rate that had never been witnessed before.

His output increased as soon as MCC elected him a member. By the end of the 1868 season, Grace's last before joining MCC, he had only scored five first-class hundreds in his entire career. W.G. scored a further six centuries in 1869, including four for MCC, as the number of first-class fixtures he played more than doubled to fifteen matches. It was 'the most wonderful series of large first-class innings ever played by one man in one season for the old club,' *Wisden* decided. All told, his series of centuries went as follows:

13–14 May – Oxford University v MCC, Oxford: 117
   ('Brilliant score', *Jackson's Oxford Journal*)

1 July – MCC v Surrey, Lord's: 138 not out ('Superb hitting innings', *Exeter Flying Post*)

7 July – MCC v Nottinghamshire, Lord's: 121 ('Magnificent', *Nottinghamshire Guardian*)

16 July – Gentlemen of the South v Players of the South, the Oval: 180 ('Extraordinary batting', *Sheffield and Rotherham Independent*)

26 July – North v South, Sheffield: 122 ('Simply irresistible', *Leeds Times*)

11 August – Kent v MCC, Canterbury: 127 ('Hitting tremendously', *Chelmsford Chronicle*)

On 16 July the *Daily Telegraph*'s anonymous correspondent at the Oval rose above the general mediocrity of mid-Victorian cricket reporting to produce a vivid sketch of Grace's innings of 180 for Gentlemen of the South:

He knew exactly where every ball he hit would go. Just the strength required was expended and no more. When the fieldsmen were placed injudiciously too deep he would quietly send a ball halfway towards them with a gentle tap and content himself with a modest single. If they came in a little nearer, the shoulders opened out and the powerful arms swung round as he lashed the first loose ball and sent it away through the crowded ring of visitors [*sic*] until one heard a big thump as it struck against the furthest fence.

Thanks to the mailboats that left every week for Australia, the colonies' newspaper readers were also starting to follow W.G.'s cricket 'doings' avidly. In Melbourne, Australia's leading theatre impresario picked up the same papers six or seven weeks later, with an idea already formed in his head. If George Coppin had his way, W.G. would be boarding a ship for Australia as soon as the English cricket season was over.

*

Corpulent and coarse, Coppin had ridden the ups and downs of Australian business life since arriving from England at the age of twenty-three in 1842 to try his luck as a comic actor. Coppin had lost money on hotels, made it again on theatres, got his fingers burned with copper mines, and bounced back as manager of the actor Charles Kean's tour of Australia and the United States in 1863–4. 'Mr Coppin is a good businessman and I believe a truly honourable and upright man,' Kean reported home to his daughter, 'but he is a *common* man and possesses a certain rudeness of manner which is very unpleasant when things do not run smoothly.'

By the late 1860s Coppin smelled money when he read about Grace's batting in the English newspapers. These stories were then reprinted by colonial papers like *The Australasian* and *The Argus* in Melbourne and the *Sydney Morning Herald*, and were eventually picked up by the country press. So it was that newspaper readers in Goulburn, a New South Wales sheep farming community, learned in October 1868 about W.G.'s 134 not out for the Gentlemen v Players at Lord's the previous June.

In Coppin's view, organising a tour with Grace as the main attraction would be no different from bringing theatre stars like Kean to the colonies. Coppin knew Felix Spiers and Christopher Pond, two English restaurateurs in Melbourne who had organised the first-ever English cricket tour of Australia in 1861–2. Spiers and Pond had returned to London in 1863, leaving the management of the second English tour by George Parr's team in 1863–4 to their employee George Shoosmith, who was also secretary of Richmond CC in Melbourne's eastern suburbs. Coppin was Richmond CC's president in 1861–2 and again in 1866–7, and knew Shoosmith well. When Shoosmith returned to his native London in the autumn of 1868 to work for Spiers and Pond, Coppin entrusted him with a mission. The impresario wanted Shoosmith to recruit a third team of top English amateurs and professionals to come to Australia in the winter of 1869–70. Coppin had only one condition: W.G. must be on the boat.

Coppin's plan had a serious flaw. He delayed giving Shoosmith a budget to organise the tour until far too late in the English cricket season, probably because Coppin had trouble finding co-investors to spread his financial risk. At the end of June 1869 Coppin finally authorised Shoosmith to draw £1000 from a London bank to cover advance payments to the professionals on the tour party. However, there was still no submarine telegraph link between Australia and England, which meant Coppin's authorisation did not reach Shoosmith via the mailboat until 9 August. Wasting no time, Shoosmith caught the train next morning to Canterbury, where the cricket festival was underway.

Shoosmith immediately sought out W.G., who was playing two matches during the Canterbury week for South v North and MCC v Kent. Shoosmith knew from his dealings with E.M. on Parr's tour in 1863–4 that W.G. would expect to be paid. Based on the stories in Melbourne about E.M. 'clearing' £500, Coppin probably offered W.G. a sum close to that amount. Shoosmith found W.G. prepared in principle to talk terms. It is plain from Shoosmith's account, published later in 1869 in the Australian press, that the Melbourne agent had already met W.G. at least once in the weeks before the Canterbury festival. W.G. could hardly fail to be tempted by a paid tour of Australia, when the alternative was grinding through another winter of lectures at Bristol Medical School. The problem was MCC.

When Shoosmith met W.G. at Canterbury on 10 August – possibly at the Fleur de Lys pub on the High Street, where W.G. liked to stay – Grace had so far played no openly professional cricket that summer for United South of England or any other team. As a newly elected MCC member, W.G. could not afford to upset MCC grandees like the Ponsonby brothers, based as usual for Canterbury week at the elegant Royal Fountain Hotel on St Margaret's Street. On its side, MCC was getting excellent value for its investment in W.G., who was about to score his fourth century for the club at Canterbury. The committee 'allowed' Grace total travel and board expenses of £7 for his first two MCC games at Oxford and Lord's, less than its standard £5 match fee for professionals, and probably continued reimbursing him at this modest rate in other fixtures.

W.G.'s willingness to risk his MCC membership by negotiating with Shoosmith probably came down to money. He was now twenty-one, and could not live indefinitely off his father. There were two other prospects – one real, the other illusory – that would have made Coppin's offer particularly appealing to W.G. When he was not chasing girls in Melbourne, E.M. stayed with his cousin William Rees in the Victoria gold-mining centre of Beechworth. Rees was the son of Martha Grace's sister Elizabeth, and other members of the Rees clan had settled in the colony, before and during the gold rush that peaked in the mid-1850s. W.G. would have plenty of invitations to catch up with his relatives.

E.M. came back from Victoria with tales of a 'golden land' and a 'glittering' colony that sounded rather more interesting than Bristol on a rainy day in February. However, E.M.'s gilded vision was well out of date when Shoosmith sat down with W.G. at Canterbury. By 1869 Victoria's gold rush was over, and a stream of doomed speculators was flowing through Melbourne's bankruptcy court. In all W.G.'s tortuous dealings with Australian promoters over the next four years, there is a sense that he did not grasp the degree to which the colony's economy was on the slide.

W.G.'s negotiating style was the opposite of his approach to batting; in discussions about money, he allowed others to take the lead. According to Shoosmith, W.G. told him at Canterbury that he 'had spoken to several gentlemen about the trip'. W.G. then advised Shoosmith 'to speak first to Mr V.E. Walker, who is the oracle amongst the gentlemen cricketers'.

Teddy Walker, colossally rich from his family's north London brewing fortune, had been W.G.'s captain at the Oval in 1866 when he allowed the teenager to compete in the hurdle race at Crystal Palace. Walker was on close terms with Fitzgerald and the rest of the MCC committee and may have asked them on Grace's behalf whether W.G. could take his discussions further with Shoosmith. W.G.'s cover was that Coppin would only officially be paying him amateur expenses. It was a convenient fiction that seemed to work. Shoosmith came away from his meeting with Walker convinced – as he put it to Coppin – that he had 'secured' Grace, 'without whom no team would be complete'. Walker 'seemed thoroughly to enter into the spirit of the thing,' Shoosmith enthused, adding that the brewer promised to 'ventilate the matter' with other gentlemen cricketers at Canterbury.

When Coppin received Shoosmith's letter at the start of October, he immediately leaked it to *The Australasian* in Melbourne and the *Sydney Morning Herald*. Coppin added a notice, inviting cricket clubs in Victoria and New South Wales to submit tenders for hosting a match against the 'All-England Eleven'. He was unaware that in England his venture had already collapsed in acrimony and confusion.

Walker was the first to disappoint Shoosmith, telling the agent at a second meeting at the Oval on 16 August that it was too late in the season to recruit any amateurs. Shoosmith was still convinced that W.G. would come to Australia, along with his younger brother Fred, already a fine cricketer at the age of seventeen. However, Shoosmith encountered another obstacle at the Oval in the form of Surrey's immovable secretary William Burrup. He refused to release four Surrey professionals for the tour without guarantees that they would be back from Australia in time for the start of the 1870 first-class cricket season. Burrup insisted that the quartet would have to deposit their tour fees in a London bank before departure. The players – Harry Jupp, James Southerton, Thomas Humphrey and Ted Pooley – then used Burrup's demand as a bargaining chip to extract better terms from Shoosmith. Negotiations broke down in early September, forcing Shoosmith to wire several northern professionals he had recruited to tell them the tour was off.

Grace's position (and presumably Fred's) was more ambiguous. On 9 September the *Bath Chronicle* stated as a matter of fact that W.G. would head a party of twelve cricketers who would depart from Liverpool to Melbourne on 20 September.

Shoosmith hastily informed the newspaper that the story was 'premature'. Yet he made it sound as if Grace had been willing to tour, provided a 'difficulty' over a medical exam could be removed. Shoosmith claimed he could easily have overcome W.G.'s 'objection'.

His tour project in ruins, Shoosmith scoured England for any other sports stars he could entice to Australia that winter with Coppin's money. At the last minute he found 'the celebrated' Frank Hewitt, of Millwall, half-mile champion; Albert Bird, of Sheffield, champion mile runner; and George Topley, the 'renowned champion walker' to put on the boat to Melbourne. For all his showman's flair, Coppin could not make the trio sound half as exciting as Grace.

Coppin was used to setbacks and could afford this one. He gave up on cricket tours and went into politics as the 'rather silent' member for East Melbourne in Victoria's Legislative Assembly. Shoosmith returned to Spiers and Pond in London, still available if other promoters in Melbourne made a second bid for W.G. As for Grace, he resumed his studies at Bristol Medical School under his tutor in surgery, Robert Tibbits.

6

SUPREMACY

W.G. and his fellow students nicknamed Tibbits 'Slasher' on account of the surgeon's showy, dramatic style on the operating table. Yet Tibbits – still in his late twenties – was not a blood-and-sawdust Victorian medical hack. The son of an engineer, Tibbits already considered himself as good as some of the best surgeons in Europe. In one operation he removed a piece of floating bone from the brain of a farm boy whose forehead had been kicked in by a horse. Tibbits used a cylindrical blade called a trephine, boasting after he saved the boy's sight that 'out of 15 cases at University College Hospital [London], only 5 were successful and that of 16 cases treated at Paris all died . . . It is a case on the success of which the operator may well be congratulated.'

Following Tibbits on his rounds, W.G. would have seen that the Bristol Infirmary's filthy wards harboured 'every disease which could be caused or fostered by foul air or insanitary conditions', as another doctor recalled. But Tibbits at least understood the connection between dirt and disease, heading a campaign in the 1870s to clean up the infirmary. He was certainly better qualified to teach W.G. than Grace's next surgery tutor, Dr Howard Marsh of St Bartholomew's Hospital in London, who 'had difficulty in accepting the germ theory of disease', according to his Royal College of Surgeons' obituary.

Grace, in short, could easily have qualified as a doctor at Bristol Medical School, working towards the not especially challenging surgeon's and physician's licentiates under Tibbits and his colleagues. Yet W.G. did not mention Tibbits at all in either of his memoirs. It was as if his time as a pupil of Tibbits was a blank. There is no evidence that W.G. sat the exam in April 1870 that he cited to Shoosmith as an obstacle to touring Australia – if indeed the exam actually existed. Tibbits already knew from the previous summer that cricket now governed W.G.'s schedule, following his pupil's admission to MCC. In 1870 W.G. would play twenty first-class matches, five more than in 1869, and five fewer than in 1871. The upward trend was plain. Increasingly in the 1870s, W.G. gave the impression that he attended medical school when he had nothing better to do.

One innings in the summer of 1870 marked W.G. in a class above any other batsman in the game's history to that point. On the morning of 13 June, W.G. walked into Lord's through the St John's Wood Road entrance shortly before the start of MCC's match against Nottinghamshire. In the summer of 1870, Grace was not yet the familiar bearded giant of later publicity portraits. He may even have been clean-shaven, for in a hirsute age W.G. seems to have dithered in his teens and early twenties about whether to grow Victorian England's most famous beard. The gentlemen cricketers Charles Lyttelton (later Lord Cobham) and Russell Walker remembered the seventeen-year-old Grace having a short stubbly beard when he made his first-class debut in 1865.

The following summer W.G. was clean-shaven when he appeared in a group photograph with his family's West Gloucestershire team. By 1868 or 1869, when he posed for a studio photograph (see page 2 of picture section), W.G. sported a set of bushy whiskers that met at the chin, plus a neat moustache. According to MCC's *Memorial Biography*, W.G. possibly then shaved the whole thing off.

Bearded or clean-shaven, the figure his MCC team-mates and their Nottinghamshire opponents saw as Grace dumped his leather cricket bag in the pavilion was far from the visibly obese Grace of the mid-1870s. W.G. seems slight, even a little thin, in his portrait from a year or two before this game; the sense of his lightness is reinforced by his strangely limp pose, taken the moment before he would normally take guard.

MCC walked out to bowl first on a pitch that looked dangerously dry, after several weeks without rain. For some reason MCC had failed to water the pitch, and the club's fast bowler Jack Platts, a newly hired professional on the ground staff, now took full advantage of the parched, cracked surface. During the first session Platts peppered the Nottinghamshire batsmen Richard Daft and George Summers with balls that 'kicked repeatedly', according to the *Nottinghamshire Guardian*, the only newspaper to publish a detailed report of the match. Its admittedly biased correspondent was outraged, adding that Platts inflicted 'repeated blows' on Daft and Summers' upper bodies as they failed to fend off his short deliveries. Platts, a twenty-one-year-old labourer from Derbyshire, was making his MCC debut, and it is hard to avoid the feeling that he was trying to impress his captain Teddy Walker and the watching MCC committee.

Platts eventually bowled Summers for 41 with a 'shooter' that skidded under his bat – another hazard of batting on the unpredictable pitch. Daft struggled on, taking more hits on his chest and arm, as he scored 117 out of a Nottinghamshire total of 267. It was a great and brave innings, which the MCC committee acknowledged by presenting the bruised Daft with a souvenir bat on his return to the pavilion.

There were fifty minutes left till the close of play when W.G. opened MCC's innings with Teddy Walker's younger brother Donny. Nottinghamshire had probably the best bowling attack in England: Jem Shaw, 'fast left-hand, with a high delivery'; William McIntyre, a 'very fast right-handed bowler'; George Wootton, left-arm fast, specialising in 'shooters'; and the exceptionally accurate medium-pacer Alfred Shaw.

Grace began slowly, mindful of the battering Daft and Summers had received earlier in the day. He drove Jem Shaw for three runs in the first over, but only scored one run from the next six overs, with Isaac Walker runless at the other end. Grace at last released the pressure with two cuts to the boundary, one of which the *Nottinghamshire Guardian* thought rather 'uppish'; as so often with reporting of Grace's batting, the journalist may have imagined that W.G. hit the ball in the air by accident, rather than deliberately into the gaps.

W.G.'s little flurry got Walker going, and the two batsmen began stealing quick singles. At 7 p.m. W.G. returned to the pavilion on 49 not out, in an overnight MCC total of 67. He looked as if he had been batting on a completely different pitch from the one that Platts had bowled on at the start of the day.

W.G. was getting changed when an incident occurred that nearly caused the match to be abandoned. Teddy Walker had injured his finger while fielding and now notified Daft that the MCC committee had allowed Walker to use a substitute batsman in his place called Henry Richardson. It was not clear from MCC's own 'laws of cricket' whether Walker had broken the rules, but Daft thought Walker was trying to gain an unfair advantage and told him so. Still nursing his bruises, Daft told Walker that Nottinghamshire would refuse to take the field next morning if MCC did not withdraw the substitute.

Grace later suggested that Daft soon climbed down as 'an act of chivalry'. The reality was far nastier. Daft was still holding firm only half an hour before the start of the second day's play (14 June), supported by his team. Meanwhile, a midweek crowd of several thousand was filing into Lords, unaware that they might soon be demanding a refund. Daft finally relented a few minutes before the scheduled start of play and agreed to let Richardson bat instead of Teddy Walker. Nottinghamshire's captain was in an impossible position. If his team abandoned the match, MCC was likely to bar Daft and the other Nottinghamshire profession-als from the full schedule of lucrative games at Lord's.

When play started, shortly after noon, Nottinghamshire's

bowlers pinned back Grace and Isaac Walker for 'over after over' on the worn, deteriorating pitch. Gradually the pair began to score more freely as the bowlers tired. MCC's total passed 100 and soon afterwards 'Grace made a tremendously hard hit to mid on, and started for a run. The ball was, however, splendidly fielded by A. Shaw, who shied down Grace's wicket so quickly that he only just recovered his ground.'

With MCC's score on 127, Jem Shaw bowled Walker for 48. Teddy's younger brother had just played the innings of his life, as the next nine MCC batsmen now demonstrated. They managed just 10 runs between them (1, 4, 0, 0, 0, 4, 0, 0, 1) as Jem Shaw and McIntyre tore through the middle and lower order. Grace responded by counter-attacking. He drove McIntyre 'magnificently' for five (all run) and then reached his century by 'lifting' the same bowler towards the grandstand for four, a characteristic over-the-top shot found in no coaching manual.

Platts, the last MCC batsman, now came out of the pavilion to join him. W.G. tried to pinch singles at the end of each over to keep his hopeless partner off strike. At length Grace drove McIntyre straight for six, and hit the left-arm fast bowler Jem Shaw (no relation to Alfred) to the pavilion for four, making his score 117. Finally McIntyre bowled Platts for 1. MCC were all out for 183, well behind Nottinghamshire's first innings total of 267. Under MCC's laws, Daft now had the right to make MCC bat again. He did so, with some relish.

W.G., probably exhausted, was soon bowled by Jem Shaw for 0. The rest of MCC's batsmen dealt better with Nottinghamshire's tiring attack, scoring 240 all out at a drearily slow rate. That left Nottinghamshire with 157 to win on the third and final day.

From the start the pitch 'bumped awfully . . . , particularly at Platts' end,' the *Nottinghamshire Guardian* reported. Its anonymous correspondent's account of what happened next has to be treated with some caution, yet his lengthy despatch, produced in 'real time' as events unfolded, was never contradicted by MCC.

At 1 p.m., with the score on 23 for one, twenty-four-year-old

George Summers walked out again to face Platts. Platts' first delivery 'struck him a violent blow on his head, the ball missing his temple by about half an inch. Summers reeled backwards senseless.'

The Cambridge amateur Charles 'Buns' Thornton remembered the moment a little differently. 'It was a fearful crack on the temple and when struck he [Summers] jumped up into the air, and then fell all of a heap.' The Kent amateur Bill Yardley, who was keeping wicket, 'never saw a ball get up with such lightning rapidity. The pitch of the ball and the blow on Summers' head appeared to be simultaneous.'

W.G. raced to the stricken batsman, felt his pulse, and established that Summers was still alive; after a minute or two he recovered consciousness. Thornton and Yardley half-carried, half-dragged Summers off the field, the batsman 'scarcely able to drag his limbs after him', according to the *Nottinghamshire Guardian*. In this fashion they got Summers to the Lord's Tavern on the boundary, where they carried him upstairs to bed.

'I shall never forget Richard Daft coming in next with a towel round his head covered with a scarf tied under his chin,' Thornton recalled. 'The first ball he had pitched half-way and went clean over his head. He did let Platts have it, and no mistake, and the bowler was taken off after that over.'

Summers got up next day (Thursday, 16 June) and rested in an armchair in front of the Tavern, watching the start of another cricket match in bright sunshine. He felt well enough by late afternoon to walk slowly round the playing field, assisted by a companion. On Friday, after a bad night, Summers agreed to take the train home to Nottingham, travelling in a special bed made up for him by the Midland Railway Company. At Nottingham station he was carried across the street to the Commercial Hotel, which his father managed. Once again Summers was put to bed, where he languished for two days, occasionally drinking 'herb beer' as a potion. At some point Summers began to have 'convulsions'; on Sunday he died.

Yardley was certain he knew why Summers had been hit.

'I am perfectly sure the ball must have struck a small stone,' he said later. 'It was impossible for it to get up in that way from the ordinary turf.' W.G. also remembered picking gravel out of the Lord's pitch – not specifically in this match, but routinely in the late 1860s. If Yardley was right, then MCC might have been liable under modern law to a charge of manslaughter. It still seems inexplicable that Fitzgerald and the committee should have paid so much attention to the pavilion and the grandstand at Lord's, while allowing the ground staff to 'prepare' such appalling, stone-pitted pitches.

MCC gave no public sign that it felt any responsibility for Summers' death. But behind closed doors Fitzgerald's committee minutes suggest there was considerable discussion of the tragedy. Summers' death was discussed twice in committee in the following weeks, with MCC eventually deciding to pay £30 'to testify their regret at the untimely accident at Lord's Ground, which cut short a career full of promise'.

The real gauge of MCC's sense of guilt was the state of the Lord's pitch, which gradually began to improve in the aftermath of what became known as 'Summers' match'.

W.G.'s great century disappeared into oblivion, barely remembered even by him.

A few weeks later Grace embarked on a run of form that prompted a burst of superlatives from the newspapers. It read as follows:

> 15–16 July – Gentlemen v Players, the Oval: 215 ('One of the longest and best innings, both offensive and defensive, that has ever been recorded', *Morning Post*)
>
> 18 July – Gentlemen v Players, Lord's: 109 out of 187 all out ('Fearless', *Nottinghamshire Guardian*)
>
> 28 July – Surrey v Gloucestershire, the Oval: 143 ('Magnificent', *Sporting Life*)
>
> 1 August – MCC v Gloucestershire, Lord's: 172 out of 276 all out ('Splendid', *The Era*)

W.G. was making a subliminal point with his centuries for Gloucestershire. In 1870 the newly formed county club acquired first-class status, without a home ground and few players of known first-class ability apart from W.G. and his brothers E.M. and Fred. Purely on the power of his batting, W.G. demonstrated that Gloucestershire (who easily beat Surrey and MCC) could hold their own against the best teams. W.G. also took fifteen wickets in the two games, mostly in partnership with Fenton Miles, a left-arm spinner who would bowl more than 2000 four-ball overs for Gloucestershire over the next nine years. Exhausted by this effort, Miles retired from first-class cricket in 1879 to focus on a less tiring career as a banker.

Gloucestershire were so poor that the entire team played as amateurs. At Lord's MCC was getting richer with each season, from two sources. One was steadily climbing gate revenues, which rose by almost a third in 1870 to about £3240; the other was the increase in the number of members, which soared from about 1000 to more than 1500 between 1870 and 1872, with an annual subscription rate of £3 per head.

MCC probably paid W.G.'s subscription. A later committee minute seems to refer to Grace's membership fee, 'which had for 14 years been paid by the club'. While MCC's subsidy was welcome, Grace does not appear to have received any other special treatment. In 1870 MCC paid him a total of £27 8s in expenses for playing six matches at Lord's, plus an away game against Oxford University. These were reasonable expenses, no more.

For now W.G. more or less kept his side of the bargain not to play openly for money. He appeared in only one major professional fixture in 1870, an MCC-hosted game at Lord's between United South and United North of England, for which he must have received the committee's approval to play. Yet his financial situation was unsustainable without playing more professional cricket or, alternatively, qualifying as a doctor. At the age of twenty-two, W.G. needed to earn a living. Once again, as the 1870 season ended, 'Slasher' Tibbits and his trephine beckoned.

7

THE CANADIAN GAMBLE

As a 'general perpetual student', W.G. was not officially obliged to attend any of Tibbits' classes and surgery demonstrations, or those of other lecturers on the school's faculty. Grace's £23 half-yearly fee simply gave him the right to turn up for the winter and summer sessions if he wished. In theory W.G. could have caught up with his studies over the winter if he really got down to work. But in December 1870 he downgraded from Tibbits' 'pupil' to 'assistant pupil', a category that did not exist in the school's prospectus. W.G. was loosening his ties with the school. Within a few months he would cease to appear in its records at all.

W.G.'s disengagement from his studies was underlined in February 1871, when he acted as the 'slipper' during two days' hare coursing on Lord Fitzhardinge's Gloucestershire estate. Of all W.G.'s sporting guises – cricketer, hurdler, golfer, bowler, shooter – his long career as a slipper was the least remarked after his death; yet it was the one which, after cricket, gave him the most pleasure. W.G.'s job was to use a slip with two collars to release two dogs at the same time once the hare was spotted, blasting away on his whistle to alert his colleagues on horseback that the chase was underway. By the end of the meeting the beagles had killed about fifty hares along the Gloucestershire side of the River Severn Estuary. One of the huntsmen made 'a suggestion . . . relative to a testimonial to the celebrated cricketer as some slight acknowledgement of his services'. In plain English, W.G. received a generous tip.

Despite such little windfalls, W.G. must have been under some pressure from his father to contribute to his upkeep at The Chestnuts. This probably explains why he played six openly professional games for United South of England in 1871. There was an obvious risk of offending MCC, but W.G.'s sheer weight of runs for the club acted as insurance against being hauled before the committee.

Grace set out his going rate for professional games in a letter he wrote in 1872 to a match promoter in the Leicestershire town of Melton Mowbray. W.G. demanded '£15.0.0 for my expenses & c.', which was probably a euphemism for a flat fee, with the promoter expected to pick up Grace's travel, bed and board costs.

At this rate in 1871, W.G. would have earned about £90 for his six USE games, slightly more than his father's annual salary as a Poor Law parish medical officer. There is no sense during the summer of 1871 that W.G. had made some strategic decision in opting to come out as a 'shamateur'. Rather, he was daring anyone – including MCC – to stop him playing for money during the greatest batting season of his life.

When W.G. arrived at Lord's on 15 May for his first MCC match of the season, the crowd outside the ground was being funnelled through two new sets of turnstiles. Lord's was acquiring the first trappings of a modern sports stadium, with W.G. the main attraction.

In bright chilly weather W.G. walked out to bat against Surrey just after midday. Through the afternoon, 'every ball that came within [his] reach was either carefully stopped or judiciously placed between the fielders for a single, or sent cracking down for six to the armoury wall or the Pavilion'. The Surrey spin bowler James Southerton finally dismissed Grace late in the afternoon for 181. 'Mr W.G. Grace, in vulgar parlance, is "at it again",' *The Australasian*'s London correspondent reported home to Melbourne. According to *The Graphic*, a London newspaper, the crowd expressed 'a general hope' that W.G. was poised for 'another brilliant season'.

Here are the highlights:

25–26 May – Gentlemen of the South v Gentlemen of the North, West Brompton: 118 ('Mammoth scoring', *Liverpool Mercury*)

29 May – South v North, Lord's: 178 ('W.G. Grace was in his best form and the bowling consequently suffered', *Sheffield and Rotherham Independent*)

1 June – Cambridge University v Gentlemen of England, Cambridge: 162 ('He at once commenced hitting in earnest', *Cambridge Independent Press*)

10 July – Married v Single, Lord's: 189 not out ('Played and hit in his best form', *Illawarra Mercury*, Wollongong, New South Wales)

21 July – Surrey v MCC, the Oval: 146 ('Mr Grace, as usual, made a leviathan score', *The Era*)

1–2 August – South v North, the Oval: 268 ('This celebrated player has eclipsed all his previous performances', *The Australasian*)

9–10 August – Kent v MCC, Canterbury: 117 ('Runs came at by no means a slow rate', *Whitstable Times and Herne Bay Herald*)

15–16 August – Gentlemen v Players, Hove: 217 ('A performance in all respects worthy of himself', *Morning Post*)

23 August – Nottinghamshire v Gloucestershire, Trent Bridge: 116 ('Defied several changes of bowling', *Sheffield Daily Telegraph*)

In total W.G. scored 2739 first-class runs in 1871 at a batting average of 78.25 runs per innings, double that of the next most successful batsman, Richard Daft of Nottinghamshire. 'Every few years produce some celebrity, but this gentleman dwarfs all who have preceded him,' the *Sydney Mail* observed of Grace's performances that year.

The reference to W.G.'s towering fame was telling, because his celebrity was to some extent magnified in the 1870s by the absence of rival stars from other sports. Football was still in its infancy, with the southern Football Association in dispute with the northern Sheffield Football Association about the rules of the game. Amid this confusion the first FA Cup Final, held at the Oval in 1872, only attracted 'a very fair muster of spectators', according to one newspaper, as if the two-thousand-strong crowd had to be rounded up.

Golf remained largely confined to Scotland, with only a handful of courses in England and none of any consequence in the United States. As for lawn tennis, it was still being invented. In 1873 Major Walter Wingfield patented 'a new and improved court for playing the ancient game of tennis', which he rebranded disastrously as 'Sphairistikè' (ancient Greek for 'pertaining to a ball game'). By 1877 tennis had sorted out its own rules sufficiently well for the All England Croquet and Lawn Tennis Club to hold its first men's singles championship at Wimbledon. 'Lawn tennis will never rank among our great games,' the winner Spencer Gore declared. 'Anybody who has played cricket or rackets will soon be choked off by the monotony.'

W.G. therefore had an almost clear field as a sporting hero in the 1870s. Yet he would never have been so famous without three developments that transformed mid-nineteenth-century Britain: the roll-out of a national railway network, the construction of a telegraph system, and the creation of a mass market press following the abolition in 1855 of stamp duty on newspapers.

One week in June 1871 illustrates W.G.'s reliance on the train to maintain his increasingly frenetic cricket schedule. On 23 June he finished a game at Lord's for MCC against Oxford University. Three days later he started a match in the Lincolnshire town of Grantham for USE which finished on 28 June. Next day he began a match at the Oval for Gentlemen of the South.

Telegrams were by now relaying news of W.G.'s latest cricket 'doings' even faster than the train. Soon he would have global coverage, thanks to the laying of submarine cables beneath the oceans. When W.G. scored 51 not out at Melbourne on Monday, 29 December 1873, readers of the *Huddersfield Chronicle* received the summary report in time for breakfast on Wednesday. It was not as if the *Huddersfield Chronicle* had a scoop. The emergence of a cheap 'penny' mass market press in the 1860s meant the public could choose from dozens of titles to read the same syndicated story. On this day (31 December) the British Library's online newspaper catalogue lists thirteen other titles that also published this report, in Sheffield, Bradford, South Shields, Glamorgan, Aberdeen, Hampshire, Liverpool, London and Dublin.

Grace's thoughts on his gathering fame can only be deduced, because he did not talk publicly about the subject. Unfortunately for his ghostwriter Methven Brownlee, W.G. did not want to talk about anything very much by the time the two of them reached the 1870s in *Cricket*. 'It is with a sigh of relief that I have finished that part of my work,' W.G. declared, after a particularly wearisome trudge through old cricket matches. 'My readers I have no doubt will be relieved too.' Not surprisingly, Brownlee cut Grace's confession from the published version of the book.

W.G. was equally keen to gloss over an episode in 1871 which he falsely claimed in the published version of *Cricket* was the only time he ever made a bet on the game. During the 1870s cricket was still steeped in a gambling culture that went back to the previous century, when peers like the Duke of Cumberland and the Earl of Sandwich staked huge sums on the outcome of prize matches. A whiff of this aristocratic taste for a bet comes across in Lord Harris's private account of his wager as captain of Oxford University with the former Cambridge Blue Charles 'Buns' Thornton about the outcome of the 1874 Varsity match at Lord's. 'I said I'd take £30 [on Oxford] but he wouldn't,' Harris wrote. Just before Oxford bowled the first ball of the game, 'Thornton ran down the steps [of the pavilion] & laid me £30 to £20 . . .' Oxford won, and so did Harris.

Gambling on the game was so commonplace that MCC's laws of cricket included special rules on how to bet on 'single-wicket' competitions, where individual batsmen took on fielding teams. Against this background, Grace would have needed exceptional restraint *not* to back himself to score runs in 1871, or any other season, especially as gambling was in his nature. He loved the turf, attending the annual races at Bath in May three days after his century against Surrey at Lord's. From horses and cards – another recreation – it was a small step to taking bets from team-mates on how many runs he might make.

At Lord's on 3 July W.G. took his usual bet with Bill Yardley over which of them would score more runs for the Gentlemen against the Players. Yardley recalled that he always 'bet W.G. Grace half a crown on my runs against his when we played on the same side against the same bowling'. On this occasion W.G. scored 50, but Yardley just won the bet with an innings of 51.

W.G. may have taken another bet during a match between South and North at the Oval that began on 31 July. The fixture was a so-called 'benefit' game for the Surrey player Heathfield Harman 'H.H.' Stephenson, who was retiring to take up a coaching job at Uppingham School in Rutland. Under the benefit system, veteran professionals like Stephenson were allowed by the host club (in this case Surrey) to keep the gate money from their game and sometimes pass a collection box round the ground.

H.H. was furious when Grace was out for 0 in the South's first innings; the whole point of having W.G. at a benefit game was to bring in the crowds and boost the collection. 'Keep your heart up, H.H.,' Grace recalled telling Stephenson on his return to the pavilion. 'I shall take care that it does not occur in the second innings.' W.G. kept his promise. He made 268, his highest first-class score so far, against an attack led by the left-arm quick bowler Jem Shaw of Nottinghamshire, before the game petered out in a draw. According to Grace, Stephenson was so 'immensely pleased' that he gave W.G. a gold ring.

The story feels sanitised, like many anecdotes in Grace's memoirs. H.H.'s present does not sound like the act of a man at a benefit match who was trying to maximise his earnings. It is more likely that Stephenson bet Grace he could not score a century (or perhaps even a double-century), to make up for the disappointment of W.G.'s 0 in the first innings. In this scenario Stephenson would have been trying to motivate Grace with a little side-bet.

A fortnight later Grace travelled to Brighton for another benefit for the retiring forty-four-year-old Sussex professional John Lillywhite, publisher of the *Cricketers' Companion* that bore his name. Lillywhite had been the umpire who gave W.G. out for 0 in the first innings of Stephenson's benefit. Now it was Lillywhite's turn to be incensed with Grace, who arrived late at the Royal Brunswick Ground in Hove and had no time for his usual pre-match practice before opening the batting for the Gentlemen v Players. Jem Shaw marked out his run-up at the sea end, with the sun glittering on the waves behind him. 'The dazzling light, the railway journey, and want of five minutes practice did it,' Grace remembered. Shaw bowled him for 0 off the third ball of the game.

W.G. returned to the thatched pavilion at the corner of the ground where Lillywhite made a bet with him. In the published version of Grace's story the wager was nonsensical. According to Grace, Lillywhite gave W.G. two sovereigns and told him to 'pay me a sixpence back for every run you make in the second innings'. Under this arrangement, W.G.'s best strategy was to get out for 0 again and keep all of Lillywhite's £2. As soon as he started scoring, the money would trickle back to Lillywhite.

The bet made much more sense in the original manuscript version of Grace's memoir. Here Lillywhite offered Grace three-pence 'or some such small coin' for every run he scored up to 100; in effect, Lillywhite was giving W.G. an incentive to score a century. Cannily, Lillywhite then received back the coins for every run over 100. Grace probably doubted that even he could score two double-centuries in a fortnight. On the other hand, he could make 150 under Lillywhite's terms, and still be in profit.

At Grace's request, Lillywhite consented to cancel the bet at the close of play, when Grace was on exactly 200 not out (he was out next day for 217). They were evens, but in a sense both of them had won. W.G. had scored another double-century, while Lillywhite had given his benefit crowd full value for the price of admission. In return, Lillywhite could expect the spectators to be generous when he passed his collection box round the ground.

A far bigger bet was about to be made on Grace, orchestrated by MCC's secretary, another keen gambler on horses. In June or July Fitzgerald met two visitors from Canada at Lord's: Thomas Patteson, a thirty-four-year-old Toronto lawyer and newspaper manager, and Captain Willoughby Wallace, an army officer stationed with the King's Royal Rifles in Halifax, Nova Scotia. Patteson, the leader of the two-man delegation, explained that a consortium of Canadian cricket clubs wanted Fitzgerald to bring an MCC team to Canada that autumn. The clubs would fund the cost of the tour, which might also include a side-trip to play in New York, Philadelphia and Boston, the three main American cricketing cities. As with Coppin's approach in 1869, the Canadians had only one non-negotiable condition: Fitzgerald had to include W.G. in MCC's tour party.

Originally from Hampshire, Patteson had much in common with Fitzgerald. He was a keen rather than outstanding cricketer, an ardent racegoer and a chaser of women, undeterred by the loss of a front tooth in a wicketkeeping accident. At some stage in his youth Patteson had also managed to fall on a pencil, '[the] point of which ran through my nose and into [the] corner of my eye'.

As a fellow entrepreneur, Fitzgerald rapidly realised that Patteson's tour proposal was about more than cricket. The Canadians thought they could make money from a tour featuring Grace, despite cricket's weak foothold in the newly independent dominion. Fitzgerald, too, hoped to make money from the venture as the author (so he hoped) of a best-selling North American tour memoir, provisionally titled *Wickets in the West*. After the disappointing sales of *Jerks in From Short Leg*, it would be the book to establish his literary reputation.

The immediate difficulty was the timing. It was too late to organise a tour before the Canadian autumn, and Fitzgerald told Patteson and Wallace they would have to wait until the late summer of 1872. Meanwhile, the key was to get W.G. on board.

Wallace now stepped into action. The thirty-two-year-old officer had a brother who was a vicar in Bristol and looked after their widowed mother, giving Wallace a good reason for visiting Gloucestershire. More significantly, he already knew E.M. quite well, having played several times with Grace's brother in the early 1860s before the King's Royal Rifles left for Canada. As Gloucestershire's acting secretary, E.M. made sure Wallace was selected for the game against Surrey at Clifton, starting on 17 August. Wallace now had three days unfettered access to W.G., who arrived at the ground from Hove.

Wallace scored 0 not out in Gloucestershire's only innings, which was more important than it looked. By not losing his wicket, he allowed Thomas Matthews, a glue merchant from Clifton, to stagger to the only double-century (or indeed century) of his first-class career. For once in his greatest season, W.G. did little, scoring just 23 as Gloucestershire easily beat Surrey by an innings.

Wallace stayed in the team for Gloucestershire's next match, away at Trent Bridge against Nottinghamshire, where he saw W.G.'s crowd-pulling power on his first-ever appearance at Trent Bridge. 'The immense attendance of spectators was ... doubtless owing to the presence of Mr W.G. Grace, the champion batsman,' reported the *Yorkshire Post*, which estimated there were about ten thousand people packed into the ground by the afternoon.

Wallace (0 and 1) saw enough of W.G. (79 and 116) to realise why a tour of Canada would flop without Grace in the side. Wallace knew from his own experience of playing cricket in

Canada that it took a lot of persuasion to get anyone to watch a match. 'Lacrosse, I was informed, was the game most patronised in Canada, thousands of spectators flocking to witness the matches,' he recalled.

Wallace left Trent Bridge (where Gloucestershire lost) in some frustration, which was shared by Patteson. Grace had still not firmly agreed to tour Canada, putting the whole project in doubt. The Canadians would have been further alarmed if they picked up any cricketing gossip that winter from Melbourne. By the spring of 1872 a group of Melbourne cricket clubs was poised to launch another bid for Grace. According to their plan, W.G. would be on a boat to Australia, not Canada, later in the year.

8

THE BIDDING WAR

W.G. was bound to consider both the Canadian and Australian bids seriously because of a sudden change in his life. Shortly before Christmas 1871 he went riding with the Beaufort Hunt on the Gloucestershire and Somerset borders. 'It is a treat to see Mr W.G. Grace running after the hounds without his coat,' the *Bath Chronicle* reported, 'then put his coat on, mount a farmer's young 'un, and pound the whole field.' W.G.'s sixty-three-year-old father Henry was on the same hunt, and caught a bad cold. He went to church with his family on Sunday, 17 December, struggled back across the road to The Chestnuts, and got himself to bed. By the middle of the week Henry Grace had pneumonia; by Saturday he was dead.

W.G. felt a double shock from his father's sudden death. There was the obvious emotional impact, and the more specific worry of whether his mother would now have enough money to make ends meet. Martha Grace was not destitute, because Dr Henry Skelton, about to marry her daughter Annie, had agreed to carry on the surgery at The Chestnuts and provide Martha with some of the income. Yet, potentially, W.G. was now his family's chief breadwinner, with rival promoters from opposite sides of the world competing for his services.

In this light, Grace's overlapping negotiations with Toronto and Melbourne in the summer of 1872 had a puzzling outcome, because he accepted the lower of the two offers. W.G.'s behaviour was more rational than it seemed. By going to Canada at the end of the 1872 season rather than Australia, W.G. ensured that eventually he got two lucrative international tours. The price he paid was a lot of bad feeling in Melbourne.

Fitzgerald had done little over the winter of 1871–2 to organise his proposed North American tour. By early May, Patteson could not wait any longer. 'I am literally besieged with "are the English gentlemen coming out?" and my life is rendered a burden to me,' he complained to Fitzgerald from Toronto. 'I have only received one letter from you, which held out hopes. Pray let me know the latest news on the subject.' Galvanised by Patteson, Fitzgerald now 'took measures to ascertain the feelings of his young friends about crossing the water with their cricket-bags'.

Fitzgerald would soon learn that W.G. had received a competing bid from Melbourne. On the afternoon of 16 May the Melbourne Cricket Club convened a special meeting at Scott's Hotel on Collins Street to consider a proposal to bring Grace and a team of amateurs to Australia in the autumn. The city's three leading clubs – Melbourne CC, East Melbourne CC and South Melbourne CC – had raised £3750 to insure against any losses from the venture. As with the Canadians, the Melbourne clubs' only stipulation was Grace's inclusion in the tour party. W.G. was the indispensable 'sine qua non', Melbourne CC's president David McArthur told the meeting.

McArthur, a prominent Melbourne banker, then gave the floor to 'the proposer of the scheme'. Richard Wardill, a thirty-one-year-old member of the Melbourne CC committee, recalled that the last English team to come to Australia in 1863–4 had 'netted nearly £7000 profit' for the promoters. An accountant by profession, Wardill reckoned that with W.G. in the team, 'there was a good chance of making a handsome profit after treating their visitors with proper hospitality'. Wardill's prospectus contained the same miscalculation as Coppin's budget in 1869. A team of self-styled English gentlemen 'amateurs' – and especially a team including W.G. – would expect to be paid.

In his essay 'The Hero and the Ham', the Australian cricket writer Gideon Haigh brilliantly captured Wardill's charming, reckless character. Born in Liverpool, Wardill arrived in Melbourne in 1858 with the rest of his emigrating family at the peak of the Victoria gold rush. By his early twenties Wardill was one of the best batsmen in the colony, scoring the first-ever first-class hundred by an Australian in a match between Victoria and New South Wales. Haigh suggests that the acclaim went to Wardill's head. He became a serious gambler, financing his addiction by embezzling money from the sugar company that employed him to keep its accounts.

Given Wardill's betting habits, his motives for proposing the 'Grace speculation' (as the colonial press soon dubbed the venture) cannot be taken at face value. Despite his rhetoric about promoting cricket, Wardill must have hoped the tour would provide further opportunities to line his own pocket. It is difficult to believe that none of the other cricketers and club officials who gathered at Scott's had an inkling of Wardill's gambling habit; some of them may even have taken money off him over the card table. Yet they took Wardill's optimistic word that a tour led by Grace would rake in cash, and gave him the go-ahead to approach W.G.

In Toronto Patteson was also busy drumming up support for the proposed Canadian tour, having finally stirred Fitzgerald into action. On 21 May Patteson sent a telegram to Fitzgerald via the St John's Wood post office: 'Large meeting enthusiastic unanimous all your propositions accepted get Thornton third August latest safe day to sail week sooner better.' The hard-hitting amateur batsman 'Buns' Thornton, in his last year at Cambridge, was still clearly a concern. On the other hand, Patteson made no enquiry about W.G.; he seems to have assumed that Grace would be on the boat to Canada in August.

Fitzgerald was now rounding up the rest of the team. At the end of May he ran into twenty-one-year-old George Harris at the Epsom Derby and asked if he could come to Canada. 'I could hardly believe it,' Harris recalled. 'Why should a humble cricketer as I thought myself, be picked out for the 1st XI of Gents that ever crossed the seas to play cricket!!' *Bell's Life* cast a suspicious eye on Fitzgerald's recruitment drive, suggesting that MCC's secretary was organising a thinly disguised commercial tour on behalf of the club. Fitzgerald fired off an indignant letter to *Bell's*, insisting 'the initiative was not taken by the MCC'.

Fitzgerald was trying to have it both ways. He certainly gave the impression it was an MCC tour to Harris, soon to be the 4th Baron Harris on the death of his father in November. Harris later wrote in an official MCC history of Lord's that the tour was 'really an MCC venture' which the committee 'entrusted' to Fitzgerald. At the same time Fitzgerald absolved MCC from any association with money-making by calling his party 'R.A. Fitzgerald's XII'.

By early June Fitzgerald faced some unwelcome competition. On 13 June George Shoosmith, the agent who had tried to recruit W.G. for Coppin, turned up at an against-the-odds match in the Leicestershire town of Melton Mowbray. Shoosmith – still employed by Spiers and Pond in London – had planned his visit well. W.G. was playing for Melton Mowbray's Twenty-Two as a lent or 'given' man, while George Parr's All-England XI featured a clutch of professionals whom Shoosmith aimed to sign up for Australia.

Shoosmith offered Grace a fee of £500, plus expenses, to lead a combined amateur-professional tour to Australia in the English winter of 1872–3. According to Shoosmith, W.G. was sufficiently interested to suggest further talks. So began what Shoosmith called a fortnight of 'considerable negotiation' with Grace.

In Melbourne Wardill and his fellow promoters had no idea that Shoosmith was in discussions with Grace because there was not yet a reliable telegraph connection with London. They still had to use the mailboat, meaning all communication between

Shoosmith and Melbourne was at least six weeks out of date when letters arrived at the other end. Patteson and Fitzgerald therefore had a crucial advantage over the Australians, as they could contact each other in hours via the transatlantic telegraph service.

By late June the Melbourne consortium was behaving as if Grace's imminent arrival in the colonies was certain. The promoters wrote to the New South Wales Cricket Association (NSWCA) asking for £1500 in return for the right to host fixtures against an England team featuring Grace. 'It appeared their association was asked to join in a speculation,' the NSWCA treasurer Albert Park observed laconically. 'The sum asked (£1500) was a large sum to give for a match in Sydney.' After some debate the NSWCA voted loftily not to obstruct Melbourne's tour venture, while having nothing to do with it.

Wardill's friend William Biddle, a vice-president of Melbourne CC, next wrote to *The Australasian* with a list of preferred names for the English touring team. In addition to Grace, Biddle named four amateurs whom Fitzgerald was trying to book for Canada. With unfounded optimism, Biddle declared it 'very possible' that the imminent telegraph service from Melbourne to London would bring news that these amateurs had signed, as well as five or six top professionals.

On 2 July, three days after *The Australasian* published Biddle's wish list, Grace scuppered any chance of him touring Australia that year. W.G. was playing for Gentlemen v Players, scoring 77 in the first innings, and he and Shoosmith met either before or after he batted. Grace stunned Shoosmith by demanding a fee of £1500, plus expenses, as his 'ultimatum' for touring Australia.

It was a colossal sum, equivalent to three hundred times the standard match fee for a professional cricketer in the early 1870s. Grace's proposed fee of £1500 seemed so large to contemporaries and later writers that it came to define his reputation as an avaricious money-grasper. Anyone who suggests that some sense of proportion and context is needed to understand Grace's financial situation is therefore venturing into sensitive territory.

But the effort has to be made, because the wilder estimates of how much W.G. 'took out' of cricket – *Wisden*'s expression in 1998 – simply do not add up. They also miss the critical point that Grace's earnings from cricket were extremely volatile and unpredictable.

Conversions of W.G.'s £1500 'ultimatum' into modern money have been increasingly distorted since the Second World War by inflation. In 1948, the centenary of Grace's birth, £1500 in 1872 money was 'worth' £3680, based on an index-linked purchasing power conversion. By 1998, his hundred and fiftieth anniversary, the modern figure had leaped to £76,000; and by 2015, the centenary of his death, the same calculation had increased the sum to £117,000. It makes much more sense to compare Grace's £1500 with contemporary earnings, the measure that W.G. and Shoosmith would have kept in their heads. They would not have benchmarked Grace against the professionals, however unfair that seems today. A better yardstick was Fitzgerald, MCC's equally money-minded secretary. Grace was asking for almost quadruple Fitzgerald's annual salary of £400, and on that basis, Shoosmith was still entitled to feel shocked.

From Grace's point of view, there were other factors behind his 'ultimatum' that he certainly did not wish to discuss in public – though he may have mentioned them to Shoosmith. In Gloucestershire he faced the prospect of helping his brothers to support their widowed mother. In London, as we will discover, he was about to become engaged to the daughter of a bankrupt. And whether he went to Australia or Canada, Grace would still remain a medical student with no earnings outside cricket. In short, he was negotiating a windfall to help him through the coming uncertain years, not a regular salary like Fitzgerald.

Grace could also reasonably argue that the Australians were hoping to make a fortune out of him. In Melbourne, Wardill was suggesting that the city's three main cricket clubs could 'net' as much as £7000 from a tour led by Grace. Applying the same, highly misleading purchasing power conversion, Wardill was projecting a profit in modern monetary values of more than half

a million pounds. In this light, W.G. would have been a fool not
to insist on the highest possible price for his services.

According to Shoosmith, Grace's demand on 2 July 'was so
greatly in excess of what I was empowered to offer him, that I
had no alternative but to refer the matter back to my Australian
friends'. W.G. said goodbye to Shoosmith and got ready for his
next appointment: a dinner that evening at Lord's, hosted by
Fitzgerald, for Grace and ten other young amateurs who had
agreed to join his North American tour. Fitzgerald – perhaps
unnerved by Shoosmith's activities – wanted to guard against
last-minute drop-outs. He made each of his guests swear they
would be 'true to the tryst' and meet him on 8 August in
Liverpool, where their berths were booked for Canada on the
steamer SS *Sarmatian*.

Next morning (3 July) W.G. put ultimatums and trysts out of
his mind for a few hours as he scored a match-winning 112 for
the Gentlemen. Yet even now Grace's business with Shoosmith
was not quite settled. On 3 or 4 July Shoosmith met a 'gentleman'
sent by Grace with some news. According to this emissary, W.G.
might be willing to go to Australia for a fee of £1000. Shoosmith
replied that 'even this amount was considerably beyond my limit'
and 'so the matter dropped'. The agent then wrote a lengthy
letter to Melbourne, explaining why he had failed to secure
Grace and requesting further instructions.

Shoosmith did not identify the gentleman in his account of the
negotiations which appeared that autumn in the English sporting
journal *Land and Water*. There was, however, one gentleman who
was extremely close to W.G., and playing in the same game at
Lord's. W.G.'s younger brother Fred, batting at number seven
for Gentlemen v Players, was the most likely candidate to relay
his brother's revised offer to Shoosmith.

W.G. knew two facts when he sent Fred, or possibly someone
else, to see the agent. First, he was definitely going to Canada;
there could be no going back on Fitzgerald's 'tryst'. Second, the
recently opened telegraph link with Melbourne had broken.

Shoosmith therefore had no chance of getting fresh instructions from Wardill and his partners until the autumn, because they would have to use the mailboat. In the light of these facts Grace's lower offer to Shoosmith looks like an attempt to keep the negotiations going with the Australians. Grace could not go to Australia in the winter of 1872–3, as the Melbourne clubs had hoped. On the other hand, he had a completely clear diary for the following winter. Wardill and his fellow promoters would just have to be patient.

The question remains why W.G. chose Canada over Australia. Ultimately, his decision seems to have been influenced by more than just money. In return for joining Fitzgerald's tour, Grace had extracted an under-the-counter payment from the Canadians. A balance sheet drawn up by Patteson after the tour showed that the Canadian clubs paid one of Fitzgerald's 'gentlemen' a fee of 880 Canadian dollars on top of his amateur expenses. Based on Fitzgerald's conversion rate (when buying furs in Montreal), the sum was equivalent to £182 in 1872 money for a scheduled two-month tour.

'There can be no question among those cognisant of the circumstances, that ... the payment made was a reasonable and proper one,' Patteson explained, 'reflecting in no way upon the gentleman who was its recipient, and amply returned by the great success that attended his play'. Only Grace matched Patteson's description, as easily the tour's most successful batsman and the player whose financial 'circumstances' were most stretched.

W.G. could have earned more by going to Australia, but he had other issues to consider. He would have destroyed his relationship with Fitzgerald and MCC by pulling out of the American tour. At worst MCC could have taken revenge on W.G. by exposing his financial dealings with Melbourne and expelling him from the club.

On 20 August Shoosmith finally managed to get a telegram through to Melbourne, leapfrogging his letter, which was chugging to Australia by the mailboat. Unfortunately, Shoosmith's cable 'suffered somewhat in transmission', the *Bendigo Advertiser* reported. 'The recipients of the information here are considerably be-fogged, inasmuch as the name of Grace in connection with sums of money and the word Canada are oddly jumbled up'.

While Australian cricket fans tried to make sense of Shoosmith's telegram, the July mailboats began to arrive in the colonies with the latest news of W.G.'s batting feats:

3 July – Gentlemen v Players, Lord's: 112 ('Superb contribution', *Leeds Times*)

4 July – Gentlemen v Players, the Oval: 117 ('Another of those splendid performances for which he stands preeminent', *Morning Post*)

8 July – 'England' v Yorkshire and Nottinghamshire, Lord's: 170 not out ('Mr Grace making his best score this season, though unfortunately that tends to lessen the interest felt in the match', *Sheffield Daily Telegraph*)

25–26 July – South v North, the Oval: 114 ('A grand innings, bar the chances referred to in our report of Thursday's play', *Daily News*)

29–30 July – Yorkshire v Gloucestershire, Sheffield: 150 ('The remainder of the Gloucestershire team were much more easily disposed of', *Sheffield and Rotherham Independent*)

Invigorated by his century against Yorkshire, W.G. went that evening to the Theatre Royal in Sheffield to watch the burlesque actresses Nellie Farren and Constance Loseby in a 'sparkling operetta'. He enjoyed the performance so much that he returned the following night.

On 8 August W.G. arrived at the Washington Hotel on Liverpool's Lime Street for lunch with Fitzgerald and his teammates. They then took carriages to the dockside, where the Allan Line's SS *Sarmatian* was ready to depart for Quebec. W.G. was about to embark on what he later described as 'one of the pleasantest experiences of my life'.

9

'X IS FOR EXPENSES'

It began nauseatingly. W.G. could not cope with the combined impact of the Atlantic Ocean and the *Sarmatian*'s first-class dinner service of 'beef, mutton, veal, pork, fowls, ducks, turkeys and goose', washed down by champagne and Madeira. He retired to his cabin, horribly seasick, emerging a few days later to observe his team-mates pestering the young ladies on deck. 'Buns' Thornton had dropped out, as had several others, leaving Fitzgerald scrambling to fill his party in the last days before departure. They were, as follows, with their first-class teams:

Arthur Appleby (29), Lancashire and MCC
Charles Francis (21), Oxford University
Walter Hadow (22), Oxford University, Middlesex and
    MCC
Albert 'Monkey' Hornby (25), Lancashire and MCC
Alfred Lubbock (26), Kent and MCC
Edgar Lubbock (25), None
Cuthbert Ottaway (22), Oxford University, wicketkeeper
Francis Pickering (21), None
William Rose (29), None

... and sheltering with W.G. beneath a lifeboat, the equally seasick Hon. George Harris (21), Oxford University and Kent.

Somewhat improbably, Harris and W.G. cemented a lifelong friendship on this tour. Harris, lean and moustachioed, was the son of a colonial governor, born in Trinidad and brought up in Madras before being sent away to prep school in England. He was lonely as a boy, 'my mother dying when I was quite a baby, I & my sister had very little of that home & family influence bearing on us which a g[rea]t many children have'. In 1859 Harris's father returned from India and the family settled at Belmont, an eighteenth-century neo-classical mansion near Faversham in Kent that the first Baron Harris had bought in 1801 with prize money from his military career.

At first glance, Harris had little in common with Grace beyond a shared distaste for the sea and a love of cricket. What drew them together was an intense seriousness about the game and its importance in life. In his long career as an MCC grandee Harris never made the mistake of patronising W.G. because of his modest background and village school education. Harris's respect for Grace's genius cut through the aristocrat's otherwise reactionary views on the benefits of cricket's distinction between 'gentlemen' and 'players' and the proper place of professionals – out of sight, in their own separate changing rooms. On Grace's side, it helped that Harris was a good first-class batsman. Crouched beneath the lifeboat, they could talk about cricket on level terms.

The two young men had something else in common: both Harris and W.G. were in love.

In April Harris had attended a fancy dress ball at Waldershare Park, another stately home in Kent, where he had met his future wife Lucy Jervis, daughter of Viscount Vincent. '[I] danced & talked with her as much as I could, & I cut out of the newspaper giving a description of the ladies' dresses, the para about her & carried it about with me for months afterwards.'

W.G.'s romantic path was more prosaic. At the start of the 1872 cricket season, a faint pencil note in MCC's subscription ledger recorded that Grace was now based at 19 Coleherne Road in the south-west London district of Earls Court. This narrow terrace house was the latest home of William Day, a failed lithographer, who was married to the daughter of Martha Grace's eldest sister. The Days had ten children living with them at this time, including their eldest surviving daughter Agnes, who turned nineteen a few days before W.G. boarded the *Sarmatian*. Grace later told Methven Brownlee that he and Agnes became engaged in 1872, at least informally. Like Harris, W.G. would be sorely tested during the next two months by all the young women who chased after the cricketers, to the MCC secretary's delight.

For now Fitzgerald had other matters on his mind as the *Sarmatian* chugged across the Atlantic. With time to kill, Fitzgerald composed a witty rhyming 'alphabet', perhaps to get his literary eye in for *Wickets in the West*, his intended best-selling tour memoir. Fitzgerald's alphabet was full of in-jokes about his young gentlemen amateurs until he came to the tricky letter 'X'. Fitzgerald thought for a moment and then jotted: 'X the Expenses in Gold to be Paid In'.

Patteson, who travelled to Quebec City to greet the team, was set to have all his financial calculations overturned by Fitzgerald's free-spending habits. 'I may say that, from the time I met the Cricketers at Quebec, till the time I bade them good-bye at the same place, my hand was seldom out of my pocket,' Patteson later lamented.

At the quayside Patteson handed Fitzgerald $230 in cash to cover the team's carriages and food in Quebec, with the Canadians agreeing to pay for the hotel. There was only one obvious flaw in the arrangement; Patteson had not in fact reserved any hotel in Quebec. For the next few hours Fitzgerald showed off his fluent French as his team, with a sheepish Patteson in tow, traipsed around the *Basse-Ville* and the *Haute-Ville*, searching for any *hôtel* or *pension* that would have them. Eventually, most of the team squeezed into the Stadacona Officers' Club on Rue d'Auteuil, where in deference to Quebec's proud Catholic,

French heritage, the club's rules banned members from discussing politics and religion.

W.G. had learned a smattering of French at the Reverend Malpas's Ridgway House school; all the same, he must have wondered why a cricket tour needed to begin in a province whose inhabitants had no interest in the baffling *jeu anglais*. There was a mad ambition to Patteson's enterprise, given cricket's precarious foothold in Canada, even in the predominantly Anglophone province of Ontario. Officially, cricket was already a Canadian national sport; the country's first Prime Minister, Sir John Macdonald, had said so in 1867. In reality the game was largely kept alive in English-speaking Canada by cricket-mad British soldiers like Captain Wallace and recently arrived immigrants from the mother country like Patteson.

Meanwhile, the new American game of baseball was spreading in Canada for the same reasons as in the United States. Baseball took less time than cricket, required little equipment, had simpler rules and was easier for newly arrived immigrants from continental Europe to understand. In contrast to cricket, baseball was ideally suited to a busy, working society with only a few hours to spare at the weekend for sport and recreation.

W.G. had no interest in such complexities. He was on a paid holiday and out to enjoy himself. Next morning he went fishing at the Montmorency Falls, a short carriage ride up the north shore of the St Lawrence River; he returned in the evening for a banquet at the Citadelle, hosted by the Governor-General of Canada, Lord Dufferin; and then shortly after midnight he set off again for the falls with Fitzgerald, Ottaway and Pickering.

At first light W.G. cast his rod and began hauling in trout, almost at will. It was all a bit too easy, so he wandered off into the forest in search of bears. This, too, seemed far more straightforward than chasing foxes and hares in south Gloucestershire. W.G. spotted a bear's paw print (or so he thought) and despatched Ottaway and Pickering in futile pursuit of the animal. Laden with trout, W.G. returned to the city just in time for some late afternoon batting practice on the Esplanade in front of the Citadelle, before a scattering of bemused Québécois. The session ended abruptly when Grace hit one ball so hard that it dislocated Walter Hadow's finger.

If Grace had been injured, Fitzgerald and Patteson would have faced a certain commercial disaster. The Canadian cricket clubs had raised $3300 (about £680) to stage fixtures from Montreal to Hamilton, Ontario, on the assumption that Grace would pull in the crowds. With Fitzgerald's assistance, Patteson also aimed to use W.G.'s fame to drum up publicity for the Great Northern Railway, controlled and managed by Frederick Cumberland, a Toronto entrepreneur and politician with multiple business interests. As manager of the *Mail*, a new Toronto daily, Patteson answered to Cumberland, the newspaper's founder.

Cumberland provided Fitzgerald's party with free or heavily discounted railway tickets on the Great Northern's overnight train from Quebec City to Montreal. To the team's delight, the steward on their reserved carriage was under orders to serve them unlimited free drinks. Cumberland's largesse allowed W.G. to sample for the first time 'the peculiar beverages which the Americans call "cock-tails"'.

Briefed by Patteson, Fitzgerald knew exactly what Cumberland expected in return for his hospitality. Cumberland was trying to raise money from investors in London to finance the Great Northern Line's westward expansion, and Fitzgerald plugged the venture shamelessly in *Wickets in the West*. The first completed viaduct of the Great Northern Line was 'of wonderful neatness and strength', he wrote of a later journey. 'Several stations of neat design were passed, the line itself well laid, and the handsome saloon carriages worthy of the line.' Fitzgerald added: 'It may be as well to state that this is the Great Northern Line', just in case readers had missed his previous reference.

The 'Grand Drunk', as Fitzgerald dubbed the train, rolled into Montreal station at 7 a.m. on 21 August. The team checked into the gigantic St Lawrence Hall Hotel on Rue Saint-Jacques, and in sticky, humid weather set off to inspect the cricket ground on Rue Saint-Catherine. Grace was appalled by the 'deplorable' state of the dry, rutted pitch and complained with his team-mates to anyone who would listen. The Montrealers were lucky. Overnight a thunderstorm allowed some belated rolling of the pitch to smooth over the cracks.

Next day, in baking heat, several thousand Montrealers watched their local Twenty-Two take on the English Twelve, led by Fitzgerald, the tour captain. W.G. scored 81 and then hit a ball straight at a close fielder who instinctively clutched his groin and caught it. The game was never remotely a contest, setting the pattern for the rest of the Canadian leg of the tour. Montreal's Twenty-Two averaged barely five runs per batsman in their two innings, as Fitzgerald's Twelve won without even trying. Despite the late dropouts, Fitzgerald's team were far too strong for any Canadian team. Grace, Harris and Hornby were future England Test players, while Appleby, Ottaway, Alfred Lubbock and Hadow were not far behind.

The cricket was so dull that Fitzgerald filled out *Wickets in the West* with lengthy passages on his young gentlemen's off-field antics, casting himself as an indulgent, fatherly bystander. Fitzgerald's account was not necessarily true or complete, but his version of the tour became the main source for a particular view of Grace in his early twenties. The MCC secretary portrayed W.G. as rather gauche socially, yet Fitzgerald's key illustration – Grace's speechmaking – does not prove the point.

At a banquet for the team in Montreal a local worthy proposed a toast to 'The Champion Batsman of Cricketdom'. Grace stood up, raised his glass and said, 'Gentlemen, I beg to thank you for the honour you have done me; I never saw better bowling than I have seen today, and I hope to see as good wherever I go.' Then he sat down. Grace's brief speech became a running joke on the tour, as he repeated the same two-liner with variations wherever the team were entertained. W.G. might substitute better 'batting' or 'fielding', as the circumstances demanded; otherwise, the template stayed the same.

Before long W.G.'s 'Canadian' speech gave rise to a belief that he was incapable of public speaking. It was a misconception that he actively encouraged, for like many celebrities, he found the whole business of speechmaking a chore. Yet when the occasion demanded, Grace could deliver speeches that were courteous, drily humorous and, once or twice, quite moving. He just ignored the Victorian convention that required guests of honour to sound off at tedious length, in the same unorthodox spirit that he disregarded the coaching manuals.

One of Grace's two-liners in Canada was also quite revealing. At a dinner in Hamilton W.G. declared that he had never seen such fine 'ladies', and he hoped to see as good wherever he went. Grace and the rather starchier Harris may have been among the cricketers spotted by a reporter in a Montreal hotel writing 'spoony' letters home to their girlfriends. Yet Harris certainly flirted or went further with the stream of young ladies who attached themselves to the tour party, despite his pangs for Lucy Jervis. 'I think Miss B [illegible], if she had (as she ought) any pleasant recollection of myself, would have sent her kind regards to me not you,' Harris replied peevishly to a letter from Fitzgerald about a girl they both met at a ball in Hamilton.

Grace had plenty of similar opportunities in Canada. At a ball in Ottawa a newspaper reported that he 'was especially noticeable for the skill and agility of his movements'. In Toronto, according to Fitzgerald, a 'deputation' of young ladies asked Grace to go further down the batting order so they could spend a little more time with him. He agreed.

By now Patteson had lost all control of his spending budget as Fitzgerald racked up his team's expenses. At Ottawa Patteson had handed over a further £60 (about $290) to cover the team's food and entertainment. They stayed at the Russell House Hotel, a grandiose establishment on the corner of Sparks and Elgin streets, where Grace went down with a stomach bug. He struggled out to bat next day against Twenty-Two of Ottawa, in front of almost four thousand spectators eager to see what cricket's enfeebled 'Leviathan' could do. With the assistance of a runner, Grace scored the worst half-century of his life, giving six chances. He might as well have stayed in bed. The Twenty-Two were so bad that they averaged barely two runs per batsman, as the English once again won easily.

Patteson now travelled on from Ottawa to Toronto to catch up on business at the *Mail*. He left Fitzgerald and his team in the care of Colonel Francis Maude, a forty-three-year-old British army officer who had recently settled in Ontario. Maude's valour was not in doubt; during the Indian Mutiny in 1857 he had shown 'nerve and coolness' under enemy fire, winning the Victoria Cross. Unfortunately, Maude was better at gunning down Indians than orienteering in Canada. He was supposed to deliver the cricketers to the small town of Belleville on Lake Ontario's north shore, where local citizens had organised a reception for the chance to see Grace. Instead, Maude ended up in Brockville, about a hundred miles from Belleville. The bemused residents decided they might as well celebrate W.G.'s unexpected appearance by opening a crate of champagne.

Maude muddled through to Toronto, where Grace scored 142 against the local Twenty-Two at the 'Taddle' cricket ground on McCaul Street, nicknamed after the nearby Taddle Creek. Grace found batting so easy that when he had made 50 he played his favourite prank on the three thousand spectators. A fielder caught the ball first bounce after W.G. hit it hard into the ground directly in front of his bat. It looked like a catch from the boundary and Grace began trudging off the field disconsolately. The crowd cheered and then groaned as W.G. turned on his heels and marched grinning back to the wicket. That was the extent of the excitement. Toronto's twenty-two batsmen collapsed like a row of dominoes, repeating the pattern set in Montreal and Ottawa.

The rest of the team's progress through Ontario degenerated into a free-spending jaunt. In London and Hamilton, Fitzgerald officially spent from Patteson's cash float 'about one-fifth of the actual expenses incurred and paid by myself or Colonel Maude', Patteson noted sourly. The English next ran up a bill of $350 (about £72) for three nights at the Clifton House, a vast hotel near Niagara Falls with 270 bedrooms, all with hot and cold running water. At the falls W.G. posed for a group photograph with Harris, Hornby, Francis, Edgar Lubbock, Patteson and his wife, plus two unidentified women (see page 4 of the picture section). Looking rather louche, Grace lounged full-length on the grass in front of the others, holding his sun-hat in one hand. One of the anonymous women looks as if she may be touching W.G.'s back. In later years he kept the photograph on his mantelpiece as a fond souvenir of Canada.

It was time to say *au revoir to* Patteson. Belatedly, a consortium of cricket clubs in Philadelphia, New York and Boston had sent him $1800 to cover the team's expenses for an American leg of the tour. Patteson handed Fitzgerald the money and deputed the willing but not very able Maude to act as the team's 'minder' and keep them out of trouble in the United States. Fitzgerald had other ideas. When they arrived in New York on 16 September, he collected a letter from an acquaintance in Canada. 'The New Yorkers ... use, I am told, every courtesy,' his correspondent warned. 'Be sure to keep the boys straight until the match is over. They will be tempted on every side.' Fitzgerald and his 'boys' checked into their hotel in Greenwich Village and then set forth for Lower Manhattan to locate the source of these temptations.

10

SHOWDOWN IN PHILADELPHIA

Fitzgerald took his team to a bar on Broadway where scantily dressed waitresses served cocktails. 'You are provoked without provocation,' he observed. 'You are disgusted in your delight.' The MCC secretary also made enquiries about how to find a Manhattan brothel. 'Any gentleman with money burning the lining of his pocket can easily obtain relief at night,' he wrote. 'By applying to any policeman, he will be directed *Alla Porta del Inferno*. Pleasantly and socially conducted, he can lose his money to his heart's will.'

Finding a decent game of cricket in New York was more difficult. On 18 September they caught the ferry across the Hudson River to take on a local Twenty-Two from New York's St George's Cricket Club at 'Elysian Fields', a large stretch of open parkland in Hoboken, New Jersey. In historical terms, Fitzgerald's team were already too late, for Elysian Fields was symbolically where baseball supplanted cricket as the summer game for east coast Americans.

During the 1850s *The New York Times* had employed a young reporter, Henry Chadwick, originally from Devon, to cover cricket games around the city, which still attracted large crowds.

In 1856 Chadwick watched a baseball game between the Mutual and Atlantic clubs at Elysian Fields and realised he had seen the coming national sport. 'Americans do not care to dawdle over a sleep-inspiring game, all through the heat of a June or July day,' Chadwick famously wrote, in what could be interpreted (from an American perspective) as a damning comment on cricket. 'What they do they want to do in a hurry. In baseball all is lightning; every action is as swift as a seabird's flight.'

W.G. liked baseball and, specifically, the competitive, aggressive attitude of baseball players. He particularly liked the keen American approach to fielding and the way baseball players threw the ball – hard and flat, quite different from the way most English cricketers chucked the ball in from the boundary. In 1888 W.G. would invite an American baseball team to Bristol to put on an exhibition game, writing to the sporting journal *Land and Water*: 'There is no doubt that the baseballers now here can set an excellent example to crick-eters by their smart fielding and accurate throwing.'

By then W.G. weighed too much to emulate the Americans' example. At Elysian Fields the spectators saw a younger, slimmer Grace who would have made a fine baseball fielder. In his mid-twenties W.G. was probably still able to sprint 100 yards in about 12 seconds, his approximate time in athletics competitions. He also had an exceptionally strong throwing arm. At the Oval in 1869 W.G. easily won a cricket ball throwing competition with an aerial distance of 117 yards. 'He was a beautiful thrower,' Charles Lyttelton remembered. 'He could run like a deer and had a very safe pair of hands.'

On Fitzgerald's team there were two other players, 'Monkey' Hornby (so called because of his long, ape-like arms) and Harris, who were as good at fielding as Grace. It may have been in this game at Elysian Fields that Harris and Hornby played a prank on the wicketkeeper Cuthbert Ottaway, whom they both thought a bit of a prig:

The Monkey (A.N. Hornby) & I arranged one day that when I was at sharp short leg & he at mid off, the first who got the ball to field should buzz at Ottaway, who was a very good wicket-keeper but a bit afraid of his fingers; the other wd be backing up & buzz back again almost before Ottaway cd turn round. We did it beautifully three or four times, Ottaway jumping about like a cat on hot bricks, ejaculating 'I say', until old Fitz's voice 'Now then, you boys, stop that fooling' made us desist.

Grace was especially struck by two brothers in the St George's Cricket Club Twenty-Two who were top baseball players. Harry Wright and his younger brother George were the sons of a cricket-playing father who had emigrated from Yorkshire to New York. 'Their fielding was – as the fielding of all base-ball players is – simply magnificent,' W.G. recalled. Today the Wrights are remembered only as baseball players who were later inducted into the sport's Hall of Fame. Yet in 1872 George and Harry were also professional cricketers, almost certainly paid to travel down from Boston (where Harry had set up the Boston Red Stockings baseball team) to play for their father's old club against Fitzgerald's team.

As soon as he turned up at Elysian Fields, W.G. would have seen what the Wrights already knew: cricket was a dying sport in America. A crowd of barely two thousand attended the match on the first day, one-tenth the attendance of the celebrated base-ball game between the Mutual and Atlantic clubs in 1865 that Chadwick watched, immortalised in a famous lithograph with the title: 'The American National Game of Base Ball'. Without W.G. as an attraction it is unlikely that more than a few hundred New Yorkers would have bothered to watch R.A. Fitzgerald's XII.

They at least saw W.G. put on a show. He scored 68 and took eleven wickets, finally persuading Fitzgerald – who had hardly let him bowl on the tour so far – that he was a useful bowler as well. It was not much of an achievement, though. Only two St George batsmen reached double figures in the whole match.

The cricket was so bad that W.G. switched the subject of his set speech at a dinner hosted by New York's Travellers' Club. He had never seen better oysters than in Manhattan, W.G. declared, and he hoped to see as good wherever he went. Based on the tour so far, W.G. could expect nothing better either at their next fixture in Philadelphia; and certainly not a cricket match that he would remember for the rest of his life.

They caught the evening train to Philadelphia, and shortly after midnight arrived at the Continental Hotel, a six-storey edifice at 9th and Chestnut Streets.

'Can you give us any news?' a reporter from *The Philadelphia Inquirer* who was waiting in the lobby asked one of the cricketers.

'No, not much,' he replied, taken aback by the intrusive manner of American journalists.

'What is your opinion of American players as far as you have met them?' the reporter persisted.

'The American cricketers play very well,' his interviewee said tactfully. 'Their fielding is excellent, but they are not good at the bat.'

With that the cricketers went upstairs to bed, leaving the reporter to file his story. 'The visitors were too much fatigued with their journey and sight-seeing in New York yesterday to enter very much into the fine points of the game,' he commented a little sadly.

Fitzgerald and his young gentlemen had just landed in the one American outpost where cricket was still played and followed with passion. Philadelphia's love affair with cricket, which lasted well into the twentieth century, is one of the most beguiling of all sporting romances because it was so improbable. The city was the birthplace of American independence and (a British observer might have ignorantly thought) naturally inclined to regard an English sport like cricket with disdain. More recently, successive waves of immigrants with no knowledge of cricket – Catholic Irish, Germans, Italians and east European Jews – had settled in Philadelphia and surrounding Pennsylvania towns. Yet until the First World War a few Philadelphia cricket clubs kept the game alive, producing a handful of players of 'a very fair lot', according to W.G.

The most persuasive explanation for why cricket flourished in Philadelphia is also the simplest. A cluster of local families were, as they said, nuts about the game, and passed their enthusiasm from one generation to the next. They included the Newhalls, the Meades and several other families that organised their cricket around four main clubs: Philadelphia, Merion, Germantown and Young America. In 1868 a combined Philadelphian Twenty-Two had lost two against-the-odds games against a visiting English side featuring top English professionals such as James Lillywhite Jr., Harry Jupp, Alfred Shaw and Ned Willsher. Now, even with W.G. in Fitzgerald's team, the Philadelphians thought they could beat the Brits. 'It is to be hoped for the glory of the Quaker City her chosen batters will do their entire duty at the bat and wicket,' *The Philadelphia Inquirer* declared. 'In the language of Lord Nelson, slightly modified, "Philadelphia expects every man (at the wicket) to do his duty."'

Philadelphia's sense of honour co-existed comfortably with the notion that the city should make as much money as possible out of its cricket 'festival'. In the weeks before the game the promoters had spent almost $500 on 2000 posters, 5000 circulars and 6000 illustrated cards and adverts in *The Philadelphia Inquirer* and its rival, the *Public Ledger*. There was one repetitive theme: W.G. Grace, 'the CHAMPION BATSMAN OF THE WORLD', was coming to town. Grace was 'the best cricketer that ever stepped and is, in fact, unapproached and unapproachable,' declared the fixture's official handbook, which hardly mentioned his teammates. 'Were it not that the tower of strength displayed by Mr Grace overshadows all competitors, the feats of other members of this visiting eleven would challenge more attention than has been bestowed on them.'

W.G. woke at the Continental Hotel to find curious locals on the sidewalk outside, straining to get a peek at him. He was, after all, the most famous Englishman to visit Philadelphia since Charles Dickens stayed at the Continental four years earlier. Gradually, these spectators joined the crowds heading north-west out of the city on chartered trains, by cab or on foot towards Germantown CC's ground in the suburbs, where the match was due to start at midday. One newspaper estimated that around ten thousand spectators attended the first day's play, but it was only counting those inside the ground, who crammed into specially erected grandstands or stood four or five deep around the boundary. Beyond the ground's high, wooden stockade fence, people climbed trees or clambered on to haystacks to catch a peek of the game.

The Philadelphians had made only one mistake in the build-up to the game. They insisted on playing a full Twenty-Two against Fitzgerald's Twelve, rather than streamlining their team down to the best players. As sometimes happened in against-the-odds cricket, the home side's numerical advantage turned out to be a weakness. Led by five Newhalls, the core of the Philadelphia team was strong. However, several of the Twenty-Two seem to have been picked (or selected themselves) because of their status as cricket officials rather than their playing ability. Dr Charles Cadwalader, chairman of the welcoming committee, was a conspicuous example, getting in the way of more athletic teammates in the field while failing twice with the bat. Philadelphia might have done better to omit Cadwalader and several other passengers and leave the field clear for their stars.

In hot sunshine, Philadelphia's captain Walter Newhall won the toss and decided to bat first. The American national flag was hoisted above the pavilion and when Philadelphia's opening batsmen marched out to the middle, a US marine band launched into 'The Star-Spangled Banner'. As far as the Philadelphians were concerned, this was a full international.

Soon the marines were playing a dirge to accompany a succession of American batting failures back to the pavilion. None of them could play the left-arm fast bowling of Arthur Appleby, who took eight wickets, or Grace, who took nine with his 'rather puzzling slows'. Philadelphia collapsed to 63 all out. So far they looked as bad as all the preceding teams on the tour.

As the band struck up 'God Save the Queen', W.G. and the Oxford Blue Cuthbert Ottaway walked out to open the English innings. W.G. was nervous; he had noticed that the dry Germantown pitch was breaking up, creating uneven bounce. For almost an hour he poked and prodded at the bowling of Charles Newhall (right-arm medium pace) and Spencer 'Pen' Meade (left-arm fast), concerned solely with survival. The crowd was perplexed; this was not the superhuman W.G. promised by the pre-match publicity, but a batsman who looked like losing his wicket at any moment. Newhall was 'one of the best trundlers I ever played against,' Grace recalled, while Meade 'kept up a wonderfully good length'.

Eventually Newhall bowled a 'shooter' at Grace that 'flew under his [Grace's] bat and sent the off stump flying into the air,' reported the *Chronicle*, another Pennsylvania newspaper: 'The greatest batsman in the world, "unapproached and unapproachable", retired with a score of 14, the most of them being obtained only by sharp running on short hits! Then what a shout arose! The crowd cheered wildly, and some of the twenty-two threw up their hats and danced for joy.' W.G. never forgot the scene. 'I have heard many a great shout go up in various parts of the globe at my dismissal, but I never remember anything quite equal to the wild roar that greeted my downfall on this occasion,' he recalled almost thirty years later.

Still, there were ten English batsmen to come after Grace. When play ended at dusk, Fitzgerald's Twelve had scored 48 for the loss of only two wickets, just fifteen runs behind the home team's first innings total. The English were on top.

Night came quickly in September in Pennsylvania. Fitzgerald and his gentlemen, with Colonel Maude in tow, now got lost in the tangle of country lanes north of Philadelphia, as they tried to locate the home of Joshua Fisher, a local philanthropist who was hosting a banquet in their honour. All Maude's skills in military navigation once again proved useless. In the end a man walking down the road showed them the way to Fisher's estate, where the host and Pen Meade's father were waiting impatiently to greet them. At the age of fifty-six, General George Meade was in considerable pain from wounds sustained during the American Civil War. Testy and impatient with pressmen, he shared one other characteristic with the bearded young 'champion cricketer of the world' who politely shook his hand. The general loved cricket almost as much as W.G did.

The next day Fitzgerald's team negotiated the torpor of Philadelphia's strictly enforced Sabbath. They wrote letters, went for a ride in the park and drank illegal 'hooch', pretending it was tea.

On Monday, with the sun beating down, another crowd of almost ten thousand descended on Germantown and saw Fitzgerald's team struggle on the crumbling pitch to a total of 105 all out, a first innings lead of 42. Once again the Philadelphians collapsed to the bowling of Grace (nine wickets) and Appleby (eight wickets). As the afternoon progressed, spectators bet 'a great deal of money' on 'the defeat of the Americans in one [English] innings'. It did not happen. The Philadelphians were all out for 74, leaving the English with the whole of the next day (23 September) to score just 33 for victory.

Sensing the game was almost over, the crowd swarmed around the pavilion as the sun set, desperate for one last glimpse of W.G. 'Cheer after cheer was given when Grace appeared, and nothing would quiet the crowd but the appearance of all the players,' wrote Fitzgerald. In his own opinion the MCC secretary then made 'a neat little speech', praising the ground and the quality of the home side's fielding. Standing next to Fitzgerald on the balcony, the Philadelphian cricketers must have felt slightly patronised.

The English had a busy evening ahead of them. First, they dropped by the New American Theater on Chestnut Street, where Robert Fox, the proprietor, had invited 'W.G. Grace Esq. & Gents of the English Eleven (cricketers)' for an evening's gala performance. It was just a ploy by Fox to use W.G. to bring in customers, for there was no 'gala performance'. W.G. acknowledged the standing ovation from the audience as the theatre band played both the British and American national anthems, and shortly afterwards the cricketers left. General Meade was waiting to welcome them at the Union League Club on South Broad Street. Some two hundred guests had paid a 'subscription' fee to attend a banquet for the English team. In cricket-crazy Philadelphia most of them just wanted to be able to tell their children and grandchildren that they had dined not with General Meade but with W.G.

In the morning W.G. would have seen from the newspapers delivered to the Continental Hotel that the local press had written off Philadelphia's chances of saving the game. He was about to discover that giving up was not in the Philadelphian cricketers' nature, any more than his. The Newhalls, Pen Meade and their team-mates believed it was better to go down fighting than merely capitulate. This was why Grace remembered them so warmly, for they were cricketers after his heart.

'Then came the tug of war,' W.G. recalled, as he and Ottaway walked out on Tuesday at noon to open the English second innings. Germantown's cricket ground shimmered in the heat of the day, as another packed house watched Philadelphia's captain Walter Newhall set a tight circle of fielders around Grace and Ottaway, designed to prevent them scoring even a single. It was a bold tactic, because Grace and Ottaway were likely to score four if they hit the ball past this inner ring towards the largely undefended boundary.

The gamble worked at first, with the batsmen hardly able to score at all off Pen Meade and Charles Newhall. W.G. hung on, as Ottaway (0) and Hornby (4) were dismissed; 'not a very promising start', in Grace's view. The Old Etonian Alfred Lubbock joined W.G., 'and though we were at the wickets together for some time, we could not get the ball away, the bowling and fielding being so excellent'. W.G. and Lubbock tried to steal some singles, but it was 'risky work' against twenty-two fielders: 'Ball after ball was sent down, which we could do nothing beyond playing, and maiden over followed maiden over in unbroken monotony.'

Lubbock (3) finally lost patience, hit out, and gave a simple return catch to Newhall. Almost immediately, Grace edged a ball from Newhall and the slip fielder held the catch. Another 'tremendous roar' went round the ground, with 'hats and umbrellas tossed in the air', at least in W.G.'s memory. He had taken almost an hour to score just 7 runs, 'about the slowest pace at which I ever remember scoring'.

Fitzgerald's team still only needed 15 runs to win, but Charles Newhall and Meade were bowling as if Philadelphia were on top. With Grace gone, the trickle of runs slowed to a drip, and then froze, as more wickets fell. Walter Newhall now brought *all* his fielders into the inner ring in an attempt to stop the English scoring any more runs. Harris released a little pressure, scoring 8 before Meade dismissed him. Francis came and went without scoring; 29 for seven wickets. The English had four wickets left, with four runs to win. Edgar Lubbock scrambled one run as the hapless Charles Cadwalader missed the ball: 30 for seven. Newhall now prepared to bowl to Appleby, a far better batsman than Lubbock.

'The atmosphere was electrical,' Grace recalled. 'I never remember a team or a crowd of spectators more excited.' Fitzgerald, who normally jabbered away to anyone, was so tense he could hardly speak. In the blur of the moment nobody remembered clearly what happened next. One reporter thought Appleby cut a delivery from Newhall. W.G. said Appleby 'opened his shoulders' at an overpitched delivery. Whatever happened, Appleby got the ball past the fielders and all the way to the open boundary for four runs. Walter Newhall's gamble had failed and the English had won.

There was another 'wild rush of thousands across the ground to the pavilion', but Fitzgerald had no time for speeches. His team were late for the overnight train to Boston, where the final tour match was due to start next day (25 September). To his hosts' disgust, Fitzgerald gathered up his 'gentlemen' and raced from the ground. Adding to the insult, the MCC secretary and his team had managed to run up $403 in 'entertainment' expenses during their stay in Philadelphia.

They still missed the through train to Boston and were obliged to spend an agreeable night at New York's Fifth Avenue Hotel; a 'magnificent structure', in Fitzgerald's view, made yet more enticing by a crowd of 'fair and young nymphs' just back from the fashionable resort of Newport, Rhode Island. The team finally reached Boston on the morning of 26 September, a day late, and checked into the Parker House Hotel on Beacon Street. Fitzgerald relished the 'good looks' of the chambermaids. It was 'miraculous' to see 'a belle bringing a bath in less than a quarter of an hour after the demand'. Oddly, Fitzgerald now announced he had business in Boston and excused himself from the start of the game. He handed the captaincy to Grace, who remembered vaguely that Fitzgerald was 'not in the best of health'. Perhaps all MCC's secretary needed was a long relaxing bath.

George and Harry Wright were waiting with the rest of Boston's Twenty-Two at the South End Grounds baseball park. It had rained heavily overnight, and W.G. thought the waterlogged field was unfit for cricket. He ploughed on, feeling a duty to offer his hosts some sort of a game. By the time Fitzgerald turned up, fully refreshed, the Twenty-Two were all out for 51 in their first innings. The English were then dismissed for the same total, as the soggy pitch became a morass. On they struggled: Boston made 43 in their second innings, leaving Fitzgerald's team 44 to win. The visitors might have lost, if Fitzgerald had not pulled the plug on the game by convincing the umpires that he could not see the ball in the gathering dusk.

Next morning they caught the train for Quebec City, minus Appleby, who was off to the West Coast for an extended holiday. Looking back on the train ride, W.G. remembered the autumnal New England scenery that passed by his carriage window: 'The beauty of the scene as the sun rose above the woodlands was a sight never to be forgotten.' He recalled as well the 'dry' state of Maine's ban on alcohol. '[We] had the curious experience of being absolutely unable to get, for love or money, anything stronger by way of refreshment than thick soup, washed down with weak tea and indifferent coffee.' W.G., who claimed to be teetotal as a young man, returned from America with a clear liking for drink.

Patteson was waiting at Quebec City to settle the tour accounts with Fitzgerald. As Fitzgerald now explained, the $1800 float for the team's expenses in the United States had not been nearly enough. Fitzgerald insisted that he and his team had made up the difference, while Colonel Maude had taken $146 from the kitty to cover his own expenses. Patteson went halfway to meet Fitzgerald, agreeing to reimburse him for Maude's additional bill. Patteson noted tartly in his tour balance sheet the $146 spent by Maude from the float was 'independent of a considerable sum disbursed by that gentleman from his own funds'.

On 8 October the team sailed into Liverpool, minus Harris, who disembarked the day before at Belfast to visit relatives in Ireland. Fitzgerald set off for Moss House, his parents-in-law's mansion near Liverpool, to rejoin his heavily pregnant wife Ettie and set to work on *Wickets in the West*. W.G. returned to Downend for another winter session at Bristol Medical School. According to the school's official history (though not its records), he was now registered as a 'physician's pupil' under Dr Frederick Brittan, another member of the faculty.

When he rejoined his classmates in Dr Brittan's tutorials, W.G. probably did not know that events in Melbourne would soon derail his studies again. In August the gambling accountant Richard Wardill had abruptly resigned from the Melbourne CC committee, offering no public explanation. Wardill's mounting betting debts were the most likely reason for his departure. William Biddle, a vice-president of Melbourne CC, now stepped forward to lead a renewed bid to bring W.G. on tour to Australia in the (English) winter of 1873–4. Biddle shared one thing in common with his friend Wardill, which W.G. only discovered later. Like Wardill, Biddle was in deep financial trouble.

11

THE MELBOURNE SPECULATOR

Sometime in the early 1870s William Biddle posed for a formal portrait in a Melbourne photographer's studio. He looked the picture of solid, bourgeois respectability, in a sober grey frock-coat, with a watch chain hanging across his portly midriff. The image was completed by his fine house in the south Melbourne suburb of St Kilda, built in 'Lombardo-Gothic' style. From the balcony, Biddle and his young family could admire their croquet ground in the front garden and then look across Port Phillip harbour to the You Yang granite ridges in the distance. The house, like the studio portrait, was a front. Behind the façade, Biddle was hurtling towards bankruptcy.

The son of a London fishmonger, Biddle had arrived in Victoria in 1854 at the age of twenty-seven. He became a manager for White Brothers, a Melbourne wine merchant, which in 1869 was sued by the Irish cognac company Hennessy & Co. Hennessy accused Biddle and his partners of diluting the firm's premium Battle-Axe brand and then sticking fake labels on the bottles. Biddle admitted adding water and 'finings' to the brandy but claimed to have done nothing illegal. As for the new label he stuck on the bottle, he said it was quite different from Hennessy's battle-axe motif.

The case was never resolved, probably because White Brothers soon went out of business. Biddle now set up as a 'broker' on Collins Street, trading largely on his own account. His real career – as it had been for most of the 1860s – was investing in gold stocks.

In 1870 Biddle and other speculators sued the optimistically named Aladdin and Try Again Gold-Mining Company after the manager stole £207 from the accounts. They won, but it was a hollow victory. Aladdin and Try Again and the Union Jack Gold-Mining Company (another of Biddle's worthless assets) were hunting for treasure that did not exist. Like dozens of other gold speculators in the early 1870s, Biddle had got his timing wrong. Victoria's gold rush was over, leaving only a patchwork of barren, disused mines across the colony.

Despite his sharp practice with Hennessy's brandy, Biddle was not an outright criminal like Wardill. He was merely a bad businessman who was capable of fooling others – and perhaps himself – about his real motives. In public Biddle insisted that he did not bring Grace's team to the colonies in 1873 'in a purely speculative spirit [but] to improve the play of the colonial cricketers'. Biddle was lying. He was banking on the profits from the tour to rescue him from ruin, but he was doing so from a far less secure starting point than the Melbourne clubs' original venture in 1872.

The clubs withdrew their institutional backing from the tour project when they learned about Grace's £1500 'ultimatum' to Shoosmith. Biddle now took on all the financial risk, along with any partners he could recruit. The identity of these fellow speculators is hard to confirm, because Biddle never publicly named them. Based on Melbourne CC committee minutes, two of Biddle's partners were Charles Croaker, a wool broker and gold speculator, and Josh Pickersgill, a wine merchant on Collins Street. Newspaper reports indicate that William Runting, an accountant who was secretary of South Melbourne CC, also joined Biddle's private consortium.

Biddle may have persuaded another investor to join his venture. Richard Wardill was still at large, stealing money from his employer, Victoria Sugar, to fund his uncontrollable betting. For a committed gambler like Wardill, Biddle's wager on Grace would have been hard to resist. All Wardill needed to do was draw a little more money from Victoria Sugar's accounts.

In England W.G.'s cricket season had scarcely begun when he got into a row with Nottinghamshire CCC's honorary secretary George Davy. The bust-up, played out in the press, illustrated why Grace was so difficult to manage in a negotiation – especially one that Biddle was about to conduct via submarine cable and mailboat. Grace had failed to check his diary and agreed to play in a benefit match in Sheffield for the Yorkshire professional Joseph Rowbotham on the same day that Gloucestershire were scheduled to play Nottinghamshire at Trent Bridge. When Davy remonstrated to E.M., Gloucestershire's secretary, W.G. fired off a letter to his county club's committee. 'I think you will agree with me that Mr Davy ... misled me and induced me to fix the match for the 28th [of July],' the same day as Rowbotham's benefit game, Grace asserted with no evidence. He went on to accuse Davy of taking 'no notice' of an earlier letter Grace had written, and generally creating 'a great deal of unpleasantness'. W.G. then refused to organise a team to play Nottinghamshire, which in any case had decided to cancel the fixture.

Davy, a wealthy Old Etonian, could look after himself; he soon quit his unpaid job, tired of dealing with types like W.G. Nonetheless, Grace's arrogance was strikingly at odds with the earlier, not necessarily accurate memories of him as a 'shy' teenager. He had changed, in a manner that suggests recent developments in his life had gone to his head. First, his father had died suddenly, removing the one person in his family who had real authority over him. Since then, Grace had been courted by the Australians and toured North America as the secretly paid star of Fitzgerald's team, a band of well-heeled young aristocrats and gentlemen who took second billing to the 'champion cricketer of the world'. Biddle was not dealing with the quiet young man who had joined MCC four years before.

On one point Biddle had no need to worry. In 1873 W.G. once again finished far ahead of any other batsman, with an average of 72.20, including six centuries. Biddle could be confident that Grace would fill cricket grounds across Victoria and other Australian colonies.

Every other issue was contentious. Grace refused to budge from his 'ultimatum' of £1500, plus expenses, despite his indirect hint to Shoosmith that he might accept a figure closer to £1000. Even worse, W.G. insisted on bringing his fiancée Agnes Day, whom he planned to marry just before departure, with Biddle's consortium paying for all her travel and board. Biddle probably did not know that Agnes's father was bankrupt, giving Grace further reason to extract as much money as possible from the proposed tour to support his penniless in-laws.

W.G. had more bad news for Biddle. On 12 June he sent a telegram to the Melbourne promoter, stating that 'in consequence of unforeseen difficulties in engaging the best gentlemen and professionals, he would have to advance considerably upon his original terms'. Outwardly, Biddle showed no sign of being concerned, as he tried to drum up bids for the right to host fixtures against Grace's team from cricket clubs in Victoria and neighbouring colonies. 'There is every probability of a cricket eleven – half gentlemen, half players – coming out at the end of the year,' Biddle airily informed the press.

W.G., too, was behaving like a man without a care. Throughout his exchanges with Biddle over the summer, he displayed a remarkable ability to ignore the distraction as soon as he put on his batting pads. At the end of June he embarked on one of his staggering bursts of form, scoring 134 at the Oval for Gentlemen of the South v Players of the South ('Capital', *Bradford Observer*); 163 for Gentlemen v Players at Lord's ('Redoubtable', *Leeds Times*); and 158 for Gentlemen v Players at the Oval ('The leviathan of the willow', *Standard*).

Grace headed to Yorkshire on 9 or 10 July for a professional USE game against Twenty-Two of Wakefield. Here, W.G. at last wired Biddle, accepting the consortium's counter-proposal 'with but a slight modification'. But some unspecified hitch now arose, because a fortnight later W.G. sent another telegram to Biddle, demanding 'further negotiations'. Wearily, Biddle sent back his latest 'final offer', as W.G. was scoring 152 at Lord's for Fitzgerald's reunited Gentlemen to Canada Touring Team against a weak MCC Fifteen.

W.G. apparently did not reply, aware that Biddle was about to receive a letter from him, despatched a few weeks earlier by mailboat. As this letter chugged towards Melbourne, W.G. got back to the more interesting job of scoring runs. On 24 July – as if to show Biddle his market worth – Grace made 192 not out for South v North at the Oval ('Electrifying', *Sheffield and Rotherham Independent*).

On 29 July Biddle had his worst day of the whole negotiation. In Sheffield W.G. scored 79 for Gloucestershire against Yorkshire. In Australia Biddle's colleagues on Melbourne CC's committee told him the club would charge £150 for use of its ground for the opening match of the tour, plus £50 for any subsequent fixtures. The committee made clear that Melbourne CC was to be 'free from all expense whatever'.

So far Biddle had no team and no fixtures. He had also just received Grace's letter, which informed him that the suggested gentlemen amateurs put forward by Biddle for the tour found his terms 'rather tight'. Grace and Biddle almost certainly had in mind some of the amateurs who had toured Canada and the United States with Fitzgerald the previous year. W.G. later explained that he 'tried to get the very best possible players, and if possible, a team of gentlemen players. But the seven months' absence from England which the trip necessitated was a stumbling block to many whom [I] would have wished to bring, and who would have been willing to come.'

Grudgingly, Biddle agreed that the team would have to include some professionals, stretching his budget even further. Biddle's reluctance to have any professionals on the tour explained their shoddy treatment in Australia, where the promoter and his partners were looking for any excuse to cut costs.

First, though, W.G. had to recruit them, with barely a month left before the end of the English cricket season.

By early August Biddle had yet to find any takers among cricket clubs in the colonies to host fixtures against W.G.'s still non-existent side. He sent out another circular, advising 'all who may wish to take advantage of this contemplated visit that it may be well to secure themselves against any risk of loss (improbable as it may appear) by obtaining guarantees to the amount of their estimated risk from wealthy residents in the locality desirous of witnessing such a display of cricket as is not likely to be afforded again in Australia for many years'. Somehow Biddle made it sound as if everything was under control.

A fortnight later Richard Wardill threw himself in the Yarra River, after confessing to the embezzlement of about £7000 from Victoria Sugar. W.G. was oblivious to the news of Wardill's suicide, which did not reach the English press till late October. But for Biddle, appalled by his friend's death, the story was an embarrassment he did not need. All of a sudden Wardill's former associates in the original 1872 tour venture looked either naive about their gambling friend or, by association, just a little bit shady.

On 27 August, as Wardill's still-undiscovered corpse floated in the Yarra, W.G. reduced his local Bristol fans to 'a chronic state of cheering' by scoring 160 not out for Gloucestershire against Surrey. He still did not have a team list for Biddle in early September, when he travelled to northern Scotland for a professional USE tour. Grace took a draft contract for the USE players he aimed to recruit, negotiating terms with five of them in Inverness and Aberdeen. They travelled south for a game in Northampton, where on 17 September, the five professionals from the Scottish tour, plus two other USE players, signed Grace's tour contract in a private room set aside by one of their hosts.

They were:

Andrew Greenwood (26), Yorkshire
Richard Humphrey (24), Surrey

Harry Jupp (31), Surrey
James Lillywhite Jr. (31), Sussex
Martin McIntyre (26), Nottinghamshire
William Oscroft (29), Nottinghamshire
James Southerton (45), Surrey

The players contracted to play fourteen matches under Grace's captaincy in Australia in return for a fee of £150, a further £20 in expenses for 'wines, spirits and other liquors', bed and board, and second-class passage there and back. These were hard terms, revealing the players' weak bargaining power and the lack of better-paid employment for most of them in England during the winter. Grace had failed to persuade several top professionals to join the tour because they thought they could earn more money by staying at home.

W.G.'s meanness towards the seven professionals became an accepted part of Grace folklore about his alleged greed. But the truth was a little more complicated. The players were free agents who knew that Grace was the '*sine qua non*' of the whole venture, as Melbourne CC's president David McArthur had put it in 1872. They also expected to earn more than their fee on the tour, despite the contract's apparently tight wording about their 'exclusive' commitment to play for Grace. On the two previous English cricket tours of Australia the professionals (and the bogus amateur E.M. Grace) had boosted their income by playing extra games around the official schedule, including single-wicket contests. They made further money from selling bats and other cricket equipment they had brought out from England.

The professionals on W.G.'s tour had exactly the same business plan; for them Grace's contract was just the starting point for earning as much as double their stated fee.

'I went out to Australia to make as much money as I could,' recalled the Nottinghamshire professional William Oscroft, a cotton framework knitter by trade. 'Before starting, Southerton wrote to me suggesting we should take out a dozen bats for sale and asking that I would see Andrew Greenwood and

McIntyre and get them to "stand in".' Oscroft decided not to join Southerton's retail consortium and by his own account 'did very well on the tour financially ... Among other things I sold were a gross of photos of myself and [Richard] Daft.' At Stawell, one of the Australian country towns on the tour, Oscroft had a nasty fright when he absent-mindedly left £70 in cash from his sales at the team's hotel while he and the other professionals stretched their legs. To his relief, the money was still there when he rushed back.

Grace still had to round up four amateurs to complete the tour party, a task he completed in early October. They were:

Arthur Bush (23), Gloucestershire
Farrington Boult (21), Surrey
Walter Gilbert (20), Gloucestershire
Fred Grace (22), Gloucestershire

Like W.G., this foursome were only amateurs in name. W.G.'s friend and later ghostwriter, the Kent amateur Bill Yardley, was among those gentlemen approached by Grace. 'I was offered an extremely handsome sum, apart from all expenses,' Yardley recalled. He decided not to go because 'I was doubtful whether it would not compromise my position as an amateur'.

Bush, Boult, Gilbert and Fred Grace – none of whom was well-off – had no such scruples. They were certainly paid fees, as well as openly playing for extra money during the tour in single-wicket and exhibition games.

W.G. had one other piece of business to settle before boarding the boat for Australia. On Thursday, 9 October, he headed for the Church of St Matthias on Warwick Avenue in West Kensington to marry twenty-year-old Agnes Day.

12

AGNES

Despite being W.G.'s second cousin, Agnes came from a completely different background. Her grandfather William Day was one of the early nineteenth century's leading lithographers, acquiring a royal warrant in the late 1820s. When Day died in 1845, Agnes's father, also called William, took over the London firm, renamed Day & Son. For the next decade and a half the business prospered. Like the first William Day, Agnes's father was a fine lithographer who kept up the company's royal connections. In 1856 the Prince of Wales and his younger brother Prince Alfred visited Day & Son's premises on Gate Street, a narrow alleyway between Holborn and Lincoln Inn's Fields, with Day proudly showing off his latest productions.

So far Day had given his wife Elizabeth, a niece of Martha Grace, no cause for concern about his ability to support their large and growing family. Agnes, born in 1853, was their fifth child and the Days would eventually have fifteen children, of whom ten survived into adulthood.

The Days' world began to fall apart in 1861, when Agnes's father agreed to print a run of illegal banknotes for Lajos Kossuth, the exiled Hungarian nationalist leader. The Austro-Hungarian government got wind of the venture, and in 1862 the Emperor Franz-Josef successfully sued Kossuth and Day in London for 'fomenting war' against his empire. Day's legal costs forced him to sell stock in his own company, and by 1867 he had lost control of the firm. With reckless ambition, he now launched a lavishly illustrated periodical, *The Chromolithograph*, which collapsed after two issues when Day was declared bankrupt. For the rest of his life, Day would be dependent on his family for support, including perhaps his cricketing son-in-law.

W.G. probably first got to know Agnes well in the mid-1860s, when the Days were living about three miles north-east of Lord's in Islington. During the summer the young W.G. needed a place to stay while he was playing cricket in London, and the Days probably offered him a bed for the night in return for some of his expenses; they were the only reasonably close relatives of the Graces who lived in the London area. Grace could have seen more of Agnes during the winter, for by the mid-1860s he had joined the London Athletic Club, based at the Lillie Bridge Grounds in West Brompton, and competed regularly at meetings in the capital.

By 1872, when W.G. formalised his arrangement with the Days – at least as far as MCC's records were concerned – Agnes was looking after her younger sisters and brothers at the family's cramped home in Earls Court. Rationally, any chance to escape her impoverished, overcrowded household would have been welcome and W.G. certainly counted as a 'catch'; he was, after all, the most famous cricketer in England. From this starting point, it was easy to conclude that Agnes was a meek Victorian housewife.

Decades later MCC's president Lord Hawke made this mistake, when Agnes overruled him and the club's committee over a matter concerning her late husband. Agnes was private, which was not quite the same as a 'dear', Hawke's patronising description. She left almost no trace of herself in newspapers, and probably destroyed all her correspondence with W.G., either before or after his death. As a result she scarcely features in the literature on Grace, unlike his rather forward mother. This would have pleased Agnes, but it was also a distortion; for as W.G. later said, 'but for her help I never would have done as well as I had, even in cricket'.

Grace's claim in his *Reminiscences* that Agnes 'consented' to the tour of Australia 'as an extension of our honeymoon' may not have done justice to her quietly determined nature. It is just as likely that Agnes saw an Australian summer as more enticing than another winter in her parents' overcrowded house at Coleherne Road and made sure W.G. married her before his departure – or else. She had been engaged to him for at least a year, and could only imagine what W.G. had got up to on Fitzgerald's North American tour.

The wedding on 9 October had the feel of a hurried affair, held on a weekday, with only a small group of close family and friends as guests. Agnes's eighteen-year-old sister Marion witnessed the marriage, while Gloucestershire's wicketkeeper Arthur Bush was best man. The ceremony was conducted in part by Grace's former tutor John Dann, now curate of Downend and the husband of Blanche, W.G.'s sister. Martha Grace watched from the pews.

A fortnight later W.G. and Agnes travelled down to Southampton for a team dinner at the South Western Hotel by the harbour. Grace 'begged' his players that 'any of them who had any cause for complaint should come to him instead of "bottling" up their grievances'. The cricketers cheered, opened more beer and there was 'another howl for Mr W.G. before that festive meal came to an end'.

All the professionals' good humour evaporated the following afternoon when the SS *Mirzapore* steamed out of Southampton. The newly married Graces and the four other fake amateurs retired to their first-class cabins. Meanwhile, the seven professionals went downstairs to the *Mirzapore*'s overcrowded, second-class 'steerage' quarters, with its stinking shared latrines and flea-ridden bunkbeds.

Two players in particular took great exception to their inferior treatment. At the age of thirty-one the Sussex bowler James Lillywhite Jr. was well cast to become the professionals' unofficial shop steward in Australia. Lillywhite was a bricklayer by trade, but like his older cousin John, he was more accurately described as a cricketing entrepreneur. He had toured North America in 1868 with Ned Willsher's professional team, lent his name to *James Lillywhite's Cricketers' Annual* (actually edited by Surrey CCC's secretary Charles Alcock) and in the early 1870s was the main match manager for the United South of England Eleven.

In this last guise Lillywhite had travelled up and down Britain with W.G. during the previous summer on USE's circuit. They stayed in the same hotels and travelled together in the same second- or third-class railway carriages. When Lillywhite saw the terms of his Australia tour contract, he made W.G. send two telegrams to Biddle requesting an upgrade for the professionals to first class. Each time Biddle had refused. With some forbearance, Lillywhite blamed Biddle, not Grace, for what he called 'this wretched second-class business'. He was right about Biddle, but, as events would prove, sadly wrong about W.G.'s attitude towards the players.

The Surrey professional bowler James Southerton was much less patient than Lillywhite. Southerton fell out with Grace as soon as he realised his captain was travelling first class. Over the next five months Southerton became the most important witness to the professionals' mistreatment by Biddle and Grace. He was a vivid writer, sending back regular despatches to the *Sporting Life* newspaper in London, as well as keeping an increasingly indiscreet diary. Far from being rough and uncultured – the clichéd image of a professional Victorian sportsman – Southerton was well-read and interested in the wider world. He particularly liked opera, going on successive nights in Launceston to watch performances of *Faust* and *Il Trovatore*, while his younger teammates went chasing women.

At forty-five Southerton was old enough to be their father, and this age gap may explain why he comes across in his diary as solitary and sometimes homesick. He missed his pregnant wife Sarah, four little girls, and teenage son. Southerton was also plainly unfit, his creaking middle-aged knees unable to cope with sunbaked Australian pitches. His mounting discontent reinforced his acid disapproval of Grace, on and off the field. 'He is a damn bad captain,' Southerton fumed to his diary on one occasion, after W.G. withdrew him from the bowling attack. Yet even Southerton regarded Biddle, not Grace, as the main culprit for the tour's mismanagement.

Southerton's first report for *Sporting Life* shone an early light on the drinking culture that spelled trouble from the start of the tour. At Ceylon they transferred from the *Mirzapore* to a smaller steamer, the *Nubia*, for the last leg of the journey to Australia. When the *Nubia* stopped at King George's Sound, a coaling station on the continent's south-western tip, the cricketers disembarked. W.G. first of all tried his hand at throwing a boomerang, nearly hitting his cousin Walter Gilbert on the return. Full of beans, W.G. then organised a practice session. 'McIntyre bowled W.G. out for the first time in his life and of course claimed the soda and brandy, which he got,' Southerton reported in matter-of-fact style. 'Some went to billiards, others for a good walk, and some good English beer was eagerly called for at 1s 6d per quart.' Slightly drunk, they reboarded the *Nubia*.

In Melbourne Biddle was clearing his desk in time to welcome the cricketers. Annoyingly, the German Consul in Victoria had just sent a cable to Berlin, warning investors to have nothing to do with Biddle's friend and business partner Friedrich Klemm. A German expatriate, Klemm was on a trip to Europe to raise capital for his and Biddle's latest gold-mining venture. In the Consul's view, Klemm was not to be trusted with anyone's money. Biddle hastily organised a joint letter to *The Argus*, in which he and fellow gold speculators affirmed their 'greatest respect and esteem' for Klemm.

On the morning of 13 December Biddle hurried down to the quayside as the *Nubia* steamed into Port Phillip harbour. He and several of his consortium partners clambered into a tug and chugged out to board the *Nubia* before it reached the dock. Grace shook hands with Biddle and introduced Agnes, who may have suspected by now that she was pregnant. Over the next three and a half months the unborn William Gilbert Grace Jr. and his mother coped well with the rigours of an Australian tour. W.G. found the whole experience far more of a struggle.

13

HUMILIATION IN MELBOURNE

Two carriages took the team through cheering crowds to the Port Phillip Club, an elegant Italianate hotel on Flinders Street. W.G. and Agnes stepped out and were ushered inside by Melbourne CC's president David McArthur. Originally from Gloucestershire, McArthur had no financial need to join Biddle's venture. Now in his mid-sixties, he was head of the Bank of Australasia and one of the best-connected businessmen in Melbourne. It may well have been McArthur who insisted on Melbourne CC ringfencing its own finances from Biddle's consortium. Certainly, McArthur kept Biddle at arm's length during the ride into Melbourne from the harbour, treating Agnes and W.G. as his personal guests.

While McArthur looked after the Graces, the other four notional amateurs got out of the second carriage and followed them into the lobby. Then the door slammed shut and the horses clattered off with the seven professionals to the cheaper Old White Hart Hotel at the corner of Bourke and Spring streets.

Grace behaved for the next week as if he did not care that the professionals had been dumped out of sight and then left to their own devices. He visited the Old White Hart for a few minutes on team business, but otherwise pursued a busy round of receptions, lunches and dinners. 'Of course being newly married, and having his wife with him, his spare time would be fully occupied,' Southerton noted sarcastically.

The local press spotted a story and followed up when the players started complaining. 'A great distinction appears to be made by Mr Grace between the "gentlemen" and the "professional" members of the eleven,' the *Bendigo Advertiser* commented. 'By what right is a distinction drawn between two sections of the team – distinction offensive to their employers, and which, we hesitate not to say, is at the bottom of the *fiasco* which the whole affair has turned out to be.' The newspapers failed to note that Biddle's consortium, not Grace, had made the distinction as a cost-saving measure.

The professionals finally decided to have words with W.G. when Biddle whisked Grace, Agnes and the amateurs off to the races, leaving them behind. 'Not one of the promoters of the undertaking up to this time had been to look or make any inquiries after the health or comfort of the professionals,' Southerton complained. It was 'a slight which they all felt keenly, as none had done anything to deserve such neglect'. They protested to Grace, who asked Biddle to organise some entertainment for the professionals. 'It would have been more satisfactory had it been done voluntarily,' grumbled Southerton.

W.G. badly needed management and advice of the kind that modern international cricketers take for granted. In particular, he needed a tour manager to deal with Biddle and a press officer to handle newspapers that were naturally biased against him. He was still only twenty-five and, after years of fawning newspaper coverage in England, had no experience of how to tackle journalists who were out for a story, regardless of the facts.

Yet Grace made a bad situation worse. He failed as a captain in Australia not because of tactical mistakes on the field (though he made a few), but because he refused to assume any responsibility as an off-field leader. He much preferred to spend time with Agnes, shoot wildlife and drink, rather than take an interest in the welfare of the professionals, who had just endured seven weeks in steerage.

The result was predictable. On their first morning of serious practice at Melbourne CC's ground, a local reporter noted that the heat 'made any great exertion from the members of the team a rather irksome duty'. It sounded like some of the players were not trying. A few days later the same correspondent decided after another session that if the English did 'not vastly improve on the play they exhibit at present, they will be easily beaten by the Victorian eighteen'.

In bright, breezy weather almost fifteen thousand spectators descended on Melbourne CC's ground by the Yarra River to watch W.G. Grace's XI, as it was called throughout the tour, play Eighteen of Victoria in the first three-day match of the tour. W.G. lost the toss and the Boxing Day crowd cheered in recognition as he led his side on to the field, his tiny yellow-and-red-striped MCC cap perched on top of his bearded head. He spent the next two hours seething at his bowlers as Bransby Cooper scored 84. This was the same Cooper who had partnered W.G. during Grace's innings of 134 in 1868 for Gentlemen v Players at Lord's. 'B.B.', so-called because of his initials, had then lived briefly in the United States, moving on to Australia where he got a job in Victoria's customs office. W.G. would learn, 'B.B.' also pursued a second career as a travelling mercenary cricketer.

W.G. could bear it no more when Victoria's total passed 200. He ordered his team into a huddle, told them to buck up, and soon decided to bring himself on to bowl. He took ten wickets with his ungainly round-arm 'slows', regretting afterwards that he did not bowl earlier. 'Our regular bowlers were conspicuously ineffective,' he recalled. 'Obviously our men were not up to their standard.' The Victoria Eighteen were all out for 266, an unexpectedly large total that sent 'a thrill of exultation through our borders', *The Argus* gushed.

Next day (27 December) W.G. and the Surrey professional Harry Jupp opened the English innings shortly before 1 p.m.:

'Cheer after cheer rose from every corner of the densely packed ring of spectators as the towering form of the champion cricketer of the world appeared in the field, and when the assembled Eighteen gave their cheer for the captain, there was one united outburst of applause, which was heard in Jolimont, in Richmond, and faintly in far off South Yarra.' In one sporting gesture the Eighteen unnerved both Grace and Jupp, as George Robertson, Victoria's astute captain, perhaps intended.

W.G. nearly ran himself out before he faced a delivery, scrambling to the other end as the fielder fumbled the ball. Gradually he and Jupp settled down and W.G. was into double figures when Robertson threw the ball to twenty-six-year-old Harry Boyle.

The son of a Bendigo cobbler, Boyle was still almost nine years away from producing one of the greatest spells of medium-pace bowling in the history of Test cricket. He looked like every Englishman's idea of an Australian: stocky, bearded and pugnacious, the type who might enter prizefights (which he did). Boyle's appearance was misleading, because with a ball in his hand he was subtle and thoughtful.

He jogged in to bowl to Grace, cheered on by a gang of mates from Bendigo, delivering the ball at a gentle speed with a round-arm action. In Boyle's first four-ball over, W.G. 'carefully placed' a shot for two runs and then pushed a single. He had now made 22 out of an English total of 40. Against most bowlers, W.G. would have been ready to accelerate towards his century.

W.G. tried and failed to score off Boyle's second over, despite 'some very hard hits' straight to the tight-set field. At some point in Boyle's third over (the press reports are unclear) he bowled a delivery to Grace that instead of cutting away – his stock ball – continued on the same line. Grace played and missed; the ball hit his leg stump; twenty thousand spectators roared; Grace loped back to the pavilion. Boyle had announced himself as a 'big wicket' bowler. It hardly mattered that he did not take another wicket in the rest of the innings. The English collapsed to 110 all out, their confidence shaken by Grace's dismissal.

At 5 p.m. the English began their second innings, still needing

156 runs to make Victoria bat again. W.G. now made a tactical mistake that was common among nineteenth-century captains. Rather than open the innings with Jupp, he sent out Andrew Greenwood and Martin McIntyre, who was principally a bowler. Grace's thinking was entirely defensive; he did not want either him or Jupp to get out in the hour before the end of the day. He ended up looking weak, as first McIntyre and then Richard Humphrey were out to soft dismissals. W.G. still declined to bat, sending out his cousin Walter Gilbert, who hung on with Greenwood till the close of play. W.G. Grace's XI were 22 for two wickets and only the Sabbath, a rest day, and the weather stood between the English and near-certain defeat.

It rained heavily on Sunday night but the sky had cleared when Grace arrived at the ground on Monday morning. He immediately asked Robertson if the damp pitch could be rolled, a blatant ruse to improve conditions for batting. Robertson refused, as he was entitled to do under the rules of cricket, explaining a few hours later that he was 'bound to play the strict game without conceding a single point'.

Robertson led his team on to the field before a crowd of about thirteen thousand, many of whom must have invented an illness in order to avoid going into work. Greenwood lasted twenty-five minutes, hardly scoring a run, until he was caught close to the wicket off the bowling of Frank Allan, a rangy left-arm fast bowler. Finally, W.G. emerged from the pavilion to join Gilbert.

Grace pushed and prodded, risking few attacking shots. Gilbert went, dismissed by Allan. Jupp soon followed, caught and bowled by the medium-pacer Sam Cosstick. Fred Grace joined W.G., and the two brothers rebuilt the innings with a partnership of 50. Then Fred was out to a sharp catch by John Conway, who bowled the next batsman, Oscroft, for 0. Grace's team now faced certain defeat.

W.G. moved on to the attack, determined to score fifty before he ran out of batting partners. He hit one ball 'clean over the chain fence' and then another 'magnificent lift' over the fielders to the boundary. Cosstick, Allan and Conway lost their accuracy under Grace's assault, with the new batsman Lillywhite also slogging a few runs. Once again Robertson turned to Boyle. He trotted in, put the ball on the same naggingly accurate spot, and bowled Lillywhite. Next he caught and bowled Southerton. Bush, the last English batsman, now strolled out to join W.G.

Arthur 'Frizzy' Bush, so nicknamed because of his luxuriant whiskers, was Grace's best friend on the team, and, when he stirred himself, a superb all-round athlete. From an old Bristol merchant family, Frizzy stood well over six feet tall and had already played rugby for England, where he was 'the giant of the team ... conspicuous in the centre of every scrimmage'. Frizzy was by repute an idle cricketer, keeping wicket for Gloucestershire because – it was muttered – he preferred to remain stationary. The rumour was perhaps unfair, because for the next few minutes in Melbourne, Victoria saw the Bush of rugby fame, 'the most feared man on the field because of his mighty frame and great pace'.

Grace tried to keep the strike and run 'whenever there was a shadow of a chance'. The left-handed Bush got the message, stealing a single 'audaciously' at one point 'in the face of the field'. Together he and W.G. scampered back and forth until Grace got to his fifty. A relieved Bush immediately hit a ball back over Boyle's head to Conway, who caught him. The English were all out for 135 just after 4 p.m. W.G. had saved his personal pride but W.G. Grace's XI had been humiliated, losing by an innings and 21 runs.

A few minutes later the two sides gathered in front of the pavilion to toast each other with champagne. Grace remarked that his team 'had not been seen in their best form', adding that he 'hoped a return match would be played on the same ground'. Robertson now gave W.G. a foretaste of how losing English captains would always be treated in Australia – with exquisite condescension. Robertson was no larrikin; a wealthy gentleman sheep farmer, educated at Rugby and Oxford (where he got a cricket Blue), Victoria's captain was at least one social class above his opposite number. He began by agreeing with Grace that the

English were 'not in form'. Robertson wondered sympathetically whether they 'felt very much the effect of the different light' in Australia, as he had done when he returned home from Oxford. Perhaps, too, the uneven, worn pitch on the last day 'had also been against the Englishmen'. On the other hand, Robertson added, 'the Victorians might have had the same thing to contend with'.

W.G. Grace's XI had not just been beaten. Even worse, the Australians were starting to feel sorry for them.

The parents

Dr Henry Grace (1808–71)
'A good upholder of Church and State', W.G.'s father was less successful at supporting his family. He died intestate, leaving a fine horse and not much else for his widow. (Dinah Bernard Collection)

Martha Grace (1812–84)
Busy and bossy, W.G.'s mother exaggerated her influence on his cricketing development. After her death, W.G. tried in vain to correct the record. (Grace Family Collection)

The cricketing brother
Ted (E.M.) Grace (1841–1911)
W.G. learned nothing from E.M.'s crude
batting technique. 'It has always been a
mystery to me how he timed the ball so
accurately.' (Copyright Marylebone Cricket Club)

The most 'analytic' mind in cricket
Aged about twenty, W.G. cuts a brooding,
intense figure in a photographer's studio near
Lord's. One Old Etonian team-mate dismissed
the young Grace as 'unanalytic', unable to
grasp how a village-educated youth could
reinvent the art of batting as a 'science'.

The MCC secretary
Robert Fitzgerald (1834–81), the 'beau Sabreur' of Victorian cricket, who engineered W.G.'s belated election to MCC. (Copyright Marylebone Cricket Club)

'Fitz' pursues the off-field interest that destroyed him at a critical moment in W.G.'s MCC career. (Copyright Marylebone Cricket Club)

'One of the pleasantest experiences of my life'
W.G. kept this photograph of an outing to Niagara Falls during Fitzgerald's 1872 cricket tour of North America. Young women attached themselves to the team at every stage of the tour; a few days later in New York, the cricketers were 'disgusted in their delight' at the scantily dressed waitresses. (Copyright Marylebone Cricket Club)

Friend in high places
Like W.G., Lord Harris (1851–1932) was prone to seasickness and thought cricket was the purpose of life. It was enough to seal a lifelong friendship on Fitzgerald's North American tour, with Harris later becoming W.G.'s main ally at MCC.

(Popperfoto / Getty Images)

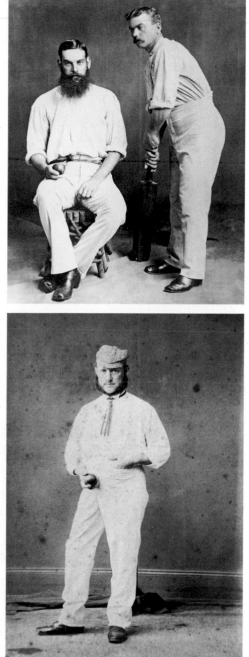

Troubled tourists
W.G. and the Surrey batsman Harry Jupp (1841–89), team-mates on Grace's miserable 1873–4 tour of Australia. W.G. relieved his stress by taking pot-shots at kangaroos, parrots and seagulls. Jupp went down with 'delirium tremens' and had to be locked in a padded room. (S&G and Barratts / Empics Sport)

Cultured and sardonic, the Surrey bowler James Southerton (1827–80) disapproved of W.G.'s boorish behaviour and neglect of the professionals on the tour. 'He is a damn bad captain,' Southerton fumed to his diary. (Copyright Marylebone Cricket Club)

Doomed speculator
William Biddle (1826–75), the main promoter of Grace's 1873–4 Australia tour, looked the part of a respected Melbourne businessman. Behind the façade, Biddle was a loser and a chancer, who hoped the tour would save him from bankruptcy. (Melbourne Cricket Club)

'I have the greatest affection for the county of my birth.'
W.G. loved Gloucestershire County Cricket Club with a passion that brooked no argument from committee men who wanted a say in selecting his side. Here W.G. sits for a team photo at Clifton in 1876 with his great friends 'Frizzy' Bush (on his right, in wicketkeeping pads) and Frank Townsend (next to Bush). Other key players include W.G.'s younger brother Fred (back row, holding a cricket ball), E.M. (to W.G.'s left), and his cousin Walter Gilbert (back row, third from left). (Roger Gibbons Collection)

The Three Graces !!
RUSSELL & SONS   CHICHESTER

Victorian dreamboat

Women wept from Tasmania to Bristol when Fred Grace (1850–80) died at the Red Lion Hotel in Basingstoke. W.G. bottled up his grief, publicly mourning his favourite brother as 'a brilliant field, a splendid batsman, and a fairly successful bowler in first-class company'.

(Boundary Books)

Black sheep

Not the 'Three Graces', but W.G. and Fred's cricketing cousin Walter Gilbert (1853–1924), standing between his relatives in 1874. Gilbert's interest in W.G.'s left pocket appears prescient. In 1886 Gilbert was jailed for stealing money from his team-mates' clothes.

(Boundary Books)

'The Demon'

Clever and chilly, Fred Spofforth (1853–1926) defied the conventional image of a brawny Australian fast bowler. 'I never had any particular difficulty in getting him out,' Spofforth recalled of his duels with W.G. 'This may have been due in part to my artfulness.'

(Melbourne Cricket Club)

On the slide

W.G. claimed implausibly to take 'a little care in my food' during the build-up to the cricket season. By 1887, when he posed for this sketch at Lord's, his eating was out of control and so was his drinking. During lunch intervals he ordered whisky and soda as fuel for the afternoon session. (Copyright Marylebone Cricket Club)

W.G. Inc.

Manufacturers used W.G. to sell everything from soap to cigarettes in New York. Despite his alleged avarice, W.G. had no idea of image rights. He once insisted on buying a Grace souvenir pipe off a passer-by in the street. (The National Archives, ref. COPY1/119 (221) / Copyright Marylebone Cricket Club)

14

THE TOUR FROM HELL

W.G. took out his frustration on Twenty-Two of Ballarat, the team's next opponents in the gold-mining centre seventy miles north-west of Melbourne. 'Grace stepped out to the slows, caught them on the full pitch, and sent ball after ball over the chain fence, the rings of spectators, and the outer fence onto the dusty road,' *The Argus* reported. He scored 126 in front of a crowd of seven thousand in baking heat. Next day, 'a perfect scorcher', Fred Grace also made a century in a colossal English total of 470.

Now it was the visitors' turn to suffer in the heat. Ballarat batted right through the third and final day to score 276 and draw the game, with the crowd expressing 'great disappointment' at the poor quality of the English bowlers. They barracked, in modern English. Southerton thought it was all a bit unfair. 'It is in consequence of their practising on such good and fast wickets they are able to hit bowling so fearlessly,' he told his diary.

It was not even as if Southerton could get a decent bath at the end of this torment. W.G., Agnes and the four amateurs were staying at Craig's Royal Hotel, a fine establishment with balconies overlooking Ballarat's main street. The seven professionals were billeted at Fussell's, a boarding house a few blocks east. Like the Melbourne consortium, the local Ballarat promoters were mindful of costs, having probably paid Biddle more than £300 for the right to host the game.

Biddle urgently needed to make deals with other clubs, for the fixture list was mostly blank, as Grace and his team must have realised by now. At the gold rush town of Castlemaine, local businessmen were preparing to open up negotiations with Biddle. In nearby Maryborough some promoters thought it was 'probable' they had secured a game, 'although the precise date is not fixed'. (It never happened.) In Sandhurst (also called Bendigo) Biddle had settled terms for a fixture but the date was 'to a great extent dependant on the engagements of the Eleven at Sydney'.

In New South Wales the towns of Maitland and Bathurst were in a blind auction for the right to play the English. Meanwhile, Grace could not even establish whether Biddle had arranged another game against Victoria in Melbourne. At the end of the Ballarat fixture W.G. only knew for certain that the team were due in the country town of Stawell and then the coastal port of Warrnambool for two more fixtures against local Twenty-Twos.

Biddle's almost empty tour schedule may explain why Grace, Agnes and the four amateurs dashed off as soon as the match finished on the Saturday afternoon (3 January) to catch the train to Melbourne. Ballarat's club officials were surprised by Grace's absence from a post-match reception, although he had sent an apology. One reason for the round trip to Melbourne was to leave Agnes behind in the city before the next, rough leg of the tour to Stawell, seventy-five miles further inland from Ballarat. She was now pregnant and W.G. – though not necessarily Agnes – wanted to park her with relatives in Melbourne.

The presence of Fred Grace, Bush, Gilbert and Boult on the train was more puzzling. If they were on a bachelor jaunt, it was bound to be short, for they did not reach Melbourne until late on Saturday evening and were back in Ballarat by Sunday evening. Their trip made more sense if W.G. brought them along because he was meeting Biddle and wanted some support. W.G. urgently needed to pin down Biddle about forthcoming fixtures. As matters stood, Grace had contracted the professionals for fourteen games in Australia, which Biddle had embarrassingly failed to deliver.

W.G. could at least tell Biddle one piece of good news. Ballarat CC had received £300 in ticket sales from the game, and the club wanted a rematch against Grace's team. There was space in the calendar, because the game in Stawell did not begin till the following Thursday. All W.G and Ballarat required was Biddle's permission for a second fixture, starting on Monday (5 January); and on a Saturday evening, with the telegraph service shut, the only way to get a response from Biddle was to see him in person.

There is no certainty that such a meeting took place. What is clear is that Grace and the four amateurs returned to Ballarat with no change to the schedule. Ballarat did not get its second game, possibly because the club's officials – some of whom were also promoters – baulked at paying Biddle another steep match-hosting fee. Whatever the truth, the professionals must have been unhappy. They had come to Australia to earn money playing cricket, not kick their heels in dismal boarding houses.

Grace had a fresh problem when he got back to Ballarat – or rather, two. On Sunday the Surrey player Richard Humphrey had badly hurt his leg in a road accident after a visit to a gold mine. It was also plain that Farrington Boult, a doctor's son from Bath, was going down with jaundice. W.G. was set to turn up in Stawell with only ten fit men.

The next ten days were among the worst of W.G.'s life. In Agnes's absence his behaviour deteriorated almost as soon as the team boarded a rickety stagecoach outside Craig's Royal Hotel on Monday morning for the journey to Stawell. W.G. climbed on top with Fred and Walter Gilbert, and once they were out of town, the trio blasted away at any wildlife they spotted on either side of the rutted track. 'Saw lots of Birds,' Southerton noted laconically, 'Magpies, Parrots, Woodpeckers, Wagtails & rabbits, the Graces and Gilbert shot some'. Even Grace was later a little ashamed about their slaughter of the 'lively and entertaining' Australian parrot.

At Stawell, a dusty gold-mining settlement, they were billeted at Cherry's Hotel on Patrick Street; 'no bath in the House, rooms very small,' Southerton tut-tutted. W.G. wandered over to Stawell's grassless, pitted ground and immediately pronounced it unfit for play. He cancelled team practice and went off kangaroo-hunting with Gilbert, leaving the professionals to stew at Cherry's.

The Stawell promoters' blamed the dreadful state of their pitch on the absence of rain in the area for several months, a normal occurrence in the Australian bush. It was not just Grace who thought the match should be called off. 'The ground here is the most fearful I ever saw,' reported B.B. Cooper, hired by Stawell to reinforce their Twenty-Two and by *The Age* as the Melbourne newspaper's match correspondent. 'I shall most probably have to telegraph you the number killed, in place of number of runs.'

Nobody got killed, but the crowd of about three thousand saw nothing resembling a game of cricket. The sheer awfulness of Stawell's ground, like a fisherman's tale, became even more awful with the years. 'One slow ball actually stuck in the dust, and never reached the batsman,' W.G. later claimed.

Fifty-two wickets fell for 269 runs as the three-day match finished in a day and a half. W.G. Grace's XI lost, not that the captain cared. He went off hunting and fishing next day with Fred, Bush and Walter Gilbert, leaving the jaundice-stricken Boult in bed at Cherry's. Meanwhile, the six fit professionals played an exhibition game for a total group fee of £25 against some of the Twenty-Two. They earned £12 10s per run, or, as the scorebook put it, were all out for a grand total of 2.

That evening crowds hooted and hissed the team all along Patrick Street and out of town as their stagecoach set off on the first leg of the journey to the port of Warrnambool, 108 miles to the south. Today Google calculates a driving time of 2 hours 9 minutes between Stawell and Warrnambool. W.G. took about

30 hours, as the carriage slogged across rough tracks that became a morass when a thunderstorm broke in the night. At Hexham, a bush town barely twenty miles from Stawell, 'fresh' horses were waiting for them. The horses went on strike (Southerton spotted 'sore shoulders') and refused to drag the coach through the mud. To lighten the load, W.G. left five of the professionals behind with the ever-available B.B. Cooper, now due to play for Warrnambool, and carried on to the coast with an advance party.

Drenched from another thunderstorm, W.G. arrived late the next evening, glad that the amateurs' hotel had fires lit in the bedrooms. 'I had just gone to sleep when a bang at the door made me jump,' he recalled. It was a local reporter, wanting an interview. W.G. told him to buzz off and went back to bed.

In the morning W.G. sent a coach back to Hexham to pick up the stragglers and then headed off with the other amateurs (probably minus the sickly Boult) on an all-day kangaroo hunt. They were still out of town when the professionals arrived in Warrnambool late in the afternoon and were deposited at another dismal, overcrowded bed and breakfast. 'There was no dinner prepared for us and they wanted to stick us two in a room, we had had enough of this ... so we let them have it,' Southerton scribbled. 'In the end we got some tea, and a room each for 4 of us at another Hotel, so we are cut up into three pieces this time, infernal rot, not to be all together.'

Once again W.G. deserved some of the press criticism that came his way for neglecting his team. Yet it was not true, as some newspapers implied, that Grace had said the separate sleeping arrangements were 'by mutual consent, both parties ensuring to themselves greater freedom thereby'. The quote was unsourced and probably came from Biddle or another member of his consortium. A press officer would have insisted on a correction. Grace had a more immediate problem to tackle. Warrnambool's 'sodden' pitch was almost as bad as Stawell's dust-track.

Biddle had sent his consortium partner Josh Pickersgill down to Warrnambool from Melbourne to keep an eye on proceedings. 'When a few of the [Warrnambool] committeemen ...

listened to Mr. Grace's ideas upon mowing and rolling between the wickets, I thereupon lost the last idea I had nurtured, viz., witnessing a pleasant match and enjoying my visit,' Pickersgill grumbled. W.G. was now so angry with everyone that he mistook Mr Tucker, Warrnambool CC's secretary, for a pressman. Shortly before the game Tucker bustled into the players' changing tent and asked Grace for his batting order. W.G. scrawled his list on a scrap of paper and thrust it in front of Tucker. Obtusely, Tucker repeated his question. 'Damn it man, can't you read?' Grace snapped, only realising a few hours later that Tucker was not one of those 'damned paper fellows'.

Southerton took 24 wickets for 57 runs as W.G. Grace's XI beat Warrnambool's Twenty-Two (top score: 11) in under two days. A more watchable contest over money now ensued between Pickersgill and the Warrnambool promoters, who probably included Tucker. According to Pickersgill, the local consortium demanded '£90 or £100' back from Biddle and his associates for lost ticket sales, because the game had finished a day early. Mr Hickling, one of the promoters, insisted they had merely asked Pickersgill to persuade Grace's team to play an extra game on the third day to bring in spectators. Otherwise, Warrnambool wanted a rebate on the £330 they had paid Biddle for the right to host the fixture.

W.G. and the amateurs voted with their feet and went off in search of the elusive kangaroo; so far their marsupial tally was 0. It was dangerous work. 'The kangaroo has one deadly weapon of defence,' W.G. later explained, as if he were describing a tiger, 'a terrible claw on its hind foot, and the hunter must be careful not to get in front of the animal or he may be ripped up.' Back at the ground the six fit professionals, minus the limping Humphrey, played another scratch game in front of a thin crowd for a purse of £25. The game 'resolved itself into skittles, no-one caring how or what was done,' Southerton reported.

Grace returned from his latest failed kangaroo hunt and straight into another public relations mess. To make more money the Warrnambool promoters had organised a subscription ball that evening for Grace's team, or at least for the amateurs. The professionals were not invited and Southerton knew whom to blame: 'There was a rumour that W.G. had been and accepted on behalf of the 5 [amateurs], saying at the same time that we should not be there as most likely we should not have suitable clothes, the people here are very much disappointed, in fact disgusted with him and the other 4 [amateurs] and speak of them as anything but Gentlemen.'

The press soon picked up the gossip. 'Mr W.G. Grace and the gentlemen players deigned to grace the ballroom with their presence, but only on condition that the professional portion of the team were excluded. Did you ever hear of anything so contemptible?' one newspaper asked. Grace denied the story two months later, but whether or not he was telling the truth, he still missed the bigger point. He should have made sure that all the team were invited, professionals as well as amateurs.

Finally, on his last day in Warrnambool, W.G. bagged three kangaroos. Late in the afternoon Southerton watched W.G. drag the carcasses up the gangway of the coastal steamer taking them back to Melbourne. Southerton reckoned his captain was drunk, and perhaps after a few beers, W.G. imagined the dead kangaroos would make a romantic trophy for Agnes. He dumped his kill, found a good position on the rear deck, got out his gun and began firing at seagulls on the water. Through Southerton's observant eyes, W.G. seemed like a young man reacting badly to an intolerable level of stress.

15

THE SPIRIT OF CRICKET

Agnes had probably been staying with her cousin Frederic Rees, who ran the Pembroke Hotel in St Kilda, just south of Melbourne. Various members of the Rees clan had emigrated from England and Wales to Victoria during the gold rush years, and W.G. and Agnes would see more of their relatives before the end of the tour. W.G. collected her from the hotel, and after a day in Melbourne the team boarded another filthy coastal steamer, the SS *Alexandra*, bound for Sydney.

As the *Alexandra* lurched through the Bass Strait, Agnes soon became seasick and retired to her cabin. McIntyre had earache. Boult's jaundice was worse. Humphrey's leg was hurting. Greenwood slept on deck in the blazing Australian sun and burned his face. W.G. took some more potshots at seagulls. Southerton noted the misery and prepared his next despatch for *Sporting Life*.

The mood lifted as soon as they reached Sydney next morning. Carriages transported the team past crowds of well-wishers to Williams Metropolitan Hotel on King Street, where they would all be staying together. There was a welcoming glass of champagne, time for a quick wash, and then they were off to

Tattersall's Hotel on Elizabeth Street for a reception hosted by Richard Driver, the Sydney politician who headed the New South Wales Cricket Association. Southerton would have preferred hot food, but the 'cold collation [was] very good, with the usual accompaniments of Cham, Hock & C'. Driver gave a warm speech; W.G. made a generous reply; they toasted 'Old England'. 'The memories of old had such a visible effect they could not restrain their tears,' Southerton remarked, looking round the room. Still, 'nearly all say they would not go back to live there'.

Six days later the Melbourne promoter William Runting accosted W.G. in the pavilion at Sydney's Albert Ground. Runting wanted W.G. to delay the start of the next day's play till 2 p.m. because the New South Wales Eighteen needed only 56 to win. In Runting's view it would be better to shorten the playing time to 'let the excitement culminate in the afternoon'.

According to Southerton, 'a scuffle' broke out between Runting and Grace, 'very unbecoming'. A journalist heard Grace call Runting 'a damned liar', at which point 'a fight' occurred; 'the combatants were separated by the spectators'. Runting brushed aside the incident. 'A slight misunderstanding only, not worth noticing!', he assured Biddle.

On the surface, Runting's 'scuffle' with W.G. was trivial; it concerned nothing more than a piece of scheduling. W.G. was already in a foul mood because for the past two days his team had been completely outplayed by a New South Wales Eighteen that included five future Test cricketers: Charles Bannerman, Nat Thomson, the brothers Ned and Dave Gregory, and a pencil-thin twenty-year-old quick bowler called Fred Spofforth. In overcast weather Grace had failed in the first innings, scoring 7. Only his and Southerton's bowling had kept the English in the game, with W.G. taking eleven wickets for 67 runs. In front of eight thousand spectators, the English had collapsed in their second innings, making 90 all out. That left New South Wales needing just 56 runs for victory.

Runting therefore picked the wrong moment to approach

W.G. Yet Biddle's consortium partner also hit a raw spot in
W.G.'s personality that went deeper than his hatred of losing.
Over the previous decade W.G. had demonstrated repeatedly
that he did not subscribe to the conventional notion of sporting manners. His fit of temper at Hove in 1864, after missing
his double-century, rather set the tone. W.G. was also a flagrant gamesman, seeking advantage wherever he could – most
recently, by trying to get the pitch rolled on the last day of the
match against Victoria at Melbourne. There was, however, an
underlying seriousness to W.G.'s approach to cricket, or any sport
he played. In his view, the rules of cricket did not need further
reform, he later told an enquiring journalist: 'The rules are all
that is wanted, but might be made plainer for the umpires who
sometimes do not quite understand them.' The same went for
promoters like Runting who tried to mess with the hours of play
to create some phony 'excitement'. As a Gloucestershire team-
mate remembered, W.G. was 'all for the rigour of the game'.

W.G. won his argument with Runting. The match resumed
next morning (27 January) at the scheduled time of 11.30 a.m.
and the English lost, although they took nine New South Wales
wickets. Ten days later, on the same ground, W.G. gamesman's
instincts collided with his respect for the 'rigour' of cricket's
laws. The outcome was a rancorous, but extremely watchable,
shambles.

First there was a tedious interlude, while they played a dire game
against Twenty-Two of Bathurst, a gold mining town 125 miles
inland from Sydney. Bathurst had earned the right to host a fixture for £300 when rainstorms flooded Maitland's ground up the
coast. Between them, Lillywhite and Southerton took 37 wickets
for 96 runs in front of a few hundred spectators who resented
the promoters' extortionate ticket price. 'There was not much
enthusiasm or excitement,' the *Sydney Morning Herald* reported,
'the rapidity with which the local favourites made their entrances
and exits no doubt having a dispiriting effect.'

The main suspense surrounded an anonymous Bathurst man's

bet with Agnes that W.G. would not hit the ball out of the ground. 'I made up my mind to do my best to win the wager – which was for a pair of gloves – and I went in for hitting,' W.G. recalled. 'I got hold of one ball, full in the bat, and sent it right over the scoring box, but unfortunately it landed just inside the ground, and so Mrs Grace lost her bet.'

They returned to Sydney on the convict-built 'zigzag' railway over the Blue Mountains for another game at the Albert Ground against a combined New South Wales and Victoria Fifteen. It promised to be the biggest fixture of the tour. 'Everyone on our side felt up to the mark,' Southerton wrote on the eve of the match. 'We wanted to show these NSW people that we could play a bit.' The Fifteen were not as strong as they should have been, because several top Victoria players were unavailable, including Harry Boyle, who was ostensibly required by his local Bendigo club. Boyle's future Test bowling partner Fred Spofforth did not play either; he was not yet the 'Demon' bowler of legend.

The Fifteen still had four future Test players, as well as a decent cricketer called William Pocock, who had scored more than half New South Wales's winning runs in the previous game at Sydney. Pocock was the stepson of W.G.'s Uncle Alfred and had grown up with his Grace cousins in Downend. In 1867 he had emigrated from Bristol to New Zealand, bringing his bankrupt stepfather with him (and, presumably, paying for Alfred's ticket). As Alfred Pocock's descendant Rosemary Marryatt has established, W.G.'s childhood coach enjoyed his own cricket 'tour' of New Zealand in 1869 and 1870. 'Uncle Pocock' played seven matches, before returning to Downend via Honolulu and North America. William Pocock then moved to Australia, settling in Sydney.

Pocock's presence in Sydney casts an interesting light on Agnes's attitude to the tour, and especially the idea that she needed cossetting. By late January she was about four months pregnant. It would have been easy for her to stay with Pocock, rather than take the perilous zigzag train to Bathurst and back. Instead, she stuck to W.G. like a limpet for the rest of the tour, joining him on hunting trips into the Tasmanian bush, sea voyages along the New South Wales and Victoria coasts, and, at the end, an overnight coach ride through South Australian scrubland. One gets the sense that Agnes had not enjoyed her solitary 'honeymoon' at the Pembroke Hotel in St Kilda.

She was at the Albert Ground at the end of the second day's play of the New South Wales/Victoria game when W.G. got into another argument that soured the rest of the match. The state of the game was as follows:

First Innings
W.G. Grace's XI: 170 all out
New South Wales and Victoria Fifteen: 98 all out

Second Innings
W.G. Grace's XI: 91 for three wickets (Grace, 56 not out)
New South Wales and Victoria Fifteen: Still to bat

With an overall lead of 163 runs, Grace's team were strongly placed to win the game on the last day. However, W.G. had a problem. Under the rules of cricket in 1874, he could not 'declare' the English innings closed; his team had to bat until the last man was out. The English had only lost three wickets and because they had to bat through till the end of the innings, they risked running out of time to dismiss NSW/Victoria and win the game.

To gain the extra time, Grace asked the home captain Joey Coates if play could start next morning at 11 a.m., an hour earlier than scheduled. W.G. was trying to adjust the playing hours in the same fashion as Runting, with one debatable difference. Grace wanted to create a competitive finish and get round the absurd ban on declarations. Runting had simply wanted to put on a better show for the punters.

A Yorkshire-born schoolmaster, Coates initially refused to budge. He eventually gave way and agreed to the earlier start time, under intense pressure from Grace and probably his own team-mates. Several newspapers reported that some of the Fifteen had put money on a draw, while the English, including W.G., had placed bets on a win for their side.

At 11 sharp next morning (Saturday, 7 February) Grace was padded up and ready to bat. He then waited for twenty minutes until the Fifteen strolled out of the pavilion, in no hurry to resume play. W.G. rapidly took his overnight score to 73 and when he was out, ordered the rest of his batsmen to lose their wickets as quickly as possible. The English already had a lead of around 200 runs, far more than the Fifteen could possibly score in the remaining hours of play.

Coates, by all accounts an honourable man, may have had little control over the antics of those team-mates who had bet on a draw. Several bowlers deliberately directed the ball wide of the stumps, while some of the fielders slouched in the field, seemingly uninterested in the game. Walter Gilbert and Frizzy Bush, who were batting together, decided to help themselves to some easy runs. Furious, W.G. stomped out to the middle and ordered them to hurry up and get out.

With some difficulty the Fifteen managed to prolong the English innings until just before 3 p.m. The Australians had three hours to hold out for a draw, on a hot, sticky day, with a Saturday afternoon crowd of about seven thousand absorbed by the contest.

Once again the incoming Australian batsmen dawdled out of the pavilion, dreaming up any excuse to slow the play. They retied shoelaces, prodded imaginary divots between deliveries, and conducted lengthy mid-wicket conferences on nothing in particular at the end of each over. Their tactics did not work. Led by Lillywhite, the English bowlers steadily dismissed the batsmen: 7 for 1 wicket, 24 for 2, 35 for 3, 35 for 4, 49 for 5, 49 for 6, 53 for 7, 61 for 8, and 82 for 9.

At this juncture Sam Cosstick, Melbourne CC's professional, wandered out to bat. He had barely settled when the square leg umpire Farrington Boult, still too ill to play, gave Cosstick out 'hit wicket'. Boult had just made 'one of the worst decisions ever given in cricket,' the Sydney *Evening News* reported impartially. Cosstick thought so too, as did his team-mates, who urged him to ask the home umpire Richard Driver for a second opinion. In protest W.G. started marching his team off the field. Driver correctly told Cosstick that Boult's decision was final and Cosstick returned self-pityingly to the pavilion, passing W.G. on the way as Grace led his side back to the middle.

From here there was no saving the Australians, who were all out at 5.35 p.m. The English had won by 218 runs with twenty-five minutes to spare.

What followed drew two completely different reactions. 'It cannot be stated that the proceedings during the close of the match were characterised by that good feeling which the cricketing public hoped to witness from first to last,' the *Sydney Morning Herald* noted. 'Square Leg', the *Sydney Mail*'s cricket columnist, blamed the whole sordid spectacle on gambling, with Grace the chief culprit: 'The accepted fact that he [Grace] had wagers on the result of the play irritated some of our men, and rendered them obstinate in their desire to make the match a drawn one, and so spoil the speculation of those who cared more for what they had on the result than for cricket itself.'

There was another accepted fact about this 'sordid spectacle'. Sydney's *The Empire* newspaper deplored 'the bad taste of very many of our citizens and countrymen ... in disheartening our players as they went to the wickets by disparaging expressions and loud hootings, where encouragement would have come with a better grace'.

As the Sydney crowd saw the matter, the Fifteen were ducking W.G.'s challenge to a fight. It was all embarrassingly un-Australian, especially after a few beers. At the end of the game the spectators surrounded the pavilion to make their point again. They shouted for Grace and his team to appear and 'submit themselves to public inspection and applause'. And then, being Australian (and perhaps a bit tipsy), the crowd forgave Coates and the rest of the Fifteen. They gave 'cheer after cheer for the players, English and Colonial, a proceeding which lasted for fully half an hour, when a pretty general move was made for the city'.

On a steamy Sydney evening the colonial press were less inclined to see W.G. and his team as heroes rather than villains. 'Tonight we shall see the last of the English Eleven,' *The Australasian*'s Sydney correspondent shuddered, as Grace's party prepared to board the SS *Rangatira*, bound for Melbourne. 'At least such is the fervent hope of all those in this city who care to see the game played in a courteous and manly spirit.'

There were still seven weeks left of this marathon tour, which now reverted drearily to type.

'The thing here in this country we [should] have at all the Hotels and most of the cricket Grounds, a good shower and plunge bath,' Southerton concluded after a particularly grim stay in Boyle's home town of Bendigo. In Hobart, the owner of the Albion Hotel was astonished that the English cricketers each drank seven or eight bottles of beer a day, and filed a lawsuit against the local promoters for unpaid bills. W.G. got more bad-tempered. 'You acted in a damned ungentlemanly way,' he yelled at one local official who questioned his right to miss the committee man's lunchtime speech (his second of three). Biddle became increasingly evasive, promising the professionals more money-earning cricket matches that never materialised.

Above all, the final weeks of the tour reinforced the sense of a wasted opportunity. At the age of twenty-five Grace was in his absolute prime. As for the Australians, they were only three years away from winning the first-ever Test against England at Melbourne, and only four years away from humiliating an MCC team at Lord's. Biddle was bound to organise some 'country' fixtures against local Twenty-Twos, because Australia's pool of cricketing talent was spread too thinly outside Melbourne and Sydney. Yet if he really had cricket's interest at heart, he should have organised more competitive fixtures between W.G. Grace's XI and cricketers of the calibre of Boyle, the Gregory brothers, Cooper and Charles Bannerman.

Strangely, the Australian press — so hostile to superior Englishmen — failed initially to realise how good their best players were. By the end of the tour some newspapers were wondering whether the likes of Boyle and Bannerman (who would score 165 in the 1877 Melbourne Test) were ready to take on the English in eleven-a-side matches. Here, though, there was another problem.

Rivalry and feuding between the two main cricketing colonies, Victoria and New South Wales, also undermined the tour. 'Australia' was only twenty-six years away from federation when W.G. arrived in Victoria in 1873. Yet when it came to cricket, Sydney and Melbourne acted more like the capitals of hostile independent countries than allies that could join forces to defeat the enemy (W.G. Grace). The absence of Boyle and other top Victoria players from the combined Fifteen in Sydney was never adequately explained. In return Biddle and his consortium made no apparent effort to suggest an equivalent 'combination' game in Melbourne.

The game that began at Melbourne CC's ground on 19 February between the English and Fifteen of Victoria epitomised this waste. Boyle and several other top players boycotted the match, probably because they were unhappy with their fees. Barely two thousand spectators turned up on each of the first two days, with most local cricket fans deterred by the absence of local stars and Biddle's 'preposterous' admission charges.

Grace's team won easily and W.G. then gave the thin crowd a glimpse of what he could do in an even eleven-a-side game, hastily arranged to fill out the time. He hit a century in less than an hour, with the smaller Victoria team unable to plug the gaps in the field with extra players. 'There is no other cricketer in the world who could accomplish that feat,' *The Argus* reported in awe.

Rain ruined a third game in Melbourne in mid-March against a full-strength Victoria Eighteen. It did, however, yield one example of real sportsmanship by the Victoria cricketers, to set against all the bad feeling at the 'combination' fixture in Sydney.

On the final day (Saturday, 14 March) *The Argus* was forced to correct an earlier story, in which the newspaper heavily implied that Fred Grace had cheated in the field by claiming he had stopped a ball inside the boundary chain. Boyle and several other team-mates pointed out that Fred was right and the umpire was wrong to signal a 'four'. 'Of course,' *The Argus* blustered, Boyle's word had to be 'accepted' but 'the very opposite was the opinion of the majority of people on the ground'.

The Argus's retraction went almost unnoticed because of an incendiary letter in the same issue from James Lillywhite. For the past three months Lillywhite had been disgusted by Biddle's disdainful treatment of the players and incompetence in organising tour fixtures. Writing on behalf of his 'brother professionals', Lillywhite set out their grievances against Biddle and his consortium. As recompense they wanted first-class passage on the boat home, like the amateurs.

Biddle retorted sarcastically in a letter to *The Argus* that he was sure readers would 'deeply sympathise with this unfortunate man in his prospects of a second-class passage to England in the P. and O. Company's Royal Mail steamship, and trust that when next he goes abroad he will be able to secure a means of transit more suitable to his merits and desserts'. Lillywhite did. As captain of the next all-professional tour to Australia in 1876–7, he insisted that the whole team travelled first class both ways.

Lillywhite's letter put W.G. in an awkward spot, especially when the professionals boycotted a farewell dinner for the team that Biddle hosted that evening (Saturday, 14 March) at the Criterion Hotel on Collins Street. Grace needed to keep on terms with Biddle for two reasons.

Firstly, Biddle had yet to pay the last instalment of the players' wages and he may also have owed W.G. and the other amateurs part of their fees. Secondly, W.G. was privately trying to organise an extra fixture in Adelaide that would follow the team's final contracted game for Biddle's consortium against Yorke

Peninsula, more than a hundred miles west of Adelaide. W.G.'s secret discussions with the South Australian Cricket Association (SACA) were bound to infuriate Biddle when he heard this news. He had agreed to give Yorke Peninsula the exclusive right to Grace's team in South Australia, in return for a fee of £800, more than double the consortium's normal rate.

At Biddle's dinner, attended by most of Victoria's leading cricket officials and players, Grace seems to have decided that he might as well fib. Replying to Biddle's toast – in which the promoter had noted the professionals' absence – W.G. said he had no idea why Lillywhite and his team-mates had boycotted the dinner. W.G. then smoothly complimented Biddle for doing 'everything in his power to make their stay in Australia a pleasant one'.

Southerton inadvertently opened the way for Grace to vent his real feelings about the professionals. Next Monday (16 March), as W.G. settled accounts with Biddle, Southerton had too much champagne at a lunch for the professionals at the White Hart Hotel hosted by several local businessmen who disliked Biddle and approved of Lillywhite's letter. Southerton blurted out that Grace had promised to travel steerage to Australia and then changed his mind when he got married. Next morning Southerton was appalled to see his comments published in *The Age*.

Grace learned about the story just as he and Agnes were preparing to leave the Port Phillip Club hotel to catch the boat to Yorke Peninsula. Fortunately, another William Day was on hand to take some rapid dictation. This William Day, aged just nineteen, was the son of Agnes's uncle, John Bellenie, and had recently emigrated from England to Victoria. More to the point, Day was a stenographer by trade. The letter that appeared under Day's name in the next issue of *The Age* was clearly Grace's work, for Day had no authority or knowledge to make any of the comments that W.G. dictated.

Grace began by accusing Southerton of 'a deliberate error', or lying:

Mr Biddle can support the assertion that the promoters were twice requested, through the medium of the cable, to give the professionals first-class passages. This was done, not because Mr Grace or anybody else who might have advised him thought they were entitled to the privilege, but because the professionals included it in their demands. Mr Biddle could not see his way to grant the request, and the professionals, sooner than lose £170, consented to journey second-class.

Grace could have stopped there, because Lillywhite had publicly exonerated him as the cause of 'this wretched second-class business'. Instead, he ploughed on at disastrous length, deriding the professionals' presumption in seeking first-class travel and accommodation: 'If the professionals had stopped at home what could they have earned? They would either have had to do nothing or else earn journeyman's wages at a trade. Is it not extremely likely, then, that they would consent to almost anything to secure £170 and live for six months in first-class style at someone else's expense ...'

Then he rounded gratuitously on Lillywhite:

It is only by a suppression of truth that he [Lillywhite] has brought himself to say that in England the professionals, when on a trip, live on an equality with the gentlemen. At the leading London grounds there is a separate pavilion for the professionals. As regards their living in the same hotels, that simply arises from the fact that for each match they obtain so much, and have to defray their expenses. This, of course, leaves them free to go where they please, and to give color to their pretension to equality they go to the same hotel as that chosen by the gentlemen, to the detriment of their pockets at the least.

It was a dreadful insult, made worse by Lillywhite's efforts to keep W.G. out of the players' dispute with Biddle. In one paragraph W.G. had lost the professionals' residual loyalty for the rest of the tour and stored up trouble for when they all returned to England. Lillywhite, Southerton and the others would soon be relaying their dismal experience under Grace in Australia to professionals like Nottinghamshire's Alfred Shaw, who had declined W.G.'s terms. In the small, gossipy world of Victorian cricket, Grace would find few friends.

Why, then, did W.G. make such a stupid blunder? He was furious, probably in a hurry to catch his boat, and perhaps his latent social unease as the grandson of servants hardened the letter's sneering tone.

The final, hellish two weeks of the tour were like an extended Victorian episode of *Men Behaving Badly*. Agnes might have done better to stay in Melbourne and check in again at the Pembroke Hotel in St Kilda. At the time, and later, W.G.'s 'betrayal' of the Yorke Peninsula cricketers by playing in Adelaide was held up as proof of his deceitful, money-grasping character. In reality nobody comes out of the saga well: Grace, Biddle, the Yorke Peninsula Cricket Association or the Adelaide match promoters.

Harry Jupp, the Surrey professional, set the delusional tone on the first evening of the voyage from Melbourne. Jupp burst on to the deck of the steamer that was taking the team to South Australia, screaming that 'persons unknown' had accused him of soiling his trousers. Fired up by shots of brandy, Jupp had a full-blown case of delirium tremens. At Adelaide he was trussed up, wheeled in a cart to a local hospital and locked in a padded room. Jupp soon escaped and, possibly with the help of more alcohol (a proven remedy for delirium tremens), recovered enough of his mind to catch a coach to Yorke Peninsula in time for the start of the match.

All sense of reality had departed from the copper-mining town of Kadina, the venue for the game. Most of the home team could not play to any recognisable standard and had hired a professional to teach them the rudiments of cricket. Dr Herbert, the match committee chairman, 'bowls underhand tolerably,' the local *Wallaroo Times* reported in a jokey feature in early March. Julius Ey, the Yorke Peninsula captain, 'has felt rather heavy on his dexter optic' but 'improves'. Overall the Twenty-Two ought to be able to 'present something like a "show" against the English Champions'. It did not occur to Yorke Peninsula's hopeless players that their 'show' would be a farce. The residents of Kadina and the nearby towns of Wallaroo and Moonta were wealthy from the copper mines that blistered the surrounding scrubland. As far as the local promoters were concerned, they had bought the rights to Grace's team, who were now obliged to perform.

W.G. tried to be diplomatic. Kadina's barren cricket ground, on a roped-off corner of the local racetrack, was pitted with stones that he and local volunteers set about removing. At lunch on the first day he congratulated his hosts on their 'pluck' in organising the fixture and suggested the appalling pitch was partly due to dry weather. No amount of tact could disguise the quality of the cricket in front of around two thousand spectators, far fewer than the Yorke Peninsula promoters had anticipated would fill their specially built grandstands. Fifteen Yorke Peninsula batsmen scored 0 in the second innings as the home team were dismissed for 13 (Lillywhite: 21 overs, 15 maidens, 7 runs, 13 wickets).

Grace then agreed to play an exhibition game for a team fee of £110, astonishing his naive hosts by demanding that the 'amateurs' were paid at the same rate as the professionals. W.G. at last extricated his players and Agnes from Kadina by cutting short the post-match dinner, which started absurdly late, probably because the promoters were trying to prevent the English from reaching Adelaide in time for their 'illegal' game next day. In this goal, at least, the copper speculators succeeded. The cricketers' coach soon got lost in the dark in the maze of tracks outside Kadina and had to park for the night in the scrubland.

Enraged by Grace's 'betrayal', the YPCA tried to have W.G. arrested for breach of contract on his arrival in the city. Adelaide's finest did not stir. Biddle threatened by telegram to cancel the team's tickets to England if the game against Twenty-Two of

South Australia went ahead. W.G. ignored these distractions, as the English beat a weak South Australia team. He had at least done something right by the professionals, who received a £10 match fee (as did the amateurs), plus a share of the gate money, on top of their extra money in Kadina.

Next day the team headed down to Port Adelaide and lugged their bags on to the waiting SS *Nubia*. W.G., Agnes and the four amateurs were shown to their first-class cabins. Downstairs, the professionals squeezed into the *Nubia*'s stifling, overcrowded steerage berths. W.G. Grace's XI travelled home as they had come out, in a thoroughly English fashion.

William Biddle's life began to disintegrate soon after Grace's team reached England. He fell ill with stomach pains, spending less time at his new office on Queen Street, where he advertised his expertise as a 'commercial broker'. In December 1874 he went bankrupt, his downfall blamed by the receivers on 'long continued illness' and 'being called upon to pay debts for which he became security, depreciation in the value of mining property, and pressure of creditors'. Those creditors included the German gold speculator Friedrich Klemm, who had lent his erstwhile partner Biddle £535, with Biddle's house in St Kilda as collateral. The house went, sold at auction by the bankruptcy court's administrator, along with the outbuildings and Biddle's cherished croquet ground.

Biddle's agony was only beginning. He and his pregnant wife moved with their children to cheap accommodation in east Melbourne, where he retired to bed. Over the next two months the strangulated hernia that blocked his bowel slowly killed him, while Biddle brooded on his disastrous business career and the suicide of his friend Richard Wardill. He died on 29 March 1875 and was buried at St Kilda cemetery, remembered in the local press for his 'genial, frank and manly straightforwardness'. With that epitaph, Biddle disappeared from Australian cricket history.

16

HARD TIMES

Four days after his return to England, W.G. travelled over from Downend to Thornbury, buckled on his pads in the Ship Inn, and marched on to the field with E.M., the village team's captain, to take on Clifton. E.M. was out of form, soon bowled for 2 by his and W.G.'s friend and Gloucestershire team-mate Frank Townsend, a Bristol schoolmaster with a taste for stripy blazers who always called W.G. 'Gilly' (short for 'Gilbert'). W.G. had more fun. He scored 259 in three hours, getting Biddle, Runting, Southerton, Lillywhite and terrible Australian pitches out of his system, as he smashed Townsend and the other Clifton bowlers into the neighbouring fields.

A few days later W.G. and Agnes said goodbye to Martha Grace and caught the train from Bristol to Paddington. W.G. had no first-class cricket fixtures in the Bristol area till mid-August and it made more sense to use the Days' London home as his base for the summer.

On 6 July Agnes gave birth to William Gilbert Grace Jr., always known in the family as Bertie. It is unlikely that W.G. Sr. was present at the birth, or even in the next room; Victorian men did not take time off work when they were about to become fathers. Grace spent most of the day at Lord's, scoring 48 for the Gentlemen against the Players. Bertie would grow up to be a gangly, bespectacled youth, better at maths than cricket, and despite heroic efforts on the playing field, a permanent letdown to his father. He took after W.G. Sr. in only one respect. Bertie was a determined, dogged trier; there all similarity ended.

A fortnight after Bertie's birth, W.G. caught a cab up the Old Brompton Road to Prince's Club in Knightsbridge for another Gentlemen v Players match. Prince's was the latest venture of George Prince and his brother James, who had launched their first club on another site in the mid-1850s as a drinking den for Guards and cavalry officers. The establishment collapsed when the membership left to fight in the Crimean War and George and James went bankrupt. At their hearing the judge decided there was not 'a single meritorious feature' in the Princes' shady business dealings. Undaunted, the brothers revived their club a decade later. They found a new home in Hans Place, just behind today's Harrods department store, recruited an aristocratic roll-call of members, and in 1871 laid out a compact little cricket ground next to the tennis and racquets courts.

W.G. liked playing at Prince's. The pitch was good, the boundaries were short, and overall it was the perfect setting to try and score his fourth first-class century of the season. He failed in the first innings, but on the next afternoon was on course for a hundred when an incident laid bare all the bad feeling between him and the professionals that lingered from his tour of Australia.

By coincidence, Princess Alexandra, the wife of the Prince of Wales, had just arrived at the ground with three of her children for a social engagement. Unlike her husband, the Danish princess knew nothing about cricket. What she witnessed probably left her with the impression that the self-styled 'manly game' was a sport for English hoodlums.

Fred Grace had just joined W.G. at the wicket, with the Gents' total on 129 for two. According to *Wisden*, Fred hit an easy catch straight back to the bowler James Lillywhite. *Wisden* then quoted an anonymous cricketer, possibly Lillywhite, who said W.G. 'palpably baulked' Lillywhite by getting between the bowler and the ball. Lillywhite appealed to the umpire to give Grace out for obstructing the field; the umpire rejected the appeal; the rest of the team then joined Lillywhite in protesting against the decision. Eventually play resumed, with W.G. carrying on to score 110 (Fred was out for 12). In *Wisden*'s version the umpiring became heavily weighted against the Players, who lost the match. 'Nearly every appeal made by the Gentlemen was decided affirmatively, and the Players' appeals were mainly met with NOT OUT,' *Wisden* noted disapprovingly.

The incident was more ambiguous than *Wisden*'s report made it sound. Not surprisingly, *James Lillywhite's Cricketers' Annual* also accused Grace of deliberate obstruction. The London *Morning Post* reported without comment that Grace 'cannoned' against Lillywhite, suggesting the obstruction could have been accidental. *John Lillywhite's Cricketers' Companion* did not report the incident at all, although it sharply criticised the standard of umpiring at Prince's.

Whatever the truth, the fracas at Prince's must have brought home to Grace that a swathe of leading professionals regarded him as arrogant and a cheat. Daft and Shaw, who were appearing for the Players, rounded on W.G., as did Jupp, Humphrey and Oscroft, who had gone with Grace to Australia. Lillywhite's position was delicate, because he and Grace travelled all over Britain in 1874 playing professionally for the United South of England Eleven. Cold business logic dictated that Lillywhite and the acerbic Southerton, another USE regular, had to mask their dislike of Grace. By the mid-1870s cricket fans were bored by against-the-odds games, which rarely attracted substantial crowds. W.G.'s star appeal was the only reason USE remained a going concern, providing Lillywhite, Southerton and other professionals with a significant source of income.

W.G.'s heavy USE schedule – he played twelve times for the team in 1874 – broadcast his now-brazen 'shamateurism'. The nearest Grace came to justifying his money-making was via his stenographer mouthpiece William Day in his letter the previous

March to Melbourne's *The Age*. Justifying Grace's Australia tour fee, Day wrote (at Grace's dictation): 'Mr Grace, by coming to Australia, is thrown back in his studies a twelve month, and as by this time he might have been in practice as a surgeon, it is fair to say he loses two years by the trip. Surely he must be compensated? That, however, does not make him a professional.'

The same sophistry could be applied to Grace's professional career in England. By playing a full season of first-class cricket as an amateur, W.G. was pleasing the public but delaying his medical studies, and by extension, his prospect of earning a living as a doctor. According to this argument, Grace needed to play against-the-odds cricket for money in order to bring in some income, especially now he had a wife and son to support. Grace never had the nerve to make such a case in public, but by the mid-1870s he seems to have calculated that MCC would not dare either to call him to account over his flagrant abuse of the amateur code.

In the spring of 1874 one senior English cricket official decided to put MCC on the spot about Grace. Captain Henry Holden, the Chief Constable of Nottinghamshire, had just become honorary secretary of Nottinghamshire CCC, the bastion of the northern professionals. Holden took a brisk policeman's approach to the issue of gentlemen amateurs playing for money. 'The time had arrived,' Holden wrote to the MCC committee, 'when some proper definition should be laid down of the term amateur, as distinct from professional.'

The committee stalled, instructing Fitzgerald to acknowledge Holden's letter while deferring the matter for another discussion. As was his habit on sensitive matters, Fitzgerald did not record when this second meeting took place. Instead, he informed Holden vaguely that the committee had 'approved of the reasons given [by it] for payment of expenses to amateurs'. Fitzgerald stressed that he was against 'anyone playing as an amateur who is essentially a professional', a precise description of Grace's status on the MCC secretary's tour of North America.

Holden leaked Fitzgerald's letter to the press, prompting

the *Nottingham Express* to ask: 'Can anyone for a moment look upon Mr W.G. Grace as being an amateur?' Other northern papers picked up the refrain, ignoring the fact that Yorkshire, Nottinghamshire and Lancashire did excellent business at the gate when Grace played. MCC also did well out of W.G.: for instance, some seven thousand spectators watched him at Lord's on the day Bertie was born, although, as it turned out, only one of Grace's eight first-class centuries in 1874 came for the club. Meanwhile, the MCC committee continued to pay Grace's expenses at his usual modest rate. In June he received a total of £20 for three games and in August less than £5 for the club's annual fixture against Kent at Canterbury.

W.G. played twelve USE games in 1874 because he needed the cash. His windfall from Australia would not last indefinitely and he did not have a winter job. His 'job', which did not inspire him, was returning to his medical studies.

W.G.'s choice of St Bartholomew's by Smithfield meat market as his next medical school owed more to his residence in London than any other reason. His anatomy tutor Dr Alphonso Cumberbatch, in his late twenties, was remembered as 'well-qualified' by the *British Medical Journal*. However, Grace's old-fashioned surgery tutor Howard Marsh, who poo-poohed the idea of infectious bacteria, was a step backwards from the go-ahead Tibbits in Bristol.

Grace never registered at Bart's, reinforcing the impression that he was a sluggish scholar. His reluctance to qualify stemmed from a particular problem. W.G. had to earn a living as a doctor, but he wanted to continue playing top cricket for many years to come. Judged from his later double career, Grace's goal was to find a medical practice that would pay well enough to allow him, with the help of locums, to play in the summer as an amateur. It made no sense for Grace to qualify until he achieved this outcome.

E.M. had already shown how to combine a GP's life with all-year-round sport. Like his father, E.M. accumulated part-time medical jobs and sinecures; the difference in E.M.'s case was that he never allowed work to get in the way of cricket or hunting.

In early 1875 E.M. set out to win a particularly juicy plum position. There was a vacancy for the post of coroner in west Gloucestershire, a part-time job that delivered an annual income of £200 for not very much work. Usually, the incumbent was required to do little more than turn up at inquests and make sure the jury rubber-stamped the local doctor's opinion on why someone had died. But there was a catch: the coronership was an elective post in the gift of local voters.

E.M.'s absurdly over-the-top election campaign provides an insight into both how badly he wanted the job and the Graces' strong family connection with the Tory establishment in the county. Far from being unpolitical, as was later suggested, W.G. was an ardent, active Tory, like the rest of his family; in 1889, for instance, Grace represented his local Conservative association at a party meeting in Bristol.

W.G. was too busy moving house and studying to lend a hand with E.M.'s campaign, but their elder brother Henry recruited a 200-strong election 'committee', chaired by the Duke of Beaufort, which amounted to a roll call of the leading Tories in Bristol and west Gloucestershire. E.M. then set about crushing his Liberal opponent, a young Bristol solicitor called Albert Essery. 'I need hardly point out to you,' E.M. reminded voters, 'how requisite it is that a coroner should be a Medical Man, as an Inquest is really to find out the cause of death.'

Essery, withdrew at the last minute to avoid being flattened by E.M.'s Conservative juggernaut. 'If Mr Essery or his friends had but asked to look at his [E.M.'s] canvassing books,' E.M. mocked in his victory speech, 'he thought that gentleman would have retired much earlier than he had.'

E.M.'s new position gave him the best nickname in Victorian cricket, 'The Coroner', and welcome extra income. On top of his coroner's salary, E.M. earned fees from private patients at his practice in Thornbury and received £60 per year as Gloucestershire's secretary. None of these part-time duties stopped E.M. playing cricket through the summer for Gloucestershire and Thornbury, and hunting through the winter with the Beaufort and the Berkeley. He seems to have been the most financially successful of all his family, living in some style from the mid-1870s with his wife and growing brood of children at Park House, a fine detached home in Thornbury looking across to the River Severn Estuary.

W.G.'s domestic arrangements were more pinched, physically as well as materially. In February 1875 he and Agnes, with little Bertie, moved into a narrow terrace house in Eardley Crescent, Earls Court, of 'desperately unhappy proportions', according to a later architectural survey. Most days W.G. travelled to Bart's for more tuition under the capable Dr Cumberbatch and the incompetent Dr Marsh. W.G. had to hope all this studying would soon lead to the kind of agreeable set-up enjoyed by E.M. in Thornbury.

Francis Berkeley, the 2nd Baron Fitzhardinge, had been thinking the same thought. Fitzhardinge lived at Berkeley Castle, a splendid medieval fortress near Thornbury, and knew W.G. and E.M. well, both as the titular head of the Berkeley Hunt, and a vice-president of Gloucestershire CCC. Fitzhardinge preferred the chase to cricket, but he knew how much the county club depended on W.G. for its winning record in the mid-1870s. For several seasons the sporting press ranked Gloucestershire as the strongest team, in what amounted to an informal and primitive county championship.

During the summer of 1874 Fitzhardinge had discussed the possibility of doing something for W.G. with Colonel Robert Kingscote, the Liberal MP for Gloucestershire West. According to Fitzhardinge, Kingscote supported the idea taking shape in Fitzhardinge's head, possibly with a nudge from W.G. and E.M. Fitzhardinge had in mind a fund that would buy W.G. a comfortable medical practice, perhaps near Berkeley Castle. Ostensibly, the purchase would be a token of gratitude for W.G.'s service to the county, now that he was 'retiring' from cricket. In reality W.G.'s practice would allow him to carry on playing full-time as a gentleman amateur, in the same way as E.M.

The plan went no further in 1874, almost certainly because the timing was awkward. Grace had just returned from his lucrative tour of Australia straight into a headwind of criticism from Captain Holden and others about his shamateurism. But in Gloucestershire, if nowhere else, Fitzhardinge's proposal was under debate. As the 1875 season began, W.G. had to remind his fans of how much he would be missed if he gave up the game for medicine.

That August Grace passed a landmark that is still the best measure of his greatness as a batsman. Playing at Clifton College's ground in Bristol, he scored 119 for Gloucestershire against Nottinghamshire. It was 'a grandly compiled innings', observed the *Standard*, which like other newspapers provided no further comment. W.G. ignored the same innings in both his ghost-written memoirs. In fact it took cricket statisticians some time to work out that his hundred at Clifton was Grace's fiftieth first-class century.

Grace was still only twenty-seven when he reached the target, just ten years after his first-class debut in 1865. He scored his centuries at a time when there were far fewer first-class fixtures; when he did not have a regular first-class club (MCC) for the first four seasons of his career; and when pitches were generally poor, and sometimes lethally dangerous. The staggering distance between Grace and everyone else was unequalled in any sport until Don Bradman reached his prime in the 1930s, on much easier batting pitches.

The statistical breakdown of these centuries – a dread phrase for any non-cricket fan – was actually quite interesting. Grace scored ten of his hundreds for MCC, between his election in May 1869 and August 1875. Gloucestershire accounted for a further ten, following MCC's granting of first-class status to his county club in 1870. Another ten centuries were scored for Gentlemen v Players, the set piece 'grand match' between the amateurs and the professionals that was the top competitive series in cricket before the advent of regular England v Australia Test matches in the 1880s. Most revealingly, W.G. scored only five first-class centuries before his election to MCC in 1869. Put the other way, Grace scored forty-five first-class centuries in the space of only seven years, when he played no first-class cricket outside England.

W.G. scored his fiftieth century in a rainy summer when he had a mediocre batting season by his standards (1498 runs; average 32.56 per innings). 'Quite naturally, critics thought "I had gone off;" but in my heart I did not think so, for I felt as fit as I ever felt in my life,' he remembered. As if to compensate, he had his best-ever bowling season, taking 191 wickets at an average of 12.94 runs per wicket.

Over the past decade W.G's bowling had gradually decelerated from medium pace to slow. To a great extent the switch to a slower style was forced on him by his increasing weight, a subject on which he held firm views. 'The great mistake of modern days is that we eat too much,' he warned schoolboys. 'Avoid late dinners and many courses. Take simple, wholesome food.' Like many medical students and doctors, W.G. proved incapable of following his own advice. One scene on his Australia tour, funny in itself, suggests he may even have had a compulsive eating disorder, which he masked by playing host at impromptu feasts and snacks. W.G. was on the SS *Rangatira*, lurching from Sydney to Melbourne, and had just 'crawled on deck' after a bout of seasickness. 'I espied some sacks of oysters which were going down to Melbourne,' he recalled. W.G. bought the lot from the fisherman, and 'in less time than it takes to write it, we had half a dozen stewards hard at work opening oysters and cutting bread and butter, while we entertained the poor sea-sick passengers to a feast of stout and oysters'. The reference to beer is also telling. From the 1870s glimpses of W.G. eating are almost always accompanied by champagne, 'hock', beer or whisky.

W.G. later reckoned that he weighed about 15 stone by the mid-1870s. The impact on his bowling was obvious. In recent years he had cut his run-up and the press now routinely described him as a bowler of 'slows'. Beyond this label, most reporters and pundits had great difficulty fathoming how W.G. managed to make top batsmen look like novices, as they thrashed and swiped at his seemingly innocuous deliveries. 'Mr W.G. Grace is fairly entitled to be considered, on a suitable wicket and in an emergency, one of the more puzzling bowlers of the day,' *John Lillywhite's Cricketers' Companion* commented on the 1874 season, when W.G. took 139 wickets. 'In a word the style is "mixed" perhaps, the "head" in it occasionally reminding the spectator of Alfred Shaw, but it gets wickets very frequently when more scientific professors of the art of trundling have failed to bring about such a desirable result.'

Lillywhite's touched on, and then veered away from, the key to understanding Grace's artful bowling. 'Bowl a bit with your head,' W.G. advised young cricketers. One exceptionally well-qualified observer grasped that W.G.'s bowling was an artful mind game:

He [Grace] seems to be able to divine what next to send, and very frequently he indeed so juggles with you that you are beaten in spite of yourself. This talent is the very finest attitude of a bowler. In these days when batting has attained to such a science and when we have men who with good sight and trained judgement are able to place a ball with almost the accuracy you get at billiards, it requires the utmost ingenuity to beat them.

The author of these rematks was Fred Spofforth, greatest and cleverest of early fast bowlers.

W.G.'s bowling performance in August 1875 for Gloucestershire against Yorkshire, a few days before his fiftieth century, epitomised what Spofforth meant. Playing at Clifton, beneath the school's looming Railway Gothic buildings, W.G. took thirteen wickets, bowling without a rest to win the game.

As always, W.G.'s approach to the wicket was designed to distract the Yorkshire batsmen. 'His run – more correctly, his scuffle – up to the wicket was short with elbows bent,' recalled

the Bristol cricket correspondent H.E. Roslyn. 'Then his right
arm would be thrust out with hand not much above the head
and the ball would roll out of his hand.' The Lancashire amateur Allan Steel described what it felt like to face Grace: 'The
batsman, seeing an enormous man rush up to the wickets, with
both elbows out, great black beard blowing on each side of him,
and a huge yellow cap on the top of a dark swarthy face expects
something more than the gentle lobbed-up ball that does come;
he cannot believe that this baby-looking bowling is really the
great man's.'

Adding to the confusion, as the ball floated towards the
batsman W.G. would dart to his left to take up an extra fielding position at short mid-off. The batsman now had to decide
whether the ball that landed unerringly on a length between
middle-and-leg justified all W.G.'s dramatics at the other end.

For W.G. the worst outcome was if the batsman treated each
delivery on its merits and pushed the ball calmly for singles and
twos. In this situation he would typically position E.M. as close
as his elder brother dared at 'point' (silly point in modern cricket)
to fool the batsman into believing the ball was spinning sharply
off the pitch. Charles Ullathorne, who opened for Yorkshire in
this 1875 match at Clifton, fell to the Graces' double act: caught
E.M., bowled W.G. for 0.

John Thewlis, Ullathorne's batting partner, was trapped by
another of W.G.'s accomplices in Gloucestershire's fine team of
fielders. Frank Townsend, whose prep school, Llantrissant House,
was next door to Clifton College, usually fielded for W.G. in
a strangely precise position not found in any coaching manual:
directly behind the umpire on the leg side and about fifteen
yards in from the boundary. Despite his taste for natty blazers,
sometimes with a matching bow-tie, Townsend normally fielded
capless in this deliberately peculiar position. Grace's tactic was
obvious. He wanted to plant the thought in the batsman's mind
that Townsend was in the wrong place; neither 'in' at mid-on, to
stop the single, nor 'out' at long-on, to save the boundary. Like
countless other batsmen, Thewlis sized up Townsend and tried

to hit the ball over the schoolteacher's capless head. Sure enough, Townsend caught him.

Frizzy Bush and Grace's double act completed Yorkshire's humiliation in the county's second innings. William Oates, the last Yorkshire batsman, charged down the pitch to another gentle delivery from W.G., swiped, missed, and turned to see Bush 'neatly' remove the bails. Oates was stumped for 1 and Yorkshire had lost by 122 runs.

One week later W.G. almost got killed by a donkey cart.

On the evening of 20 August W.G. set off in a horse-and-trap from the Swan Hotel in Tunbridge Wells with his friend Robert Lipscomb, an amateur bowler, at the reins. Grace had just finished a game for South v North on Tunbridge Wells' Higher Common ground and was staying the night at Lipscomb's farm in a nearby village. Rounding a blind corner, the trap crashed into a donkey-and-cart driven by a costermonger heading the other way. W.G. and Lipscomb were thrown 'with considerable force' on to the country lane, shaken but uninjured. They got up, saw the costermonger was all right and then looked at Lipscomb's horse. It lay dead in the road, speared through the neck by one of the shafts from the unhinged donkey cart. Picking his way through the overturned fruit and vegetables, the world's greatest batsman went off with Lipscomb in search of help.

17

SHOWTIME: AUGUST 1876

A month before Grace's traffic accident the newspapers got wind of another story about him. 'It is stated – we know not with what truth – that Mr Grace intends at the end of the season to bring his cricketing career to a close,' the *Western Daily Press* reported in July. In August the *Bradford Daily Telegraph* predicted that W.G. would only play occasionally in 1876 because of his commitment to medicine. Both rumours were untrue. Grace or someone close to him was trying to focus minds on how he could continue playing full-time cricket once he qualified as a doctor.

As secretary of MCC, Fitzgerald ought to have played a central role in settling the issue of Grace's future. However, by the autumn of 1875 Fitzgerald was distracted by another matter. He could not move his left arm properly, and in December consulted two doctors in Mayfair. Fitzgerald left Dr Rees and Dr Henderson's consulting rooms in Albemarle Street with no reassurance. The doctors recommended to the MCC committee that Fitzgerald should rest 'for some months from all work that might in any way press upon his mental faculties'. Privately, Fitzgerald took a more melodramatic view of his plight. 'My first warning,' he wrote. 'I placed my resignation in the hand of the Committee this afternoon [but] was too affected to read my own death warrant.'

In fact the committee granted Fitzgerald a stay of execution, asking him to continue in office till the club's annual general meeting in May 1876, while providing him with additional clerical assistance. Fitzgerald struggled on till March, but the effort was too much. He departed on sick leave to the Greek islands, where he sketched the idea for a Byronic epic, 'The Childe Fitz', in his 'Quidnunc' scrapbook. 'Like Byron I know not where my Pen will guide me,' he declared of his unwritten masterpiece.

Henry Perkins, recruited to help the ailing Fitzgerald, now took over the MCC secretaryship. Like Fitzgerald, the forty-three-year-old Perkins was a Cambridge cricket Blue and a qualified barrister. '"Perkino", short of stature, with the ugliest and scraggiest of beards, a somewhat uncommon cast of countenance, a confirmed stoop, an inveterate habit of rubbing his hands together, and a complete carelessness as to his attire, presented a weird aspect,' recalled the Yorkshire and MCC grandee Lord Hawke. Sydney Pardon, *Wisden*'s editor, alluded tactfully to Perkins' 'foibles'. The new MCC secretary had one particular foible that would almost wreck Gloucestershire and MCC's eventual testimonial fund for Grace. In contrast to Fitzgerald, 'Perkino' was an idler who preferred to lie low, avoiding any unnecessary additional work.

During the winter of 1875–6, as Fitzgerald consulted the doctors, W.G. shuttled back and forth between Bart's and Eardley Crescent. Agnes was pregnant with their second child, making more urgent the business of sorting out his future. To his chagrin, W.G. could see in the mirror that he was getting older and, frankly, fatter. By his own admission, he weighed about 15 stone (95 kilograms) at the start of the 1876 season, confessing that it took him 'longer to get into form and condition than in previous years. Increase of years and increase of weight may account for it.'

W.G. was at the start of a long and completely unsuccessful career as a 'dieter'. In *Cricket* Grace suggested that during his build-up to the new season, he 'even' observed 'a little care in my food'. He then cut the sentence from the published version, probably because he knew that nobody would believe him. His increasingly visible fatness after his return from Australia had some bearing on Fitzhardinge's still-vague plans for a testimonial fund, because W.G.'s obesity reinforced the impression left by his mediocre batting form in 1875 that he was past his peak. As he lumbered after the ball in the field, or wheezed for breath following a quick single, he was in danger of planting an inconvenient question in the public's mind: if Grace's best years were over, why worry about his threatened retirement?

W.G. did little in the first half of the summer of 1876 to dispel this impression, scoring only one first-class century in May and June. The weather warmed up and, as so often, he found his form with the sun on his back, making 169 for Gentlemen v Players at Lord's at the start of July. A week later W.G. travelled to Grimsby for a USE fixture that assumed far more importance in subsequent Grace folklore than it really deserved.

W.G.'s 400 not out against Twenty-Two of Grimsby summed up why against-the-odds cricket was so dull to watch. At the end of the first day, when W.G. had reached 130, Grimsby's umpire cheerfully admitted in the bar that he should have given W.G. out leg before wicket when his score was only 6. Mr Mortlock felt it 'inadvisable' to dismiss W.G. so early in the game.

W.G. carried on relentlessly through the second day, fortified by champagne to celebrate the birth of his and Agnes's second son Edgar. Everyone toasted Mrs Grace's health and W.G. announced with jovial menace that he would like to celebrate with a record score. By close of play he was 314 not out and Grimsby's cricket fans had seen enough. 'The third day, financially, was an awful one,' recalled Bob Lincoln, one of the Grimsby players. 'The public, undoubtedly, were tired of seeing him at the wickets and stayed away.' Strictly speaking, W.G. failed to reach 400. When the last USE wicket fell, Grimsby's scorer had Grace on 399 not out. 'Oh, make it 400,' W.G. reportedly called to the scorer.

Lincoln, a decorator by trade, then added a fictitious single in the scorebook and Grace's quadruple-century became fact.

In an odd way W.G.'s colossal score at Grimsby underlined his general indifference to his performances in these professional games for USE. During the 1870s W.G. consistently underperformed for USE compared with his batting record in first-class cricket. He scored only eight hundreds in 91 USE games between 1870 and 1878, a ratio of about one century for every 11 matches. In the same period W.G. scored 50 centuries in 207 first-class matches, or about one in every four fixtures. It was true that by the mid-1870s most first-class pitches were of a higher standard than the rough local club grounds on USE's circuit. Yet W.G. had proved in the 1860s that he could score runs on all surfaces. W.G. was a natural trier, but his overall record in against-the-odds cricket suggests he sometimes found it hard to apply himself with the same rigour as when playing a first-class fixture.

The real show began three weeks after the Grimsby game on the other side of the River Humber in Hull. On a rain-damaged pitch, W.G. scored 126 for USE against United North of England in a proper, eleven-a-side match, with the other batsmen managing just 28 runs between them against a strong bowling attack led by Alfred Shaw. Grace's innings ended with fitting violence when he accidentally smashed his bat into the stumps attempting a cut. The ground dried out, batting became easier, and the match ended in a tame draw on Saturday, 5 August. Grace (who scored 82 in the second innings) caught the train to London, passed by Eardley Crescent to collect some clean kit and say hello to Agnes, Bertie and Edgar. Then he was off again to Canterbury for the start of the city's cricket week on Monday.

As always, Kent society was out in force for the annual festival at the St Lawrence Ground on the Dover Road. Hot weather was forecast all week, and as the sun blazed down, 'delightful little parties' began to form in the carriages and private tents that ringed the boundary, with 'the fair sex predominating'.

Normally, Fitzgerald would have been conspicuous among the fashionable young ladies. But he was stranded in Salzburg, consulting the suitably named Dr Carl Grassberger about the grass that the MCC secretary imagined was sprouting through his skin.

Grace's week got off to a bad start as soon as he went out to bat for a combined Kent and Gloucestershire team against an All-England XI. He made 9 runs and spent the rest of the day in the heatwave watching his cousin Walter Gilbert score a century. W.G. did better in the second innings, scoring 91 as the game petered out in a draw.

It was now Wednesday, and the festival's main fixture began: a twelve-a-side match between Kent, captained by Lord Harris, and MCC, led by Grace. Harris won the toss and chose to bat, and with the temperature hovering around 90° Fahrenheit, W.G. spent most of the afternoon watching helplessly as his aristo-cratic friend scored 154. For the politically ambitious Harris, life could not get any better. His innings was full of dashing 'Old Etonian' strokes, played in front of his home crowd, a clutch of well-connected Kentish politicians and peers, and his admiring young wife Lucy.

On Thursday – another hot, almost cloudless day – W.G. scored just 17 as his weak MCC team collapsed to 144 all out. They were 239 runs behind Kent's first innings score and at about 4.50 p.m. Under the rules of cricket at the time, MCC was now obliged to follow on and try to erase the deficit.

Grace walked out to open MCC's second innings with the Surrey amateur Alfred Lucas. In the baking afternoon heat Grace was probably wearing a floppy white sun hat rather than his usual MCC cap. Otherwise the sight confronting the Kent bowler Charlie Absolom was a familiar one. When the sun shone W.G. dressed to bat in a white, long-sleeved silk shirt, rolled to the elbows; cream flannel trousers with no pockets, which he tied round his girth with a string cord or ribbon; black rubber protective gloves; canvas batting pads stuffed with cotton wool; and brown or two-tone leather cricket shoes with spikes.

According to his settled habit, W.G. would have made
Absolom, Harris and the rest of the Kent team wait while he
went through a methodical routine. He scrutinised the pitch
intently and surveyed the field, verifying the position of each
fielder. Next, W.G. asked the umpire for a middle or middle-
and-leg batting guard. He then removed a bail from the stump
and scratched a mark behind the batting crease, double-checked
his guard with the umpire and replaced the bail, taking care it
was properly aligned with the other bail. Finally he took guard;
W.G. was ready.

Grace later suggested in his memoirs that he was keen to catch
a train to London that Friday evening and gain a rest day in
Bristol before his next game, starting on Monday at Clifton; in
effect, he would throw away his wicket and the match by taking
undue risks. This is hard to believe. W.G. was either implying
that Kent would take all eleven MCC wickets in an hour and
forty-five minutes, or that he would abandon his team and head
for the station once he was out.

In an earlier essay, W.G. left a more convincing account of
his thinking as he prepared to take on Kent's attack on a perfect
batting pitch. 'I made up my mind to play a fast game, knowing
that the bowler could get little or no work on the ball, and that
any attempt to play carefully for a draw would be useless,' he said.
This version was consistent with Grace's competitive character.
Apart from Lucas, a future Test player, the rest of MCC's batting
was extremely weak, as the team had demonstrated in the first
innings. W.G. could not rely on anyone staying with him for
long, so it made sense to attack and get runs as quickly as possible.
As a bonus, he might wipe the smirk off Harris's face.

What happened between 5 p.m. and the close of play at 6.45
p.m. left *Wisden* sounding as if it had attended a sado-masochistic
orgy rather than a game of cricket. W.G. unleashed 'hitting
almost unexampled in its brilliant severity,' *Wisden* wrote. The
almanack's heated prose did not quite capture the full terror for
bowlers when faced with W.G. in this mood. Kent's bowlers
were not confronted by an instinctive hitter who might make

a stupid mistake. Grace's assault on Harris's bowlers was calm, deliberate and 'scientific'.

When play ended W.G. had scored 133 not out in an MCC total of 217 for four. Harris retired with Lady Harris to the fancy Rose Hotel on Canterbury's Parade. Around the city that evening, Canterbury's 'hotels, clubs and other public places of resort' had only one 'subject of general conversation, the extraordinarily brilliant batting of Mr Grace'. At the Fleur de Lys pub on the High Street (cheaper than the Rose), W.G. went to bed for a good night's sleep. He had plenty more work to do.

As Grace knew, Kent were still in a strong winning position on Saturday, the final day of the festival. MCC had no serious front-line batsmen left, with W.G.'s overnight partner twenty-one-year-old Percy Crutchley, just down from Cambridge. The good news was that Crutchley had won a Blue that summer. The less good news for W.G. was that young Percy's Blue was for tennis. He had hardly played any cricket since going up to Cambridge.

At midday, beneath another fierce sun, W.G. and Crutchley resumed MCC's innings, both feeling rather nervous. Surprisingly, Crutchley settled sooner than W.G. and began to score freely. At the other end W.G. was 'fidgety' for the first half-hour, as the crowd at the St Lawrence Ground grew to become another full house of about seven thousand spectators. He was just getting into his stride when he broke his bat. To his irritation, Grace found the handle on his replacement bat too thin, a problem that Sir Spencer Ponsonby-Fane was determined to fix when W.G. and Crutchley came off the field for lunch. Sir Spencer grabbed W.G.'s bat and busily wrapped thick twine around the handle. He was not going to see 'the fun and their outing spoiled for want of a little attention of *that* kind,' joked Sir Spencer, who had added his mother's family name of Fane to his own one on inheriting her estates in Somerset.

They went out again at 3 p.m. in the heat of the afternoon. W.G. passed his double-century and Crutchley looked set for a hundred. Kent's bowlers wilted and W.G. became thirsty as he raced towards his triple-century. Mercifully, 'relief came pretty often from the Officers' Tent in the form of Champagne and Seltzer'. Or so Grace recalled in the first draft of his 1891 memoirs. In the published version he made it sound as if the soldiers who were entertaining the young ladies on the boundary only came out once to refresh him.

Throughout the day the military band outside the tent had been serenading W.G.'s onslaught in the shimmering heat. 'The band kept on playing an air,' recalled one of the spectators, the Reverend Robert Holmes. 'That air and W.G.'s batting on that afternoon are forever linked in memory.'

Crutchley was out for 85, just before 4 p.m., easily the top score of his three-match first-class career; he spent the rest of his long life dining out on the day he batted with W.G. A draw was now the only possible result because neither side had enough time to win the game. At stake was whether W.G. could score the first-ever first-class triple-century (he did) and perhaps even a quadruple-century.

At about 5 p.m., in a spirit of *noblesse oblige*, Harris brought himself on to bowl. W.G. sized up Harris's medium-pace trundlers and hit one delivery into a neighbouring wheat field. Absolom came back after a rest; W.G. pulled him to the boundary. Harris plugged away; W.G. hit him for two successive fours. Finally, at 5.35 p.m., Grace mistimed a drive off Harris. The ball looped in a gentle arc towards mid-off where the Kent fielder Vero Shaw rushed forward and held the catch just above the ground. Harris danced a little jig for joy; Grace tore off his sweat-soaked batting gloves, furious with himself. He was out for 344, and to Harris of all bowlers.

He spent Sunday on a stifling train to Bristol, got a good night's sleep at The Chestnuts, and on Monday morning (14 August) travelled over with his mother to Clifton College for the start of Gloucestershire's game against Nottinghamshire. At around noon, with no end in sight to the heatwave, W.G. walked out to open the innings with E.M. To his fury, W.G just missed out on a double-century. He scored 177 in three hours and then foolishly got caught in the deep off the occasional bowling of John Selby – one of only five first-class wickets that Selby ever took.

There was more frustration for W.G. at the end of the day, when, as he prepared to bowl the final over, the Nottinghamshire batsman Robert Tolley deliberately wasted time by painstakingly adjusting his pads.

'W.G., eager for another over, called to Tolley to play cricket,' the *Bristol Times and Mirror* reported. 'Tolley still went on and W.G. continued to complain in a loud tone against the waste of time, then were general cries of "Play" but when the clock struck the players left the ground to groans and hisses.' Grace got his revenge in Nottinghamshire's second innings, dismissing Tolley and seven other batsmen to win the game for Gloucestershire.

Next stop: Cheltenham. On Thursday morning thirteen-year-old Harold Webb arrived early at Cheltenham College's ground, hoping to sneak in and catch a glimpse of his hero before the start of Gloucestershire's game against Yorkshire. Harold was in luck. He walked straight through the unattended gate and ran over to join a group of boys who were waiting for W.G. to emerge from the changing room. '[He] came out to the practice nets, throwing broadcast a few balls and putting us in paradise by an invitation to bowl at him,' Webb remembered. 'A burly, stooping, blackheaded giant he seemed to us, wearing a loose, unbuttoned shirt, which showed a chest clothed with dense hair; rolled up sleeves, which revealed equally hirsute arms, and a tiny MCC cap surmounting an enormous head.'

W.G. was 216 not out by the end of this humid day, against a Yorkshire bowling attack that included four players who would appear at Melbourne the following March in the first-ever Test match. During lunch and tea breaks he played cards with his team-mates or chatted to his mother in the little tent he and his brothers had erected for her by the boundary.

Rain delayed the start of play on Friday, as the heatwave finally broke. When play resumed, Gloucestershire's lower order collapsed. W.G., still rueing the double- and perhaps triple-century he had missed at Clifton, cursed his luck again as Gloucestershire's last man strolled out to join him. All would be fine, Frizzy Bush reassured W.G. – and so it was. Bush scored 32, confounding W.G.'s fixed belief that his friend was too lazy to score runs. W.G. ended on 318 not out, his second triple-century in the space of six days.

The rain came back and the game ended in a draw. Grace had made 834 runs in three innings over eight days, a performance that went unnoticed by the most important cricket patron of his early career. At the Manor House lunatic asylum in Chiswick, south-west London, doctors were assessing a newly arrived patient from Salzburg. 'The well known secretary of the Marylebone Cricket Club' has a 'highly nervous temperament' and a 'well-shaped' head, they noted. Over the next month Fitzgerald scribbled with increasing urgency 'songs and letters of an erotic character' and other literary works, his pen racing across the pages of his Quidnunc scrapbook.

By late September despair began to grip him as he sensed the onrush of madness: 'With Insanity, the Demon Spider weaves but one web for his victims & it is only the Rough Broom which clears not only Spider but web & victim for ever and ever.' The asylum doctors diagnosed Fitzgerald as suffering from tertiary syphilis, for which there was no known cure. That autumn Fitzgerald took leave off his remaining senses just as the task of organising a fund for W.G. landed on Henry Perkins' desk at Lord's.

18

THE FUND THAT FLOPPED

In December 1876, as Fitzgerald raved, 'dirty and noisy', in his asylum room, the MCC committee agreed unanimously that 'Mr W.G. Grace is deserving of a testimonial [fund] in acknowledgement of his extraordinary performances & that the time has arrived for presenting such testimonial.'

Perkins' minute made it seem as if the idea came from Lord's. In reality the proposal originated in Gloucestershire and Perkins wanted the county to take the lead. 'I hear that your Lordship takes an interest in this matter,' Perkins wrote to Lord Fitzhardinge shortly before Christmas. 'If so, will you kindly inform me what plan you would advise.' Perkins also enquired with the Duke of Beaufort, the county club's president and MCC's incoming president for 1877.

The Duke now referred the matter back to Fitzhardinge. Gloucestershire were 'likely to be more keen' than any other county about the proposed testimonial for Grace, the Duke wrote to Fitzhardinge on 21 January. A fortnight later Fitzhardinge chaired a meeting of Gloucestershire cricket officials and local dignitaries in Berkeley Castle's medieval great hall to set the fund in motion.

Gloucestershire could not afford to lose their dominant player to medicine, a prospect that E.M. Grace, as the club's secretary, now pretended was imminent. 'He had not heard his brother intended playing this year,' E.M. told the meeting, adding that he thought W.G. would retire from cricket after sitting his qualifying exams in the autumn. On that basis Fitzhardinge set a deadline of September 1877 for Gloucestershire to send a contribution to MCC's still non-existent fund. A brief whip-round in the great hall yielded £25 from Fitzhardinge, 10 guineas from the Mayor of Bristol, and around a dozen smaller contributions; even Frizzy Bush, who was not rich, gave 3 guineas. Only E.M. kept his hand in his pocket, perhaps feeling he was doing enough as the Gloucestershire fund's manager.

A fortnight after the meeting the *Cheltenham Chronicle* ran an odd little diary item, which stated confidently that W.G. would soon be installed as 'a county surgeon and perhaps an officer of health in the fair vale of Berkeley'. W.G.'s prospective job sounded remarkably similar to E.M.'s agreeably undemanding medical practice a few miles away in Thornbury. Yet as Fitzhardinge implied, Gloucestershire could not possibly raise the money to buy Grace a practice single-handedly. By the 1880s GPs in affluent neighbourhoods often earned more than £500 per year from fee-paying patients, meaning the practice's potential value could be far higher. The county needed MCC's assistance to give the Grace testimonial national momentum. It proved a task that was quite beyond Perkins' limited ability.

At Lord's Perkins talked vaguely about setting up a testimonial committee composed of 'influential persons from all parts of the country'. Nothing had happened by May 1877, when the Duke of Beaufort began his year's term as MCC president, an appointment probably timed to coincide with the Grace testimonial. Annoyed by Perkins' inertia, the Duke wrote directly to W.G. to establish whether he really was about to retire. Put on the spot, Grace equivocated. W.G. 'intended to follow his profession after this season, though he should continue to play for his county and MCC', the Duke reported back to the MCC committee. Grace had given the game away. He did not mean to retire from first-class cricket when he was still the undisputed 'champion batsman of the world'.

Agnes watched her husband on 31 May as W.G. batted all day at Prince's, scoring 252 not out for South v North. By now, the Prince brothers were more interested in selling off parts of their Knightsbridge ground to property developers than maintaining a full-size playing area. W.G. swatted many of his 'boundaries' into the construction sites around Hans Place, where builders were erecting the mansion blocks that would soon encircle the venue. Agnes had brought a Dutch lady friend along with her to enjoy the cricket – a surprising cosmopolitan touch for a woman regarded as a little Victorian wife. Agnes gave proof as well of a dry sense of humour. A clergyman sitting next to them got so excited by Grace's innings that he insisted she have a closer look through his binoculars at the great batsman in action. 'Which she did, very carefully, very gravely – without remark! Matters became slightly embarrassing when W.G., his innings over, went seeking for the light of his home.'

The public wanted to watch W.G., but he was confronted by the humbling reality that, by and large, they did *not* want to show their gratitude by contributing to his testimonial fund. By June 1877 E.M. was letting it be known that the county had received about £400 'in promises and money', which begged the question of whether the promises would materialise into hard cash. E.M. had a tough job on his hands, given his brother's poor public image as an avaricious shamateur. Even W.G.'s most ardent fans might reasonably ask why someone who was about to earn a living as a doctor – like E.M., in fact – needed even more money.

At Lord's, Perkins finally opened a bank account for MCC's overlapping 'national' fund, with the club contributing 100 guineas. The Duke of Beaufort also made sure that MCC appointed Fitzhardinge as the club's president for 1878, a move that would allow Gloucestershire to keep an eye on Perkins' management of the testimonial if it slipped into a second year. Embarrassingly, Fitzhardinge had forgotten to pay his MCC member's subscription for several years. The baron hastily provided the committee with a 'satisfactory' explanation and his presidency was confirmed.

By August E.M. was resorting to gimmicks to get Gloucestershire's hard-nosed public to boost the county's fund for W.G. He placed a notice in the Bristol press, announcing that all the gate money from the county's forthcoming match against Yorkshire at Clifton would go to W.G.'s testimonial; in the event of an early finish, W.G. and his team-mates would play a novelty game using broomsticks as bats.

In early September W.G. went on a shooting weekend in Northamptonshire, where he blundered in front of the guns and was hit near one of his eyes. He could have been killed, but the injury turned out to be minor, as the press soon confirmed. Within days of the accident he had recovered completely, scoring 71 in a professional game in Sussex. It was a further reminder of why the Grace testimonial was in such poor shape. Once again W.G. was playing openly for money, with his appearance against Eighteen of Hastings his tenth USE engagement of the season.

By October the MCC's grandly named national fund had received two pledges of £50 each from Yorkshire CCC and Kent CCC, and little else. The MCC committee quietly decided to shelve the whole project till the following spring. In Bristol E.M. placed another advert in the local press, stating disingenuously that Gloucestershire's fund would remain open till the summer of 1878, 'in order to give those who have not already subscribed an opportunity of doing so'.

With his testimonial on hold, W.G. delayed his qualification as a doctor even further by leaving Bart's. In the autumn of 1877 he moved with Agnes, who was pregnant again, Bertie and Edgar into a cottage in the village of Kingswood, near Downend, where his eldest brother Henry had his medical practice.

It is generally assumed that W.G. spent a year in Kingswood in order to gain some practical medical experience as Henry Grace's assistant. This seems implausible. As a teenager W.G. had already spent plenty of time watching his father at work in the surgery at The Chestnuts and it would have been easy for him to follow one of the physicians at Bart's on their visits to outpatients. W.G. took exactly this course when he returned to London in the autumn of 1878 and transferred to Westminster Medical School.

It is more likely that W.G.'s sabbatical with Henry was a ruse to slow down his progress towards qualification while he waited to see how much money his faltering testimonial would raise. By the autumn of 1877 W.G. was close to fulfilling the qualifying requirement of thirty months' attendance at a medical school. His time spent with Henry stopped the clock, guaranteeing it would take him another year to become eligible to sit for his physician's and surgeon's licentiates.

Henry was also a useful contact if W.G.'s testimonial fund failed to raise enough money to buy him a practice, as seemed increasingly likely. W.G.'s brother was a public vaccinator for the Barton Regis Union (previously the Clifton Union), the local Poor Law union for whom their father had worked as a medical officer. The union administered Poor Law relief across a sprawling area that stretched from central Bristol to villages like Kingswood, and vacancies for parish medical officers arose from time to time. As his brother's assistant, W.G. could keep an eye out for any openings with the union.

At the start of the 1878 season a banker's son from New South Wales gave Grace the shock of his cricketing life and effectively threw down a challenge. W.G. could retire from cricket and become a full-time doctor or he could test himself in the coming years against the greatest bowler he would ever face.

Shortly after midday on Monday, 27 May, W.G. and 'Monkey' Hornby opened the batting for MCC at Lord's against the visiting Australian team. Grace was soon out to Frank Allan, the left-arm fast bowler who played against him several times on the 1873–4 tour. A few minutes later Grace watched from the pavilion as twenty-four-year-old Fred Spofforth marked out his run.

Before arriving in England, Spofforth had posed for his portrait in a photographer's studio. Tall and lean, with a slightly raffish moustache, he is quite the dandy; one hand clutches a bowler hat, the other a rolled umbrella, while a patterned handkerchief peeks out of his frock-coat. To contemporaries, Spofforth did not look like a brutish fast bowler, and he did not behave like one either. His natural Australian heir was Dennis Lillee, who looked the part but who realised, like Spofforth, that truly great fast bowling required intense mental effort. 'The Demon' Spofforth had 'a head like an almanac, he was always dodging you', 'Buns' Thornton recalled. According to Lord Harris, Spofforth bowled 'judgmatically', an arresting image that captured the thought behind every delivery and the batsman's dread of his imminent execution.

MCC's score stood at 25 for two wickets as Spofforth began his short, sprinting run-up, culminating in a high, 'over the shoulder' cartwheel action quite different from the prevailing round-arm style of most bowlers. Spofforth's sixth ball bowled Hornby. His ninth delivery bowled the young Oxford and Middlesex amateur A.J. 'Webbie' Webbe. In his fourth over he took a hat-trick (Hearne, Shaw and Vernon). Next over he caught and bowled Flowers, the last batsman. MCC were all out for 33. Spofforth had taken six wickets for 4 runs in 23 deliveries.

The press could not make sense of Spofforth's bafflingly unpredictable bowling. Sometimes he bowled 'tremendously fast' and sometimes he slipped out a 'slow one' with no perceptible change of action. Some deliveries 'broke' (deviated) sharply towards the stumps, others cut away, and, strangest of all, two of the hapless MCC batsmen were stumped, with Spofforth ordering the Australian keeper Billy Murdoch to stand right up to the wicket.

MCC's two main bowlers, Alfred Shaw and his left-handed Nottinghamshire team-mate Fred Morley, now set out to prove what they could do on a poor, rain-damaged Lord's pitch. They took full advantage, rapidly dismissing the Australians for 41. At about 4 p.m. Grace and Hornby began MCC's second innings, with a slender lead of 8 runs. This time Spofforth opened the bowling.

His first delivery 'evidently puzzled' Grace, according to the *Standard*'s correspondent. Spofforth's second delivery, 'rather a slow one that came across from the leg, clean bowled him'. The moment was symbolic: at one end Grace, overweight and slightly past his best; at the other end Spofforth, lean and approaching his peak.

Spofforth took three more wickets but for once played second string to his bowling partner. After years of toil on baked, concrete-hard Australian pitches, Harry Boyle had just discovered the joy of bowling on a damp English wicket that was 'doing a bit'. He took six wickets for 3 runs, as MCC collapsed to 19 all out. The Australians needed just 12 runs for victory – which they made, carefully, for the loss of one wicket.

Having failed twice against the Australians on the field, W.G. spent the rest of the summer trying to get his revenge by winding them up. He lost this contest as well. The day after the game at Lord's, Agnes gave birth at Kingswood to a daughter, Bessie. W.G. dashed down to Bristol to see his new-born girl, played in a county trial game at Cirencester for the latest batch of promising Gloucestershire teenagers, and was back in London by the start of June for his next round of games in the capital.

On 20 June W.G. and the Australians almost came to blows in a dispute which became so foul-tempered that neither side afterwards could produce a reliable version of events. Billy Midwinter, a good all-rounder, was down to play for both the Australians against Middlesex at Lord's and Gloucestershire against Surrey at the Oval. On his 1873–4 tour of Australia W.G. had learned that Midwinter came originally from the Forest of Dean, before moving to Australia, and on that basis was eligible to play for Gloucestershire. Grace had invited Midwinter to England in 1877 as the county's first professional, and the Australian then returned for another season with Gloucestershire in 1878. However, Midwinter was also picked for the Australians' tour, setting up a tussle over his services.

W.G. claimed that on 20 June, having discovered Midwinter's absence from Gloucestershire's team at the Oval, he turned up at Lord's and 'after some persuasion', brought Billy back with him for the county game. The Australian cricketer Tom Horan, who was also a journalist, reported a different sequence of events.

Horan said the Australian manager John Conway, with Boyle (an accomplished boxer) and the captain Dave Gregory as his seconds, caught a cab to the Oval 'to acquaint W.G. with Mid's decision' to play at Lord's. In Horan's version, Grace was 'mightily riled' and told Conway the Australians were a 'lot of sneaks'. Conway and W.G. may have shaped to punch each other, but the scorecard shows that W.G. had already won the first round. Midwinter played for Gloucestershire, scoring 4 and 0 as his adopted county lost the match.

Conway was not finished. He and W.G. had form going back to Biddle's farewell banquet for Grace's team in Melbourne in March 1874. On that occasion Conway had told the English they should stop whingeing about their treatment by the Australian press. Now he wrote to Gloucestershire demanding that Grace send him a personal apology. W.G. provoked Conway a little more by blandly expressing his regret for any misunderstanding. Conway wrote back, threatening that if W.G. did not send him a *full* apology, the Australians would cancel their fixture against Gloucestershire in early September.

W.G. needled Conway again by directing his next reply to Dave Gregory, as if he had washed his hands of the Australian manager. 'I am sorry that my former expression of regret to the Australian cricketers has not been considered satisfactory,' Grace said. Seizing the high ground, he assured Gregory that he wished 'to let bygones be bygones'. He offered 'extreme regret' for 'use of unparliamentary language to Mr Conway', along with the promise of a 'hearty welcome' when the Australians came to Clifton.

The Australians dropped their threatened boycott in favour of letting Spofforth teach W.G. a lesson. Spofforth took twelve wickets in the game against Gloucestershire, though Grace in fact survived him. Spofforth also scored 44 in the Australians' first innings, happily slogging Grace for several boundaries; and then, just for his amusement, Spofforth opened the batting in the second innings to help score the 17 runs needed for victory. It was thrillingly vengeful cricket, and Gloucestershire's first-ever defeat at Clifton.

*

W.G. was finishing the worst batting season of his career. He only scored one first-class century in 1878 and finished the summer with an average of just 28.77 runs per innings. In theory he was due to receive his testimonial cheque in November. As the deadline approached, E.M. placed yet another notice in the Bristol press, soliciting 'early payment' to Gloucestershire's fund 'which has been before the public for two seasons'. It sounded like a complaint rather than an appeal. Still short of contributions, Gloucestershire and MCC quietly postponed W.G.'s award for a second year running.

Over the winter two controversies involving W.G. almost stalled the whole testimonial project. In November, responding to renewed press comment about 'shamateurism', MCC ruled that 'no gentleman [i.e. amateur] ought to make a profit by his services in the cricket field'. In future, 'no cricketer who takes more than his expenses in any match shall be qualified to play for the Gentlemen against the Players at Lord's'.

This was too much for *John Lillywhite's Cricketers' Companion*, which cited Grace as proof of MCC's hypocrisy. 'One well-known cricketer in particular has not been an absentee from the GENTLEMEN'S eleven at LORD'S for many years past, and that he has made larger profits by playing cricket than any other Professional ever made is an acknowledged fact,' the *Companion* declared. 'How the MARYLEBONE CLUB can reconcile their statement with this fact, even with any reasonable amount of word-twisting, we are unable to conceive.'

In January 1879, a dispute at Gloucestershire destroyed W.G.'s pretence that he was a genuine amateur. Nominally, the issue concerned whether E.M. had overcharged Surrey the previous summer when billing the county for an away match at the Oval. E.M.'s invoice included £20 expenses for himself as Gloucestershire's secretary and £15 for W.G. A special meeting of Gloucestershire CCC members at the Grand Hotel on Bristol's Broad Street rapidly degenerated into a faction fight over the Graces' power within the club. W.G. remarked in a wounded tone that he was 'aware from the very starting of the club of the personal feeling against some of their family'. Indeed, 'even when a little boy [I] could recollect it'.

After the meeting a committee member revealed to the press that W.G. and his two brothers, plus their cousin Walter Gilbert, received expenses 'on a special scale' that was higher than the rate for Gloucestershire's other amateurs. W.G. agreed to end his premium arrangement, but the damage was done. 'He has become a very well-paid amateur, to the dissatisfaction, I will not say disgust, of his professional brethren and his brother amateurs,' the *Leicester Chronicle* commented. It was a fair description of Grace's standing among his fellow cricketers, with only six months to go till his scheduled testimonial award.

Grace was now back in London and enrolled at Westminster Medical School under Dr William Allchin, a far more capable surgery tutor than Dr Marsh at Bart's. During the day, W.G. also visited outpatients with his general practice tutor Dr Francis de Havilland Hall, making the long journey each day from his latest rented home in the west London suburb of Acton. Grace's brief residence at 1 Leamington Park, a grim semi-detached house, is on the face of it inexplicable. He was miles from the Westminster Medical School and Agnes's family in Earls Court and it is not even clear whether she and the children joined him there. He must have known his time in Acton would be brief, for he was now on course both to qualify as a doctor and to receive his testimonial fund in July 1879.

As his testimonial loomed, Grace tried to make peace with his critics. He announced that he would not play for USE in 1879, a decision that gave the London *Standard* another chance to draw attention to MCC's hypocrisy. W.G. had been 'treated with an amount of indulgence in a financial sense which the cricket world would not and will not accord to any one else,' it said. Grace also persuaded MCC to donate all the gate money from his testimonial match in July to Alfred Shaw, whose recent benefit game at Lord's had been ruined by rain. His gesture was generous and diplomatic, repairing some of the damage caused by his various fallings-out with professionals since going to Australia.

In May W.G.'s friend Harris urged MCC to replace its proposed testimonial game between 'Over Thirties', led by Grace, and 'Under Thirties' with a more competitive match that might draw a bigger crowd for a game scheduled to start on a working Monday. Harris suggested instead that the team he would lead on a tour of Australia the following winter should play an 'England' eleven captained by Grace. The MCC committee decided that Harris's proposed match would be too much trouble for Perkins to organise, and voted 'that the original fixture, *viz* over & under 30, must be adhered to'.

By now 'Mr. W. J. Gordon' was managing the combined Gloucestershire and MCC funds and contactable at Lord's for any late contributions. William Gordon was well qualified on two fronts to take over the administration of the testimonial from Perkins. He was a professional accountant and also Grace's brother-in-law, married to Agnes's younger sister Marian. With Gordon installed at Lord's, Fitzhardinge issued another invitation to W.G.'s admirers in Gloucestershire 'to gladly join in hearty good wishes for his [W.G.'s] future welfare'. The press smelled an impending fiasco. 'We hear this week that the national testimonial to Mr W.G. Grace does not progress so successfully as could be desired,' the *York Herald* commented archly at the end of June.

In the second week of July W.G. dashed up to Edinburgh to sit for his qualifying physician's licentiate. Here was another strange move; why not sit the exam in London? W.G. was following a family tradition, for E.M. had also received his physician's degree from the Royal College of Physicians of Edinburgh. There was a perception south of the border, strongly denied by the RCPE, that Scottish licentiates were easier to obtain than northern ones. It is unlikely, though, that W.G. found his main examiner a soft touch. Dr Charles Bell came from one of Scotland's most eminent medical families, as a descendant of the pioneering early nineteenth-century surgeon and neurologist of the same name.

W.G. survived his ordeal with Bell and received his physician's licentiate. He then caught the train back to London in time to play in James Southerton's benefit match at the Oval. As with Shaw, there is a sense that W.G. was trying make his peace with the professionals. Southerton was now fifty-one and poised to retire to the Surrey suburb of Mitcham, where he ran a pub. W.G.'s presence in this game between South and North certainly boosted the gate and, with it, Southerton's benefit windfall, which came only just in time for his wife and children. The opera-loving, literary Southerton died less than a year later from pleurisy.

It poured all the following Monday, the first day of Grace's 'Over Thirties' v 'Under Thirties' testimonial match at Lord's. Grace sat with the other players in the pavilion as the rain swept across the deserted ground. Next morning he took a cab to the Royal College of Surgeons in Lincoln's Inn Fields to take the oral exam for his surgeon's licentiate, the other qualifying degree to practise medicine.

Like his stay in Edinburgh, W.G.'s seemingly last-minute trip to the college raised a question. If he had failed his surgeon's viva voce, Grace would have returned to Lord's to collect his testimonial cheque with the embarrassing news that he was still not a qualified doctor. Yet by fixing the exam on the same day as his testimonial, Grace behaved as though he regarded the oral as a formality. In an age of medical reform, the Royal College of Surgeons did not issue special licentiates for celebrities. W.G.'s apparent confidence that he would pass the viva voce suggests he felt right on top of the subject. It is even possible that he could have sat the exam a few years earlier.

Grace did not miss a single ball of his testimonial game, because the 'wet and muddy state' of Lord's delayed the start of play till 1.20 p.m. The 'Under Thirties' had hardly begun batting in grey, drizzly weather before a scattering of spectators when the teams came off for lunch, followed by the testimonial presentation ceremony in front of the pavilion. Fitzhardinge made 'a business-like speech', in which he revealed that the fund would not after all buy Grace a practice. In one version of his speech, Fitzhardinge joked that he and the Duke of Beaufort 'thought that Mr Grace was old enough and strong enough to choose a practice for himself'. The peer now revealed the total size of Gloucestershire and MCC's combined funds: £1458, including a donation from the Prince of Wales, a keen, though dreadful cricketer. According to Fitzhardinge's arithmetic, Gloucestershire had contributed more than half the money. MCC, the game's richest club, was a junior partner in the enterprise.

Grace made a courteous speech of thanks and put in a word for Alfred Shaw, whom he said deserved a second benefit later in the season to compensate for another game spoiled by rain. He then accepted his cheque, plus a fine marble clock and accompanying bronze obelisks. There was no sign of the promised album containing the names of subscribers. For whatever reason, Gloucestershire and MCC decided the cheque and the clock were enough.

Grace's 1879 testimonial was not an outright failure. Somehow Fitzhardinge, the Duke of Beaufort and E.M. managed to overcome MCC's ineptitude to collect a sum that amounted to three and a half times Perkins' £400 annual salary. Professionals like Southerton, Shaw and Lillywhite could only dream of this kind of money.

W.G.'s prospects as a newly qualified doctor were hardly hopeless, even if his testimonial fund had fallen short of its original target to buy him a practice. During the summer of 1879, Dr William Day (no relation) resigned as the Poor Law medical officer for the northern half of the Bristol parish of St Philip and St Jacob. Eight years earlier, Dr Day had succeeded to the post on the death of W.G.'s father. Grace was ideally positioned to take over from Day, especially as his elder brother Henry was on the union's payroll as a public vaccinator.

In October, the union confirmed W.G.'s appointment. By Christmas, Grace and his family had moved into a small house at 61 Stapleton Road owned by an Irish cattle merchant.

19

DOCTOR AT LARGE

W.G.'s new home was only a fifteen-minute walk from the centre of Bristol, where handsome buildings such as The Exchange on Corn Street spoke of the city's civic pride and prosperity. Yet Stapleton Road, winding north-east from the centre, was another world, filled with the flotsam of Victorian society. Pedlars, prostitutes and tramps came and went, often ending up at the Eastville workhouse on Fishponds Road, halfway to the village of Stapleton. They were disdained by the district's settled inhabitants, who clawed a living as tradesmen and artisans; people like Thomas Higgs, a maltster at number 65, or William Griffiths, a tailor round the corner at 5 Clifton Place.

W.G. soon learned that his neighbours consulted the doctor as little as possible because they disliked the fees. 'You will be glad to hear I have started a practice here, and have had between 700 and 800 fresh patients since Jan 1st,' he wrote in April 1880 to the secretary of the Royal College of Surgeons. 'Unfortunately, they do not all pay.'

As a Poor Law medical officer, W.G. answered to the Board of Guardians of the Barton Regis Union, which met most Fridays at the Eastville workhouse. For two decades the guardians would exercise considerable power over W.G.'s professional life off the field. It was Grace's misfortune that some of these builders, brewers and other local worthies disapproved of his long absences playing cricket. They thought W.G. should be on call throughout the year to help the union administer poverty relief across a swathe of central and northern Bristol and a ring of outlying villages. Under the 1834 Poor Law Amendment Act, a sick person could only be seen by a medical officer at the parish's expense after the local 'relieving officer' had established that there was no one in the patient's immediate family who could pay for a private doctor. The union paid W.G. £90 per year to perform this service in a densely populated inner city area containing almost twenty-five thousand people. This was the same salary his father had earned in 1871 as a medical officer for the Clifton Union, the Barton Regis Union's predecessor.

W.G. was not the workhouse doctor, as was sometimes assumed later; that job belonged to his brother-in-law David Bernard, the husband of W.G.'s sister Alice. On the other hand, Grace did treat plenty of patients at risk of being sent to the workhouse, and could recommend whether or not they should be admitted, based on their health and financial circumstances. When he began practising in Bristol, the Eastville workhouse – like many others – still resembled the grim, fictitious institution described by Charles Dickens more than forty years earlier in *Oliver Twist*. At Eastville, beggars and 'paupers' were seen as shirkers who refused to work, reflecting the Victorian view that poverty was a moral rather than a social issue. As for tramps, the men were set to work breaking stones, while homeless women untangled old shipping rope, in order to qualify for a meal of bread and gruel.

From the outset, W.G. was unhappy with his medical officer's salary, especially as the union paid David Bernard £40 a year more than him. Yet his post was a desirable plum for a hardworking GP, because, as W.G.'s father had shown, a parish medical officer could use his position to gain private, fee-paying patients. As the historian of medicine Anne Digby writes: 'The appointment of poor-law medical officer, although low-paid, was eagerly contested by local GPs. Doctors building up a practice were keen to become known through holding a public office and well-established doctors would take a local office (however ill-paid), rather than see a stranger take it and begin to build up a competing practice.'

W.G. was reasonably placed to develop a private practice. His area of the parish was a bit rough in parts, but it was not a slum district, another later misperception. There were enough people willing to pay for a doctor, provided he was reliable and available. Year after year Grace would fail this test, as he disappeared each May to play cricket around the country, not returning full-time to his surgery until the autumn. Two guardians in particular soon took a dim view of the way W.G. hired locums to cover for his long absences over the summer, with the board's grudging agreement. In January 1884, when W.G. requested a pay rise of £40 per year, Samuel Shield, a laundry owner, wanted to know 'what proportion of the cases had been attended to by Mr Grace [in the past year], and how many had been attended by his assistant'. The request was deferred and then shelved.

John Bastow, a local builder, also became fed up with Grace's habit of pushing the rules for Poor Law doctors, just as he did on the cricket field. In the early 1880s, W.G.'s main locum was Horace Elliot, a young doctor from the Midlands who liked the job well enough to do two stints. By agreement with Gloucestershire CCC, Grace charged the club £36 in expenses to cover Elliot's wages. Just before the 1884 cricket season, W.G. infuriated Bastow, Shield and several other guardians by asking for authority to hire a second locum to help Elliot during the 'few days' that W.G. would be away from his surgery playing cricket. They 'protested against Dr Grace being allowed to absent himself from his duties during the cricket season'. W.G.'s Irish landlord Joseph Hennessy, who was also a guardian, came to his rescue. The cattle merchant carried a motion granting W.G.'s request on the understanding that 'on no future occasion will it be allowed'.

W.G. was well aware that the guardians could shut down his cricket career at any time, simply by refusing to allow him a locum. 'Patients don't like an assistant, never mind how good he is,' he wrote in September 1884, in reply to a questionnaire submitted to him by the *Pall Mall Gazette*. 'You see, I have a good practice which increases every winter when I am at home, and decreases in the summer when I am away from home. That is the real reason I shall not play much away from home next season.'

As usual his assurances meant nothing. W.G. played nineteen first-class matches outside Gloucestershire in 1885, the same number as in 1884. He was barely in Bristol between late May and early August, leaving Shields, Bastow and the rest of the anti-W.G. faction on the board with a choice. They could refuse him his locums, and risk the fury of MCC, Gloucestershire and cricket fans at home and abroad, or they could carry on making an exception in his case. The guardians took the latter course, while expressing their displeasure in an elegant fashion. During twenty years as the union's most famous employee, W.G. never got a pay rise.

Grace's working conditions reflected his modest income. His first home as a Bristol GP at 61 Stapleton Road was so small that in the autumn of 1879 he rented a second property at number 4, Frenchay Villas, a short walk along the street, for a rent of £22 a year. W.G. may have used this address as his surgery to provide more space for his growing household.

In addition to Agnes, Bertie, Edgar and Bessie, the 1881 census showed Agnes's twenty-year-old brother Stewart, a medical student, living at Stapleton Road, probably to gain experience in W.G.'s surgery. Two servants, Harriet Fowler and Elizabeth Pullin, were in the house, along with a couple who misleadingly described themselves as 'visitors'.

Since 1851 Agnes's sixty-one-year-old Aunt Caroline, the sister of William Day, and her sixty-eight-year-old husband John Nicholls, had been popping up as 'visitors' at census time in the households of the Days and then the Graces. Some time between the end of 1879 and the spring of 1881, the Nicholls turned up at Stapleton Road to stay for 'a fortnight', or so W.G.'s young son Edgar was told. As Edgar would recall, 'Uncle and Aunt Nicholls' then settled down with the family for the rest of their lives.

The childless couple's residence in such a cramped home was curious, because the Nicholls were the only members of W.G. and Agnes's extended families who were independently well-off. John owned land as far afield as Hampshire and Lincolnshire and when he died in 1889, with W.G. signing the death certificate, he left Caroline an estate valued at almost £14,500 in the money of the time. Nicholls' will contained detailed instructions about financial assistance to William Day and his family if Caroline died before her penniless brother. It is likely that John Nicholls and his widow were the main support for Agnes's parents after William Day's bankruptcy. If so, W.G. probably felt accommodating them at Stapleton Road was well worth the price.

Agnes became pregnant again in the summer of 1881 with her fourth child. By now, the Graces had moved two doors along the street to a larger property at 57 Stapleton Road which Joseph Hennessy also owned. Thrissell House, named after the original owner, had enough space on the ground floor for W.G. to convert a room into his surgery, allowing him to give up his bolthole at Frenchay Villas. Upstairs, he and Agnes had their drawing room and bedroom and there was space on the two upper floors for four more bedrooms. The house had an extension, Thrissell Cottage, which may have been where the Nicholls lived. Altogether, W.G. paid Hennessy £70 a year to rent the property on a fourteen-year lease. He also agreed to spend at least £60 on repairs and decoration, suggesting that Thrissell House was in a decrepit state when he took it over.

For W.G., the best part of Thrissell House was its large back garden, where he soon laid out a practice cricket net. It was here that he tried out his 'colts': a steady stream of nervous young local cricketers who hoped to impress him enough to gain selection for the full Gloucestershire county team. Time and again, W.G.

would fox the latest teenager with his crafty 'slows', and hit the youth's bowling all round the garden (the cook eventually put protective bars across the kitchen window). W.G. would usually decide well before the end of the session that the boy was not up to scratch.

Over the years W.G. drew plenty of criticism from Gloucestershire CCC members for preferring (as they saw it) posh young gentlemen with connections to the county rather than local talent. The sniping was unfair, because, in addition to his intimidating back garden trials at Thrissell House, W.G. gleaned plenty of intelligence about cricket in the area through his ties with two village clubs, Stapleton and Bedminster, just south of the River Avon from Bristol. In 1866 and 1867 W.G. had captained Stapleton, and during the 1870s and 1880s he played occasionally for both Stapleton and Bedminster, where he was one of the club's vice-presidents.

Even illness did not prevent W.G. from turning out for these village sides. In the spring of 1882, shortly after Agnes gave birth to their youngest son Charlie, W.G. went down with a bad case of mumps. Like many doctors he was a terrible patient, and after about ten days he could no longer bear the tedium of staying indoors at Thrissell House. (Agnes had probably had enough of him as well.) Still feeling awful, W.G. set off for Bedminster to watch his team in a game against Clifton.

When W.G. arrived at the start of the match, the Bedminster and Clifton players were shocked by the sight of him. Bedminster's vice-president had lost at least a stone (over six kilos) in weight and obviously should have been in bed. W.G. was shocked as well; Clifton's side, bar two players, were all regular members of Gloucestershire's first-class team. *His* side, Bedminster, were about to be thrashed; it was more than W.G. could bear.

W.G. approached Bedminster's captain to offer 'what help he could' by playing, despite his enfeebled state. The captain could hardly say no, and, after checking with Clifton, W.G. was allowed to use a runner when he came out to bat at number seven. It made no difference. W.G. was out for 6, dismissed by one of only two Clifton players who did not appear for Gloucestershire. The other, Major George Rumsey who held the catch, was a senior guardian with the Barton Regis Union. Clifton won, and W.G. struggled home to Thrissell House.

The story has an enigmatic footnote. Both W.G. and Agnes came from large families and Grace clearly loved small children. From about this time glimpses of W.G.'s encounters with awe-struck little boys and girls begin to accumulate. Yet he and Agnes had no more children after Charlie. Perhaps they chose to stop there, but it is possible that Grace's attack of mumps had left him infertile.

W.G. looked the part of a local GP as he went on his rounds, dressed in a frock-coat and grey trousers, with either his crumpled Quaker hat popped on his head or a 'topper' for visiting smarter patients. At Thrissell House his surgery cabinet was stocked with the standard Victorian remedies for illnesses and ailments that the Barton Regis Union issued to all its medical officers. W.G. dispensed cod liver oil for patients who needed fortifying, quinine to deal with muscle cramps, linseed meal for a weak heart and tincture of digitalis for fevers.

Hennessy, W.G.'s landlord, insisted to more sceptical colleagues on the Barton Regis Union's Board of Guardians that all W.G.'s patients spoke 'most highly of him'. The cattle trader had a vested interest in keeping his tenant, but his comment raised an interesting question: was Grace a good or even competent doctor?

By his own account, Grace disappointed his patients when he was away, and the time he took to qualify is strong circumstantial evidence that he lacked any real vocation for the job. Yet W.G. also possessed a formidable work ethic, in cricket or any other activity.

One source lends weight to the impression that W.G. tried to be a good doctor, although there were times when he could have done better. During the 1880s and 1890s, the Bristol press carried regular reports of local inquests, which the city's long-serving coroner Henry Wasbrough often convened in the meeting rooms of pubs. W.G. was sometimes called to testify about deaths on his watch, and these cases suggest he was a doctor who – while not perfect – tried to do the job properly within the limits of his medical knowledge.

On Sunday evening, 19 February 1882, Francis Best, a forty-five-year-old French polisher, went into the Gladstone Arms, just round the corner from Thrissell House, and ordered a pint of Burton Ale. 'Before the landlord could serve him with it, Best fell down in the bar and expired immediately,' the inquest heard. Another drinker rushed to fetch W.G., who hurried down the street to the Gladstone Arms and realised immediately that Best was dead. According to Grace, the polisher had suffered 'a fatal syncope' (loss of consciousness from falling blood pressure).

After recording the death, W.G. returned home and went to bed. Next morning he was summoned to the nearby home of Eliza Eales, a seventy-four-year-old widow who lived near Stapleton Road with her sixty-six-year-old companion and lodger, Ann Vowles. It was probably Ann who came to Thrissell House after finding Eliza unconscious in bed. Once again W.G. was too late, reporting at the inquest next day in the Beaufort Arms that she had suffered an 'apoplectic seizure'.

Sometimes Grace's poorest patients got snared by the tight Poor Law rules regarding medical assistance 'on the parish'. One Thursday evening in February 1883, forty-two-year-old Ellen Mansfield, who lived just north-west of Stapleton Road, complained of 'severe pains in the stomach'. She ate 'a bit of bread and bacon' with a cup of tea, while her daughter and son-in-law went to the local Poor Law relieving officer to ask for a medical note, which would allow them to call for W.G. at the parish's expense. The officer refused, saying they first had to ask Ellen's estranged husband Joseph, a hotel porter, to pay for a doctor privately. Joseph Mansfield also refused, on the grounds that Ellen was 'addicted to drink' and spent most of his money on alcohol.

Next day, Ellen's daughter returned to the relieving officer who at last scribbled the sought-after medical note.

It was now Friday evening. When Ellen's daughter arrived at Thrissell House, W.G. considered what she told him about her mother's condition and decided Ellen was not in immediate danger. He said he would visit Ellen on Saturday morning and decide whether she should be transferred to the Eastville work-house, which had an infirmary. He made a bad mistake. An hour later, Ellen's sister hammered on the door of Thrissell House and announced that Ellen was dying. When W.G. reached the cottage on Pennywell Road she was dead, with blood-tinged froth around her mouth.

W.G.'s testimony at the inquest was defensive and vague. He stated that Ellen's daughter had said nothing to suggest her mother's life was at risk. As to the cause of death, W.G. thought Ellen had some lung or heart disease and he could not tell whether she was 'a drinking woman', as Joseph Mansfield had alleged. Under further questioning from Wasbrough, Grace firmed up his verdict to probable death from heart disease. It was not his finest hour as a doctor.

Other press reports of Dr Grace at work reveal him in a better light. In February 1886 a gas leak caused an explosion at Easton Colliery, near Stapleton Road, killing four coal miners. W.G. raced to the scene along with other doctors, probably including his brother-in-law David Bernard, who lived only a few minutes' walk away. As the injured miners were brought to the surface, W.G. dressed their wounds as best he could and then despatched them to Bristol Royal Infirmary.

Much later some of W.G.'s former patients and neighbours filled out the picture of a more-or-less conscientious, essentially kind local GP. In 1933 the *Bristol Evening World* newspaper had the clever idea of asking older readers for their reminiscences of Grace. Each day the reader who wrote what the editor judged to be the best letter would win a small cash prize. A flood of correspondence poured in, including fifteen letters that recalled W.G.'s time as a parish medical officer.

Memory played tricks over the decades, and several of the letters described incidents that could not have happened exactly as told by the correspondent. A snowball fight involving W.G. outside Thrissell House supposedly occurred when he was still a medical student in London. Most of the other letters bore the hallmark of many unreliable anecdotes about W.G., where the correspondent heard the tale at second-hand or even as folklore and often exaggerated their familiarity with Grace. But there was one letter that stood out for its quiet authority; significantly, the writer did not give her full name.

'E. Chappell' had been the district nurse in W.G.'s parish when he lived at Thrissell House: 'I often had occasion to go to his surgery for my poor people and he was always most kind,' she remembered. 'On one occasion, I remember, he gave me money to get food for some poor people. His patients loved him. I am more than 80 years old now, but I shall never forget his kindness.'

It may be stretching a point to say that W.G.'s youthful arrogance, which rebounded so disastrously on his tour of Australia, was tempered by his years as a doctor on Stapleton Road. Yet there is enough evidence to suggest that his underlying decency did shine through as he went about his medical business in the parish. While never 'humble' in a crawling fashion, he displayed an engaging humility, perhaps under Agnes's influence. Edgar, their second son, remembered every Christmas time, when W.G. and Agnes would play open house for their poorer neighbours who could not afford a proper lunch: 'The institution grew and grew till in one year there were as many as a hundred guests,' Edgar told Grace's biographer Bernard Darwin. 'Everybody had to bring two pudding-basins. Into one was put roast beef and greens, and into the other plum pudding ... while it was the children's business to hand out the oranges and apples.'

Apart from filing expenses for locums, W.G. kept his doctoring and cricketing lives largely separate. The more well-worn anecdotes about W.G.'s use of his medical skills during matches came from other cricketers who sometimes over-dramatised the story. After W.G.'s death, the former Gloucestershire amateur Arthur Croome told a tale about how Grace had supposedly saved his life during a game against Lancashire in Manchester in 1887. Croome gashed his neck on a metal boundary rail spike while chasing a ball. With hindsight, Croome concluded that in 'all human probability' he only survived because W.G. held the 'deep wound' together while a colleague fetched a needle and thread to stitch it up. At the time, the *Manchester Courier* reported that the wound missed all Croome's 'vital' organs, and was 'not a dangerous one'.

The usually clear line between medicine (winter) and cricket (summer) in W.G.'s annual routine may explain why he was caught off guard on a rare occasion when someone took advantage of his open door at Thrissell House. One Thursday in May 1884 a young man called Vincent Kelsey showed up, asking to see Grace. Kelsey explained to W.G.'s locum Horace Elliot that he, too, was a cricketing doctor, from New York, and wanted to swap notes with the great batsman. As it happened, W.G. was away at Lord's, scoring a century against the visiting Australians. Elliot told Kelsey that W.G. would be back on Saturday evening, when once again Kelsey knocked on the door. W.G. agreed to see Kelsey in his surgery, where they chatted for a while about cricket in New York. Kelsey then left.

Grace did not realise until Monday morning that Kelsey had stolen his valuable case of surgical instruments. Kelsey had deposited the case at a pawnbroker and then, rather oddly, returned to the vicinity of Thrissell House. He was arrested on Tuesday by a police sergeant and brought before the local police court, where it emerged that some of his story was true. Kelsey had lived in New York and probably played cricket there, before returning to his native Bristol. He apologised to the magistrates, who gave him the minimum fourteen days in jail, sensing that Kelsey was mentally disturbed.

When W.G. closed the door to his surgery and collected his cricket bag, he moved into another world. Each summer in the

1880s his neighbours on Stapleton Road witnessed a familiar tableau. John Spurrier, the local livery man, parked his hansom cab outside Thrissell House and helped W.G. lift his cricket bag into the carriage. W.G. climbed in, Spurrier jigged the reins, and off the horses trotted to Bristol Temple Meads railway station a mile away, where Grace caught the train to London.

Spurrier picked up W.G. when he came back from playing at Lord's, the Oval or one of the other county grounds. 'It was a common thing to see people waiting to see Mr Spurrier and his hansom coming along Stapleton Road with "W.G." returning home,' recalled one former resident. 'They wanted first-hand news about the matches and the doctor was always ready to oblige.'

20

FIRST TEST

On many days the postman also brought letters to Stapleton Road from cricket fans around the world. In the spring of 1880 W.G. had only just settled into his new job as a parish medical officer when he received one such letter that particularly irritated him.

'Dear Mr Joseph,' he replied on 12 April to a Sydney business-man visiting London, 'I think it is a great pity that the Australians are not going to play at Lord's and the other places. They have no-one to blame but themselves.'

When W.G. despatched this letter, a visiting Australian team were en route to England, with no prospect of any first-class matches. From their point of view, the English were finding any excuse to freeze them out. In 1877, at Melbourne, Australia had beaten an 'England' team in what was later deemed the first-ever full international 'Test' match. Lord Harris had then led a tour to Australia in the winter of 1878–9, which W.G. had missed because of his medical studies. At Sydney in February 1879, Harris had been struck by a spectator during a pitch invasion over an umpiring decision. 'We never expect to see such a scene of disorder again – we can never forget this one,' an enraged Harris wrote to his friend Teddy Walker, the well-connected MCC and Middlesex amateur. As Harris intended, Walker then leaked the letter to the *Daily Telegraph*.

Harris had now received 'an adequate apology', MCC's secretary Henry Perkins explained in April 1880 to Edward Joseph, the Sydney merchant who was trying to get first-class fixtures for the Australians. Unfortunately, Perkins added, there was another problem: MCC had only learned about a planned Australian tour in 1880 after the club and the counties had settled the first-class fixture list for the season.

In Bristol, Grace made a couple more points to Joseph. Officially the Australians were amateurs but they planned to take all the turnstile revenue from matches, cover the costs, and then split the profit between themselves. 'The MCC will not sanction this sort of thing,' W.G. declared. 'The Australians must play as gentlemen or as professionals and it ought to be understood before they came, who play as professionals and who as amateurs.' As for the so-called 'Sydney Riot', 'it could and would not happen at Lord's,' W.G. told Joseph. 'The Australian cricketers must learn 'that the decision of the umpire is final, whether right or wrong'. W.G.'s hypocrisy was so outrageous that it is hard to escape the sense that he was deliberately provoking the Australian team, with whom Joseph was in correspondence.

Grace soon changed his mind about playing the Australians. Led by Billy Murdoch, they arrived in early May and, with no first-class fixtures, spent the first half of the summer trudging around England playing a series of dismally one-sided against-the-odds fixtures against local clubs. By the end of June Spofforth – probably bored out of his mind – had taken 175 wickets, an average of almost 16 wickets per match.

W.G.'s younger brother Fred, now aged twenty-nine, had appeared as a guest professional for local clubs in four of these early tour games. He now helped change W.G.'s mind about offering the Australians first-class fixtures, including a full international Test match.

Like W.G., Fred stretched the definition of a gentleman

amateur to breaking point. After desultory medical studies at Bristol and Aberdeen, Fred was in theory on course to qualify as a doctor. To help calm Fred's nerves, W.G. asked the secretary of the Royal College of Surgeons in April 1880 if Fred could be pushed up the list of students sitting the college's oral exam. Fred never took the exam because, as usual, cricket got in the way of his studies. By 1880 he was one of the best batsmen in England, as well as being a brilliant outfielder, and a decent change bowler. He played as an amateur for Gloucestershire and as a professional for any team that would pay him.

In the summer of 1880 Fred may have needed to boost his income because he was about to get married. With dreamy eyes and a competitive moustache and whiskers, Fred fitted the bill for a Victorian pin-up and took full advantage of his attractiveness to women. Six years earlier he had missed the last two games of W.G.'s Australia tour to return to Tasmania to meet up with his latest girlfriend. Now he was engaged to Annie Robinson, from a prominent Bristol family that ran a successful printing firm. The Robinsons were keen cricket fans who later put out their own family team in a match against the Graces. They were also considerably richer than the Graces and Fred must have wondered how he could maintain Annie's comfortable lifestyle without depending on her parents.

W.G. was far fonder of Fred than E.M., who was almost eight years older than him, and with whom he maintained a testy, competitive relationship. During the 1870s, Fred became W.G.'s best friend in cricket, closer even than Frizzy Bush and Frank Townsend at Gloucestershire. The two brothers spent long summers playing cricket up and down the country, with Fred acting as W.G.'s professional match manager and his most trusted confidant.

Fred was therefore ideally placed in the early summer of 1880 to tell W.G. he was wrong to take such a dismissive attitude towards the visiting Australians. Based on his own experience, Fred could report back to W.G. that Murdoch's team deserved better opposition than Eighteen of Burnley and District

(Spofforth – 23 wickets for 46 runs) or Eighteen of Rochdale (Boyle – 18 wickets for 73 runs).

In early July W.G. suggested to the MCC committee that the club should organise a fixture between an England XI, captained by him, and the Australians. The committee agreed, but a stumbling block arose in the form of W.G.'s future employer, the Crystal Palace Company, which had booked the Australians for a game in south London on the same day as the proposed Lord's fixture. The company refused to cancel, ending MCC's chance of hosting the first-ever Test match in England.

W.G. at least gave the Australians a fixture against Gloucestershire at Clifton in early August. He took eleven wickets with his artful bowling, but the Australians won comfortably. Spofforth took ten wickets, trapping Grace leg before wicket for 3 in Gloucestershire's second innings. 'I never had any particular difficulty in getting him out,' Spofforth recalled of his duels with W.G. 'This may have been due in part to my artfulness.'

After this defeat, W.G. was even keener to arrange a full 'England' game against the Australians. Two friends now became key allies. Charles Alcock, the thirty-seven-year-old secretary of Surrey CCC, had all the entrepreneurial flair and energy that Henry Perkins lacked. Alcock saw that a match between England and Australia at the Oval would be a money-spinner for Surrey. In early September he cleared a space in the fixture schedule by persuading Sussex CCC to drop its game at the Oval against Surrey, in return for £105 in compensation. With less than a month to assemble a team, Alcock began searching for available players.

At Belmont, his stately home west of Canterbury, Harris had at last stopped sulking about the 'Sydney Riot'. 'Since their [the Australians'] arrival this year I have said I had no objection to playing ag[ain]st them provided my existing arrangements were not interfered with,' Harris wrote on 20 August to the Lancashire amateur Allan Steel, who was grouse shooting in Scotland. 'Now I think the best team that can possibly be got together ought to be opposed to them & I write this to ask you

to play ag[ain]st them if the Surrey Club ask you, which they
are sure to do.'

Full of false modesty, Harris made clear that he would captain
the team, regardless of his batting form, which was actually quite
good: 'Without conceit I may say that it has been made a *"sine
qua non"* that I shd play ... You will I am sure understand that
I am not pushing myself forward as an English cricketer, for I
know I'm not good enough to play in a representative team; but
as having been captain of the 79–80 eleven to Australia.'

Alcock and Harris, with help from Grace, eventually put
together the following team, in batting order for the first innings:

E.M. Grace (38), Gloucestershire
W.G. Grace (32), Gloucestershire
Alfred Lucas (23), Surrey
William Barnes (28), Nottinghamshire
Lord Harris (29), Kent, captain
Frank Penn (29), Kent
Allan Steel (21), Lancashire
Alfred Lyttelton (23), Middlesex, wicketkeeper
Fred Grace (29), Gloucestershire
Alfred Shaw (38), Nottinghamshire
Fred Morley (29), Nottinghamshire

It was not the best possible England team but it was still very
strong. W.G. warmed up for the Test match by going shooting
in Berkshire with his friend John Porter, the leading race-
horse trainer, and then playing for Porter's cricket team against
Newbury CC. By then, news had reached London that a tear-
away club fast bowler had broken Fred Spofforth's right hand in
a game at Scarborough. 'The Demon' would miss the big game.

On Monday, 6 September, in bright sunshine, almost twenty
thousand people squeezed into the Oval for the first day of the
match.

'Thousands who could not possibly get more than an

occasional glimpse of the players, and some not even that, stood throughout the day,' the *Sydney Morning Herald* reported. 'Stands were improvised from water-carts and steps, from office stools and chairs, from orange boxes, from piles of dirt, which were hastily thrown up and had to be stoutly defended against attack.'

An 'ingenious waggon proprietor' rented space on his cart, which his horse then wheeled around the boundary, allowing passengers to view the game above the other spectators' heads. In the narrow streets around the Oval, more people watched from every available window, balcony and rooftop: 'Every now and again the police attempted to dislodge some of the more adventurous; no sooner had they turned their backs than the coveted position was again stormed and taken possession of.'

The 1880 Oval Test match was the first great modern international between two teams in any sport. Six months earlier, Scotland had beaten England at Hampden Park, Glasgow, in the latest annual football match between the two countries. A crowd of about fifteen thousand attended the game, but football was still competing for attention with rival codes. As the *Yorkshire Post* observed: 'While Manchester is generally admitted to be the centre of the Rugby code, there can be no doubt that a larger gate can be obtained to witness an important Association contest in Glasgow than in any other part of the kingdom.'

Across the Atlantic, baseball had so far bridged just one national frontier, northwards into Canada. In continental Europe, representative national sports teams barely existed. Cricket, briefly, had a chance to stage a spectacle that showed why international sport would become the supreme examination of a player's skill and character. Presciently, several newspapers would call it a 'test', the label soon attached to all England v Australia cricket fixtures.

Strictly speaking, the Oval match was not a contest between two nations. 'Australia' was welded together from two rival colonies, Victoria and New South Wales, with Harry Boyle (Victoria) and Billy Murdoch (New South Wales) jointly organising selection for the tour. Harris's petulance, MCC's obduracy and W.G.'s sublime ability to annoy Australians had already combined to unite the tourists. Spofforth's late injury ensured they turned up at the Oval with a distinctively Australian backs-to-the-wall team spirit.

Harris won the toss and decided to bat. As W.G. walked down the Oval pavilion steps at just after 11.30 a.m., he entered the stage he had craved for more than a decade: twenty thousand spectators cheering him and E.M. to the wicket, Harry Boyle marking out his run-up, the press corps poised with their pens. Only Spofforth was missing. 'The Demon' was lurking in the pavilion, nursing his damaged hand.

E.M. hit Boyle's second ball for a single and then pulled a ball from 'Joey' Palmer for a boundary. W.G. began more cautiously, and at the start of Palmer's second over was 'as nearly as possible bowled' by a delivery 'which only missed his leg stump by a shave'. W.G. played Palmer's second ball defensively, the next ball to leg for three runs and, soon after, cut Palmer 'grandly' for four. His first Test innings was underway.

For the next four hours batsmen came and went at the other end. E.M. was out for a streaky 36. The Cambridge Blue Alfred Lucas scored 55 in elegant, 'Cantab' style. The Nottinghamshire professional Barnes joined Grace, full of nerves and riding his luck as he 'snicked' Alick Bannerman twice for runs. Barnes was bowled for 28. In came Harris, starting with a flourish as he drove and cut two balls to the boundary.

All the while, W.G. played in a manner that the press struggled to sum up. He would hit a boundary, or run three, and then defend for the next few minutes in a puzzlingly quiet manner. In Boyle's second spell, W.G. cut one delivery for four, but 'this was the only big hit for several overs'. Shortly before 3 p.m. W.G. reached his century, to a general cheer around the ground. Only now did he begin to accelerate.

On 135, Grace drove a ball from Alick Bannerman in the air towards George Alexander, Australia's manager and Spofforth's late replacement, who was fielding near the pavilion. Alexander 'jumped in and got to the ball, but failed to hold it'. W.G. moved up another gear, driving Palmer for four and Alexander for two more boundaries in the same over. Finally, 'a good ball from Palmer just took Mr Grace's off stump a couple of inches below the bail'. W.G. 'retired amidst tremendous applause for a splendidly played 152'.

Alongside his team-mates' cameo performances, Grace had produced a complete Test match innings. It had a beginning (watchful), a long central section (measured) and an attacking finale that reinforced England's dominant position.

It rained overnight, allowing the Australian press to complain about how the unfair weather damaged the pitch. 'For the first two hours of the second day the wicket played most bumpily, and was very treacherous,' one reporter complained.

In bright sunshine it soon became plain that Australia would fall well short of England's first innings total of 420 all out. Murdoch went immediately for 0, and while Alick Bannerman (32), Percy McDonnell (27) and Boyle (36 not out) made decent scores, none of Australia's batsmen looked capable of staying for long. The most memorable moment occurred when Australia's number seven George Bonnor, an even bigger man than W.G., heaved the ball high in the air towards the boundary. The ball rose so far that Bonnor had time to run two as Fred Grace raced to where he thought it would land. Everyone's money was on the ball, but somehow Fred caught it, an astounding piece of fielding. It made up a little for Fred's 0 in England's first innings.

By mid-afternoon the Australians were all out for 149, giving England a first innings lead of 271 runs. The Australians were now forced to bat again and see if they could wipe out their first innings deficit. At some point that afternoon Billy Murdoch approached W.G. and bet him a sovereign (£1) that he could beat Grace's score of 152. W.G. took him on. The timing of Murdoch's wager is unclear. His bet was extremely brave if he made it before the start of Australia's second innings, rather less so by the close of play, when Murdoch was 79 not out. In either case, Murdoch's bet was psychologically astute, forcing him to up his game. It was also entirely in keeping with Murdoch's fighting mentality.

Squat and bullish, with a flamboyant waxed moustache, Billy Murdoch would later become W.G.'s best Australian mate. In 1880 he was a bankrupt, trying to recoup his losses from the collapse of Murdoch & Murdoch, the Sydney law firm he had run with his brother until a client failed to pay a large bill. Murdoch's broad back was firmly to the wall at the start of Australia's second innings. He had failed first time round and his team looked like certain losers. From his perspective, it was the perfect moment to try and upstage W.G.

He walked out to bat with Australia's score on 8 for one wicket, which soon became 14 for three. Percy McDonnell, aged just nineteen, stayed with Murdoch for a while, and then W.G. trapped McDonnell leg before wicket for 43. By the end of the day Australia were 170 for six, still 101 runs short of making England bat again, with only four wickets remaining. Murdoch looked like he had lost his bet.

Next day (8 September) the public decided the game was effectively over. There were only about six thousand spectators inside the ground at the start of play to watch Murdoch and Bonnor continue the Australian innings in overcast weather. Murdoch instantly went on the attack, hitting Steel for four to the leg-side boundary and scoring another four in the next over. Bonnor soon went, followed rapidly by Palmer; Australia were 187 for eight.

George Alexander, batting ten, now did his best to stay with Murdoch and at least let the captain get to his century. For some minutes, W.G. had been pestering Harris to let him bowl. Finally Harris relented. Murdoch froze, sensing danger in every gentle floater that W.G. released for Australia's captain to ponder. 'He [Grace] was dead on the wicket, and Murdoch could make nothing of his bowling.'

Murdoch crawled to 99. At this point the left-arm fast bowler Fred Morley bowled a delivery that 'struck the gallant batsman full in the stomach; he staggered a few steps, fell in agony, and then seemed for a few minutes in a faint'. In plain English, Murdoch had been hit in the balls. Doctors W.G. and E.M. Grace rushed to attend him, and a third doctor jogged out of the pavilion, followed by a waiter carrying a jug of water and a glass on a tray. Murdoch took a few sips, thanked the doctors, struggled to his feet and took guard again. It was an emblematic Australian moment, repeated often in the years to come; the stricken batsman toughing it out and carrying on through the pain.

Two minutes later Murdoch scored a single to reach his century. The crowd cheered, Murdoch saluted them . . . and then Alexander was out: 239 for nine.

Australia's last man William Moule, on the threshold of a distinguished legal career at the Melbourne bar, was a completely hopeless batsman. Moule clung on, as Australia's score crept up. Murdoch and Moule passed Australia's first target, which was to make England bat again, and 'the Australian spectators fairly stood on their legs and yelled with delight'. Fired up by his captain, Moule moved into double figures, alien batting territory. He even started to play some shots, to his own and Murdoch's astonishment. W.G., thoroughly alarmed, conducted 'many consultations' with Harris about bowling and fielding changes. Every minute, more spectators filtered into the Oval, as news of Australia's fightback spread round London.

At last W.G. argued his way back on to bowl. Murdoch hit Grace's third ball for four, bringing his score to 140, twelve runs short of W.G.'s 152. He pushed a single and then drove another four; 145. Moule hit a single and then a two: 'again Lord Harris and Dr Grace had a consultation'. Murdoch nudged and prodded his score up to 151. A 'neat snick' got him to 152, level with W.G.'s score.

And then, since this was a cricket match, they all left the field for lunch.

At 2.50 p.m. the players came out again. Murdoch watched as Moule hit Steel for two. Calmly, Murdoch scored a single off

Barnes to win his bet. It was all too much for Moule, who was immediately bowled for 34, the highest score of his first-class career. Australia were all out for 327, leaving England needing 57 runs to win the game.

Heavy cloud loomed above the Oval and the light was worsening as England prepared to bat again. In these difficult conditions, Harris now made a bad tactical error, repeating W.G.'s mistake at Melbourne in 1873. Harris decided to hold back his best player, W.G., as well as E.M., and promote the England wicketkeeper Alfred Lyttelton and Fred Grace to open the innings. His thinking was misguidedly defensive. He wanted to keep his most experienced batsmen in reserve in case anything went wrong. It did.

Fred Grace was bowled for 0. Lucas went next, caught for 2. Lyttelton was soon out: 22 for three wickets. Next Boyle dismissed Barnes: 31 for four. E.M. appeared. Boyle bowled him second ball: 31 for five, 'and the excitement something terrible'.

At last W.G. emerged from the pavilion to join the Kent batsman Frank Penn, who was taking risks in the gloom and getting away with it. While Penn slogged, W.G. drained all the suspense from the game, treating the bowlers as though he were having a net practice. He hit a couple of singles; Penn hit two boundaries; Penn and W.G. both hit singles; Penn hit a boundary; Grace cut a short delivery for four.

At 4.15 p.m. W.G. hit one last single to get England over the finishing line. They had won by five wickets, and the two teams had just played the best game of cricket ever. None of the newpapers noted that W.G. had also made the best 9 not out of all time.

Six days later, Fred Grace stood on a platform at Reading station, nursing a bad cough and a cold. He should have been in bed, but Fred was due to play in a benefit game in Winchester and did not want to let down his team-mates.

Fred spent the night at the Red Lion Hotel in Basingstoke. In the morning he was about to leave for the game when he realised he was too ill. He went back to bed and next day, still feeling terrible, asked to see a doctor, who decided there might be a problem with his right lung. The news was relayed by telegram to The Chestnuts and Fred's cousin Walter Gilbert caught the train to Basingstoke. Fred's elder brother Henry soon followed, bringing his doctor's bag, and over the weekend decided the patient was getting better. On Monday, Henry returned to Bristol, leaving Gilbert at the hotel.

It was a mistake. Two days later Fred's condition suddenly worsened, prompting Gilbert and the Basingstoke doctor to send an urgent telegram to Downend. Fred's sister Blanche and her husband John Dann, the vicar of Downend, set off first. Henry Grace left next, accompanied by W.G., who was staying at The Chestnuts. The two brothers caught a cab to Bradford on Avon station near Bath, in order to board the next 'up' train to Reading, and then on to Basingstoke. They were waiting by the platform when a postboy ran up with yet another telegram. Fred had just died of pneumonia.

Several thousand people lined the streets of Downend for Fred's funeral, a measure both of the Graces' celebrity and of the Victorian fascination with untimely death. John Dann gave a short address at Fred's graveside about the uncertainty of life. Martha, W.G. and the rest of the Graces looked on. Then Dann, like many others in the churchyard, broke down and wept.

21

ULTIMATE TEST

That autumn Fitzgerald was dying as well, oblivious to the great match at the Oval or the death of W.G.'s brother. In 1878 Fitzgerald had left the Manor House asylum, as his more violent delusions began to subside. Unable to tolerate the sight of his wife Ettie, he stayed with his widowed mother at her country home in Buckinghamshire, still convinced on bad days that he was MCC's secretary. On better days, he cut out pictures of comely young women to stick in his Quidnunc scrapbook, but as the years went by he gradually weakened. By the spring of 1881 Fitzgerald was back with his family at their home in Hertfordshire, too ill to cause Ettie any more trouble. He died there in October 1881 from 'softening of [the] brain', a common Victorian euphemism for tertiary syphilis.

In May 1882 the MCC committee paid tribute to Fitzgerald, noting that the club's prosperity was largely due to his exertions. Then the club's annual meeting turned to present business. If Fitzgerald had still been secretary, the club would certainly have ensured that the Australians, about to arrive in London for another tour, played a Test match at Lord's. Perkins had let the opportunity slip. Once again, the only Test match of the summer would take place at the Oval.

Fred Spofforth amused himself on the boat to England by fighting a duel with a French passenger whom he had insulted, choosing two buckets as the 'blood-letting weapons'. The team's fancy dress party caused another distraction; the 'Demon' came as Mephistopheles, the collector of damned souls. Like the rest of the Australian team, led again by Murdoch, Spofforth reached England thoroughly bored with life at sea, and ready for cricket.

He started slowly, but was at his best by late August, when the Australians played Gloucestershire at Clifton for the second time that month (they won by an innings in the first match). Spofforth took five wickets in a rain-ruined draw, including W.G. for only 4.

W.G. was having the worst batting season of his career. He had failed to score a century and only managed two half-centuries in six matches against the Australians for various teams. Even so, it was inconceivable that W.G. would be dropped from the England team for the Oval Test match, which immediately followed the game at Clifton. In batting order, the side read as follows:

Dick Barlow (31), Lancashire
W.G. Grace (34), Gloucestershire
George Ulyett (30), Yorkshire
Alfred Lucas (25), Surrey
Alfred Lyttelton (25), Middlesex, wicketkeeper
Charles 'C.T.' Studd (21), Cambridge University
Maurice Read (23), Surrey
William Barnes (30), Nottinghamshire
Allan Steel (23), Lancashire
Albert 'Monkey' Hornby (35), Lancashire, captain
Ted Peate (27), Yorkshire

The team, chosen by a joint MCC and Surrey selection committee, was peculiar in several respects. Harris, one of the selectors, had ruled himself out, although in good batting form. The side was still absurdly overloaded with ten front-line batsmen, betraying the selectors' fear of Spofforth, Boyle and the other Australian bowlers. The choice of Hornby as captain, rather than Grace, seemed equally odd.

'Monkey' Hornby was not a subtle man. From a Lancashire mill-owning family, he captained his county with the rigid authority of a parade-ground sergeant, barking orders at his largely professional team. Harris despised Hornby, whom the peer accused of picking fast bowlers who 'threw' the ball with an illegal action, at least in Harris's view. 'I ... remonstrated with "Monkey" Hornby ... but he w[ould] not yield,' Harris recalled of one attempt to stop the Lancashire captain selecting these bowlers for a game against Kent.

Harris's disapproval had been enough to ensure that Lancashire's star fast bowler Jack Crossland ('a low blackguard', according to Harris) was not picked for the Test team, almost certainly because of his dubious action. So why did Harris, as the most influential selector, choose Hornby to captain the side rather than W.G.? For all his failings as a man-manager, W.G. had a better tactical brain than Hornby and unlike Lancashire's captain, did not panic in a crisis. The most plausible explanation is that the Old Etonian Harris felt the Old Harrovian Hornby was better qualified to captain England than an alumnus of Ridgway House school in Stapleton.

On the night before the game the Australians had more urgent worries. Joey Palmer, their third main bowler after Spofforth and Boyle, was injured and unlikely to play. Spofforth swanned around the team's hotel in Covent Garden, remarking to journalists that while he was 'wonderfully fit and well ... I may not come off (although I feel I shall) and if not, where shall we be without Palmer?' One can almost hear his apprehensive teammates telling 'Spof' to shut up.

'Heavy banks of cloud' hung over south London on Monday, 28 August, the first day of the Test. As in 1880, almost twenty thousand spectators packed into the Oval, with thousands more finding vantage points on balconies and rooftops around the ground. When the Australian team arrived an hour or so before the game, Joey Palmer tried to bowl a few practice deliveries, but immediately started limping, probably from a groin strain (the newspapers decorously skirted round the injury's precise location). Australia now had only three front-line bowlers: Tom Garrett, who bowled medium pace, Boyle and Spofforth.

Murdoch won the toss and chose to bat in murky light and intermittent drizzle. He regretted his decision immediately, as the Australians collapsed to 59 for nine wickets against the slow left-arm spin of Peate and the medium pace of Barlow. Spofforth, number eleven, came out to join young Sam Jones, just twenty-one, the not out batsman. 'They want you to slog,' Spofforth told Jones imperiously, as though issuing an order from the dressing room. Jones promptly hit a catch straight to Grace. When Jones got back to the pavilion, Murdoch asked him why he had played such a stupid shot. Spofforth had lied, as he later admitted to Jones. He merely wanted the disastrous Australian innings to finish as quickly as possible so he could get at the English batsmen on the rain-damaged pitch.

At 3.30 p.m. Barlow, taking first ball, and W.G. prepared to face Spofforth who marked out his run-up at the Gasworks End (now the Vauxhall End), tamping down sawdust to keep his footing on the damp grass. W.G. lasted fifteen deliveries before Spofforth speared a full-pitched yorker under his bat; out for 4 runs. None of the other England batsmen could cope with Spofforth. Barlow was caught; Ulyett missed a disguised slower ball; Studd fell to one of Spofforth's 'breakbacks', known as an 'off-cutter' today; Lyttelton was caught; Hornby was bowled by a faster delivery; Peate was caught. At 5.55 p.m. England were all out for 101, a lead of 38 runs. Spofforth (seven wickets for 47 runs) had hauled Australia back into the game.

A storm early next morning gave way to dark clouds that hung over the Oval all day. Despite the weather, the crowd was another sell-out:

The ring round the ground was seven or eight deep, and behind the ring came another body quite as dense on the high bank inside the palings. On walking round the ground there was found to be a slight space between the two rings, but viewed from the Pavilion the interval could not be discerned, and it appeared as though the ground were one vast amphitheatre, with a bank of spectators 60 or 70 feet deep.

Australia's opening batsman Hugh Massie, a twenty-eight-year-old banker from Victoria, continued the fightback begun by Spofforth. Massie scored 55 in an hour, but after he got out, Australia lost wickets steadily until Billy Murdoch and Sam Jones, batting with the 'utmost caution', dug in and gradually inched Australia's total to 113 for six.

Up to this point the match had been ferociously competitive but generally well-tempered. W.G., fielding close, now changed the whole mood of the game.

Murdoch hit a delivery from Steel, bowling from the Pavilion End, gently on to the leg side and set off for a run, bringing Jones to the striker's end. Lyttelton, England's wicketkeeper, jogged out to retrieve the ball because there was no fielder near it. Lyttelton threw the ball to Peate, now standing in the wicket-keeper's position. Peate dropped the ball. Jones thought the ball was 'dead', which was not strictly the case; theoretically it was still 'live', because the passage of play had not been completed. He wandered out of his ground to pat a divot on the pitch with his bat. Grace, standing near the wicket, picked up the ball, broke the stumps and appealed to the umpire for a run out. Reluctantly, the umpire Bob Thoms said that if W.G. was making a formal appeal then Jones was definitely out.

Grace did not back down, because, as the *Sydney Morning Herald* observed, 'he was purely within his rights, and it was the strict game'. But should Grace have observed normal cricket etiquette and warned Jones that he was out of his ground and would be run out if he repeated his absent-minded error? *Wisden*, batting metaphorically for England, agreed with spectators in the pavilion who thought W.G. had taught the foolish Jones a lesson in the rules of the game: 'There was a good deal of truth in what a gentleman in the pavilion remarked, amidst some laughter, that Jones ought to thank the champion for teaching him something.'

Some Australian commentators condemned Grace's quick thinking as 'cricket, but dirty'. Today, W.G.'s behaviour just seems remarkably modern, no better or worse than a Test batsman refusing to walk for a catch behind when he knows he has snicked it, or a slip fielder claiming a catch on the half-volley. W.G. was not playing the 'manly game', as conceived by Victorian cricket's muscular Christian moralists. He was playing to win, which was far more exciting to watch.

From that moment, every time W.G. fielded the ball the Australians in the crowd barracked him. Spofforth came out to bat, swung furiously at a ball from Peate, and was clean bowled. Enraged by Jones's dismissal, Murdoch called for a ridiculous single and was run out. Boyle, his mind elsewhere, was bowled first ball by Steel. It was 3.25 p.m. Australia were all out for 122. More heavy cloud had started banking up behind the Oval gas-works and the light was fading. Batting would be difficult, but England needed just 85 runs to win.

The Australian team spent the interval moaning to each other about the 'Jones affair'; everyone, that is, except Spofforth. According to a much later, second-hand version told by Hugh Massie's son, Spofforth marched into England's dressing room and told W.G. he was 'a bloody cheat'. Spofforth reportedly carried on abusing Grace for 'a full five minutes' and, as he stormed out, flung back a threat: 'This will lose you the match.'

As Spofforth's entry in the *Australian Dictionary of Biography* notes, he was 'an entertaining raconteur of "tall stories"'. Spofforth was clearly absent from the Australian dressing room for several minutes, and when he returned, he told Massie and other team-mates that he had just come from berating Grace. Yet none of the Australians witnessed Spofforth's alleged tirade and none of the England team ever corroborated his story; he could just as easily have paid a quiet trip to the lavatory.

Besides, W.G. had little, if any time to listen to Spofforth during the interval, because he had to deal with a more pressing matter. At 3.30 p.m. George Spendlove, a forty-eight-year-old servant from Kennington who was watching the game with a friend, suddenly began 'vomiting blood'. W.G. was summoned from the dressing room and, along with another doctor on the ground, arranged for Spendlove to be carried to a room at the top of the pavilion where he died a few minutes later. In view of the emergency, the umpires allowed a ten-minute delay. W.G. went back to the dressing room, strapped on his pads and walked out to open England's batting.

In a characteristically bold move, Hornby had decided to promote himself to lead England's charge to victory. All the same, he and W.G. agreed that Grace would take first ball, to be delivered by Spofforth from the Gasworks End. Spofforth's possibly 'tall tale' about a bust-up with Grace served the same psychological purpose as Murdoch's bet with W.G. two years earlier. Spofforth and the rest of the Australian team were out for revenge as he turned and sprinted towards W.G.

In his first over, Spofforth bowled four very fast deliveries, which W.G. calmly defended. At about 4 p.m., with England's total on 15, Spofforth bowled Hornby. Next ball he bowled Barlow; 15 for two wickets. Sensing a crisis, Grace counter-attacked. He drove Garrett for three and Spofforth in the air for two, and then went after Spofforth with a three and a four in one over.

Spofforth switched to the Pavilion End; Grace now drove him to the off for two. Harry Boyle came on at the Gasworks End; Grace hit him to the square leg boundary. Ulyett, W.G.'s batting partner, hit the first ball of Spofforth's next over to square leg for four. The crisis eased and then evaporated. At 4.40 p.m. England reached 50, just 35 runs short of victory, with seven men still to bat.

Ulyett snicked a ball by Spofforth and was caught behind by the wicketkeeper Jack Blackham: 51 for three. Australia had got a breakthrough, but W.G. was still not out and going well. Boyle trotted in from the Gasworks End to bowl to W.G., who cut him for two runs. Boyle turned again, jogged in, and bowled a delivery that may have been imperceptibly slower. W.G. drove early, straight in the air to Alick Bannerman at mid-off, who clung on to the catch. The Australians let out a collective roar, for they knew the significance of the moment. England were 53 for four and, more to the point, W.G. was out for 32.

Slowly, Lyttelton and Lucas clawed England back on top, adding twelve more runs by 5 p.m; 65 for four. Spofforth, sensing the game slipping England's way, now bowled a 'very nasty' over to Lucas, which put both batsmen into their shell. For the next half-hour Spofforth and Boyle reeled off a succession of four-ball maiden overs, the tension building in deteriorating light. At last, Lyttelton got a single off Boyle, bringing him down to the Gasworks End to face Spofforth, bowling from the Pavilion End. The change of ends proved fatal. Spofforth bowled Lyttelton with a breakback: 66 for five.

Steel, the next batsman, played too early at a (possibly slower) ball from Spofforth and gave him an easy return catch: 70 for six. Two balls later Spofforth bowled Read with another breakback: 70 for seven. By now, each time Spofforth turned and began his run-up, 'a shudder of fear for the wicket of the defender seemed to go round the ground'. Barnes and Lucas added five more runs, three of them due to a fumble by the usually nerveless Blackham. Spofforth came in again and bowled Lucas: 75 for eight.

England needed just ten runs to win, as the tall, ascetic figure of the twenty-one-year-old Cambridge all-rounder Charles Thomas Studd arrived to join Barnes. 'C.T.' had pledged his life to Christ as a schoolboy at Eton, but cricket had since lured him away from God with such spectacular effect that he was now tipped by some pundits to become the next W.G. Grace. At this precise moment, Studd was a victim of Hornby's panicky reshuffling of the batting order. In the first innings, Studd had batted at number six. However, each time Spofforth took another wicket in the second innings, Hornby had demoted Studd down the order, either because he did not trust the Cambridge student to handle the situation, or because he wanted to hold back one

of his best batsmen as the crisis deepened. Hornby's muddled
thinking made no immediate difference, since Spofforth had just
completed an over. Studd waited at the non-striker's end. It was
Boyle's turn to bowl.

For almost an hour Harry Boyle had been under more pressure
than anyone else on the field. If England lost, their batsmen could
spread the blame around the team. If Australia lost, Spofforth
would still be a hero, as the 'Demon' bowler who nearly pulled
off an incredible victory. But if Boyle gave away runs and
England won, he would go down in history as the bowler who
lost the game for Australia. Over after over, Boyle had pinned
down England's batsmen with formidable mental and technical
discipline, providing no respite from Spofforth's assault.

Boyle's first delivery to Barnes bounced a little higher than
normal and glanced off the batsman's glove. Billy Murdoch,
fielding close at silly point, held the catch: 75 for nine. Ted Peate,
England's last batsman, emerged from the pavilion, with the light
getting worse by the minute. The left-handed Peate was a tail-
end slogger who a month before, playing for Yorkshire against
the Australians, had flailed away for a few minutes and scored a
lucky 20. Boyle had eventually bowled Peate, and knew how to
get him out now.

According to Sam Jones, Boyle bowled a slower ball, daring
Peate to smash the delivery to the boundary. Peate swung early
at the ball, just connected, and 'fluked' the ball over the leg-side
ring of fielders. Peate and Studd scrambled two runs: eight to
win. Possibly unnerved, Studd had made the wrong call. He
should have run just a single to get the high-risk Peate off strike.

Boyle now bowled one of the most courageous deliveries in
Test match history – a 'masterpiece of deceit', in Jones's memory.
With England only seven runs short of victory, Boyle sent down
another slow tempter. Once again, Peate swung too early. He
missed. In the hush of the crowd, Peate heard the ball hit the
stumps behind him. It was 5.45 p.m. England were all out for
77 and Australia had won by seven runs. Studd, the finest young
batsman in England, had not even faced a ball.

Afterwards, memories blurred into each other. Charlie Beal, Australia's manager, knocked over the pavilion gateman as he raced on to the ground to 'crush Spoff to his manly breast & chest'. Hornby came into the Australian dressing room and handed round a 'loving cup' for the victors to drink. Spofforth, Murdoch, Massie and Boyle went out on to the balcony and waved to the cheering crowd below. Finally it was time to go, the Australians' carriage crawling through hordes of well-wishers along Kennington Road while 'ladies from their windows ... waved their handkerchiefs to us'.

W.G. was conspicuously absent from these scenes, which led directly to the creation of the 'Ashes', via a mock obituary for English cricket in a London newspaper and the burning of some bails in Melbourne. In the course of two hours, Spofforth and Boyle had swept W.G. off the stage. One Australian newspaper said W.G.'s innings of 32 displayed his 'ancient power and skill', a revealingly patronising remark. In reality, W.G.'s Test career had already peaked at the age of thirty-four. Over the next seventeen years, he scored only one other Test match century, when the Australians dropped several chances. Grace's overall international batting average (32.29) was merely good, not great.

His tragedy was to arrive at the threshold of modern international cricket just as he passed his prime. The Oval Test in 1882 marked a symbolic turning point. As the Australians returned in triumph to their hotel in Covent Garden, the 'greatest batsman of his or any other age' was sliding further into a long, distressing decline.

22

THE 'OLD MAN'

In the autumn of 1884 *the Pall Mall Gazette* asked W.G. in a written questionnaire whether he was still as good a cricketer as in his youth. 'My defence is as good,' W.G. replied, 'but I cannot punish the bowling as I used to and as you get older you cannot field as well. You lose your activity.'

Have you ever been badly hurt at cricket? the newspaper asked: 'Never seriously. Split finger now and again, once sprained my ankle. This year I have had more accidents than all the years I have played cricket. Fingers split open twice, and a sprained leg, which laid me up, or rather ought to have laid me up, but I never stopped playing for a day, although very lame.'

W.G.'s decline was relative, because he was falling from a level never before reached by any batsman. In the right mood, Grace was still a formidable batsman in his late thirties, but as W.G. knew, his younger self would have scored more runs, more consistently, on the better surfaces of the late 1880s. Instead, he had to settle for being good in some years and merely average in others; he was mortal after all:

1884: 1361 runs; 34.02 runs per innings; 3 centuries
1885: 1688 runs; 43.28 runs per innings; 4 centuries
1886: 1846 runs; 35.50 runs per innings; 4 centuries
1887: 2062 runs; 54.26 runs per innings; 6 centuries
1888: 1886 runs; 32.51 runs per innings; 4 centuries

At this level of achievement, W.G.'s supremacy faced a threat from younger challengers. The first of them, C.T. Studd, was en route to China to become a missionary when W.G. answered the *Pall Mall Gazette*'s questionnaire. In the summer of 1884 Studd had recommitted himself to God after his cricketing brother George (Cambridge University, Middlesex and England) suffered a nearly fatal illness: 'Formerly, I had as much love for cricket as any man could have,' C.T. recalled, 'but when the Lord Jesus came into my heart I found that I had something infinitely better than cricket. My heart was no longer in the game; I wanted to win souls for the Lord.'

By the mid-1880s a more potent rival to W.G. as the world's best batsman had come to the fore. Arthur Shrewsbury was a bundle of neuroses. The son of a Nottinghamshire publican, Shrewsbury fretted about his baldness, imaginary illnesses and money, while devoting himself to batting with the same attention to detail that he brought to the sports retail business he ran with the retired Nottinghamshire bowler Alfred Shaw. There is no direct evidence that W.G. ever said 'Give me Arthur', when asked to name the next best batsman after himself. Even if Grace made this comment, Shrewsbury was arguably better than W.G. by the late 1880s, judged purely by the number of runs he scored:

1885: 1130 runs; 56.50 runs per innings; 4 centuries
1886: 1404 runs; 42.54 runs per innings; 3 centuries
1886–7 (Australia tour): 721 runs; 48.06 runs per innings;
    2 centuries
1887: 1653 runs; 78.71 runs per innings; 8 centuries
1887–8 (Australia tour): 766 runs; 58.92 runs per innings;
    2 centuries

Given that he was physically so unfit, W.G.'s ability to remain a front-rank batsman testified to his ferocious urge to compete. By the late 1880s he would be left gasping for breath if he ran a quick third run: W.G. would 'place his hands on the top of his bat handle and bend over it to recover his breath,' the Bristol cricket correspondent H.E. Roslyn remembered. In 1888, when he was still only thirty-nine, a provincial newspaper referred matter-of-factly to W.G. as the 'Grand Old Cricketer' – the 'Grand' also serving as a diplomatic euphemism for 'fat'.

As a doctor, Grace knew there was nothing inevitable about his startling physical decline. Fred Spofforth remained lean and athletic through middle age, and so sure of his prowess that in 1896, at the age of forty-two, he tried unsuccessfully to convince Australia's captain Harry Trott to select him for a Test match at the Oval. Lord Harris was another of Grace's cricketing contemporaries who remained in trim shape into old age, his appetite possibly tempered by heavy smoking.

W.G., by contrast, was acutely aware that he ate far too much. In a revealing omission, he cut a first-draft reference to 'observing a little care in my food' as part of his pre-season training regime from the published edition of his 1891 memoir *Cricket*. 'He is a tremendous lot fatter,' an Australian reporter observed the same year, on seeing W.G. in the flesh for the first time since his 1873–4 tour. Yet W.G. seemed incapable of addressing *why* he could not stop eating. The Cambridge University cricketer Freddie Wilson, who knew Grace well from the late 1890s, left a memorable image of W.G. lunching in the pavilion at Crystal Palace Park in south London:

> He was a fine Trencherman was W.G. He had a red-haired waiter called Joe at the Crystal Palace whom he used to keep fairly on the hop ... If he enjoyed his lunch he saw that everyone else did the same. 'Here, you,' he would shout to some nervous youngster, 'how are you going to get that hundred for me this afternoon if you've got nothing to eat. You have a bit of that cold beef, like I'm going to.'

The element of compulsion, for Grace as much as the 'nervous' youngster, is striking.

Wilson noticed as well how 'all through lunch his eyes were never still'. And he saw something else: "'Here – you have another drop of that hock," W.G. would call across the table to a member of the opposition. "They'll never hear you calling out for leg before against me if you can't speak."'

In the 1880s, W.G. concealed his increasingly heavy drinking with such success that he was claimed by the Victorian temperance movement as a champion teetotaller. For in public, W.G. was all for people drinking less or abstaining altogether. The Reverend Dixon Spain was among those fooled by Grace, announcing to a temperance meeting in Bristol in January 1887 that he had received a letter from W.G. on 'the advantages of abstinence from alcoholic drinks'. A few months later, the president of a temperance society in Bury St Edmunds confirmed to another meeting that 'Mr W.G. Grace, one of the most famous cricketers of modern times, was a teetotaller.'

W.G. and his fellow cricketers knew better. There is a curious passage in the published version of *Cricket* where W.G. notes that the Graces 'have always been a temperate family. Intemperate smoking, in my opinion, has more to do with nervousness and small scores than moderate drinking.' Grace then abruptly switches the subject to the need for 'constant exercise' as part of a cricketer's fitness routine. In the original manuscript W.G. elaborated on what he meant by moderate alcohol consumption. When batting, a glass or a 'little thimbleful' of wine or spirits was 'helpful at certain times'. Furthermore, 'when the innings is over a little wine or spirits is undoubtedly useful.' He was still not being entirely candid. From the early 1880s, W.G. routinely ordered a whisky and soda to keep him going through the afternoon.

Anyone who played for or against W.G. soon learned about his drinking habits. During a match at Oxford in June 1886, W.G. let his student opponents ply him with glass after glass of champagne over dinner. They were trying to get him drunk so he would have a hangover when he resumed his innings the next day; but, as one of Grace's team-mates remembered, 'a bottle or even two bottles of champagne could have no more effect on his mighty frame than a liqueur glass of Kummel on a bunker on a golf course'. Next morning, W.G. completed his century.

Taken individually, some of the glimpses of Grace in his cups have a surface bonhomie; cumulatively, they paint an unsettling picture of someone out of control. 'He drank something of everything, before and during dinner, and afterwards he sent for the whisky,' a fellow guest recalled of W.G.'s behaviour during a banquet in Bristol in his honour in 1895. The story was told long after the event by the Somerset cricketer Sammy Woods to the journalist Raymond Robertson-Glasgow, who may in turn have embellished Woods's account. But for once an unreliable anecdote about W.G. corrected a myth. W.G. at the table was not a merry, Falstaffian giant. Grabbing the next bottle, or sawing off a hunk of cold beef, he comes across as a man seeking release in food and drink from considerable internal stress.

In his sad way, the great Arthur Shrewsbury provides one clue to the strain W.G. was under from the mid-1880s. On 19 May 1903, convinced that his best days were over as a batsman (which was true) and that he had a fatal disease (which was not), Shrewsbury shot himself in the chest at his home in Nottingham. The normally meticulous Shrewsbury missed his mark, because the bullet failed to kill him. He grasped the pistol again, put it to his head and blew out his brains.

Grace was not suicidal or even morbid; he exuded ebullience and conviviality. Yet he and Shrewsbury confronted the dilemma of all sporting geniuses: how to cope when your powers begin to wane? In W.G.'s case, the strain of being past his peak was compounded by an external crisis. Gloucestershire County Cricket Club had begun a potentially terminal decline.

W.G. loved Gloucestershire CCC with a passion that brooked no argument. Where his relationship with MCC was essentially a business affair, W.G.'s bond with Gloucestershire resembled a tempestuous marriage, full of rows where the couple (in this case

Grace and the Gloucestershire committee) tried hard to kiss and make up, but sometimes did not succeed.

'Dear Arrowsmith', W.G. scribbled furiously one Wednesday evening from Thrissell House, 'What's up with you and Clarke, I saw Clarke only last night with Frank Townsend and everything seemed going on all right. I was awfully surprised at your joint telegram.'

James Arrowsmith, a prominent Bristol publisher and Gloucestershire CCC committee man, was used to such notes. During the 1880s, W.G. used Arrowsmith as his first point of contact for his frequent run-ins with the committee. 'I will be at your office at 9:15 [a.m.],' W.G. signed off menacingly in this instance. Arrowsmith knew what awaited him in the morning.

Many times W.G. would turn up at Arrowsmith's office on Quay Street, one hand clutching his crushed Quaker hat, the other tugging irritably at his beard. He would launch into his latest grievance against the committee, while the emollient Arrowsmith tried in vain to soothe him. W.G. would then stomp out of the publisher's offices, perhaps allowing himself a few minutes in his friend Herbert Gibbs's gun shop on Corn Street in order to calm down. Arrowsmith (forty-one in 1881) would subsequently pass on Grace's complaints to the publisher's friends on the committee, Edward Clarke (forty-seven), an accountant, and Harry Beloe (thirty-two), a grain and flour merchant. The three of them would have to decide whether to sit tight until W.G.'s rage subsided or try to meet him halfway.

W.G.'s anger was an expression of love betrayed. By the mid-1880s, the club his family had done so much to create was letting him down badly. In the 1870s Gloucestershire had been one of the strongest first-class teams, winning or sharing the informal county championship four times. A decade later, Gloucestershire were on a losing streak that got progressively worse. The county's record between 1880 and 1889 read as follows:

Played: 117
Won: 20

Drawn: 35
Lost: 62

Gloucestershire's decline reflected the county's dependence in the 1870s on the 'three Graces': W.G., E.M. (still an occasional match-winner) and Fred. By the 1880s, Fred's death and E.M.'s descent into arthritic middle age exposed gaps in Gloucestershire's ranks that the county club struggled to fill because of its small recruitment base and modest income. It did not help either that MCC continued to enforce strict birth and residency rules for county cricketers.

As captain and sole selector, W.G. was open to any ruse to get good players 'qualified' for Gloucestershire. His cousin Walter Gilbert, who was born in London, had played a few games for Middlesex in the early 1870s and then spent a couple of years at The Chestnuts becoming a born and bred Gloucestershire man. The Australian Billy Midwinter played six seasons for Gloucestershire between 1877 and 1882 on the basis of being born in the Forest of Dean.

However, W.G. could do nothing about Gloucestershire's lack of money. The club had no home ground and its income from ticket sales was further reduced by the rent it paid Clifton College and Cheltenham College to use their playing fields during the schools' summer holidays. It was poverty, rather than snobbery, that caused Gloucestershire to continue to put out predominantly amateur sides, because the club could only afford to hire one or two professionals.

W.G. held Gloucestershire's batting together with the help of a small pool of young Oxford and Cambridge amateurs who had connections to the county. They included three Oxford Blues: Joseph Brain, a Clifton old boy; Herbert Page, who returned to Cheltenham College as a teacher; and Arthur Croome, another schoolmaster. Gloucestershire's shortage of bowlers caused a bigger headache, following the retirement of the amateur Fenton Miles (left-arm slow), the death of Fred Grace (medium pace) and the return to Australia of Midwinter (medium pace). Victorian amateurs generally disdained bowling as journeymen's work and, apart from Page, who bowled occasional medium pace, none of Gloucestershire's young gentlemen offered much help to W.G. Instead, spectators at Gloucestershire's games got used to the sight of W.G. bowling for hours on end, usually in tandem with an uncomplaining professional at the other end.

William 'Woofie' Woof started as a left-arm fast bowler and then switched to 'slows', a wise decision given the burden he would bear. In 1884, his most successful season, Woof bowled 4033 deliveries for Gloucestershire, far more than Grace (2447), the team's only other front-line bowler. While accurate, Woof was not much of a match-winner; yet hour after hour he soldiered on, 'holding an end' as Grace alternated with Page's second-string bowling.

Gloucestershire's dire performances lent a bleak humour to the club's annual meetings, held every spring at the Grand Hotel on Broad Street. In April 1885, one member observed how sad it was 'to see a club, once of such importance, sunk so low amongst the counties'. Another member added to 'laughter and applause' that everyone in the room 'would be glad to hear there was a prospect of its former glory being revived'.

'We shall not do worse than last year,' W.G. chipped in, to more laughter.

'Have you any bowlers?' Harry Beloe asked.

'Lots. But no good ones,' replied W.G., who seemed to have forgotten Woof.

Behind the public good cheer, many members grumbled about W.G.'s insistence on personally selecting the team, with no involvement by the committee. A view took root among cricket clubs in the Bristol area, and elsewhere in Gloucestershire, that W.G. chose former public schoolboys and university 'gentlemen' for the county team because he was prejudiced against local players. W.G. retorted that he was always keen to try out the latest promising teenager in his net at Thrissell House. Unfortunately, young players 'were never much use at first'.

In May that year a team of twenty-three Gloucestershire

'Colts' made W.G.'s point for him in the annual trial match against the full county team. The game 'yielded little, if any better batting on the part of the Gloucestershire Colts than in former years,' Gloucester's *The Citizen* reported. The Colts were struggling on 17 for eleven wickets in their second innings when rain swept across Durdham Down, high above the River Avon gorge, forcing the game to be abandoned. For W.G., and for everyone else, it was all a bit depressing.

It said something for Gloucestershire's mediocrity in the 1880s that the two most dramatic episodes concerning W.G. and his team took place off the field.

Shortly after 3 p.m. on 25 July 1884, W.G. was waiting to bat in Lancashire's pavilion at Old Trafford when E.M. hit the ball high into the air and was caught on the boundary. At this moment, someone thrust a telegram into W.G.'s hand. He opened it and learned that his mother had just died unexpectedly at The Chestnuts. In a daze, W.G. continued on his way to the middle, possibly too stunned even to tell E.M. as they passed each other.

He scored a single before realising he was in the wrong place. At the end of the over a visibly distressed W.G. approached 'Monkey' Hornby, Lancashire's captain, and explained the situation. Hornby summoned his team and with his usual brisk authority abandoned the game immediately. W.G., E.M. and their cousin Walter Gilbert hurried off to the station to catch the first train to Bristol, while messengers passed around Old Trafford, explaining to the crowd what had happened.

Hornby's action was a measure of W.G.'s standing, for no other cricketer could have ended a first-class match because of the death of his mother. Martha's funeral in Downend was not quite a state occasion, but the local newspapers reported several hundred people lining the streets outside the village church, as they had done for Fred Grace four years earlier.

Walter Gilbert, who stood with the rest of the family as Martha was buried, would soon present W.G. with the biggest embarrassment of his career. Gilbert was the son of George Mowbray Gilbert, Martha's brother-in-law, who had been bankrupted with Alfred Pocock in 1864 when their lead-making business collapsed. The elder Gilbert had died almost penniless in 1877, followed in 1879 by his widow Rose (Martha's sister), whose meagre estate was put in the hands of a local creditor. Soon after his parents' deaths, Walter Gilbert's chief source of income dried up when the United South of England team disintegrated in the early 1880s.

In 1883 Gilbert married Sarah Lillywhite, a daughter of one of the Lillywhite cricket clan. With a wife to support, Gilbert started pestering Gloucestershire's committee for more expenses, even when he could not play for the club. For a while the committee remained sympathetic, agreeing in October 1884 to make him 'a present of £24 on account of his having been injured'. But the following summer the committee refused Gilbert's request for 'an additional sum per match' in expenses. He had only one bargaining chip: as one of Gloucestershire's better batsmen, he knew the county could not afford to lose him. At the start of 1886 the committee yielded again to Gilbert, offering to make another donation of £25 if he played in all the county's matches during the summer.

Gilbert could not wait that long. He announced that he was turning professional, in effect coming clean about his true position at Gloucestershire. At the same time he joined the minor East Gloucestershire Cricket Club in Cheltenham, playing weekend cricket for a match fee whenever the county did not need him. Gilbert's East Gloucestershire team-mates soon noticed money disappearing from the dressing room and set a trap. On Saturday, 5 June, Sergeant Woolford, a local policeman, clambered on to the dressing room roof and watched through a spyhole as Gilbert rifled through his team-mates' clothes and took two marked half-sovereign coins. Woolford jumped down, rushed into the dressing room and arrested Gilbert, who was 'quietly conveyed' in a cab to the police station.

Gilbert almost certainly did not see W.G. between his arrest on Saturday afternoon and his appearance in Cheltenham's police court the following Monday. Grace finished a game a day early at Lord's at 5 p.m. on Friday and was due in Brighton by Monday morning for the start of his next match between Gloucestershire and Sussex. In theory, he could have caught a train to Bristol on Friday evening or Saturday morning. But such a journey would have made little sense, given W.G.'s need to be in Brighton two days later. It is more likely that he stayed in London over the weekend with friends – as he did many times – before taking the train to Brighton

W.G. may not even have learned of Gilbert's arrest until Monday, because of the difficulty of sending telegrams on a Saturday or Sunday, when post offices were shut. It is possible that Charles Margrett, a baker in Cheltenham and a former Gloucestershire Colt, brought W.G. the news when he turned up in Brighton as a late replacement for Gilbert.

While W.G. was scoring 51 at Hove, Gilbert made a full con-fession to the magistrates sitting at Cheltenham's police court. He 'expressed sorrow, and said that if they would forgive him he would go to Australia'. W.G. must have been alarmed by Gilbert's plan. His cousin was well known in Australia as a member of Grace's touring team in 1873–4, and the colonial press – natu-rally hostile to Grace – would have hounded Gilbert as soon as he got off the boat. During Gilbert's month-long prison sentence, the Graces persuaded him to depart with his family to Canada. Even then Gilbert did not disappear into oblivion. The Canadian press had already picked up news of the scandal from the London papers, so there would be no question of Gilbert beginning a completely new life.

W.G. did not cut off contact with Gilbert, who eventually became a government land agent while continuing to play cricket. In 1897, Arthur Shrewsbury responded to a request by Gilbert from Montreal for a new bat. 'Am sending you a Bat through Dr Grace and hope you will get a lot of scores with it, don't blame the bat if you don't,' Shrewsbury wrote wryly.

From W.G.'s perspective, Gilbert had been a fool and a

let-down, leaving Gloucestershire in the lurch just when the county needed him badly. His cousin also constituted an unpleasant reminder of just how easy it was to slip over the financial edge. By the time Gilbert left for Canada, W.G. had probably exhausted the money he received from his 1873–4 Australia tour and his 1879 testimonial. He had also lost the income he earned in the 1870s playing professional cricket for USE. Apart from his doctor's salary, he had no other substantial earnings. At about the time of Gilbert's disgrace, W.G. began to pay more attention to the business of exploiting his fame for money. He approached the task with all the entrepreneurial flair of a man who came from a family of chancers and losers.

23

W.G. INC.

Everybody was feeling the pinch in the 1880s, as increased competition from the United States, Germany and other rising industrial economies took its toll on Britain's export-driven factories. 'The slump of the eighties, following so soon after that of the seventies and linked to it by the unlifted depression in agriculture, gave Victorian courage and optimism the severest shock that it had yet received,' the historian Sir Robert Ensor wrote half a century later.

Lord Harris, squeezed by falling farm rents and prices, leased out his stately home in Kent and moved with his wife into a boarding house near London's Victoria station. 'We were there off & on for some years and never lived more comfortably or economically,' he remembered. 'We paid £2. 2. 0 a week per head for our board & £1. 1 for our servants, guests so much per meal, & everything was excellent.'

Money worries nagged at W.G., too, but he lacked his friend Harris's financial discipline. On his daily rounds he was a strikingly generous tipper for someone depicted by his critics as a money-grasper. In 1891 Thomas Renwick, a telegraph messenger boy, found a purse on a street near Thrissell House with Grace's name and address stamped on the outside. 'My father and I went at once down to Dr. Grace's surgery where my father asked Dr. Grace if he had lost a purse. Plunging his hands into both trouser pockets, Dr. Grace said, "Yes." After examining the purse and its contents Dr. Grace presented me with the purse and the money; one half-sovereign, three half-crowns and four pennies.'

Albert Bole, a local boy from near Downend, recalled how as an eleven-year-old he was handed a half crown by W.G. after Grace played a practical joke on him. W.G. dressed Bole up in blue Tory colours to go and buy a newspaper during the 1886 election, knowing the newsagent was a 'red-hot Liberal'.

While he was spraying half-crown tips around Bristol, W.G. probably also had calls on his wallet closer to home. After Martha's death, there were other members of Grace's family who still counted as hard-up. W.G.'s unmarried sister Fanny, who had been Martha's companion, moved out of The Chestnuts into another house in Downend, where she took in boarders. Despite this income, Fanny may have needed additional support from her brothers to make ends meet. W.G. may also have helped his elder brother Henry look after their penniless uncle Alfred Pocock, Grace's childhood cricket coach, who fancifully described himself as a 'collector of debts' in the 1891 census.

Yet W.G.'s own domestic situation was not particularly secure. In July 1887 his cattle-trading landlord Joseph Hennessy died and when Hennessy's son and two trustees decided to auction the freehold, W.G. obligingly allowed prospective purchasers to inspect his home and surgery. It provided a vivid illustration of W.G.'s double life and the on-off nature of Victorian celebrity; simultaneously, he was the most famous sportsman in the British Empire and 'Dr Grace, the tenant', as the auction notice described him. James Farmer, a window blind maker on Stapleton Road, bought the freehold at auction for £1905, giving W.G. a new landlord. Farmer, who soon moved his business next door to Thrissell House, would prove a more troublesome landlord than Hennessy.

*

Grace saw enough poverty on his daily medical rounds in Bristol
to want to be a responsible, prudent head of his household. He
held a life insurance policy with Equitable Life and was also a
member of two mutual societies with strong Tory, monarchist
roots: the Ancient Order of Druids and the Loyal Order of
Ancient Shepherds.

But he lacked any grasp of how to make money beyond the
fees and expenses he charged for playing cricket. He was terrible
at marketing, as customers who dealt with W.G. in his guise as
a director of the Gloucestershire County Ground Company Ltd
soon discovered. The company was set up in 1888 to buy and
manage the club's first ground at Ashley Down, on the northern
outskirts of Bristol. In theory, W.G. was supposed to increase
the company's revenues by hiring out the ground to local sports
teams. In practice, he treated Ashley Down as his personal fief-
dom, taking the view that the customer was generally wrong.
'Some cricketers, who are not good judges, think that a ground
that looks green and nice is better to play on, than a well rolled
bare wicket,' he wrote angrily to the *Western Daily Press* in June
1888, after two local cricket clubs complained about the pitch
he had prepared for them. The pitch was 'a little fiery from
being so hard,' W.G. conceded, 'but no other fault could be
found with it.'

In March 1889, W.G. opened up Ashley Down for a far more
congenial sports team. A few days earlier, 'fairly done up' after
a rough sea crossing from France, the former baseball pitcher Al
Spalding arrived at London's Victoria station, delighted to hear
he would soon be meeting the most famous living Englishman.
Spalding and a party of twenty National League baseball players
were on the final leg of a world tour aimed at exporting the game
beyond North America. As a keen baseball fan, W.G. insisted that
Spalding's team should come down to Bristol straight away to
show the locals how to play and demonstrate to his lackadaisical
Gloucestershire team what smart fielding meant.

After lunch at the Grand Hotel, W.G. escorted Spalding
and his baseballers to Ashley Down. Around five thousand

spectators turned up – far more than for most of the county's cricket matches – to watch the first major sporting event at Gloucestershire's new ground. For an hour or so Spalding's team put on an exhibition, and then W.G. and several others 'tried their hands at baseball with much success'. W.G. was not finished on the subject of baseball. 'There is no doubt that the baseballers now here can set an excellent example to cricketers by their smart fielding and accurate throwing,' he wrote to the sporting journal *Land and Water*. He pointed out knowledgeably that bowlers, because they kept their arm straight, would never be able to deliver a curve ball.

W.G. had less welcome visitors at Ashley Down two months later in the form of some 'colts' who ignored his notice warning cricketers not to use the practice nets following a spell of rain. He was so enraged when he spotted them that he struck one of the teenagers, and although he later apologised to the parents, the father threatened to sue. As so often, W.G. subcontracted the problem to the uncomplaining Arrowsmith. 'I shall certainly not stand Black Mail being levied on me, which I fancy the father has been put up to, by some of his friends,' W.G. wrote to the publisher. Arrowsmith seems to have persuaded the father to back down, because the case never went to court.

In business matters, W.G. had a deeper problem than a violent temper and insensitivity to criticism. Plenty of modern superstars have no idea about the complexities of image rights or how to make themselves marketable. Instead, agents and public relations firms do the job for them. Grace had no such help, because none was available in the late nineteenth century. Nor did he possess the kind of brazen flair for self-promotion displayed by Spalding on his world baseball tour, which provided a platform to build one of America's most famous sporting brands. By contrast, W.G.'s efforts to make money out of his name had a kind of homely incompetence, as though he could not figure out how to sell himself and did not care for the whole business anyway.

W.G. was not the only Victorian athletic star who squandered his own brand potential. In the late 1870s and early 1880s, W.G.'s fame was briefly rivalled by Captain Matthew Webb, the first swimmer to cross the English Channel unassisted. After his epic feat in 1875, Webb drifted from appearances on the cover of matchboxes, through weird tank 'flotation' stunts, to a bid in 1883 to swim across the Whirlpool Rapids beneath the Niagara Falls. Potential sponsors thought Webb's final money-making scheme so suicidally dangerous that they refused to put up any cash. They were right. As soon as he plunged into the rapids, the current sucked him underwater and smashed him against the rocks. Webb's battered corpse was washed up a few miles downstream.

W.G.'s commercial starting point was far more favourable than Webb's, for in several ways he was an advertiser's dream. His instantly recognisable beard, massive size and record scores were the most obvious elements of the W.G. package. Grace could anger easily, but he combined his short temper with natural warmth, especially in the company of children, whom he adored. Ten-year-old Mabel Catley, playing with her cricket bat on the boundary, received the full W.G. treatment during the lunch interval of a game at Scarborough in 1889. An enormous man with a huge beard walked out of the pavilion and approached her. 'I would like to try that bat,' W.G. said gravely to Mabel, pointing at her matchstick. 'Then the master and the little girl walked together to the outfield, she solemnly to bowl underhand, he to play straight and serious with the child's bat, much to the delight of the crowd surrounding them.'

Unfortunately for W.G., he proved no match for Victorian England's booming souvenir and novelty industry, which had no qualms about using famous faces without paying their owners. One Sunday morning in the late 1880s, Grace was strolling along a Bristol street when he spotted young Edward Bankin, a coal miner's teenage son, puffing a 'W.G.' novelty clay pipe with the cricketer's bearded features carved on the bowl: 'He [W.G.] nudged his friend, as if to say, "Twig that", and after I had gone about ten yards past him, I heard his stentorian voice shout out, "Hi",' Bankin remembered:

On looking around, I saw him pulling his whiskers. With a shake of his head, he called me back, and asked me if he could look at the pipe. Proudly I handed it to him. He asked me how much it cost, and when I told him twopence, he said, 'It cost more than that to get it as black as that.' I smiled and he then asked me if I would sell it. I tried to tell him he could have it with pleasure, but before a word could come he had put 2s. 6d. in my hands and turned on his heels, laughing.

When W.G. consciously lent his name to products, his choices had a weirdly random flavour, suggesting he was unable to distinguish between obvious duds and surefire winners. 'I shall certainly recommend it to my friends,' W.G. wrote obligingly in 1884 of 'Stapleton', a revolutionary new 'outdoor game' invented by an ironmonger on Stapleton Road. 'Stapleton' sunk without trace, obliterated by the new craze for lawn tennis.

Some years later W.G. endorsed another strange new pastime called 'Cricket, A Table Game', invented by an acquaintance in south London. In November 1902 W.G. and his youngest son Charlie turned up at *Wisden*'s offices near Leicester Square for the sales promotion (see photograph, back cover). While the press took photographs, W.G. and Charlie pretended to have fun hitting a ball the size of a pellet with miniature bats past 'nine little nets' placed in 'ordinary fielding positions'. A perimeter net, the 'boundary', stopped the ball falling off the edge of the table on to the floor below. Cricket, A Table Game did not catch on, despite being an early forerunner of Subbuteo table cricket (and football).

A more promising venture for W.G. came along in 1888, when the sports kit manufacturer W.H. Cook & Company set up a subsidiary to produce a brand-name 'Magic Bat'. Cook & Co. offered W.G. shares in the business and signed him up as a non-executive director, along with other commercially minded amateurs, including 'Monkey' Hornby and the MCC and Yorkshire grandee Lord Hawke. The company failed to anticipate W.G.'s willingness to promote competitors, especially when they were old cricketing comrades. In 1890, while the 'Magic Bat' was still at the prototype phase, W.G. visited the Cheltenham workshop of the former Gloucestershire bowler 'Woofie' Woof, who had designed and patented a 'special bat' with a curling rubber spring inside the handle for 'better balance'. W.G. 'expressed a very decided opinion as to its merits ... wishing some to be made and sent on to him,' the *Cheltenham Chronicle* reported.

W.G.'s questionnaire from the *Pall Mall Gazette* was almost as strange an exercise in money-making as his endorsements of 'Stapleton', 'Cricket, A Table Game', and the 'Magic Bat'. Grace refused to give a face-to-face interview, declining an invitation to stay the night at the Bayswater home of Marion Spielmann, the young art critic who compiled the questions – an obvious ruse on Spielmann's part to get him to talk. Instead, Spielmann dressed up the 'interview' to make it seem as if he had met W.G. at Lord's, which at least helped to stretch some alarmingly thin material a little further.

'Your fiancée announced that she could not marry you – a dishonest man – as she had heard you had "stolen a run" & had been so ungallant as to "bowl a maiden over"?' Spielmann wrote, in a laboured attempt to get a witty response from Grace.

'This is of course not true,' replied W.G., who had no desire to drag Agnes into the public eye.

In the early 1880s W.G. also wrote several pieces on the subject of 'Cricket, and How to Excel in it' for the *Boy's Own Paper*, a new journal launched by the evangelical Religious Tract Society, which aimed to encourage literacy and wholesome Christian values among the working class. W.G. quickly picked up one of the tricks of the journalist's trade. In 1887, he recycled some of his *Boy's Own* material when the Duke of Beaufort commissioned him to write an article on batting for the cricket volume in the Duke's *Badminton Library of Sports and Pastimes* series.

The eventual Badminton article, a fourteen-page essay called 'How to Score', nonetheless disproved the myth that Grace could not write. There is no evidence that he had any assistance, and

his prose is clear and lucid, shorn of the pomposities and circum-
locutions that disfigure his two largely ghostwritten memoirs.
No detail was too small for W.G. when it came to the serious
business of batting:

> You must . . . not only bear in mind the vast importance of
> reaching the ground in good time, but the greater impor-
> tance of getting five or ten minutes batting practice before
> the innings begins . . . There is this also to be said in favour
> of five or ten minutes' batting practice before a match, that
> it enables you to test pads, gloves, and shoes. To have the
> fastening of a glove or pad break off when you are well set
> is a disagreeable and annoying interruption.

W.G. did not find writing about how to play cricket a chore. A
few years later, he expanded his *Boy's Own* journalism into an
absorbing, thirty-page essay for a boys' sporting encyclopedia
on the wider theme of 'excelling' at cricket. In the article, W.G.
invented a fictitious cricket match to demonstrate his points,
with 'Slashington', 'Tomson' and 'Slate' playing on one side and
'Dickson' and 'Lawson' on the opposition:

> Lawson's slows are taken off; Dickson is the next change
> bowler put on, and Lawson goes to cover point. This is an
> improvement. Dickson's command of the ball is great, he
> seems able to put it where he pleases; he bowls with his
> head, calculating and varying every ball that he delivers.
> But the defence is obstinate, the batsmen cannot be parted.

So it goes on, as W.G.'s imagination runs away with him and
he becomes completely absorbed by who will win this exciting
match. Afterwards, he added a four-page article on the important
subject of 'Cricket clubs: Their formation and management'.
    What W.G. hated writing about was himself, as his curt replies
to the more probing questions from Spielmann indicated. He
was an emotional man, incapable of reining in his passions, but

in print, he was as reluctant to spill the beans about his private life as most Victorian celebrities. Grace therefore shut down one avenue – the tell-all autobiography – that could have earned him a fortune. Instead, it fell to one of his whist partners to extract what juice he could from W.G. in two literary joint ventures.

Methven Brownlee, a cricket-loving Scot, arrived in Bristol from Airdrie in 1872 to work for Dunlop, Mackie & Co., a local wine merchant. By the early 1880s Brownlee was an active member of Gloucestershire CCC, and while the Scot was only a club stand-ard cricketer, he soon became part of W.G.'s inner circle because of his ability at cards. Grace hosted frequent evening whist par-ties at Thrissell House and Brownlee became a regular partner, playing with W.G., Grace's brother-in-law David Bernard and other local doctors.

In the winter of 1886–7, Brownlee persuaded W.G. that they should work together on the first biography of the great crick-eter. The cooperative nature of the enterprise was made plain in the book's frontispiece, which reproduced a handwritten letter by W.G. to the publisher Iliffe & Son. 'The Biography by Mr Brownlee, my personal friend, has my entire approval,' W.G. announced. To encourage buyers, he explained that 'the per-sonal incidents' contained in the book 'are entirely new to the public'. So far he was more or less willing to submit to Brownlee's interrogations.

Brownlee was not a rigorous researcher. His Caledonian ears, confused by Grace's accent, misheard W.G.'s school as 'Rudgway' House, rather than 'Ridgway' while Brownlee mistakenly imagined that Grace's father-in-law William Day was also his first cousin. Yet Brownlee got more out of Grace than any pro-fessional journalist, largely because he and W.G. were friends. W.G. trusted Brownlee enough, as did Agnes, to let him use several extremely short extracts from W.G.'s diary on his voyage to Australia in 1873. With Grace's approval, Brownlee even dared to offer little character sketches of W.G. and Agnes's four children which brought them to life.

The biography sold sufficient copies for Iliffe & Son to publish a second edition. Encouraged by their success, Brownlee proposed a new project to W.G.: a memoir of his 'forty years of cricket', with Brownlee acting as ghostwriter and Arrowsmith as publisher.

From the outset, W.G. got into a tug-of-war with Brownlee and Arrowsmith over the content of the book. The publisher and the ghostwriter wanted Grace to dictate a proper autobiography, full of personal reminiscences and anecdotes. W.G. wanted to write about cricket, and in a way he won. *Cricket*, the book's eventual title, was largely a trudge through cricket history, cricket games and cricketers. Try as he might, Brownlee could never get W.G. off the subject of cricket for long enough to provide more than a handful of serviceable (though often unreliable) anecdotes.

Grace found the whole process a chore. 'I find that I really cannot spare the time to go to Cardiff as I have so much writing etc. to do ...,' he wrote to an acquaintance there. 'I wanted Brownlee to let me off, but he cannot.' To pad out the book, Brownlee added a section on cricket 'records and curiosities', compiled by another wine merchant, Charles Green, a keen amateur cricket statistician. If readers were not yet exhausted, they could then wade through an 82-page appendix listing cricket records and the 'laws' of the game.

Initially, W.G. was far more engaged by another project underway at Lord's: 'Dear Perkins,' he wrote to MCC's secretary on 14 October 1888, 'Will you make arrangements with Mr Stewart Wortley for next Friday, I can then give him a sitting, and again on Saturday if early in day. What am I to be painted in, what position, and what size, I think a small size will spoil the whole thing.'

In the summer of 1888, as W.G. turned forty, the MCC committee had decided it was time to commission a portrait of its most famous member. As the *Bristol Mercury* noted, the painting would be 'in recognition of the pluck and skill he still displays in maintaining his well-won reputation as England's foremost cricketer'. It was also a chance for the forty-one-year-old society portrait painter Archibald Stuart-Wortley (not 'Stewart Wortley', as W.G. wrote) to make a name by painting the most famous sportsman of the age.

Stuart-Wortley negotiated a fee of £300 with MCC, some of which may have been earmarked to pay Grace, who did not usually give his time for free. However, as Stuart-Wortley soon realised, W.G. was better at talking about visiting the artist's Chelsea studio than actually showing up. Lacking Grace in the flesh, Stuart-Wortley borrowed a picture from MCC of a recent Oxford v Cambridge match, and over the winter of 1888–9 used it as the background for his canvas. Stuart-Wortley's plan was to superimpose W.G. on the scene afterwards.

The painting still had a W.G.-sized hole in the middle by the summer of 1889. 'I am rather afraid I cannot give you much time this week our match at Oval is over Friday, then I could give you a field day Saturday,' he wrote again at some point during the season. 'I will call round tomorrow morning at 10 o'clock and talk the matter over. I cannot then wait to give you a sitting.' Eventually, Stuart-Wortley managed to grab W.G. for long enough to finish his portrait in time for the Royal Academy Spring Exhibition in May 1890.

At this point MCC agreed to raise Stuart-Wortley's fee to £350, and also add £50 for unexplained expenses – possibly another fee for his subject. For Grace had now become fully involved in Stuart-Wortley's venture, jointly signing the first proofs of reproductions of the painting, printed on Japanese vellum. Stuart-Wortley then sold these high-quality prints on the open market.

Stuart-Wortley's much-loved portrait of Grace, which now hangs in the Lord's pavilion, failed to capture W.G.'s genius as a batsman for several reasons. One was W.G.'s refusal to give the artist more of his time; he looks, inescapably, as if he has been stuck on the background at the last minute. Another was W.G.'s obesity; even Stuart-Wortley's neighbour in Chelsea, the portrait artist James McNeill Whistler, could not have made the portly, middle-aged Grace seem athletic.

But the fundamental problem was Grace's posture, frozen at the moment before he bent his shoulders and knees to face the bowler. The result is a static image, where Grace stands stiffly with his weight planted on the back foot; at first glance he looks in danger of toppling backwards on to the stumps. Stuart-Wortley was not really to blame. W.G. could not possibly have held his true batting position for long without seizing up, because his guard was the prelude to movement. It was possible to sketch Grace in his next position – shoulders hunched, front foot cocked (as in Stuart-Wortley's painting), ready to move back or forward – but the artist had to be quick. In 1895, the cartoonist Harry Furniss captured all W.G.'s pent-up dynamism at the crease while sketching him during an innings at Lord's. By then, sadly, W.G. was even fatter (see illustration, page 9 in picture section).

Over the summer of 1890, as Grace's picture hung at the Royal Academy, newspapers ran the first instalments of *Cricket*, even as W.G. and Brownlee raced to finish the book. In Australia the *Sydney Mail* bought the twenty-six extracts 'at considerable cost'. The *Nottinghamshire Guardian* acquired the same package, announcing that it was 'confidently anticipated' W.G.'s magnum opus would prove 'the most popular history of our national game ever written'. W.G. received £100 as his share of the serialisation rights, although Arrowsmith withheld £25 to cover the publisher's 'expenses'.

The book sold well, not because it was readable but because of W.G.'s fame. On that assumption, Arrowsmith decided on a large initial print run of eight thousand copies in April 1891, with a cover price of 6 shillings. The book trade snapped up most of this first edition run immediately. Aware that *Cricket* was a book to treasure rather than enjoy, Arrowsmith also produced a special deluxe edition, personally signed by Grace in a limited run of 652 copies. The publisher sent out a circular to targeted readers, explaining it was a collector's item. In his personal message W.G. failed to grasp the need to flatter potential customers. 'Kindly read this circular and if you wish to subscribe reply as soon as possible,' he instructed a shooting chum in a one-line note.

Relations were still fine between Arrowsmith and W.G. in May 1891, when the publisher hosted a dinner in Bristol to celebrate the publication of *Cricket*. Arrowsmith used the menu card, written in mock 'Olde English', to show off his company's fancy typefaces, as the guests were served with 'ye Souppe from ye pungent Tomato' and 'Ye Salmone from ye loved River offe ye Severne'.

The trouble began almost five months later, after Grace learned that Arrowsmith planned to spin off three chapters on batting, bowling and fielding as a separate book. These chapters contained Grace's advice for young cricketers on the sport's main disciplines and were far better written than the rest of the book for a reason: W.G. was obviously the author. Once more, Grace set out everything in practical detail: the correct weight for a boy's bat ('It is better to err on the side of having one too light, for with a heavy one you cannot cut or time the ball'); how to bat on a wet wicket ('In playing forward you must not play too quickly, as the ball sometimes hangs a bit'); why it is 'a huge mistake' to bowl short to a batsman at the start of his innings ('It is the one ball which he sees best of all, and he rarely fails to play it'); or how to back up a wild throw from another fielder ('Do not go too near to the wicket-keeper or bowler, or you will miss it: about eight yards is the best distance to be from each other in backing up').

It is hard to understand why Grace's observations in these chapters were later dismissed as 'overly earnest' and even unintentionally comic. More than sixty years later, in *The Art of Cricket*, Bradman would offer equally earnest advice to young players. 'No batsman should run the risk of playing without one of these confidence producers,' Sir Donald Bradman (as he had become) wrote of the box that protected his groin. For boots that have 'no inner sole for cushioning, it will probably pay you to invest in a pair of rubber insoles or at least sponge rubbers for the heels'. *The Art of Cricket* is rightly regarded as a classic of the genre, for its author had earned the right to be taken seriously on all aspects of the sport. Bradman's publisher Hodder and Stoughton did him proud. Even the photograph of Bradman in the frontispiece underlined the book's authority. Wearing a grey three-piece suit, one hand on chin, the other holding an opened volume, 'The Don' actually looks like a don as he gazes reflectively away from the camera. Hodder and Stoughton got only one detail wrong: the book in Bradman's hand is not Plutarch's *Lives* but *West Indian Adventure*, a tour memoir.

Grace had no such luck with Arrowsmith, who, as far as W.G. was concerned, set about demolishing the very chapters that were meant to be the cornerstones of *Cricket*. To Grace's horror, Arrowsmith proposed publishing the chapters separately as a cheap throwaway edition for sale at railway station bookstalls and other popular outlets.

'Dear Arrowsmith,' W.G. wrote from Thrissell House on 31 August. 'You seem to have commenced this book without my knowing exactly what you intend to do. I must see the binding and covers before giving my consent, as it must be done nicely or not at all.'

Arrowsmith replied immediately, prompting Grace to write another note on the same day: 'I do not at all understand the tone of your letter and think with you that you had better not at present proceed any further in the matter.'

In early September, W.G. scribbled another note to Arrowsmith: 'I am just off to Hastings, if you do not mean to publish the little book let the matter drop. If you do, I must approve of what you do, whether it is customary or not.'

Arrowsmith must have been sure of his contractual rights because he went ahead with the spin-off. On 1 October, W.G. wrote a final note to the publisher from William Day's latest bolthole off London's Oxford Street, where he, Agnes, Bessie and Charlie were staying for the night. 'I have put your letters in the fire, and hope our private friendship will be the same as before, although on business matters we do not agree.'

W.G. had plenty of time over the next month to seethe about Arrowsmith's cheap venture. Next day, he and Agnes, accompanied by Bessie and Charlie, boarded the SS *Arcadia* at London's Albert Dock. Eighteen years after his last turbulent visit, W.G. was leading a second English cricket team to Australia.

24

THE MAJOR AND THE EARL

W.G. could have returned to Australia much sooner than 1891. In 1876, a passing reference by the secretary of Melbourne CC suggests that the club was hoping to organise a tour by 'Mr Grace's Eleven' for the following (English) winter. A decade later, the Nottinghamshire players Alfred Shaw and Arthur Shrewsbury tried to persuade W.G. to join a mixed team of amateurs and professionals for a tour of Australia and New Zealand in 1886–7. Meanwhile Ben Wardill, manager of the Australian team visiting England that summer, also approached Grace about joining a rival tour organised by Melbourne CC, where Wardill was also secretary. W.G. declined both offers, probably because he did not dare risk his relationship with the Barton Regis Union's Board of Guardians. An all-professional tour led by Shaw went ahead, while Wardill put his own plans on hold.

In bidding for W.G., Wardill had several obstacles to overcome, beginning with his family name. Born in 1842, Ben Wardill was the younger brother of Richard Wardill, whose failed attempt to bring W.G. to Australia in 1872 had swiftly been followed by financial disgrace and suicide. Ben had become

Melbourne CC's secretary in 1878, running the club efficiently while ensuring that not a whiff of scandal surrounded his own affairs. 'Major Wardill', as he styled himself, was a volunteer officer in Melbourne's Harbor Trust Garrison Battery and, unlike his late brother, a man whose word was his bond.

In this spirit, Wardill wrote again to W.G. in February 1887 on behalf of Melbourne CC regarding a proposed tour to Australia in 1887–8 to be led by the Middlesex amateur George Vernon. Grace had turned down Vernon, and also relayed this news to Wardill, whom he had met in England the previous summer. Wardill decided to have another go. 'My Dear Doctor,' he began warmly:

> Your kind messages to self and Mrs. Wardill to hand. I am sorry that you have made up your mind not to come & [illegible] at the old terms, as I cabled to George Vernon on Monday to try and get you with the team we have determined this year to bring, and I don't think that any team without you old man would be representative. We all want to see you once more on this side and really it's no distance now – the steamers are very different articles to those of 10 years ago and are replete with every comfort and convenience including a cricket ground where matches can be played every day of the voyage, almost!

Next day, Wardill wrote a blunter letter to Vernon that laid bare the pretence that Grace was an amateur: 'Engage best obtainable amateurs. Telegraph names. Should include Grace, if not too expensive, telegraph lowest terms.'

Wardill continued: 'I got a letter from Dr Grace today. He says he will not come unless he gets what he asked me, but I trust you will be able to induce him to come at something more reasonable, especially when he finds your team is coming.'

By the start of the 1887 English cricket season, Wardill and Vernon had run into another problem. Shrewsbury – just back from the Antipodes – was busy organising a second tour to

Australia and New Zealand over the (English) winter of 1887–8. W.G. now sent two further letters to Wardill in Melbourne, apparently reiterating his financial demands for joining Vernon's tour.

'My dear Doctor,' Wardill wrote again on 16 May. 'I am awfully afraid that you have determined not to pay us another visit. With the advent of two teams I don't see it possible for the M[elbourne] CC to pay expenses, even with an ordinary rate of expenditure and if we assumed an extra item of £1500 or £2000, there would be a dead loss of more than this amount.'

In the end it required an exceptionally rich cricket fan to entice W.G. back to Australia in 1891. Henry Holroyd, 3rd Earl of Sheffield, loved the sport so much that when he succeeded his father in 1876, he built his own cricket ground at Sheffield Park, his country estate near Uckfield in Sussex. During the 1880s, Lord Sheffield's XI took on visiting Australian teams whenever they toured England, while the Earl opened his park free of charge to spectators. The Earl was equally generous with the players' expenses, ensuring that W.G. regularly turned out for his team. In 1884, the *Manchester Courier* reported the 'very peculiar' fact that Sheffield had paid Grace £50 to lead the Earl's side against the Australians, with a further £250 going to the visitors, plus 'first-class railway fares and refreshments provided', and no admission charge for spectators.

The Earl began to dream of an altogether grander cricketing enterprise: a tour of Australia, led by W.G., entirely at his lord-ship's expense. Several individuals encouraged Lord Sheffield to advance his scheme. One was Alfred Shaw, who became the Earl's cricket manager in 1887, immediately after his return from Australia. Another was Shaw's business partner Arthur Shrewsbury, who in February 1891 drafted a costing for Lord Sheffield of an Australian tour, based on the assumption that W.G. would travel. 'His presence would at the very least make a difference of £1500 or £2000 in the takings,' Shrewsbury estimated in his covering note.

W.G. was perhaps a third persuader; he enjoyed the Earl's

hospitality to the full whenever he played at Sheffield Park. In
May 1890 Grace turned up again, fishing in the lakes at the park,
before leading Lord Sheffield's eleven against the latest Australian
team. He had no success on either front. 'The fish were as
difficult to obtain as runs against Australian bowling, and the
champion wended his way back with an empty creel, although
the water was said to contain some thirty potenders,' a newspaper
reported. The Australians easily beat Lord Sheffield's side, who
could not cope with the left-arm medium-pace bowling of John
Ferris, looking to earn a living from cricket in England.

It is not clear exactly when W.G. began to negotiate in earnest
with Lord Sheffield, but discussions were probably underway by
the time of this game. W.G. appears to have demanded £3000,
plus all expenses; furthermore, he wanted the Earl to pay for
Agnes and their two youngest children Bessie and Charlie to
come on the trip as well. Lord Sheffield succumbed because he
had no choice. As his Australian correspondents made clear, the
whole point of the tour was to give the colonies another chance
to see W.G.

At the start of the 1891 cricket season W.G. and Shaw – signed
up as tour manager – began recruiting a team on the Earl's
behalf. Meanwhile, Lord Sheffield fretted about whether Grace
was fit enough for the tour. 'I can very plainly see how a crop
of troubles may spring up from W.G.'s knee,' he wrote to his
nephew Aubrey Harcourt on 15 July, as Grace hobbled through
the summer with his latest load-bearing injury.

The earl may not have realised that a much bigger potential
obstacle than Grace's dicky knee lay between W.G. and a tour
of Australia. Over the past decade, the Barton Regis Union
had become grudgingly accustomed to its most famous medical officer's long absences during the English cricket season.
However, Lord Sheffield's tour threatened to deprive the union
of Grace's services for the whole winter as well. On 28 August,
the union's Board of Guardians met for their regular meeting at
the Eastville workhouse. There were two pressing items on the
agenda. George Rumsey, chairman of the board, regretted to

inform his fellow guardians that the workhouse's Irish chaplain had earlier in the day 'committed suicide by cutting his throat with a razor'. Once they had digested this news, the board turned to consider a letter from Dr W.G. Grace. He asked the board's permission 'to place a *locum tenens* in charge of his district, so that he might accompany the English cricketing team to Australia, from October next to May 1892'.

One guardian, the builder John Bastow, had a track record of opposing W.G.'s annual requests to use locums as cover during the English cricket season. Bastow realised that Grace was in effect asking for almost a full year's leave of absence, since it was certain he would play another season of cricket in England on his return from Australia. Rumsey, a retired soldier, overrode Bastow's objections and persuaded a majority of his colleagues to approve W.G.'s request. 'The Chairman remarked that it was an exceptional case, as their medical officer was the champion cricketer of England,' Rumsey observed. 'He was sure that the board would not stand in the way of Dr Grace in his desire to uphold the honour of England in the colonies. (Laughter.)'

On 2 October the Peninsula and Oriental mail ship RMS *Arcadia* steamed out of London's Albert Dock, as Lord Harris and other cricket dignitaries and officials stood on the quayside waving goodbye to Lord Sheffield and his tour party. Once the *Arcadia* reached the calmer Mediterranean, W.G. got down to business as chairman of the ship's entertainment committee.

In one of those bizarre conjunctures that happened to W.G., another eminent Victorian happened to be on a train heading south through Italy to board the *Arcadia*. The explorer Henry Morton Stanley, fresh from discussing Congolese affairs in Brussels with the imperially minded King of the Belgians, had nearly reached Brindisi when his train crashed into a goods train at the nearby town of Carovigno. Stanley's wife and mother-in-law, who were joining him on a speaking tour of Australia, were uninjured. As for Stanley, he hobbled on to the *Arcadia* with the help of a crutch, obviously unfit for the intensive schedule of deck cricket and other sports that W.G. had lined up for the passengers.

One member of Lord Sheffield's tour party was up for anything. Miss A.B. 'Bessie' Grace, now thirteen, won the ladies' egg-and-spoon race and then teamed up with the Cambridge University wicketkeeper Gregor MacGregor to take the needle-and-cigar race. Later on the journey, she made the highest score (24) in a match between the daughters and the sons of the first-class passengers. Just to rub it in, Bessie then took all the boys' wickets, to the 'keen delight' of the umpire (W.G. Grace).

For W.G. the highlight of the voyage was yet to come. On the evening before the *Arcadia* reached Western Australia, he 'blacked' up his face, whitened his beard and put on a large white wig to compere the cricketers' 'Christy Minstrel' show, a forerunner of the Black and White Minstrel Show. Stanley probably steered clear of the performance, and since neither celebrity mentioned the other in later memoirs, it is generally assumed they never met. Yet W.G. and Stanley would both have been high on the captain's list of guests for his table and besides, they shared the same sponsor. During their visit to Australia the explorer and the cricketer would both be endorsing Goodfellow's Coca Water, 'a medicinal stimulant ... unequalled for the treatment of vomiting, alcoholism [and] fevers'.

25

A TOUR TOO FAR

On form alone, W.G. did not deserve his place on Lord Sheffield's tour party, which read as follows:

Bobby Abel (33), Surrey
William Attewell (30), Nottinghamshire
George Bean (27), Nottinghamshire
Johnny Briggs (28), Lancashire
W.G. Grace (43), Gloucestershire
George Lohmann (26), Surrey
Gregor MacGregor (22), Cambridge University
Bobby Peel (34), Yorkshire
Hylton Philipson (25), MCC
Maurice Read (32), Surrey
Goldney Radcliffe (31), Gloucestershire
John Sharpe (24), Surrey
Andrew Stoddart (28), Middlesex

Shrewsbury had not been joking when he said the team would have been stronger without Grace. Hampered by his knee, W.G. had averaged under 20 runs per innings during the 1891 English cricket season; judged by this benchmark, he was the ninth best batsman in the tour party. The team would have been better with Shrewsbury, who decided to stay in England for the winter managing his sports equipment firm. Yet even in Shrewsbury's absence, two members of Lord Sheffield's team highlighted the contrast with Grace's first tour of Australia in 1873–4, when he was by far the best player.

Andrew Stoddart was an outstanding all-round sportsman, already capped for England at rugby and on the brink of several seasons for Middlesex when he was the best amateur batsman in the country. 'Stod' also played for Hampstead CC in north London, where his fine moustache and dashing lifestyle – he once scored a quadruple-century after an all-night game of cards – dazzled the ladies who turned up to watch him put their husbands in the shade. Yet Stod was not quite what he seemed. The son of a wine merchant, he lived beyond his means and was beset by constant money worries. In this regard he was a bit like W.G.

Appearances were also deceptive with George Lohmann. On paper, Lohmann ought to have been a gentleman amateur, as the son of a London stockbroker. But Lohmann was hard up, playing as a professional for Surrey, where in the late 1880s he had established himself as the best bowler in England. He took more than two hundred wickets in 1888, 1889 and 1890, and 177 in 1891, bowling medium pace, a description that fails to capture his craft and intelligence. In spirit Lohmann was close to Spofforth, using his clever head to fool the batsman with subtle changes of pace and other tricks and dodges. Like Spofforth too, Lohmann had a mind of his own and little time for captains he did not respect. By the end of Lord Sheffield's tour W.G. had become one of them.

W.G.'s own playing record on the tour was a lot better than Lord Sheffield had feared or Shrewsbury had anticipated. He scored almost as many runs in first-class games (448) as Stoddart (450) and held his own as a batsman in the three Test matches at Melbourne, Sydney and Adelaide, making two fifties and averaging 32.8 runs per innings. Yet he was a liability in the field, depending on younger team-mates to chase the ball for him, and hardly needed at all as a bowler. Grace's indispensability lay in his box office appeal. The tour happened because – in the local promoters' thinking – the Australian public wanted a last chance to see W.G. before he retired from first-class cricket. It was a throwback to Grace's 1873–4 tour, with one crucial distinction. Lord Sheffield's seemingly limitless resources and habit of tipping the professionals for fine performances ensured there would be no significant rows about money.

The absence during the tour of his great Australian rivals from the late 1870s and early 1880s reinforced the feeling that W.G. had outlived his time. Spofforth, the 'Demon' bowler, had transmogrified into a London city gent. On the Australians' 1884 tour of England, Spofforth had fallen in love with the daughter of a wealthy Derbyshire tea importer. He returned to marry her and after playing a little for Derbyshire CCC (and enjoying a row with MCC about his eligibility), Spofforth had settled in West Hampstead, going back and forth each day to the City, where he managed his father-in-law's tea business. Spofforth joined forces with Stoddart at Hampstead CC, convinced that at half the pace, but with double the tricks, he was twice as good as in his Test-playing days.

W.G.'s friend Billy Murdoch had also moved with his wife and children to England, where he planned to qualify by residence as a professional for Sussex. Bizarrely, the winter of 1891–2 found the mercenary Murdoch playing for another 'England' team in South Africa led by the Surrey amateur Walter Read. Meanwhile in Australia, Harry Boyle – W.G.'s nemesis in the 1882 Oval Test match – still turned out for his beloved local team in Bendigo, but had retired from top-class cricket.

W.G.'s second tour of Australia therefore acquired the character of a fractious royal progress, where his 'doings' off the field frequently attracted more attention from the press than his largely unmemorable batting. For in one particular W.G. had not changed. Try as he might – and he did not try very hard – he could not help annoying a familiar gallery of puffed-up Australian cricket officials and opinionated press pundits. He behaved, at times, extremely badly. It made great copy.

'Great Scott – such feet!,' an Australian reporter marvelled when he saw W.G. for the first time since the 1873–4 tour. 'He could get two pounds a week and his tucker merely to walk about in the grasshopper districts to kill off the pest . . . When fielding he stands point, where he does not have to run, and any ball within possible reach is sure to find a resting place in one of his vast, carpet bag-like hands.'

Fatter and slower, W.G. soon began to push himself about in a manner that was bound to infuriate his hosts. In the second game of the tour against Victoria at Melbourne he had to respond during the lunch interval to a toast from a local bigwig. Keen to get on with the cricket, W.G. announced 'that the time at his disposal was hardly sufficient for such a speech as he was accustomed to make, and, under the circumstances, it was scarcely worth while commencing'. Victoria's batting had collapsed before lunch and by the scheduled tea interval W.G. was at the wicket and looking good. 'At 4 o'clock the bell rang for the usual adjournment, but although some of the Victorians showed a desire to leave, Grace ignored it and went on batting [Cheers from the crowd].' W.G. scored 159 not out, his only century of the tour.

On Christmas Day, W.G. sent world-weary greetings from Melbourne's Oriental Hotel to his cousin William Rees, who had settled in New Zealand. 'Cricket is played out here in a very bad spirit, which if continued will ruin the game, as after all it is a game of pleasure,' Grace complained. 'Here everyone suspects his opponents of cheating and trying to best one another. The umpires are all bad and some are unfair as well.'

W.G. probably had two incidents in mind when he wrote his unseasonal letter. On 4 December, 'a most vexatious delay' occurred before the start of the game against New South Wales at Sydney, when the home team objected to the Melbourne professional Denis Cotter standing as an umpire for the English.

Several members of the New South Wales side thought Cotter had been biased against them in the recent inter-colonial match at Melbourne against Victoria. 'This little episode at the beginning of the match was not pleasant, and the Englishmen displayed a generous feeling in giving way, Shaw being appointed umpire in place of Cotter,' the Sydney *Evening News* reported. In the next game against Eighteen of Cumberland County, Grace got into a row with the home captain about who had won the toss. W.G. insisted he had won and marched off the field in a huff.

W.G. was therefore in a mood to suspect Australian players and officials of any low-down trick when the first Test match of the three-Test series began at Melbourne on New Year's Day. Immediately before the start of play, Australia's captain and wicket-keeper Jack Blackham managed to confirm W.G.'s suspicion that he was dealing with cricketing equivalents of card-sharps.

Blackham was desperate to bat when he met W.G. in the pavilion to toss for choice of innings. The pitch looked good, the weather was perfect for batting, and Australia's star fast bowler Charles Turner was ill with a stomach upset. Melbourne's *The Argus* reported that Blackham 'fossicked an old and battered penny out of his pocket, which bore evidence of having been tossed many a time, and sometimes heavily'. In *The Australasian*'s account, W.G. remarked with surprise, 'There's a thing to toss with.' Blackham tossed and because the coin was so tarnished, went 'down on his hands and knees [and] found after close inspection that he had won'. The wicketkeeper got to his feet and announced he would bat, allowing Turner to go back to bed at the team's hotel. Grace then took the coin and tossed it 'experimentally' several times to check it was not loaded.

There *was* something rather odd about Blackham producing a coin at the start of an international match where, as one former Australian Test player pointed out, 'you [could] hardly tell the head from the tail'. Some newspapers suggested that Blackham's coin was his 'lucky one'; yet if that was the case, why did Blackham not use it when tossing as captain of Victoria in the second game of the tour?

So did Blackham cheat? Scrabbling around on his hands and knees, it was entirely Blackham's fault that W.G. could not be sure.

The Australians did not take full advantage of Blackham's lucky toss. In front of a sell-out crowd of about twenty thousand, they struggled to 191 for seven wickets by the close of play, with Turner the next man due to bat. To add to Blackham's worries, the New South Wales player Harry Moses had wrenched his left leg going for a quick single and could only carry on batting with the help of a runner. In a small act of chivalry, largely unnoticed by the Australian press, 'Dr W.G. Grace' had a look at Moses' injury that evening at the Oriental Hotel.

Turner, fully recovered, scored 29 on the next day, which in a tight game turned out to be crucial runs. W.G. now showed both the best and the worst side of his competitive nature. He opened the batting and scored 50, and then watched as George Bean and Maurice Read took the score to 171 for three, only 69 runs behind Australia's first innings total. Bean had just reached 50 when he pulled a ball in the air towards the local Melbourne player William Bruce, fielding on the boundary. Bruce raced in and caught the ball just above the ground. It was a critical moment, turning the game Australia's way. By the end of the day, England had subsided to 248 for seven.

When Bruce reached the pavilion, W.G. confronted the fielder and suggested aggressively that he had in fact scooped up the ball after it hit the ground. Bruce denied he had cheated and went straight to his friends in the Australian press to give his side of the story. Grace had gone too far – a fact he may have realised when he refused to talk to the same reporters. To get it all out of his system, W.G. spent the evening watching an inter-colonial boxing contest at the Melbourne Athletic Club.

On Monday (4 January), Bruce got his own back on Grace, fielding dangerously close at silly point. Bruce scored 40, under orders to grind out a winning total, however slowly it took. At the other end, the Australian opener Alick Bannerman infuriated W.G. and stupefied the crowd by taking almost four hours to score 41.

On Tuesday afternoon England finally dismissed Australia for a total of 236 and the spectators could wake up again. England needed 213 to win with one more day to play. Once again, W.G. resorted to the muddled tactic of reshuffling England's batting order, as Harris and Hornby had done unsuccessfully in the 1880 and 1882 Oval Test matches. Stoddart, a natural attacker, opened the batting, while the more defensive Abel dropped to number five. W.G. was worried by a poor weather forecast for Wednesday and was 'sending in his hitting batsmen to force runs while the wicket and weather held good, a sound policy under the circumstances,' *The Argus* commented. Yet Abel was good enough to change his normal game; it was as if W.G. did not trust the Surrey professional.

For a while all went well as Grace and Stoddart rapidly took the total to 60. Then everything went horribly wrong. W.G. and Stoddart were dismissed and England collapsed to 104 for seven at the close, facing almost certain defeat.

It took Australia only half an hour on Wednesday to win the match by 54 runs. Grace was furious: with his batsmen for letting him down, and with the Australian press for wanting to talk to him. 'England's greatest cricketer was in a very bad temper over the defeat of the Englishmen, and when questioned said: "I have nothing to say to the Press, especially the evening Press. They do not know when to tell the truth."' W.G. was alluding to his spat with Bruce, who now summoned anonymous 'friends' (probably including Bruce himself) to declare they were 'very indignant at the action of the ungracious Grace'.

One New South Wales editorial writer (also anonymous) ratcheted up the indignation for his own and his readers' entertainment: 'Grace has proved himself to be a thorough-paced prig and one of these days when he is engaged in his favourite pastime of putting on airs and sneering at the "professional" players in those "blawsted colonial teams", he will get landed on the nasal organ so suddenly that he will see a whole display of Pain's fireworks free of charge.'

*

The Australian player Harry Moses had still not fully recovered from his leg injury when the second Test began at Sydney on 29 January. Before the game, according to the *Sydney Morning Herald*, Grace had told Blackham that 'if Moses broke down, neither fielder nor substitute to run for him would be allowed, the injury having been received in a former match'. Moses did break down when he batted on the first day, prompting W.G. to approach Blackham. According to the wicketkeeper, W.G. said, 'Jack, you can have a man to run for Moses.' The same runner then acted as a fielding substitute for the injured Australian batsman. 'This was ... simply an act of courtesy,' the *Herald* noted, 'because Grace would have been within his rights in declining any substitute for him.' He was not such a 'thorough-paced prig' after all.

At this stage, England looked on course for victory. Lohmann, in perhaps the best bowling spell of his life, took eight wickets for 58 runs in Australia's total of 144 all out. Bobby Abel then scored 132 not out in a total of 307 all out. Grace's team therefore spent Sunday in Sydney going to church, writing letters home and looking forward to Australia's likely defeat. He did not yet know it, but W.G. was about to endure three of the worst days of his cricketing life.

On Monday, the South Australian John Lyons scored 134 in even time, while at the other end Alick Bannerman dug in so deep that he almost burrowed his way back to the 'mother country'. Bannerman took more than seven hours to score 91, while W.G.'s *bête noire* Bruce scored 72. England eventually bowled out Australia on Tuesday afternoon for 391. Grace's team required 236 runs to win, with a little more than a day's play left.

During Australia's innings the elder brother of the Victoria cricketer Bob McLeod had suddenly died of flu. McLeod batted and then left the ground to return to Melbourne for the funeral. Before the start of England's innings, Grace sought out Blackham again and said the Australians could use a second substitute fielder for McLeod, as well as the one for Moses. It was another small example of W.G.'s sportsmanship which most of the Australian press failed to notice.

His business done, W.G. walked out to open with Bobby Abel in worsening light. First Abel went, caught for 1, then George Bean went, caught for 4. Then W.G. went, caught by Blackham for 5. Twenty thousand spectators roared at Grace's dismissal: 'Hats, sticks, umbrellas, coats and all sorts of paraphernalia were hoisted into the air ... W.G. returned to the pavilion with a heavier step than usual.' And then it started to rain, with play abandoned for the rest of the day.

Next day Stoddart gave the Australians a foretaste of his brilliance, scoring 69 in an innings that showed he could defend as well as attack. It was too late. England lost by 72 runs, and with it the Test series. In victory, Blackham went out of his way to quash wild newspaper allegations that W.G. had behaved badly towards the Australians. On the contrary, Blackham said, Grace had offered the home team two substitutes and acted like a 'genuine sportsman'.

Blackham's chivalry, which erased the stain of his 'fossicked' coin at Melbourne, failed to stop a fresh assault on Grace from *The Truth*, a republican newspaper in Sydney. *The Truth* had already made up its mind about Grace's character and had just republished a proven lie to bring its version of the truth to light: a fabricated letter that W.G. had purportedly written during his first 1873–4 tour. In it, 'W.G. Grace' abused Australians and the professionals in his team as beneath his social dignity.

The real W.G. had already dealt with this crude forgery in 1874 by sending warning notes to the few British newspapers that dared to reprint the letter. Now he wrote again from the Grand Hotel on Castlereagh Street to Sydney's *Evening News*:

> I trust that my position in life and in the cricket world is too well known for it to be believed by right-minded people that I could demean myself by descending to such scurrilous abuse as is contained in that letter ... I ask you to permit me through your columns to publish this my positive and most emphatic denial of being the author or writer of the letter referred to.

Reading *The Truth*, Grace must have felt there was nothing he could do in Australia to stop such character assassination. Yet he failed utterly to understand how he let down his Australian friends as well. Major Ben Wardill, Melbourne CC's capable secretary, was about to become W.G.'s next unintended victim.

Wardill had effectively been acting as Lord Sheffield's tour manager. Alfred Shaw, the official manager, was too busy flogging cricket bats and dealing with his partner Shrewsbury's constant correspondence to worry about tedious details such as booking hotels, trains and coastal steamers, or finalising cricket fixtures. From his base in Melbourne, Wardill valiantly held the tour together, peppering Lord Sheffield, Shaw and W.G. by telegram and letter with the latest information about dates, match venues and accommodation as the team travelled around Victoria and New South Wales.

Wardill had agreed with W.G. that the team would return to Melbourne from Sydney after the second Test match. They would go to the horse races (a particular request by W.G.) and then travel to Tasmania to play a couple of games, before returning to Melbourne. Without telling Wardill, W.G. decided instead to go direct by steamer from Sydney to Hobart at the end of February. 'After all the telegrams, letter's arrangements & rearrangements both here and in Tasmania to alter the dates to suit you & the amateurs to see the Races, you are not coming!!!' the normally affable Wardill scribbled to W.G. ''Pon my soul, you all deserve I don't know what.'

W.G. did not care. On the day he probably received Wardill's note, he and Agnes travelled out to Westleigh Park on the western outskirts of Sydney to watch Bessie play for the Ladies of Neutral Bay against the Gentlemen. Bessie got the top score of 20 and then took fourteen wickets in the gentlemen's two innings to win the game for the ladies. It was 'more than a fair record for the young lady under the blaze of an Australian sun,' a 'lady correspondent' in Sydney reported.

For Grace, Bessie's impressive display gave him a brief respite from the nuisances and annoyances that seemed to be coming from all directions. The next one was Mr Briscoe, the local umpire for the team's final match in Sydney against New South Wales. On the third day Briscoe – a government land agent by profession – rejected an appeal by MacGregor, the English wicketkeeper, for a catch off the bowling of Lohmann. Briscoe said he was unsighted by Lohmann following through and obstructing his view of the batsman.

W.G. approached Briscoe and protested against the umpire's decision. Oddly, in view of his later indignation, Briscoe carried on umpiring till the end of the New South Wales innings and then walked off the field and out of the ground; the land agent was staging a personal one-man strike. Alick Bannerman's brother Charles now took Briscoe's place for the rest of the game, which the English won easily.

Briscoe's protest against W.G.'s vile slur on the umpire's integrity had only just begun. 'Dr Grace, in no unmeasured terms, told me my decision was "unpardonable, that I would not give anyone out, and that I must be blind, and that his team had better go home at once",' Briscoe told *The Referee*, a Sydney sports newspaper. Briscoe was a committee member of the New South Wales Cricket Association and he also sent his colleagues a letter demanding action against W.G. The committee duly decided that 'a copy of Mr Briscoe's letter be forwarded to Dr Grace with a view to that gentleman furnishing the Committee with any remarks he may deem necessary on the statements therein made'. Grace's reply was direct: 'I did not insult Mr Briscoe, nor did I think him a cheat,' he wrote.

Sterner measures against Grace were required. At a special meeting of the NSWCA it was resolved that 'Dr Grace be asked to more clearly reply to the statements made by Mr Briscoe; and to give a direct answer as to whether he did, or did not, make use of the expressions complained of, & if it is true, that, he in no measured terms, questioned the decision of the umpire on the occasion referred to'. Furthermore, the committee proposed to collect evidence from the two New South Wales batsmen 'who were at the wickets at the time', from the other umpire, and from the New South Wales captain, 'to enable the Comtee to thoroughly investigate the matter'. It did not occur to the NSWCA that Grace had no interest in the committee's opinion.

A pause in the Briscoe affair ensued, as W.G. attended to the less important matter (from the NSWCA's point of view) of the final Test match in Adelaide. He and the team offended the Mayor of Adelaide before the game by failing to show up for a civic reception. W.G. claimed it was all the fault of the secretary of the South Australian Cricket Association, who had failed to alert them in time at the hotel about the invitation to drinks with the mayor. 'Three of us were having baths and two others were waiting to have one,' he insisted.

On the field, W.G. scored a farewell 58 in front of a crowd of about ten thousand, after surviving some early nerves and 'streaky' shots. He was upstaged by Stoddart, who made 134 with the kind of supercharged batting associated with W.G. in his prime. Briggs, Lohmann and Attewell then bowled out Australia so easily that England won by the huge margin of an innings and 230 runs. At the end of the game, 'most of the young urchins on the ground rushed to get near the doctor and touch him, indeed the champion found it difficult to make a passage to the reserve'.

It only remained to deal with Mr Briscoe once and for all. 'I did tell Mr Briscoe that his decision was unpardonable, and that he must pay more attention,' W.G. wrote testily to the NSWCA from Adelaide's Botanic Hotel. 'I did not insult Briscoe, nor do I think him a cheat, but I am sorry to say he is not a good umpire.' With that parting shot, W.G. gathered up Agnes, Bessie and Charlie, plus a large bundle of colonial newspapers, and left Australia for ever.

26

CLIFTON MAN

On the evening W.G. returned to Bristol, a young local reporter called Archie Powell knocked on the door of Thrissell House, hoping to get an interview. W.G. let him in and 'was very kind and talkative on a variety of subjects that wasn't cricket, but I failed to get anything out of him about the tour'. As Powell was leaving, W.G. explained that he had to 'reserve his impressions' of the tour for a London journal, the reason he had brought home all those Australian newspapers.

Grace's article in *The Cricket Field* contained little of interest. He had another dig at Briscoe, whose great matter was still under consideration in Sydney, and indeed still is; Briscoe's case was never officially closed. W.G. generously acknowledged that the Australians deserved to win the series, but the article's flat, plodding prose betrayed his boredom when writing about the past.

Grace did not need the money anyway because for the first time in his life he was unquestionably rich. Sales of *Cricket* were going well, with about eighteen thousand copies sold by early 1893. Brownlee now produced a shorter 'continental' edition of *Cricket* for the French publisher Hachette & Leo, which probably intended selling the book to British expatriates in Paris.

All of this income, real or potential, was dwarfed by the £3000, plus expenses, that Grace received from Lord Sheffield for the 1891–2 Australia tour. W.G. hardly had to touch this money during the tour, when the Earl or local hosts paid for all his family's expenses. Freed from financial worry, W.G. decided it was time to move up in the world, and specifically, from Thrissell House to a more affluent part of Bristol. Besides, W.G and Agnes's home for the past decade was under siege from the builders.

In the autumn of 1892 work began on a new church meeting hall at the corner of Thrissell Street and Stapleton Road on land that had previously formed part of W.G.'s garden. Grace came to an amicable arrangement with the freeholder James Farmer (his next-door neighbour) over the development, which suggests W.G. received some compensation. Nonetheless, Thrissell House would soon adjoin a large public building, while W.G. would have less space in the back garden for his cricket net. He and Agnes started house-hunting.

In February 1893 they moved into a handsome three-storey house at the corner of Victoria Square in Clifton, which Grace rented through Messrs Lewis and Sons, a local estate agent. W.G.'s choice of residence undercuts the later myth that he was a countryman at heart. With Lord Sheffield's money in the bank, he could have afforded a fine country house in south Gloucestershire. Instead, he chose to live in the smartest part of Bristol, while satisfying the 'rural' side of his character through his regular outings with the Clifton Beagles and his shooting weekends with his gunmaker friend Herbert Gibbs.

Despite his move to Clifton, W.G. had no intention of giving up his Poor Law medical officer's post with the Barton Regis Union. Following his tour of Australia, Grace's opponents on the board of guardians abandoned any lingering hope that he might become a full-time medical officer. 'Who is this Dr Smith?' the builder and Poor Law guardian John Bastow sarcastically enquired in February 1893 when W.G. proposed his latest locum as cover for the next cricket season. 'We have heard of Brown, Jones and Robinson, and might just as well elect one of them. (Laughter).' Bastow and several other guardians pointedly abstained when the rest of the board voted to allow Smith's appointment.

Smith and from time to time W.G. still worked from the surgery at Thrissell House, with Grace probably subletting the rest of the building to his locums or other tenants to bring in more money. However, in March 1894, twelve months before Grace's lease expired, W.G.'s landlord James Farmer gave him a year's notice to quit. Farmer, now based next door at 59 Stapleton Road, was a window-blind maker and may have wanted more space for his business. In any case, Grace stayed put, probably by agreeing to extend the leasehold at a higher annual rate. Farmer soon abandoned his window-blind shop, retiring to Weston-super-Mare.

W.G. led an extraordinary double life as he shuttled back and forth between Victoria Square and Stapleton Road. At work he was still a modest parish doctor, seeing patients at the lower end of Victorian society. A particularly nasty case came up in November 1894 when Grace treated Rosa Gannaway, who had left her violent, drunken husband. Fred Gannaway was then indicted for attempted sexual assault on their daughter Sarah. At the Bristol assize, W.G. certified to Mr Justice Grantham that Rosa was too unwell to give evidence. Grace had only just left the witness box when a court official hurried up to him with an urgent request from the judge: could W.G. see Mr Justice Grantham in his chamber immediately. Puzzled, Grace did as he was told. Mr Justice Grantham produced a large book, opened it and handed Grace a pen. The judge wanted the signature of the world's most famous cricketer for his personal autograph collection.

W.G.'s home life at Clifton was altogether more agreeable. During the summer, he entertained visiting 'gentlemen' amateurs from the county teams that came to play Gloucestershire. When he closed the door on his last guest, W.G. retired to bed as master of a household that was far more spaciously accommodated than at Thrissell House. Agnes's widowed Aunt Caroline had moved with them to Victoria Square, while Bertie, Bessie and Charlie were all still living at home. Only Edgar, now a junior naval officer, had left for good, with a bedroom always ready for him when he was granted shore leave.

W.G. tried to be a good parent. Yet despite Agnes's calming influence, his mixed record as a father brought to mind his chief flaw as a cricket captain: an inability to see the world from someone else's point of view. In particular, Grace could not understand why two of his sons, Bertie and Charlie, failed to rise above what he saw as inexcusable mediocrity.

No son of a Victorian hero lived under such a crushing weight of paternal expectation as the bespectacled William Gilbert Grace Jr. 'Will your cricket reputation be handed on to any other bearing your name?' the *Pall Mall Gazette* had asked W.G. in 1884, when Bertie was only ten. 'I think my son W.G. Grace, jun, will,' W.G. wrote. 'He promises to be a very good cricketer.' The press soon picked up Grace's cue. 'There will be another W.G. Grace among the great cricketers if the eldest offspring of the famous Gloucestershire man should continue as he has begun,' one newspaper reported in May 1888, seizing on the fact that Bertie had taken fifteen wickets in a village game against Twenty-Four of Bedminster.

W.G. did not heed the early warning signs that Bertie was an earnest trier at sports rather than a natural winner. In the spring of 1893, Grace entered Bertie for the Public Schools' national quarter-mile championship, enlisting John Toms, a local Bristol athlete, to help with his son's training. 'Come on, lazybones!' W.G. roared from the sidelines, as Bertie pounded round the county cricket ground at Ashley Down. W.G. and Bertie travelled up to London for the race at Stamford Bridge (now Chelsea Football Club's ground). As always, Bertie did his best. He finished third, with the joy of the long train journey back to Bristol with his father yet to come.

Bertie was equally disappointing at cricket, at least from

W.G.'s point of view. In 1896, Bertie obligingly took guard in a posed photograph during a game at Hove. The picture (see page 12 of picture section) could have been used by any coach to demonstrate 'how not to bat'. Bertie's elbows and back are stiff, while his bat is far away from his pads, offering the bowler an inviting gap to target the stumps. He looks out of place peering through his spectacles, as if he would rather be in a library.

Bertie was in fact a capable student, winning a scholarship to Clifton in 1887 worth £30 per year (almost half the annual fee for day boys) from the prep school he attended next to the college with his younger brother Edgar. Yet even at his studies, Bertie suffered the burden of being his father's son. 'As a mathematician he is said to show remarkable promise,' a newspaper columnist ventured in 1888, when Bertie was fourteen. 'He is only a boy, and youthful geniuses do not always come up to expectation; but in the opinion of those who were qualified to judge, there is the making of a Senior Wrangler in him.' Bertie was good, not great at maths, as his school reports indicated. 'His mathematics have [sic] made considerable progress,' a teacher noted in April 1890. 'Has done some good problem papers,' another report observed in June; but then in July, a teacher 'complains of maths'.

Bertie persevered, one character trait he certainly inherited from W.G. In October 1893 he went up to read maths at Pembroke College, Cambridge, on a scholarship, having finished at Clifton as captain of both the cricket and rugby teams. Alarmingly for Bertie, W.G. was sure his son would gain a cricket Blue the following summer.

Edgar, two years younger than Bertie, attended Bristol Grammar School from 1886 to 1888 and then spent the rest of his life putting clear blue water between himself and his domineering father. Unlike W.G., who felt ill at the sight of a boat, Edgar loved the sea and joined the navy in 1890 as a cadet on board the training ship HMS *Britannia*, stationed at Dartmouth. Alone among W.G.'s extended family, Edgar felt at home in large bureaucratic organisations, rising relentlessly through the ranks over the coming decades until he became an admiral. From a distance, W.G. was proud of his naval son, even though Edgar unaccountably preferred tennis to cricket.

In early 1892, Edgar completed his cadetship at Dartmouth and was assigned as a midshipman to the battleship HMS *Victoria*, based in Malta. W.G. and Agnes hoped to meet Edgar at Malta on their way back from Australia, and then did not expect to see him again for several years. Fortunately, they saw him much sooner. In June 1893, HMS *Victoria* accidentally collided with another British naval ship off the coast of Tripoli and sank. Three hundred and fifty-eight crew members drowned in the disaster, including Vice-Admiral Sir George Tryon, commander of the Mediterranean fleet. Edgar was not among them, having returned to Bristol on sick leave. He attributed his lucky escape to God, reinforcing the evangelical streak that already coursed through his soul.

Agnes and W.G.'s third son Charlie, born in 1882, was not academic and therefore identified as dim, in the narrow Victorian definition of intelligence. E.M.'s son Edgar remembered Charlie as 'not as bright as his brothers'. There is some circumstantial evidence that W.G. took steps to rectify Charlie's perceived lack of brainpower. In 1896, the head of a school for 'backward or delicate boys' in the Gloucestershire village of Ashleworth named Grace in a newspaper advertisement as someone who could supply references for the institution. By then Charlie had scraped into Clifton, where he was soon bringing dreadful reports from his teachers back to Victoria Square. 'Knows very little classics & is shy and faint-hearted,' one teacher complained at the end of Charlie's first term. On a brighter note, Charlie's conduct was 'good'.

No such worries attached to Bessie, who turned fourteen immediately after her return from Australia. She returned to Clifton High School for Girls, a short walk from Victoria Square, where her academic grades suggest she was an average rather than an excellent scholar. Besse's forte was sport, and especially cricket, and she became a mainstay of the school's team. 'She is the very picture of a well-built, athletic British maiden,' *Woman* magazine reported, 'as she stands at the wicket in her spotless cream flannels and straw hat. Spectators who have come to scoff remain to wonder at the easy way in which she masters the bowling.' According to *Woman*, 'among the ranks of her admiring school-fellows may be seen occasionally, on a half-holiday, the black-bearded, stalwart figure of the champion applauding his daughters "fours", and revelling in her inherited prowess'.

If you were Bertie, it was all a bit unfair. Bessie's batting performances for the school in 1893 and 1894 were actually quite poor, with a fair number of ducks and single-digit scores recorded against the likes of Miss Fyffe's XI and Mrs Baker's XI. But she was W.G.'s favourite child and could do no wrong in his eyes. 'My own daughter was a real good bat, a splendid fielder and a fair under-hand bowler,' he wrote in an article for the *Pall Mall Gazette* in June 1895. Sadly for Bessie, W.G. had now forced his daughter to retire: 'As to the innovation of ladies cricket, I consider it only a game for school-girls ... As she [Bessie] is now 17 her cricket days are over.' W.G.'s firm views on the place of women in cricket – behind the boundary rope, and definitely not in the pavilion – cast a revealing light on his mother's alleged role as his childhood cricket tutor. It is unlikely that the young Gilbert Grace would have paid any attention to Martha Grace's analysis of his batting technique, simply because she was a woman.

W.G. also looked close to retirement during the 1894 season. His autocratic leadership of a failing Gloucestershire was now openly ridiculed, outside and inside the county. All W.G.'s cunning plans to strengthen the side seemed to flop, his biggest embarrassment being the recruitment of the Australian left-arm medium-pace bowler John Ferris. In 1890, Grace had found Ferris a job with a Bristol stockbroker, allowing the Australian to qualify by residence for Gloucestershire. Ferris then emerged from his enforced sabbatical minus most of his bowling powers.

The Ferris fiasco steeled Gloucestershire's committee to try and impose a selection panel on W.G. in the winter of 1892–3.

Grace was so angry that he spent the next few months resigning the captaincy, early and often. He resigned before the 1893
season, carried on captaining anyway, withdrew his resignation
at the end of the season, thought about the matter, resigned
again and withdrew his resignation for a second time when the
committee begged him to reconsider.

Through this mayhem, W.G. remained unmoved on one
point. 'With regard to the Selection Committee I will have
nothing to do with it,' he wrote to the main committee in
1893. 'I do not think it will help us to win matches, or that it
would work at all satisfactorily, what is more, most if not all of
the playing members of the Club are of my opinion.' This was
not necessarily true. During 1893, Gloucestershire's small band
of poorly paid professionals expressed increasing unhappiness at
Grace's habit of dropping one or more of them from the side.

To add to his misery, Grace's two best friends at
Gloucestershire, Frizzy Bush and Frank Townsend, had both
retired. Bush had quit in 1890, to concentrate on the family's
warehouse business and his resplendent part-time career as
Bristol's civic sword bearer. Townsend's departure was sadder.
At the end of 1892 he was declared bankrupt, when his prepara-
tory school next to Clifton College went bust. All Townsend's
assets were sold off and to avoid further shame he and his family
decamped to the Devon seaside town of Barnstaple, where he
became a private tutor. The committee voted Townsend and his
wife a 'gift of 100 guineas ... as a slight acknowledgement' of
his services to the county. Gloucestershire's committee minutes,
written by E.M., offer no clue about what the county's badly paid
professionals thought of Townsend's 'gift'.

Townsend's personal financial crisis seems to have had
no impact on his wardrobe. Shortly before his bankruptcy,
Townsend posed with his two sons Charlie and Frank Jr. and
W.G. outside a cricket pavilion (see page 10 of picture section).
Townsend looks dapper in a striped blazer and matching bow
tie. One would not know from the picture that W.G. was nine
months younger than Townsend. Grace seems old, his beard now

mostly grey, his huge girth scarcely concealed by his bulging blazer.

After Lord Sheffield's tour, W.G.'s cricketing decline accelerated. He scored a total of only four first-class centuries and took just 82 first-class wickets from the start of the 1892 season to the end of 1894. By then, the promising young Gloucestershire amateur Gilbert Jessop thought it was 'game over' for forty-six-year-old W.G. 'Even home supporters despaired of his ever regaining form,' Jessop recalled.

However, W.G. had been counting. In June 1894 he had scored the 97th first-class century of his career against a weak Cambridge University attack, and another hundred soon afterwards brought his tally to 98. No batsman had ever scored a hundred first-class centuries and no one apart from W.G. had ever come close. His nearest rival, Arthur Shrewsbury, had 'only' made 41 first-class hundreds by the end of 1894. As W.G. saw the matter, it was definitely not 'game over'.

27

THE NATIONAL TREASURE

On 17 May 1895, in fine but chilly weather, W.G. walked out to the middle at Ashley Down with his eighteen-year-old godson Charlie Townsend to continue their partnership against Somerset. A week earlier, W.G. had scored his 99th century, against Sussex, and now his overnight score stood at 32. Agnes and Bessie, wrapped up against the icy wind, were watching from the members' enclosure, but on this working Friday, only a few hundred other spectators ringed the ground.

W.G. and Charlie were soon scoring freely against Somerset's weak bowling attack. Boundaries to the leg, to the off and over the bowler's head were frequent, one or two balls being sent 'right over the track', the *Bristol Mercury* reported. Shortly after he passed 90, W.G. yelled to the scorer to check his and Townsend's respective totals. The scorer confirmed that W.G. was on 98.

Somerset's bowler and captain Sammy Woods now had an uncharacteristic attack of nerves. Born in Australia, Woods was by nature and talent the prototype of a much later Somerset all-rounder, Ian Botham. Like Botham, Woods was a big, athletic man, who bowled fast when the mood took him, but also relied on variations of speed, length and movement through the air and off the seam. Like Botham, too, Woods was a brilliant, aggressive middle-order batsman, and sociable off the field. During three years at Cambridge, Woods cheerfully claimed that he never had time to read a book in between all the parties he attended.

At this moment, Woods froze at the thought he might dismiss W.G. on the brink of Grace's 100th hundred. Woods walked nervously back to his mark, jogged in slowly and bowled the most depressing delivery of W.G.'s career: a deliberate easy ball to leg, which W.G. hit to the boundary to bring up his landmark century.

Agnes and Bessie cheered with the rest of the scattered spectators, as E.M. trotted out from the pavilion with an enormous jeroboam of champagne. Woods and the Somerset players toasted W.G., who now revealed one reason why his tally of hundreds was so much greater than any other batsman in history. In Victorian cricket's gentlemanly code of honour, most batsmen would have returned Woods's chivalrous gesture and got out. Grace responded quite differently. As he drank his bubbly, W.G. looked at the tiring Woods and Somerset's other, weaker bowlers and must have thought: Why not?

About two hours later (the press reports are unclear), E.M. trotted out with more champagne. W.G. had reached 200. W.G. cruised on, while E.M. possibly began making enquiries about nearby wine merchants who might have emergency supplies of bubbly. W.G. had scored 288 when he mistimed a drive off Woods and was caught near the boundary by the Somerset professional Edwin Tyler. Grace was disgusted at his stupidity, just twelve runs short of a triple-century.

Next day, Gloucestershire easily beat Somerset and W.G. caught a late afternoon train to London. He was off to the Café Monaco on Piccadilly Circus – not to celebrate his 100th hundred but to join a welcome-home dinner for Andrew Stoddart, who had just led England to a thrilling 3-2 victory in the latest Test series in Australia. W.G. finally reached the Café Monaco at

9 p.m. and, as he entered the restaurant, Stoddart and his fellow guests rose to applaud him; even Spofforth, present in his latest incarnation as Hampstead CC's captain.

Unfortunately for Grace, the press and the general public had failed to grasp the magnitude of his achievement. One widely syndicated report of W.G's 288 described him as 'the hero of yesterday's play' without mentioning that he had scored his 100th first-class hundred. In a longer report, the London *Daily News* buried the 'interesting' fact that W.G. had 'now, in first-class cricket, played a hundred three-figure innings' in the last line of the story. During the next few days, the national press gradually gave Grace's landmark more coverage, but it was not particularly big news. In its round-up of the previous week's 'wonderful scoring', for example, the Dundee *Evening Telegraph* dealt with W.G.'s 100th hundred after Nottinghamshire's record-breaking total of 726 against Sussex.

A week after his innings against Somerset, W.G. dropped a heavy hint that the cricket world really ought to take more notice. On 24 May he scored 257 for Gloucestershire against Kent at Gravesend. Here was 'further proof which the champion cricketer of all time afforded of his wonderful vitality,' observed a syndicated report, which merely mentioned in passing that it was W.G.'s 'third three-figure innings this year, and his 101st in first-class cricket'. In Gloucestershire's second innings W.G. scored 73 not out in just over an hour to win the game. Hubert Preston, a future editor of *Wisden*, recalled seeing W.G. trotting at the end of the match 'from the dressing tent in his tweed tail suit and hard felt hat, carrying his heavy cricket bag to a four-wheeler cab which took him to the station'.

W.G. was on a roll, yet the press beyond the Bristol area still refused to accept that anything of national note had happened. In late May John Le Sage, the editor of the *Daily Telegraph*, received a proposal from a Bristol solicitor called Haythorne Latcham suggesting 'a World-wide 1s subscription' fund to present to W.G. to mark his achievement in scoring 100 centuries. Le Sage came from Bristol, which is probably why Latcham approached him. However, the editor was a former war correspondent with no great interest in cricket. He instructed an assistant to reply that 'the Editor must respectfully decline to take charge of this subscription'.

All the pressure for a second Grace testimonial fund came once again from Gloucestershire, as it had done for the first such fund in the late 1870s. James Arrowsmith and Methven Brownlee took the lead, with support from E.M. as Gloucestershire's secretary, and W.G.'s almost certain involvement. Nobody's motives in this murky saga were entirely altruistic. Even Gloucestershire CCC had a vested interest in a Grace testimonial as a useful vehicle for attracting publicity and members to the club.

The challenge was getting the attention of anyone outside Bristol. In late May, Gloucestershire CCC's committee voted to send a 'memorial' to MCC proposing that Lord's should organise a national fund. If MCC failed to cooperate, Gloucestershire would start a national fund of its own. The committee further voted £100 from the club's meagre resources. At the same time, the Mayor of Bristol and other civic dignitaries proposed a 'distinctly national and substantial testimonial' to W.G. 'in recognition of his cricket achievements'. On 30 May, two senior Gloucestershire members – probably Arrowsmith and Brownlee – visited Lord's to press the county's plan on the MCC committee. They arrived in time to watch W.G. score 169 for Gloucestershire against Middlesex in front of a large Lord's crowd, in the process becoming the first batsman ever to score 1000 first-class runs in May.

At last someone of national standing took note of W.G.'s performances: Queen Victoria's son Bertie, the Prince of Wales, who had been a lifelong fan of W.G. The heir to the throne now commanded his private secretary to write to his cricketing hero Grace. 'His Royal Highness cannot allow an event of such interest to all lovers of our great national game to pass unnoticed by him, and he has desired me to offer you his hearty congratulations upon this magnificent performance,' Sir Francis

Knollys wrote to Grace on Saturday, 1 June. Critically, Knollys made clear the prince's congratulations covered both W.G.'s 1000 runs in May (a baffling statistic to non-cricket lovers) *and* his 100 hundreds (easy to understand).

Knollys was not in the habit of leaking the Prince of Wales's personal correspondence to the press. Yet the letter to Grace was all over the London and provincial newspapers on the following Monday (3 June), from the *Morning Post* to the *Hartlepool Mail*. There is only possible conclusion: either Grace or someone close to him must have leaked the letter, probably to spur MCC into action. If so, the ploy failed. When the MCC committee met later on Monday, it postponed any decision about W.G.'s testimonial until the following week. In Bristol, a local newspaper picked up rumours that the committee could not 'see their way to undertaking the organisation of such a fund'.

By dithering, MCC lost control of the plot. On 6 June Brownlee returned to Lord's to lobby the committee again. On the same day, or the next one, an immensely wealthy Yorkshire businessman, John Thomas North, sent a cheque for £50 to the still non-existent Grace testimonial fund, via *The Sportsman* newspaper. Helpfully, *The Sportsman* said it would forward North's cheque to Lord's or Bristol, depending on which was the right forwarding address. *The Sportsman* also offered to act as a receiving agency for any further contributions from the public.

By now Le Sage, the *Daily Telegraph*'s editor, had changed his mind about Latcham's proposal, mindful of the interest sparked by the Prince of Wales's letter and North's £50 donation. Le Sage went to the newspaper's proprietor Sir Edward Lawson (later Lord Burnham) and suggested that a fund for Grace organised by the newspaper would be an excellent way to increase circulation. As sometimes happens with newspaper editors, Le Sage suggested that the 'shilling' fund was his own idea, not Latcham's. In later years, Le Sage even fibbed that the thought had come to him while watching W.G. at Lord's.

On Saturday (8 June) the *Daily Telegraph* opened its national testimonial 'shilling' fund for Grace. 'Let us all unite to furnish

proof of the love which still attends in England and her depend-
encies a recognised specimen of true and trained English
manhood,' the *Telegraph* declared, as though W.G. were a ped-
igree bull. W.G. knew what was expected in return. 'I think I
should be less than human if I did not wish it [the shilling fund]
unbounded success, however unworthy I may be that it should
be so,' he wrote from Victoria Square.

MCC was now in serious danger of being written out of
the script completely. On Monday, 10 June, a full week after
the leaking of Knollys' letter, the committee ponderously confirmed that 'in reference to the desire which has been generally
expressed that a National Testimonial shall be presented to W.G.
Grace, the MCC approve the same and are willing to undertake
the direction & management'. It took another week for the club
to make a donation of 200 guineas (£210) to what it imperiously described as a national fund 'under the authority of the
Marylebone Cricket Club'.

By early 1896, Gloucestershire, MCC and the *Daily Telegraph* had
collectively raised £9073 8s 3d for W.G. from their three separate
funds. As with his much smaller 1879 testimonial, converting
this sum into modern money gives an inflated idea of Grace's
windfall. By 1948, the centenary of Grace's birth, £9073 was
'worth' about £29,000, based on retail price inflation. In 1998,
the modern conversion had grown to almost £600,000 and by
2015, the centenary of Grace's death, it had almost reached £1
million. A better comparative benchmark is wages at the time.
Shortly after W.G.'s testimonial the economist Arthur Bowley
estimated that in the mid–1890s workers in the mining, building,
printing and iron industries earned on average about £70 per
year. W.G. received almost 130 times this amount, still a fortune
by almost any contempoary reckoning.

How did a testimonial that began so uncertainly in June 1895
raise so much cash in barely six months? Part of the answer lay in
Grace's bat: for almost two months after his 288 against Somerset

he enjoyed a streak of form that distantly recalled his batting rampages of twenty years before.

On 14 June he scored 125 for MCC v Kent at Lord's ('A brilliant innings', *Manchester Courier*), following up on the same ground eight days later with 101 not out for Gents of England v I Zingari. The *Morning Post* reported of this latest innings: 'Grace's success was, of course, extremely popular, and the crowd after the player had retired cheered him persistently until he bowed his acknowledgements from a window in the pavilion.'

On 4 July W.G. was at Lord's again in his top hat and tails, this time with Agnes. After failing to make the Cambridge team as a freshman, Bertie had clawed his way into the side for the Varsity match against Oxford. In dull weather, before a crowd of more than ten thousand, Bertie jabbed and prodded his way to a 'very creditable' 40 as his proud parents looked on. 'The son of the Champion made some queer strokes, but, on the whole, his display was far from being a poor one,' the *Standard* noted diplomatically.

Five days later, Grace completed his seventh century of the season for the Gentlemen against the Players at Lord's, while the cartoonist Harry Furniss drew him in action. Furniss's fluid, vivid sketches of W.G. on this hot summer's day provide the only convincing visual evidence of Grace's dynamic batting style. Furniss also could not resist poking affectionate fun at W.G. as he drew the great batsman at rest, leaning on his bat to catch his breath, wiping the sweat off his forehead with a large handker-chief or clutching his stomach to get rid of a stitch. Indeed, there *was* something comically endearing as well as uplifting about a grossly overweight forty-six-year-old man scoring a hundred on a difficult Lord's pitch against Tom Richardson and Arthur Mold, two of the quickest bowlers in England. Here was another element of W.G.'s extraordinary appeal in the summer of 1895.

Grace's apotheosis came on the evening of 24 June when he arrived at Clifton's neo-classical Victoria Rooms for a banquet in his honour, wearing 'an enormous expanse of white shirt'. The banquet was a fundraiser, attended by about four hundred guests, most of whom had paid a subscription fee for the chance to dine with their hero.

Amid various flights of oratory, the newly appointed Bishop of Hereford John Percival (formerly the first headmaster of Clifton College) took wing with fanciful imaginings of W.G. as an ancient Greek warrior or a medieval crusader. Percival was actually playing for laughs, as the detailed report of his speech in the Bristol press next morning made clear. After his comic conceit, Percival made a serious point. W.G. had been born for 'something happier' than killing infidels: 'He was, perhaps, the man best known of all Englishmen wherever the English language was spoken, and he had set a great example, not only of physical strength, but of moral strength, the strength that kept a man going in the front of a great amusement, year after year.'

W.G.'s speech of thanks offered further proof that he was a capable public speaker. He was brief, courteous and self-deprecatingly funny about his ability as a cricketer (not bad) and his merits as a football referee (doubtful). W.G. also went out of his way to mention his friend Andrew Stoddart's 'great achievement' the previous winter in leading England to victory in the five-match series against Australia. Talking like a cricket fan rather than a star, W.G. recalled how 'he never knew more excitement than followed those contests'.

The next evening, W.G. attended another local dinner in his honour at the Century Club on Colston Street. Restricted to a hundred members, the club had been founded at the start of the decade to promote the interests of sport in the city. On this night Brownlee, W.G.'s shooting pal Herbert Gibbs and other friends saluted the guest of honour with a specially written song. Like the poetry of William McGonagall, the lyrics of 'The Nestor of the Bat' were memorably dire:

> From myriad throats a rousing cheer
> Salutes each hundredth run;
> From Prince and Peasant, knight and peer,
> Leaps forth the cry, 'Well done!'

Time spins his wheel with fury on,
But what recks [sic] Grace of that?
We hail him Great 'Centurion'
The Nestor of the Bat.

A month later, the publisher W. Upcott Gill rushed out Grace's *History of a Hundred Centuries*, available at all the best railway station bookstands for 6d. Here, according to the publicity, was a treat for every cricket fan: W.G.'s personal recollection of each individual century. In reality W.G. paid scant attention to the draft, which was rapidly churned out in his name by Bill Yardley, a former Kent cricketer turned burlesque dramatist. In the preface Yardley's 'W.G. Grace' offered his 'sincerest thanks to Mr Wisden of Cranbourn Street, Leicester Square' for providing copies of *Wisden Cricketers' Almanack* to assist with research for the book. Neither 'Mr Wisden' nor the real W.G. ever read this dedication. As Grace knew perfectly well, John Wisden, the 'Little Wonder' had died in 1884.

Outside the cricket world, W.G.'s extraordinary popularity in the summer of 1895 was less easy to explain. The *Daily Telegraph*'s fund, which collected about £5000, was a straightforward circulation booster, and there was a clear pattern of self-interest in many of the letters the newspaper published from contributors who sent in their money. Some of them were blatant publicity seekers.

'Being one of the softer sex, I *cannot*, therefore, play cricket,' wrote Phyllis Broughton, a chorus girl at London's Gaiety Theatre, 'but as a woman I admire superiority in a man, and I beg to send you twenty-one shillings for the Dr W.G. Grace Testimonial.' The actresses Mrs Patrick Campbell and Ellen Terry, looking to stay in the public eye, also sent 1 guinea apiece. Bram Stoker, soon to publish *Dracula*, informed the press that the Shakespearian actor Sir Henry Irving was 'delighted to add to the Grace Fund' the sum of 100 shillings.

It all became too much for the *Manchester Courier*, which

protested against 'the columns of nauseous nonsense that the public are every day invited to wade through in connection with the subscription ... One of the most remarkable features in the daily outpouring of correspondence is the prominence of actors' names in it, and only one degree less remarkable is the extreme silliness of the actors' attempts at wit and humour.'

There was a general election that summer, so W.G.'s testimonial also attracted politicians looking to gain some easy popularity. Lord Salisbury, the Conservative leader of the opposition, sent £5, a modest sum for the owner of substantial tracts of Dorset and Hertfordshire. The Liberal Prime Minister Lord Rosebery preferred horse racing to cricket, but after Salisbury's gesture he felt obliged to contribute £25. Rosebery lost the election anyway. Some opportunists seized on Grace's testimonial as a chance to use his name for their own profit. 'Dr W.G. Grace is the head of the Cricket World, and John A. Cooper takes the first position among Practical Furriers in the Provinces,' a notice announced in the *Sheffield Evening Telegraph*. Put another way, John A. Cooper was the W.G. Grace of provincial 'Practical Furriers'.

The Norwich mustard company Colman's probably decided to put Grace on a souvenir mustard tin after his testimonial got underway. It is not certain that W.G. was ever paid by Colman's for what became the most famous advertising image associated with him. Unilever, which now owns the brand, has no record of a contract or any other information about the tin in its archive. Colman's picture of Grace was clever on several levels. W.G. walks down the pavilion steps, several stones lighter than his real self, with 'As Good as Grace' emblazoned on his cricket shirt and what looks like an MCC cap on his head. Only a sharp-eyed MCC member would spot that Colman's had tinged the club's garish red and yellow stripes to fit the slightly darker hues on its mustard packaging. In another ingenious touch, Colman's put more women than men in the pavilion enclosure, even though ladies were never allowed in this all-male setting. It was overwhelmingly women who bought Colman's Mustard and were therefore the target audience.

Yet personal and commercial self-interest alone cannot explain the extraordinary range of contributors to W.G.'s three testimonial funds. Le Sage's flowery prospectus for the *Daily Telegraph*'s fund, suffused with muscular Christianity and narrow-minded nationalism, offered no convincing answer. Foreigners, Le Sage asserted, would never understand cricket or its role in 'sustaining the Empire'. They would have been baffled as well by Le Sage's description of the grossly overweight W.G. as a perfect 'specimen' of British manhood.

The Bishop of Hereford came closer than anyone to identifying the source of Grace's immense popular appeal when he referred to W.G.'s longevity. By 1895, W.G. had been 'in the front of a great amusement' for thirty years, and now, miraculously, just as the know-alls had written him off, here he was conquering fresh heights. In this heroic narrative, it did not matter that Grace's 100 first-class centuries across three decades on steadily improving pitches was a less impressive cricketing achievement than his first 50 hundreds in just eleven seasons. Fat and lame, W.G. was perfectly cast to touch a sentimental British public who warmed to improbable middle-aged comeback stories rather more readily than specimens of perfect manhood.

Amid the celebrities and self-promoters, many people gave money to W.G. who had little income of their own. William Sansum, an agricultural labourer in Berkshire, sent in his shilling, as did his wife Caroline, a laundress, and their nineteen-year-old daughter Ann. Logically, the Sansums' charitable gesture was pointless; they would have done better to spend the cash on themselves. Yet they were clearly grateful to W.G. for somehow adding to their happiness.

28

HANGING ON

In February 1896, W.G. and Agnes made the short walk from Victoria Square to the Clifton Club on The Mall for a dinner to mark his record-breaking summer. The Duke of Beaufort presented W.G. with a gold chronometer watch and Agnes with an 'elegant silver kettle' as 'the honoured and beloved wife of our famous champion'. W.G. then rose to his feet and, looking at Agnes, declared that 'but for her help I never would have done as well as I had, even in cricket'. Agnes may have wondered what her husband had done well apart from the cricket, but she was duly grateful.

The evening could not fail to underline the passing of time. Henry, W.G.'s eldest brother, had died two months earlier from a seizure during a shooting trip in Devon. Alfred, his next brother, was a guest at the dinner, still in robust health and jokingly described as the 'hunting doctor' by his patients in Chipping Sodbury, who rarely saw him. But E.M., sitting across the table, was now an arthritic fifty-four-year-old, who would play his last game for Gloucestershire in a few months' time. Arrowsmith, Brownlee and the other Gloucestershire CCC officials at the dinner almost certainly assumed that W.G. would soon retire as well.

W.G. carried on in the late 1890s for reasons that were straightforward: while never recapturing his form of 1895, he was still on his day a wonderful batsman. He would score a total of eleven centuries in 1896, 1897 and 1898, including one innings for Gloucestershire against Sussex at Ashley Down in August 1896 that must have been excruciating for his eldest son Bertie to witness. Bertie had just graduated from Cambridge with a second-class degree in maths and, less impressively, a pair (0 and 0) in the Varsity match at Lord's. He returned to Bristol for the rest of the summer and W.G. selected Bertie to open the batting with him in the Sussex game. Bertie was out for 1 and spent the next day and a half watching 'W.G. Grace Sr.' score 301 against Sussex's weak bowling attack.

There was a deeper reason why W.G. refused to follow E.M.'s example and retire from the first-class game. Cricket had become so fundamental to W.G.'s identity that he could not stop, even though he was grossly unfit. It led to an inevitable outcome: W.G.'s first-class career ended not in triumph, as it should have done, but in misery and humiliation.

In 1896, W.G. resumed the captaincy of England from Stoddart for the first Test at Lord's against the visiting Australians. By rights Stoddart should have kept the job as the winning captain in Australia the previous winter and, in most people's view, a much better leader than Grace. However, W.G. had become by now an institution, undroppable as both captain and player. England won comfortably, in a game overshadowed by MCC's refusal to pick the brilliant Indian expatriate batsman Ranjitsinhji because he was not 'of British extraction'.

Lancashire CCC, the host county, then selected Ranji for the second Test at Manchester, where he scored 62 and 154 not out as England narrowly lost the match. W.G., who scored 2 and 11, faced the first rumblings that he was not worth his place in the team. Two weeks before the deciding match at the Oval, the *Yorkshire Post* published a letter from an anonymous reader who along with some friends had selected their strongest England side for the game. W.G. was only 'first reserve'. 'Alas, poor W.G.!' the *Post* remarked.

W.G. kept his place, but became embroiled in an ugly expenses row. Five professionals, including four who played for Surrey, refused to play in the third Test unless their match fee was doubled to £20. Among several grievances, they suspected that the amateurs in the England team sometimes received more in expenses than the professionals did in fees. W.G.'s friend Charles Alcock, Surrey CCC's secretary, refused to budge and in the end four of the players backed down and were selected. The fifth player, George Lohmann, who was not picked, apologised to Surrey's committee for failing to explain that he had also withdrawn his protest.

W.G. was infuriated when the press insinuated that Surrey would pay him a great deal more in expenses for the Test than the players would receive in fees. He got Alcock to issue a press statement confirming that 'during many years' Surrey CCC had only paid him £10 for Gentlemen v Players and England v Australia matches at the Oval 'to cover his expenses in coming to and remaining in London during the three days. Beyond this amount Dr Grace has not received, directly or indirectly, one farthing for playing in a match at the Oval.' Alcock's statement was almost certainly true. There is no evidence in Surrey's admittedly sparse records that Grace received a special expenses rate from the county for matches at the Oval.

Unfortunately for W.G., the press had long since made up its mind on the issue. The *Derby Daily Telegraph* was not surprised by the professionals' revolt before the Test match, given 'the heavy expenses which it is well known will be paid to Mr W.G. Grace'. Sydney Pardon, *Wisden*'s editor, made the same assumption in more diplomatic language. 'Mr W.G. Grace's position has for years, as everyone knows, been an anomalous one,' Pardon wrote, 'but "nice customs curtsey to great kings", as the saying goes, and the work he has done in popularising cricket outweighs a hundredfold every other consideration.'

W.G.'s continuing place in the England team constituted the

real anomaly. He scored 24 and 9 at the Oval in a low-scoring
game that England won. As a player he no longer belonged in
this company.

A banquet in September 1896 summed up W.G.'s eclipse by
Ranji as cricket's superstar. Held at the Guildhall in Cambridge,
and attended by Ranji, it celebrated an amazing summer, in
which Ranji had scored ten centuries. Grace sent his apologies
for not being there to fête the new hero. 'We are just getting
into a new house,' he wrote to Ranji, 'and I cannot possibly
get away.'

W.G. left unexplained why he was moving from his
fancy rented house in Victoria Square to a cheaper home at
Ashley Grange in north Bristol so soon after his testimonial.
Surprisingly, he may have been worried about his finances. Long
after Grace's death, the cricket writer Sir Home Gordon said the
Daily Telegraph's owner Sir Edward Lawson (also dead) had told
him that W.G. used 'a substantial portion' of the newspaper's
national shilling fund to pay off betting debts. Gordon's word
was not to be trusted, as he later demonstrated when he edited
Grace's *Memorial Biography* for MCC. Yet there may have been
some substance to Lawson's allegation, even if he or Gordon
exaggerated Grace's gambling losses. Gilbert Jessop, then a junior
member of Gloucestershire's team, later remembered how W.G.
regularly laid money on horses. 'Though not a betting man – in
the sense of distributing fivers haphazardly – he [Grace] took a
keen interest in racing and when occasionally, as did happen, he
received information of a reliable description, he generally found
a sovereign or two to satiate his optimism.'

W.G. had a more obvious reason for feeling financially
insecure in 1896: he had just returned around two-thirds of
his total testimonial receipts of just over £9000 to MCC and
Gloucestershire to invest on his behalf. Grace did not trust
himself to manage his windfall responsibly, regardless of any
betting debts. The bigger question was whether anyone on
Gloucestershire's committee or at Lord's was better qualified

than W.G. to invest his money wisely, given the volatile and confusing state of the markets.

To a racegoer like W.G., selecting stocks and bonds in the mid-1890s must have looked even chancier than picking the winner of the Derby. In 1893, a financial panic that began in the United States had reverberated in Britain. On the other hand, a decades-long 'Great Depression' of falling agricultural and industrial prices had run its course by the mid-1890s. If you were an optimist, South African gold promised huge returns. If you were a pessimist, the same gold mines could lead to war between the Boers and British speculators. It seems from later evidence that whoever managed W.G.'s portfolio decided to go 'long', and long-term, in gold and commodities like rubber.

Ashley Grange, which W.G. leased, had two other advantages compared with Victoria Square. His new house was only a short walk down the hill from Gloucestershire's ground at Ashley Down, and it had a large garden to lay out a practice cricket area. W.G. quite liked flowers and shrubs, so long as they did not disrupt the main function of a garden. One chilly day in April 1897, the Bristol cricket correspondent Henry Roslyn came to Ashley Grange to watch W.G. organise a pre-season practice session for Gloucestershire. Roslyn found W.G. ordering the team to saw off an overhanging branch that got in the way of his net.

That spring, W.G.'s uncle and childhood coach Alfred Pocock died, having spent his final years under the care of John and Blanche Dann at the vicarage in Downend. W.G. travelled over to Downend for Alfred's funeral and then returned to the serious business of preparing for the new season. Uncle Pocock would have thoroughly approved.

Yet W.G.'s star was fading. In June, he agreed to take a Gloucestershire team across the Irish Sea after the students (who probably did not tell him) failed to persuade Ranji to bring a side. Grace was not entirely deluded. He knew that he was a once-great batsman dragged down by age and crushing weight. In 1897, as in previous summers, he visited the Turkish baths on

St George's Road in Bristol several times a week, hoping to shed
a few pounds. W.G. 'always weighed himself most carefully on
going in and coming out', the amateur batsman Walter Troup
remembered. 'If there was a reduction he was always in high
spirits and a good temper; if he had gained an ounce or two, it
worried him to death.'

W.G. liked to bring along Troup, Jessop and the other younger
Gloucestershire players for these futile weight-loss sessions in
order to keep him company. When they peered at him through
the steam, they saw a man who seemed to be heading, metaphorically, for the exit door. But nobody at Gloucestershire had
the nerve to suggest he ought to start thinking about retirement.

In the autumn of 1897, *The Sportsman* proposed a 'jubilee' for
the following summer to mark W.G.'s fiftieth birthday. Queen
Victoria had just celebrated her Diamond Jubilee and W.G. surely
deserved a similar send-off before he inevitably quit the stage.
Such, at least, was the rationale, and even MCC was amenable.
The MCC committee agreed to rejig the first-class fixture
schedule for 1898 so that the annual Gentlemen v Players match
at Lord's fell on 18 July, W.G.'s birthday. No one anticipated
W.G.'s refusal to behave like an august national institution.
He celebrated his fiftieth the only way he knew: in ferociously
competitive style.

W.G. built up to the big day by taking centre stage in the most
bad-tempered game of county cricket anyone could remember.
On 7 July 1898 Gloucestershire began a match against Essex at
Leyton in the north-eastern outskirts of London. Essex batted
first and W.G. took seven wickets, to the disbelief of one local
teenager, Chris Massie, watching in the crowd of several thousand. Massie later recalled Grace 'lumbering up to the crease to
bowl, an ambling giant, and the attempts of the Essex batsmen
to play the poor stuff he was sending down were ludicrous in
the extreme'.

Neither Massie nor the press at the ground noted the
alleged piece of cheating by W.G. that inflamed the rest of
the game. According to Gilbert Jessop, who was fielding for

Gloucestershire, the Essex batsman Percy Perrin hit a delivery from W.G. straight back to Grace in the air. W.G. bent down, scooped up the ball as it seemed to land and appealed for a catch. The umpire gave Perrin out, to the batsman's disgust and Jessop's disbelief. As far as Essex were concerned, W.G. had cheated, even though the evidence was ambiguous. Essex were all out for just 128 and still incensed when W.G. walked out to open Gloucestershire's first innings.

Charles Kortright now had his chance to rough up W.G. 'Korty' was an Essex gentleman of private means whose vocation was to be the world's fastest bowler, a title he disputed with Australia's Ernest 'Jonah' Jones. Two years earlier Jonah had allegedly bounced a delivery straight through W.G.'s beard – an incident so shocking that no one could agree afterwards about exactly when or where it happened. 'Korty' now unleashed himself on W.G. at such terrifying pace that a legend was born. In W.G. v 'Korty', a snarling Kortright vented all his team's fury on the ageing titan, after more outrageous cheating by Grace. In contemporary newspaper reports, a quite different, more complicated story emerges.

Half a century later, Kortright recalled that W.G. repeatedly allowed the Essex fast bowler's deliveries to hit his 'thick felt gloves', which Grace used instead of his bat to 'punch' the ball through the slip area to the boundary. If this was really true, W.G. would have broken his fingers. Massie painted a more convincing picture of W.G.'s supposed counter-attack against Kortright:

He drove and cut Kortright where he stood, with consummate ease. He appeared not to use much footwork, but battered the bowling as if he were a hammerman. There were no elegancies such as Ranji had brought into the game, no delicate leg glances. It was a display of pure hitting, eye and arm together in perfect coordination ... He had put on a lot of weight and couldn't run very well; but he saw to it that running was reduced to the minimum.

Yet Massie's description was also misleading. The scorecard shows that Kortright did not give away many runs, taking five wickets for 41 off 24 five-ball overs. Kortright did not take W.G.'s wicket (which he never claimed) and it seems W.G. did not go after Kortright; Grace reserved most of his 'hammerman' shots for the other Essex bowlers. Without W.G., Gloucestershire would have been sunk. He scored 128 in a first-innings total of 231, with only Charlie Townsend (51) among the rest of Gloucestershire's batsmen making runs. Essex (250) then left Gloucestershire needing 148 to win, with a little more than a day to go.

At 5.15 p.m. Grace walked out to open Gloucestershire's second innings with Jack Board, the team's wicketkeeper, in front of a Friday crowd of about seven thousand. Kortright immediately bowled Board for 0, followed by Troup for 0, and then delivered a ball to Grace that hit him in the stomach. 'The horrid thud of the impact could be distinctly heard in the pavilion,' Jessop wrote later with a Gothic flourish.

Even if Jessop exaggerated, the incident surely alerted the local newspaper reporters on the ground that they needed to pay close attention to every ball that Kortright sent down to W.G. Yet at the time, they missed entirely two incidents that were central to later accounts of Korty's epic confrontation with Grace. *After* the game (but not during it), several unnamed members of the Essex team complained to the *Essex County Chronicle* that W.G. hit a clear return catch to the bowler Walter Mead when he had scored about 30. Mead appealed, but the umpire gave Grace not out. Clearly, some such incident took place. It just did not appear particularly dramatic to the *Chronicle*'s correspondent.

When W.G. reached 49, Kortright began an over that entered cricket folklore. According to myth, Kortright bowled one ball where he was convinced W.G. was out leg before wicket. The umpire rejected Kortright's appeal. Grace edged Kortright's next delivery to the wicketkeeper and refused to 'walk'; again the umpire rejected Kortright's appeal. Kortright's third ball bowled Grace, hitting two of the stumps. As Grace started walking back to the pavilion, Kortright said: 'Surely you're not going, Doc? There's still one stump standing.'

In 1898 the press failed to report any such exchange between Kortright and Grace, or mention Kortright's two preceding deliveries before he bowled W.G., which supposedly made him so angry. Kortright was certainly worked up, and said something like, 'Is *that* out, Mr Grace?'; these were the words he or one of his team-mates gave to the *Essex County Chronicle* after the game, with the newspaper then publishing the story several days later. The anecdote then went the rounds for half a century, until the writer A.A. Thomson published it as 'one of the classic apocryphal stories' in 1954. It was all there in Thomson's unashamedly apocryphal version: the build-up as W.G. refused to walk twice, followed by Kortright's implausibly neat 'there's still one stump standing' remark when he flattened the other two stumps.

This is not to say that W.G. behaved impeccably. Essex's captain Hugh Owen, the son of a vicar, was clear in his own mind that Grace was a cheat. Owen told the *Essex County Chronicle* with reference to Grace's conduct that Essex had 'morally gained the victory'. For those who cared about the result (e.g. W.G.), the scorebook showed that Gloucestershire had won by just one wicket. W.G. had made another point that the Leyton crowd certainly understood. Even – and perhaps especially – at his most obnoxious, he was still terrific entertainment.

A week later, wearing a silk top hat and frock-coat, W.G. turned up at Lord's with Agnes and Bessie for his fiftieth birthday jubilee match. W.G's 'birthday party', as the historian David Kynaston describes it, was set to be a rose-tinted event. Everything was in place: the sun was shining, Lord's was packed with around seventeen thousand spectators, and even Kortright had stopped sulking and agreed to play for the Gentlemen. 'People began to pour through the turnstiles about ten o'clock,' the *Pall Mall Gazette* reported. On the St John's Wood Road 'there was a converging procession of hansoms, busses, bicycles and all kinds of conveyances, and thousands of people braved the asphyxiating dangers of the underground'.

W.G. settled Agnes and Bessie in their reserved box; struggled past hundreds of well-wishers to pick up his congratulatory telegrams at the Lord's post office; changed out of his ludicrous penguin suit into his cricket clothes; doffed his cap at a film cameraman who caught a brief, flickering image of the two teams walking past; lost the toss and had to field; and, just to show he had no hard feelings about Leyton, gave Kortright an extended opening spell both sides of lunch that completely exhausted the Essex bowler.

At the end of the second day, Sir Richard Webster, the Attorney-General, hosted a dinner in W.G.'s honour at the Sports Club off Piccadilly. Andrew Stoddart, Billy Murdoch and Sammy Woods were there, as was W.G.'s new best friend 'Korty'. The First Lord of the Treasury Arthur Balfour, who was detained on affairs of state, sent W.G. a message with the remarkable news that he, Balfour, was exactly the same age. W.G. revealed for the first time in public that his hurdles 'triumph' at Crystal Palace in 1866 had actually been a one-man race.

And then he spoke from the heart: 'I can only say you have tonight done me the greatest honour you have ever done me. When I look round, and see the friends and cricketers near me – ("hear, hear") – I wish I had Stoddart's happy knack of saying the right words in the right place. If I can't say the right words, I feel them.' ('Cheers.')

W.G. did not want to bat next day as the baking weather continued. He had received 'a nasty smack on the left hand' and had also hurt his heel. But the Players under Arthur Shrewsbury had a far stronger team. His team had collapsed to 77 for seven wickets when W.G. limped out to the middle with one goal in mind: he wanted to save the game. The situation looked hopeless when two more wickets fell. At this point Kortright, the Gentlemen's last batsman, walked out of the pavilion to join W.G.

Kortright was a good enough batsman to score two first-class centuries during his career. Together, he and W.G. 'juggled on' till 6.30 p.m., when Kortright discovered to his horror that they still had half an hour to go; W.G. had agreed to play till 7 if either side had a chance of winning, which the Players obviously did. W.G. continued to bat calmly, although he could hardly run. With three minutes to go, Kortright's nerve finally failed him. He made 'a half-hearted flick' at a ball and watched it loop over the head of the Yorkshire professional Schofield Haigh, who ran back and caught it.

Next morning, the London *Standard* observed that 'the great object of the game was fully achieved ... as marking the Jubilee of the greatest cricketer of this or any other age'. W.G. probably thought the great object of the game had *not* been achieved; for there, beneath the *Standard*'s report, the scorecard showed that the Players had won by 137 runs. Kortright returned to Essex, having said sorry to W.G. for letting him down. W.G. caught the train to Nottingham for his next game at Trent Bridge. His heel and hand were still injured, but no matter: W.G. spent the next day and a bit getting his disappointment at Lord's out of his system by scoring 168 against Nottinghamshire.

29

BESSIE

In October 1898, W.G. and Agnes went on a house-hunting expedition in the south-east London suburb of Sydenham. They were dismayed by the prices. 'I am afraid we shall have great trouble in getting a comfortable house, at a reasonable rent, close to the [Crystal] Palace,' W.G. wrote to his friend Alexander 'Webbie' Webbe, the captain of Middlesex. 'I was . . . hunting all yesterday afternoon, but could only find one suitable, and that was about twice the rent we ought to give.'

W.G. had just taken a new job as the Crystal Palace Company's cricket manager after resigning his post as a medical officer for the Barton Regis Union. Ostensibly, Grace objected to a take-over of his parish by the neighbouring Bristol Poor Law Union. He probably would have quit anyway. Cricket, not medicine, was his vocation, and the Crystal Palace Company had offered him an annual salary of £600 to set up and manage a new first-class club called London County CC.

Yet W.G. had not properly considered one problem: how to continue playing for Gloucestershire while attending to his new cricket venture in Crystal Palace Park. According to one of the company's directors, Grace's contract was 'very binding' and his retirement from Gloucestershire an obvious 'deduction'. The Duke of Beaufort made the same deduction shortly before Christmas at a farewell dinner for W.G. in Clifton. He felt 'pain in thinking that an old friend, whom he had known from his birth, who had lived amongst them all his life, and had made himself celebrated through the whole of the world as the first cricketer in England, was going to leave them'.

W.G. saw the matter differently. 'He had had a very good innings,' Grace responded, and 'he hoped to have more before he gave up Gloucestershire cricket'. In W.G.'s optimistic mind, he could play for both London County and Gloucestershire in 1899 because the two teams had no fixture clashes. Put more accurately, London County so far had no team, no ground worth the name, and therefore no matches. Trouble would loom as soon as Grace sorted out these minor details.

A few days later, W.G., Agnes, Bessie, Charlie and Aunt Caroline moved into St Andrew's, a modern detached house on Lawrie Park Road, only five minutes' walk from Crystal Palace Park. From W.G.'s perspective, the location was perfect. He was just round the corner from Sydenham station, from where he could easily reach central London when he was playing at Lord's or the Oval. Agnes was closer to her recently widowed father, who was living with one of her sisters in a mansion block in Westminster. Charlie, now sixteen, and 'very dull and feeble' according to his latest school report, had been promised a place at the Crystal Palace Company's engineering school. As for Bessie, almost twenty, she was by all accounts 'delighted in the change from the West of England to the popular London suburb'.

On 20 December, full of vim, W.G. grabbed his hat and headed over to Crystal Palace Park as quickly as possible. He had heard that some cross-Channel balloonists were about to set off from the park towards France: 'A casual recognition, a few hearty words of welcome, and an explanation of the objects of the excursion were enough to enlist the energies of the Champion of cricket ... The spectacle of the great cricketer carrying bundles of rugs and bottles of seltzer water to the [balloon] was one which nobody could forget.'

Suddenly, a gust of wind caused the balloon to lurch in the air before the passengers had boarded:

> Dr Grace relieved the situation by stepping forward and grasping one of the ropes which held the car in position. He was attired in the conventional frock coat and high hat; but the effect of his vigorous grasp upon the rope was sufficient to bring the car to its moorings, and he was heartily cheered by the workmen for his assistance ... He raised his hat as the balloon ascended, with a hearty 'God-speed' to the adventurous aeronauts.

When the balloon disappeared over the horizon, W.G. walked back home to St Andrew's. Life was good.

Two days later Bessie fell ill with typhoid. She was put straight to bed, well away from the rest of the household, apart from her distraught parents.

As W.G. and Agnes tried to comfort Bessie, they must have wondered about the coincidence of her catching the disease just after their move to Sydenham. Bessie had grown up amid the filthy drains and sewers of Bristol, yet in 1897 the Kent town of Maidstone, twenty miles from Sydenham, had suffered Britain's worst-ever typhoid outbreak. An inquiry into the epidemic warned about the dangers of unclean water piped from London. It is just possible that the home W.G. had so carefully chosen for his family was a death trap for Bessie

At first the family thought Bessie had only suffered a mild attack. She seemed to be recovering, but in late January the fever gripped her again. Bessie died in the early hours of 6 February, with her father by her bedside; Agnes was almost certainly there too.

Next day, a hearse carried Bessie's coffin down Lawrie Park Road, round the bottom of Crystal Palace Park and on to Elmers End cemetery in Beckenham. A few friends and fellow cricketers, alerted at the last minute, managed to get to Beckenham in time for the service. W.G. thanked one of them for his 'kind sympathy with us in our great trouble, and for so kindly attending the funeral on such a dreadful day'.

In Bristol, Bessie was remembered as a familiar sight at 'many a county match ... carefully following the game and keeping score'. She was 'a typical, bright, active English girl, who frequently accompanied her father when he went out after the Clifton Beagles'.

Bessie was buried in a plot near the front entrance of Elmers End cemetery. Then Agnes and W.G. returned home and closed their door on the world.

In the normal course of Victorian mourning they would have been allowed to grieve in private. Instead, three times a week W.G. had to endure a twenty-six-year-old journalist called Arthur Porritt knocking on his door. It was not really Porritt's fault. The publisher James Bowden had hired Porritt as an emergency ghostwriter after W.G. failed to deliver an autobiography originally commissioned to coincide with his 1898 jubilee year. Porritt normally covered religious affairs, but he had some cricket reporting experience and lived just across Crystal Palace Park in Streatham. Short of handing back his advance, Grace had little choice except to suffer Porritt's regular intrusions to rescue a book that would be called *Cricketing Reminiscences and Personal Recollections*.

Porritt could not understand why it was so difficult to 'lure' Grace into 'a flow of reminiscence. Many days I drew a blank and came away with scarcely sufficient material for a paragraph.' It is hard to believe that Porritt was unaware of Bessie's death, but perhaps this was so; Grace never spoke about her loss outside his family and a close circle of friends.

Bowden's exceptionally tight deadline presented Porritt with another challenge as he tried to produce a readable manuscript. In the spring of 1899, Porritt was horrified to discover that Bowden had just sold the serialisation rights, with newspapers planning to publish the first extracts in May. To his credit, W.G. gradually opened up. However, 'he never stuck to any train of recollection, but would jump from an event in the 1860s to something that happened in, say, the last Test match. Often I left his house in absolute despair.'

Porritt later gave the impression that W.G. checked the man-uscript in detail, citing one instance when Grace demanded the removal of 'inimical', a word he never used. In reality, Grace appears to have paid only fitful attention to Porritt's draft. It is hard, for instance, to imagine the plain-speaking W.G. talking about an alteration to his Australian tour schedule in 1874 as follows: 'The change of arrangements was by no means unwel-come to us as it obviated the necessity for another of the short sea voyages, of which we had already had a surfeit.'

By May 1899, Grace had largely abandoned the project, apart from writing a weekly 'Cricket Notes' column as part of Bowden's serialisation package. W.G. approached this task with a ruthless disregard for the reader. Typically, he cut and pasted chunks of the previous week's first-class match reports, inserted some banal comments about Smith or Jones looking in top form, and added the odd 'reminiscence' from the draft that Porritt was churning out. W.G.'s heart was elsewhere; at this terrible time he wanted to play cricket, not write about it.

On 11 May, W.G. travelled the short distance from Sydenham to Blackheath to captain Gloucestershire against Kent. 'It is my last year,' W.G. wrote to an acquaintance, adding that he was 'in hopes of leading Gloucestershire to a few victories in the season'. Belatedly, W.G. had recognised that he could not run London County CC and continue playing for Gloucestershire.

The county got off to a good start by beating Kent, but at the end of the game W.G. told his team-mates that he would not appear in Gloucestershire's next fixture against Yorkshire, starting in Bristol on 15 May. W.G. assigned the twenty-nine-year-old amateur batsman Walter Troup to captain the team in his absence, leaving Troup strict orders about the team's composition.

Grace's abrupt withdrawal took Gloucestershire's committee by surprise. For the record, W.G. let it be known he would not play at Ashley Down because of the new advertisement hoardings, which he said were distracting to batsmen. Privately, Bessie may have been the reason why W.G. wanted to avoid Bristol. It would have been hard for him to meet old friends such as Arrowsmith, Brownlee and Frizzy Bush, all of whom had known Bessie as a young girl. He would also have to endure the well-meant condolences of Gloucestershire CCC members and spectators at Ashley Down.

Lastly, and most importantly, Agnes needed W.G. Much later, the Sussex and England cricketer Charles 'C.B.' Fry heard that W.G. refused to stay 'even a night' away from home because Agnes was so distressed by Bessie's death. Fry's story, like many others he told, does not accord with the facts, because Grace did travel a little later in the summer of 1899, possibly taking Agnes with him. However, in mid-May, barely three months since Bessie's death, W.G. possibly felt it was too soon to leave Agnes on her own in Sydenham.

Gloucestershire's committee faced a dilemma. In effect, the county had a part-time, absentee captain who insisted on maintaining long-distance control of team selection. During the Yorkshire game, which Gloucestershire lost heavily, the committee instructed E.M., as the club's secretary, to establish with W.G. 'exactly what matches he intends playing in for the county during the year'. More cautiously, the committee told E.M. to wait until after Gloucestershire's next three away games against Surrey, Sussex and Middlesex, for which W.G. had confirmed he was available. W.G. was therefore completely in the dark, and E.M. did nothing to enlighten him. It appears that E.M., like the rest of the committee, had become exasperated by his brother's behaviour.

W.G.'s manoeuvrings with Gloucestershire now became entangled with an increasingly public debate about his captaincy of England's Test team. On Saturday, 20 May, he finished Gloucestershire's drawn game against Surrey at the Oval (in which he scored 0) and headed across the river to the Belgravia home of the Yorkshire captain Lord Hawke. Grace, Hawke and the Warwickshire captain Herbert Bainbridge were meeting as the senior selectors to discuss England's team for the first Test against Australia at Nottingham, starting on 1 June.

Most of the press already doubted that W.G. deserved to be in the team on merit. 'A place may be found for that once great cricketer, still great considering his years, W.G. Grace, in the first [Test] match for sentimental reasons alone,' the *Sheffield Daily Telegraph* commented.

Having completed his Test selection duties, Grace travelled down to Brighton for Gloucestershire's game against Sussex. He failed with the bat, but Gloucestershire won. The team returned to London for the game against Middlesex at Lord's. W.G. scored a patient 33 in Gloucestershire's second innings – not enough to save his county from defeat on a rain-damaged pitch.

Finally, E.M. despatched the committee's delayed enquiry about W.G.'s availability for the rest of the season. On Sunday, 28 May, W.G. sent his wounded response:

Gentlemen,

In answer to yours of the 26th re resolution passed on the 16th, and kept back from me for reasons best known to yourselves, I beg to state that I had intended to play in nearly all our matches, but in consequence of the resolution passed and other actions of some of the committee, I send in my resignation as captain, and must ask the committee to choose the teams for the future matches, as I shall not get them up.

I have always tried my very best to promote the interests of the Gloucestershire County Club, and it is with deep regret I resign the captaincy. I have the greatest affection for the county of my birth, but for the committee, as a body, the greatest contempt.

I am yours truly,
W.G. Grace

At first glance, it looked as though Grace had severed all his ties with Gloucestershire CCC. Yet W.G. had chosen his words quite carefully, until his final expression of 'contempt'. He had resigned the captaincy and transferred all selection duties to the committee, but he had not resigned from the team. Without his withering sign-off, W.G. might still have found a way back to playing for his beloved county.

Grace probably wrote the letter en route to Worcester, where he was due to lead his new London County CC against Worcestershire, in a game that started on 29 May. For this fixture, London County was better described as 'Gloucestershire Wanderers'. As well as W.G., the team included five other Gloucestershire players, and in particular Walter Troup, Grace's designated successor. Seizing the moment, Troup and Frizzy Bush, who travelled over from Bristol, spent a long night at the team's hotel trying in vain to get W.G. to withdraw his 'contempt' comment. W.G. replied that the committee should underline the word *contempt* 'a hundred times'.

On 31 May, Grace caught a train to Nottingham to lead England against Australia. 'Why does not W.G. retire?' the *Yorkshire Evening Post* asked rhetorically. 'Even a man of his extraordinary powers and endurance must drop out of international cricket some day, and it would be the wiser and more graceful act on his part to do so voluntarily.'

On the second day (2 June), after Australia were all out for 252, he opened England's batting with C.B. Fry in front of a crowd of about thirteen thousand. Like Grace in his youth, the trim, fit twenty-seven-year-old Fry was an outstanding athlete. Grace scored 28 in a partnership of 75, as Fry grew increasingly frustrated with his plodding partner. 'We lost innumerable singles on the off side, and I never dared called W.G. for a second run to the long field,' Fry remembered. 'W.G.'s embarrassment got worse when England (all out for 193) fielded again. 'A section of the crowd behaved very rudely to W.G. Grace, hooting him if a ball went anywhere near him and was not fielded, and cheering him derisively when he stopped a simple hit,' the *Sheffield and Rotherham Independent* reported.

On this shameful day – for W.G., and for the spectators who jeered him – Gloucestershire released a statement declaring that they had tried without success to persuade Grace to retract his letter. With 'deep regret', the committee reluctantly accepted his resignation. Only now, it appears, did Grace realise the implication of his refusal to back down. He fired off telegrams to *The Times* and the *Bristol Mercury*, making clear that he had *not* severed his connection with Gloucestershire. In Grace's view he was still a Gloucestershire player; he just did not want to be captain.

The Test match ended as a draw on 3 June with Australia on top. W.G. scored only 1 in the second innings, when England were saved from likely defeat by Ranji, who made 93 not out. 'Old Ebor', the *Yorkshire Evening Post*'s cricket columnist, had already decided that Grace should be dropped for the second Test at Lord's, starting on 15 June. 'It would be a graceful act on the great cricketer's part to voluntarily withdraw from the remaining matches,' the columnist suggested. The *Morning Post* agreed. 'Sentimental considerations should not be permitted to weaken our side,' it argued, 'and the opinion must be bluntly expressed that Mr Grace, great and various as are his abilities even now, is no longer a source of strength.'

Grace read the papers and knew his time was up. On Saturday, 10 June, he arrived for the next selectors' meeting at the Sports Club in London's St James's Square and promptly told Hawke and Bainbridge that he was dropping himself from the Test team. C.B. Fry, who turned up late for the meeting, subsequently claimed that W.G. tricked him into approving Grace's resignation, seemingly over Hawke and Bainbridge's objections. Fry's story had only two flaws. For a start, Fry was not in the room when Grace discussed the matter with Hawke and Bainbridge. Fry also omitted to mention that he was a junior selector on the two-tier panel, whose opinion carried less weight than the judgement of W.G. and his senior colleagues.

W.G.'s retirement from Test cricket hardly made the news.

'That Grace would be omitted from the team was generally anticipated in view of his comparative failure at Nottingham,' the *Derby Daily Telegraph* commented. Tactfully skirting round W.G.'s immense weight, the newspaper praised him for recognising 'the necessity of giving way to younger and more active men'. W.G. was more preoccupied by his rupture with Gloucestershire. 'I am glad to hear I am not the only one who the committee dislike,' W.G. wrote in July to the Gloucestershire amateur Cyril Sewell, who had some complaint of his own. 'From what I hear they cannot speak the truth, they are a bad lot, and the less you have to say to them the better for you.'

In this miserable mood, W.G. brought to a close the worst six months of his life. He had lost Bessie, and in great personal distress had then wrecked his relationship with Gloucestershire. Still dazed with grief, W.G. had also stumbled into a final Test match he should never have played.

Later in the season, Troup received a telegram from an 'old Gloucestershire cricketer' saying that W.G. was willing to play for the county as an ordinary player under Troup's captaincy. The committee would not hear of it. Another chance for a reconciliation passed that summer when W.G. and Agnes returned to Bristol for Edgar's marriage to Kittie Slaughter, a local Clifton girl.

W.G.'s retreat to the margins of top-class cricket was brought home on 27 July. In Huddersfield, Gloucestershire began their match against a Yorkshire team that included the future England captain Stanley Jackson and the young left-arm spinner Wilfred Rhodes, at the start of his illustrious Test career. At Crystal Palace Park, W.G. scored 13 for his new club against Wiltshire, a minor county. W.G. then watched in frustration as the Middlesex amateur Robert Lucas, a guest for London County, made an easy century against Wiltshire's second-rate bowlers.

30

THE PALACE YEARS

W.G.'s tenure as the Crystal Palace Company's cricket manager from 1899 to 1905 was a strange blend of mediocrity and glamour. He had launched his new venture in May 1899 with a top-drawer game between South of England (so called because London County still lacked first-class status) and the visiting Australian team. A crowd of about six thousand turned up each day to watch Fry (the rising star) score 81, Ranji (the established star) score 63 and W.G. (the fading star) score 47. The Australian batsmen Syd Gregory and Monty Noble both scored centuries as the game ended in a draw. Yet the match lacked any real edge, because South of England or London County were nothing more than Grace's invitation eleven.

A better businessman than W.G. would have realised immediately that London County CC had no future as a serious first-class club or a profitable venture. The Crystal Palace Company was almost bust, after repeated failures to fill the colossal glass Great Exhibition hall that had been transferred to Sydenham Hill. In the directors' minds, Grace and his London County CC would lure crowds to Sydenham in the summer, which would then stay to enjoy the palace's delights, ranging from a 4500-pipe 'Great

Organ' to livestock auctions. However, MCC only allowed London County first-class status from 1900 and refused to admit the club to the county championship. Surrey, a well-supported county club, was just up the road at the Oval, while Kent played regularly in nearby Blackheath and Gravesend.

For a while, W.G. managed to lure enough top cricketers to Crystal Palace to mask his team's dependence on local club players and (when available) his sons Bertie and Charlie. It helped that W.G., using his showman's flair, created a fitting stage for some of the greatest Edwardian cricket stars on a flat stretch of land directly beneath the Great Exhibition hall. On sunny days, as the palace glittered high above W.G.'s ground, spectators could sometimes enjoy the sight of Fry, Jessop and other top players from cricket's so-called 'golden age' making guest appearances for London County.

More durably, Grace also persuaded his old mate Billy Murdoch to come and play in Sydenham. The former captain of Australia was forty-five in 1899 when he realised, after seven years with Sussex CCC, that he was finished as a serious first-class cricketer. Murdoch left Sussex and moved with his wife Jemima and their children to a house on Lawrie Park Road, just down the street from the Graces. According to his 1901 census return, Murdoch was a 'retired solicitor'. Everyone on the cricket circuit knew he was paid to play for London County. Other cricketers recruited by Grace to his eclectic team included the left-handed all-rounder Carst Posthuma, from the Dutch town of Haarlem, who played regularly for London County CC in 1903 and is remembered in the Netherlands as 'the Dutch W.G.'

W.G. insisted that London County was a 'proper' first-class club, but he knew that in leaving Gloucestershire and retiring from Test cricket, he had departed from the game's top table. At Lawrie Park Road, he still kept a keen, sometimes critical eye on any slippage in standards at Lord's, on or off the field. He was especially fed up with MCC for losing a pair of pads belonging to the famous early nineteenth-century cricketer Alfred Mynn, which W.G. had donated to the club. 'They did not seem to appreciate them,' W.G. complained to Harris in 1900. 'I should know them again, if I saw them, they might be just hidden away with a lot of rubbish, or they might be destroyed.'

W.G. also monitored *Wisden* for any sloppy mistakes, as soon as the latest edition of cricket's quasi-official annual 'Bible' arrived at Lawrie Park Road. 'I see they have put Sladen the Lancashire bowler down as Slades, a bad mistake,' W.G. tactlessly wrote in January 1903 to the cricket statistician Frederick Ashley-Cooper, the almanack's chief fact-checker. 'I have not yet had time to go through *Wisden*, I dare say I shall find a few more slips.'

From his Sydenham outpost, W.G. stayed in touch with the greatest bowler he had ever faced. 'My dear Spof,' he wrote in 1901, 'I am sorry to say I am not playing at Hampstead so cannot accept your kind invitation to dine afterwards.' 'The Demon' was still captain of Hampstead CC, and happy to receive W.G. the following year, when according to another London County player, Percy Gale, 'each bowled the other out, and curiously enough, each of them took no other wicket in the innings'. Gale was wrong that Spofforth and Grace never met again. They were not close friends, but as W.G's 'dear Spof' salutation indicates, they encountered each other from time to time at Test matches between England and Australia.

The imperious Spofforth would never have fitted into the vaudeville culture of London County, where a trail of celebrities found themselves playing with or against W.G. In August 1900 it was the detective writer Arthur Conan Doyle's turn, playing for MCC against London County at Lord's. Conan Doyle, a slow bowler, wrote a comic ditty about his joy when he took W.G.'s wicket:

> Out – beyond question or wrangle!
> Homeward he lurched to his lunch!
> His bat was tucked up at an angle,
> His great shoulders curved to a hunch.

Conan Doyle's poem, which went on and on, omitted one crucial detail: Grace had already scored a century.

Grace had to wait two years for his revenge, when the creator of Sherlock Holmes batted for MCC in a return match at Crystal Palace Park. Conan Doyle had just scored two boundaries off W.G.'s 'delightful slows' and was feeling full of confidence: 'Out I danced to reach the next one on the half volley. It was tossed a little higher up in the air, which gave the delusion that it was coming right up to the bat, but as a matter of fact it pitched well short of my reach, broke sharply across and Lilley, the wicketkeeper, had my bails off in a twinkling.'

Sherlock Holmes would have spotted Conan Doyle's error immediately. The wicketkeeper was Edward French, an obscure amateur, not the Test player Dick Lilley.

There were plenty of other distractions at Crystal Palace if the cricket ever got dull. During the same game, W.G. and Conan Doyle sauntered over to the nearby polo ground to congratulate Mrs Spencer, who had just navigated an airship above the park. When there were no airships or hot-air balloons to inspect, there was fun to be had in the dressing room. 'The inner group of the London County Club was like a happy family,' remembered Percy Gale, an accountant from Croydon who was one of W.G.'s local club recruits. 'Grace himself was known as Father, W.L. Murdoch as Muvver, 'Livey' [Livingstone] Walker as the Babe and I as Granny – why I was given that nickname I do not remember, unless it was because I was slow in the field.'

Yet it is hard to see how W.G. could have been happy, given all his private grief. He and Agnes were still deep in mourning for Bessie in 1900 when two of Grace's sisters died: Alice, whose husband Henry Skelton had taken over the surgery at The Chestnuts, and Fanny, who had never married. Their deaths, coming so soon after Bessie, may have been one reason why Grace's drinking became noticeably heavier around this time. The Derbyshire amateur Albert Lawton, then twenty-two, remembered being on a train to Birmingham for a London County game in 1901 when the steward brought the wine list for dinner. W.G. passed the list to Lawton, who recommended a French vintage.

'W.G. said he had never heard of it but ordered a bottle to see what it was like. A small quantity was poured into his glass, he took a sniff at it, sipped it and then drank it down. Then came his decision – "Bring four more bottles".'

One wound was partly healed in 1902. W.G.'s godson Charlie Townsend, who played occasionally for London County, persuaded W.G. to bring a team to Ashley Down to raise money for the National Society for the Prevention of Cruelty to Children. Gloucestershire CCC lent the ground for free, while Arrowsmith printed all the scorecards for no charge. Frizzy Bush came out of retirement to play for Townsend's team and, best of all, W.G. scored 68 not out, reminding the crowd of what the county had lost. He was touched by his reception. 'After the kind way you treated us at Bristol last season, I must say I should like to come again,' W.G. wrote to Arrowsmith in November. 'I have written Harry Beloe fully on the subject.' W.G. also wanted Gloucestershire to play an away match against London County in 1903. 'Hoping you and Harry will be able to work it.'

Gloucestershire came to Crystal Palace Park in June 1903. W.G. was in 'high spirits' throughout the game, recalled Henry Roslyn, 'behaving like one who was proudly showing old pals over a new home'. Yet Roslyn saw that W.G. was nervous. 'Each day throughout the meal he talked incessantly. I could not help noticing that he deliberately steered clear of the past; his conversation was solely concerned with the present and the future.' For W.G., there was only one way to celebrate this reconciliation with his beloved county. He took a look at Gloucestershire's bowling attack, did not think much of it, and scored 150. Gloucestershire lost by seven wickets.

W.G. soon wrote again to Arrowsmith, following a return match in Gloucester that London County also won. 'You will be glad to hear that Bertie has been appointed one of the assistant masters at the Osborne Royal Naval College, tell Beloe when you see him and anyone who you think might like to know.'

Bertie was now twenty-nine, still unmarried, and available for his father's club when the naval college in Queen Victoria's former home on the Isle of Wight closed for the summer holidays. In August 1904 Bertie played his only game of the season for London County against Wiltshire at Crystal Palace Park. Opening the batting, he scored 75 in a total of 198 all out, one of the rare occasions when he outperformed everyone, including W.G. Shortly afterwards Bertie caught the train to Portsmouth, ready to switch from cricket to coaching the cadets at rugby over the winter.

The following February, Bertie fell ill with appendicitis. He never recovered, dying on the naval surgeon's operating table in the early hours of 2 March. Later that day, W.G. and Agnes travelled down to the Isle of Wight to collect Bertie's coffin from Osborne House and bring him back to Sydenham. They were escorted back to the harbour by a procession of naval officers, a thoughtful gesture that only added to their agony.

Remember Bertie's 'fixity of purpose', the college's chaplain instructed the cadets. 'He let nothing turn him from his work, from what he felt to be his duty.' If Bertie had not been W.G.'s son, one newspaper noted unkindly, 'very little would have been heard of him in connection with the summer game'. Yet if he had been anyone else's son, Bertie's short life would have counted as a success. Academically, he had gone far further than all his many Grace and Pocock ancestors, even the schoolteachers. He was clever, with a good degree in maths from Cambridge, and he was liked by the boys he taught at Oundle and Osborne. In a way Bertie was his father's son, because as the chaplain also noted, 'he was a very *thorough* man in all he did. Whether it was his teaching or his organising and arranging your games, in which he took so great an interest, he did it with his might.' Perhaps W.G. also saw this quality in his dogged, bespectacled son.

Agnes and W.G. buried Bertie next to Bessie in Elmers End cemetery. 'We know what it is to lose those that are dear to us,' W.G. wrote with fellow feeling in 1907 to his friend James Arrowsmith, who had just lost his wife. By then, Agnes's father William Day had also died. Day was still a figure of some significance in the art publishing world, remembered by *The Modern Lithographer, a trade journal,* as 'a grand old man of the craft for which we all have a sneaking kindness'.

Amid so much sadness, W.G. and Agnes's two surviving sons pursued markedly different paths. In 1902 Charlie had graduated from the Crystal Palace School of Practical Engineering and left home to work as a switchboard attendant for the Mansfield Corporation in Nottinghamshire. A keen cricketer, Charlie joined Mansfield CC, winning a prize in 1903 as the club's best batsman. In 1907, Charlie got a job at the government dockyard in Chatham on the Thames Estuary, where he supervised the installation of a new telephone system. Now in his mid-twenties, he moved back to his parents' home in Sydenham, seemingly content to remain a bachelor, and ever available to turn out for London County.

Edgar, a competitive tennis player, had no intention of getting roped in to play cricket for his father. In 1906 he received his first command, the battleship *Majestic*, based at Portsmouth and then on the Thames Estuary until the summer of 1908, when Edgar moved with his ship to Devonport. During this period, W.G. and Agnes saw a lot of Edgar and his wife Kitty's four small children: Edgar, Alice, Gladys and Primrose ('Prim'). There is no evidence, but it is easy to imagine Agnes taking the little ones to the Oval on 18 July 1906 to watch their grandfather enjoying his fifty-eighth birthday with a vengeance.

At the start of the 1906 season, Surrey CCC had invited W.G. to captain the Gentlemen against the Players at the Oval. His appointment was sentimental. W.G. had utterly dominated the fixture in the late 1860s and 1870s, when it functioned as the nearest equivalent to a Test match. He had played in at least one Gentlemen v Players fixture every year from 1865 to 1903, but had then not been chosen at all in 1904 and 1905, probably because he was deemed too old. By coincidence, the last day of the Oval fixture in 1906 fell on W.G.'s birthday and the Surrey committee decided to offer the Oval public a last chance to say goodbye to the 'Champion'.

So it was that shortly before lunch on 18 July, in baking sunshine, W.G. walked out of the Oval pavilion with the Leicestershire amateur Cecil Wood to open the Gentlemen's second innings. The Gentlemen faced defeat, having been set an impossible 443 to win in under four hours against a Players' bowling attack that included three past or present Test bowlers: Walter Lees, John Gunn and Albert Trott. In the Gentlemen's first innings, W.G. had modestly put himself down the batting order at number seven and failed, scoring only 4. Now he wanted to celebrate his birthday and – if he could – save the game.

W.G. dug in. He hardly scored a run before lunch, and for some time afterwards barely managed to 'chop away from the wicket many balls that almost bowled him'. When he reached 20, the Leicestershire fast bowler Thomas Jayes struck him a 'nasty knock on the arm'. Slowly, W.G. found his touch, using one signature shot in particular. 'When he cut, the strong wrists [sent] the ball at a good speed towards third man, or squarer, with nothing more than a flick.'

It took him an hour and forty minutes to reach his fifty, when he was 'tremendously cheered' by the crowd of around six thousand. Some minutes later 'he cut a ball down to deep third man and just walked along the wicket [for] his 58th run', his birthday target. 'The crowd went fairly mad,' recalled Albert Lawton, who was waiting to bat. W.G 'rather naturally sagged after that' as the spectators willed him towards a 127th first-class century. 'He is now very slow between the wickets,' one correspondent observed, as if W.G. were an aged elephant, 'and in consequence something like 20 per cent of the runs he really deserved were lost'.

W.G. struggled on to 74, when he played a tired shot off Jayes to Albert Trott, who caught him. Utterly spent, W.G. saluted the crowd and dragged himself off the ground, the game now a certain draw. Back in the pavilion, hot and happy, he told his team-mates he was finally ready to stop playing. Nobody believed him.

A fortnight later, W.G. signed a new contract with the Crystal Palace Company, on the same £600 annual salary, as manager of the company's cricket and bowls clubs. In truth, London County CC had largely ceased to function. At the end of the 1904 season, short of top players and fixtures, the club had lost its first-class status. It pottered on as a local team, with W.G. leading the side in 1906 and 1907 against the likes of Banstead, Kensington and Guy's Hospital. He also played several first-class games for W.G. Grace's XI and 'Gentlemen of England' against the universities, a visiting West Indian team and Surrey CCC, while continuing to appear in minor fixtures for MCC in the London area. But by his sixtieth birthday in 1908, W.G. was at heart a local club cricketer, lugging his kit to Clapham, Forest Hill and other grounds in the south London suburbs, never far from Agnes in Sydenham.

Grace had also just retired as captain of England in a completely different sport: bowls. W.G. took up bowls before he left Bristol in 1899, because Gloucestershire's ground at Ashley Down also included a bowling green. When he arrived in Sydenham, W.G. persuaded the Crystal Palace Company to convert the tennis courts near his cricket ground into a bowling green – a modest proposal, except W.G. was thinking big. In 1901, he invited more than five hundred bowlers, including the visiting Australian and New Zealand teams, to attend the opening of the London County Bowling Green, hosted by the newly formed London County Bowling Club (Captain: W.G. Grace).

W.G. realised that the sport was better organised in Scotland, where the country's bowling association claimed the copyright of the rules, to the annoyance of the rival English body, the Imperial Bowling Association (IBA). Seizing his opportunity, W.G. affiliated London County Bowling Club with the Scottish association, which sent a representative team to Crystal Palace in 1901 and 1902. That August, W.G. took his London County team to Edinburgh, Glasgow and Ayr, prompting another thought to occur to him. The IBA was clearly a shambles, but fortunately W.G. had the solution. In June 1903, with the help of like-minded friends, he formed the English Bowling Association (President: W.G. Grace). A month later 'England' (Captain: W.G. Grace) played its first match against teams from Scotland, Ireland and Wales. Entirely because of his empire-building, W.G. thus joined the select band of England cricketers who have represented their country in another sport.

W.G.'s fellow bowls players soon learned that he was not just a famous figurehead. As with London County CC, W.G. threw himself into the minutiae of organising fixtures and match day arrangements: 'We shall be ready for you at 4 o'clock, as soon after as you can arrive,' he wrote to the secretary of Hurst Bowling Club in Berkshire in May 1904. 'I fancy it will perhaps be best to say 4.30 sharp to commence. I enclose tickets of admission to Palace. Come to the Cricket ground, you can change boots there, the Bowling Green is close ... We have arranged for a cold meat tea as soon as the game is over.'

Two years later, when London County Bowling Club visited Hurst, W.G. sent a helpful note to Hurst's secretary: 'We propose leaving London at 1.45 Wednesday, arrive Reading at 2.27. I trust this will meet your arrangement. We must catch the 7.35 back.'

W.G was less good at golf, which he took up in earnest around the time he became England's bowls captain. 'He played golf with a mixture of keen seriousness and cheerful noisiness which was peculiar to him,' W.G.'s future biographer, the golf writer Bernard Darwin, recalled of his rounds with Grace at the Walton Heath course in Surrey. 'There would come from him periodically, immense shouts of laughter, or loud greetings to some friend playing another hole.'

Bowls and golf were mere diversions. In 1909, as American explorers reached the North Pole and Japan occupied Korea, W.G. turned once more to the great issue of the age: how to score runs. *W.G.'s Little Book*, despite its slimness and modest

title, ought to have dispelled for ever the idea that Grace did not
think deeply about cricket. W.G.'s publisher George Newnes
insisted on the usual laboured anecdotes and 'reminiscences',
dutifully extracted by Grace's latest ghostwriter, the amateur
cricketer and journalist Edward Sewell. However, the book's
four main chapters on batting, bowling, the 'new bowling' and
fielding were clearly Grace's work, written in his typically plain,
direct prose. Tucked into his *Little Book* were four little gems,
which nobody really noticed.

W.G.'s chapter on the 'new bowling', meaning googlies, was
a pure example of his approach to a cricketing problem: absolute
rigour in identifying the challenge, combined with complete flexi-
bility in proposing a solution. The googly had first been developed
in the late 1890s by Bernard Bosanquet, a student cricketer at
Oxford, who discovered how to bowl an off-break (spinning right
to left from a right-handed batsman's perspective) using the same
back-of-the-hand action as for a leg-break (left to right).

With hindsight, Grace's analysis of the googly was wrong in
several respects. He probably had the inaccurate Bosanquet in
mind when he predicted that the googly would never become
'universal' because 'the bowling of "googlies" well – and there
is nothing easier to score from when they are bowled badly – is
a much greater physical strain than is any other kind of bowling'.
Within a few years the great Australian leg-break and googly
bowler Clarrie Grimmett would show how it was possible with
hard practice to bowl the 'bosie' (after 'Bosanquet') with tremendous accuracy.

Grace was also wrong that a googly bowler could never be
sure which way he was spinning the ball, and that a batsman
could never read the spin by watching the bowler's action. Shane
Warne, the greatest of all leg-break and googly bowlers, had
complete control of a spectrum of spin that he varied according
to the pitch and the state of the game. Yet the greatest batsmen,
at their best, could read Warne's spin by looking for minute
changes in his bowling action, such as the position of his wrist
and shoulder at the moment of delivery.

Grace, however, was concerned with the googly problem as presented by the bowlers of his time. He particularly had in mind the South African googly-bowling quartet of Albert Vogler, Reggie Schwarz, Aubrey Faulkner and Gordon White, who toured England in 1907. In his *Little Book*, W.G. pointed out that the batsman could take advantage of the googly bowler's need to spread his fielders to cover both the leg-break and the googly, a disguised off-break. 'The genuine "googlie" [*sic*] bowler is bound to have his field scattered,' W.G. noted. 'This means gaps, and gaps mean singles and twos to an observant and good batsman.'

Grace's pragmatic analysis illustrated his ability to simplify a seemingly intractable cricketing problem and then adapt his conclusions according to further experience. Cricket, for him, had always been a work in progress, with scope for new thinking about the latest innovation: in this case, a weird invention by the nephew of a Hegelian philosopher (also called Bernard Bosanquet).

W.G.'s Little Book, like Arrowsmith's spin-off from *Cricket*, came out as a cheap edition for sale at railway bookstores and general newsstands. To grab the attention of customers, W.G. stared out from the garish red front cover like a rather menacing Santa Claus. Once again the packaging of W.G. made it hard to take him seriously as a thinker on the game.

In his preface, Grace betrayed his main reason for submitting to another bout of book-writing. His previous two books had both 'met with great success', he claimed, but 'were not what might be called popular editions'. In direct terms, W.G. felt the need to make some money.

31

CLOSE OF PLAY

W.G. probably knew when he agreed to write his *Little Book* that he was about to lose his job. In May 1909, after years of increasing debt, the Crystal Palace Company finally collapsed and went bankrupt. Several months later, W.G. moved from Sydenham to a new home in the village of Mottingham, four miles east, which he rented from a local publican on a short-term lease for £110 per year.

W.G. clearly felt financially insecure following the loss of his £600 annual salary from the Crystal Palace Company. 'I only have a small income,' he wrote to his friend Lord Harris in 1910, seeking advice about gold stocks. 'I naturally would like to get as much interest as I can with a fair amount of safety.' W.G.'s letter to Harris, now chairman of Consolidated Gold Fields, is the best evidence that the 1895 testimonial money Grace handed back to MCC and Gloucestershire to manage on his behalf was not successfully invested.

W.G. evidently wanted to take charge of at least some of his portfolio, although it is possible that MCC and Gloucestershire continued to invest on his behalf. When he died in 1915 his portfolio was worth about £2500, less than half the approximately

£6000 he had returned after his testimonial. It could be that Harris gave Grace poor advice, or that W.G. made his own poor investment decisions. Yet he was quite cautious, paying close attention to 'safety' by holding railway, rubber and gold stocks, plus bonds, rather than riskier short-term equities.

At the heart of all W.G.'s fretting and fussing about money in his final years lay a puzzle. In 1891, when he toured Australia under Lord Sheffield, and in 1895, when he celebrated his second testimonial, Grace had received two colossal windfalls, amounting to a grand total of more than £12,000 in the money of the day. Competently managed, the income from this capital ought to have provided W.G. and Agnes with financial security, yet Grace continued to behave as if hard times were just around the corner. Perhaps he could not shake off the ingrained mentality of someone who came from a family that lived close to the edge, for in reality he was not poor, especially when compared with the top professional sports stars of his time, who earned a pittance.

During the early 1900s, the FA imposed a wage ceiling of £4 a week on players who belonged to Football League clubs. Professional cricketers were paid barely more in real terms on the eve of the First World War than during the 1860s and 1870s. Grace, in contrast, had enough money in his last years to pursue the life of a retired but active sporting gentleman of modest means. He had a small doctor's pension of about £70 per year from the Barton Regis Union, about the same as a labourer's annual salary, plus a little extra from book royalties. Yet he lacked money in his hand and was concerned about touching his capital, because he wanted to ensure that Agnes had enough to live on after his death.

Fairmount, W.G. and Agnes's new home in Mottingham, was a modern detached, red-brick house set back from a quiet lane that meandered out of the village into the surrounding countryside. For W.G., the best part of the property was the large rear garden, where he had enough space to lay out a practice cricket net before the ground sloped gently away.

Indoors, W.G. had only women for company whenever Charlie was away working at the Chatham Dockyard. By 1911, W.G.'s elderly, widowed cousin Marian Coleman was living with the family, paying for her bed and board. Aunt Caroline, now ninety-one, was still going strong, and there was also a maid, a parlourmaid and a cook. As best he could, W.G. introduced some masculine touches into this feminine domestic scene. Several stuffed birds, possibly shot by W.G., stared at visitors from their mounted glass boxes in the hall. There was more dead wildlife in the drawing room in the form of a tiger skin and two bear-skins – the latter probably brought back by W.G. from Canada in 1872. His treasured souvenir plate from 1895, recording his 100 hundreds, took pride of place on the mantelpiece, next to the baseball that Harry Wright had given him in Boston all those years ago.

Fairmount became a homely retreat for W.G. and Agnes. They had two matching walnut easy chairs in the drawing room, along with a walnut writing table to deal with their correspondence. An early adopter of new technology, W.G. soon installed a telephone (Lee Green 1293), perhaps getting Charlie to sort out the connection. There was an upright grand piano by the wall, possibly bought originally for Bessie, and more than a hundred books on cricket and other subjects, spread around the drawing room and the billiard room and morning room across the hall. No guest, leafing through W.G.'s well-thumbed volumes, would make the mistake of assuming that he never read a book in his life.

Upstairs, Agnes had her own, sparsely furnished bedroom with a single bed and occasional table, while W.G. slept in the back bedroom on the second floor. This arrangement was quite common for Victorian couples and did not mean that W.G. and Agnes always slept apart. The bed in the back bedroom was five feet wide, large enough for both of them. When W.G. started snoring, Agnes could slip away to her own bed.

For the first time in his life, W.G. was a permanent man of leisure, free to pursue his favourite pastimes. He kept his prized

READY FOR ANY BOWLING.

What MCC members see . . .
W.G. stands rigidly in Archibald Stuart–Wortley's famous 1890 painting at Lord's, frozen at the moment before he takes guard to face the bowler. (Time Life Pictures / Getty Images)

. . . and what they don't
The cartoonist Harry Furniss captures W.G.'s dynamic batting stance during a century at Lord's in 1895.

'Great scores at cricket, like great work of any kind, are, as a rule, the result of years of careful and judicious training and not accidental occurrences.' W.G. Grace, 'How to Score' (1888)

The bankrupt and the godson
Grace with his schoolmaster friend Frank Townsend (right) and Frank's sons Charlie (standing, left) and Arthur (front). Frank went bankrupt in 1892 and was forced to leave Gloucestershire. Three years later Charlie was W.G.'s batting partner when Grace scored his hundredth first-class century. Charlie later became the Graces' family solicitor. (Boundary Books)

From a back garden in Bristol . . .
W.G. lines up with the rest of his Grace Family XI before a game in August 1891 against the Robinsons, a prominent Bristol business family. Grace's side included his elder brothers Henry (back row, second from left), Alfred (front row, third from left) and E.M. (second from right). W.G.'s son Bertie (front row, far left) also played, while the boy on E.M.'s knee is probably W.G.'s youngest son Charlie. (Dinah Bernard Collection)

. . . to the Adelaide Botanic Garden

Three months later W. G. looks the wrong way in an incongruous bowler hat as captain of Lord Sheffield's 1891–2 team to Australia. Alfred Shaw, the tour manager (back row, far left), was warned that W. G. 'would drink enough to sink a ship'. The dazzling batsman Andrew Stoddart (back row, second from left) upstaged W. G. in the Test matches.

The rest of the team: Maurice Read (back row, third from left), Hylton Philipson, Goldney Radcliffe.

Front row, from left: Bobby Abel, George Lohmann, Gregor McGregor, Johnny Briggs, Bobby Peel, W.G., William Attewell, George Bean, John Sharpe. (Bob Thomas / Popperfoto / Getty Images)

The children

Bertie (1874–1905)
'How not to bat': bespectacled Bertie, disastrously christened W.G. Grace Jr., tried hard at cricket but was better at maths. He became a teacher, letting 'nothing turn him from his work' until appendicitis killed him.
(Bob Thomas / Popperfoto / Getty Images)

Edgar (1876–1937)
Unlike his father, Edgar loved the sea, rising through the Navy ranks to retire as an admiral. A fervent Christian, Edgar saw life as a Test match 'where it was no use complaining of bodyline tactics or sticky wickets'. (Dinah Bernard Collection)

Bessie (1878–99)
Sporty and keen, Bessie played cricket until her doting father decided the game was unsuitable for a young lady. Then Bessie broke her parents' hearts, dying of typhoid with W.G. by her bedside. (Grace Family Collection)

Charlie (1882–1938)
Charlie's teachers thought him 'dull and feeble' and he may have spent time at a school for 'backward and delicate boys'. He grew up to be a successful engineer and a local batting hero, dying at the crease straight after seeing his side to a record-breaking total. (Dinah Bernard Collection)

Love of his life
Agnes (1853–1930): the daughter of a bankrupt, W.G.'s wife was easily underestimated, as MCC learned to its cost. W.G. knew better. 'But for her help I never would have done as well as I have, even in cricket.' (Popperfoto / Getty Images)

Deceptive approach
W.G. shuffles up to the crease to bowl another of his artful 'slows', which fooled even Test batsmen. Spofforth admired the mind games W.G. played with his victims. 'He indeed so juggles with you that you are beaten in spite of yourself.'

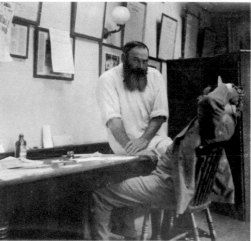

Swapping notes
W.G. chats in the dressing room with the Indian batting maestro K.S. Ranjitsinhji (1872–1933), who eclipsed him as cricket's superstar in the late 1890s. Like Grace, Ranji was an inventive genius and financially insecure. There all similarity ended. (Copyright Marylebone Cricket Club)

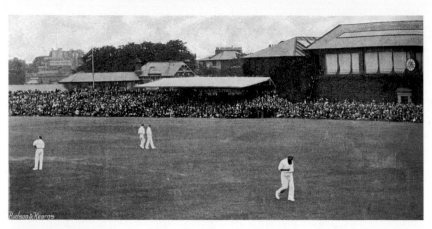

Out, but not down
Grace limps back to the Lord's pavilion with an injured heel during in his fiftieth birthday
'jubilee' match in July 1898. He got over his frustration at losing this game by scoring 168 at
Nottingham the following day. (Country Life)

Cricket at the Palace
W.G. lounges on the grass at Crystal Palace Park, home to his London County Cricket Club in
the early 1900s. Beneath the jollity, he and Agnes were still mourning the loss of their daughter
Bessie. (Hulton Archive / Stringer / Getty Images)

'Give me your answer, do'
Daisy, Countess of Warwick, pops a question to W.G. during a lull in play. Grace's celebrity fan club stretched from the American Civil War commander General George Meade to Daisy's ex-lover King Edward VII. (Copyright Marylebone Cricket Club)

Early adopter
W.G.'s fascination with cars and airships confounded his false image as a traditional countryman. 'He had only to pass through a village street in a motor car for windows to be thrown up and fingers to be pointed, but he seemed, and really was, as nearly as possible unaware of it, unless his admirer was a small child, to whom he liked to wave his hand.'

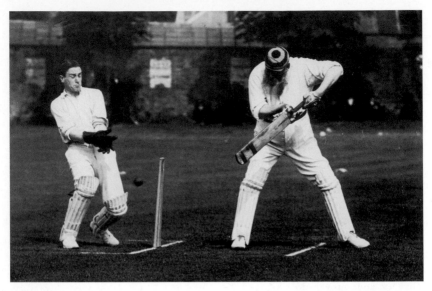

Old master
W.G. demonstrates his distinctive backward cut shot at Gravesend CC's ground in 1913. 'At the last moment he pressed down quickly with his wrists, with an almost vertical swing, and away sped the ball past all catching, just clear of second or third slip.' (Look and Learn / Elgar Collection / Bridgeman Images)

Adieu, October 1915
W.G.'s funeral at Elmers End Cemetery, south-east London. Bobby Abel, the shortest pallbearer, nearly dropped Grace's massive coffin. Frank Townsend shrieked 'Goodbye' as W.G. was lowered into the family grave. King George V sent his condolences – to MCC, not Agnes. (Topical Press Agency / Getty Images)

twelve-bore gun in a locked case in the morning room, a gift from the gunmaker James Purdey Jr. Purdey saw the advantage of the British Empire's most famous sportsman being seen at shooting weekends with one of the firm's models. W.G. was grateful, but a problem arose: while he blasted away at the birds, he needed a reserve gun that was instantly on hand, loaded by an assistant, when he ran out of ammunition. A word with Purdey and the problem went away. The gunmaker lent W.G. another weapon to satisfy his shooting needs.

During the winter, W.G. also went out beagling with the Halstead Place Beagles, about five miles south-east of Mottingham in rural Kent. 'I was out with the Beagles at Chelsfield on Saturday, had good sport for the hounds, running about 2 and a half hours,' he wrote to a friend in Halstead in an undated note. Later, he joined the West Kent Beagles in Hawkhurst as one of their 'slippers', paying no attention to members who disliked his whistle-happy style when he thought he spotted a hare. W.G. 'blew his whistle so often he became a nuisance to the members who implored the huntsman to take no notice of him,' recalled his nephew Edgar (E.M.'s son), who once or twice went beagling with W.G. in Hawkhurst.

When he was not out with his guns or his dogs, W.G. often set off for one of the golf courses that had started to sprout around the Home Counties in the early 1900s. One of his partners was Sir George Riddell, who owned the *News of the World* and, more relevantly for W.G., a handsome motor car, which took them as far afield as Huntercombe Golf Club near Oxford. On one occasion, the car broke down while W.G. and Riddell were on their way to Huntercombe. According to Riddell, W.G. used the time while the car was mended (presumably by the magnate's chauffeur) to practise his golf shots in a field by the road.

Bernard Darwin remembered Riddell arriving in his car with W.G. in about 1911 to collect Darwin from his Chelsea home for a round or two at Walton Heath in Surrey. W.G. 'saw my daughter, then aged two, flattening a pudgy nose against the window, and kissed his hand to her with an air so pretty and gracious'. On these outings, Darwin observed W.G.'s indifference to his own celebrity: 'He had only to pass through a village street in a motor car for windows to be thrown up and fingers to be pointed, but he seemed, and really was, as nearly as possible unaware of it, unless his admirer was a small child, to whom he liked to wave his hand.'

In this busy schedule, one sport remained W.G.'s dominant passion, as visitors could see when he showed them his back garden. There, ruining the lawn, was his matting practice wicket, with a net to protect the surrounding flowerbeds. Most weeks, in winter as well as summer, W.G. would ask Robert Haywood, the club professional at Eltham CC, and his teenage son Archie, to come over to Fairmount to bowl at the oldest and keenest member of the club.

On the face of it, Grace's decision to settle in Mottingham was hard to explain. He had no obvious connection with the village and it may be that he and Agnes simply found a house they both liked. Yet one scrap of circumstantial evidence suggests that W.G. moved to Mottingham because he wanted to play for Eltham CC, whose ground in a rented farm field was less than a mile from Fairmount.

In 1895, the stupendously wealthy John Thomas North had been the first contributor to W.G.'s 1895 testimonial, writing a cheque for £50. A grateful W.G. had then dedicated his ghost-written potboiler *The History of a Hundred Centuries* to the tycoon, who died a few months later. North had lived at Avery Hill, a mansion about a mile from Mottingham, and in the years leading up to the First World War his son Arthur played regularly for Eltham CC and served on the club committee. It seems possible that after W.G. lost his job at Crystal Palace, Arthur North persuaded him that Eltham CC might be a congenial cricketing home to play just one last season – W.G.'s serial refrain since failing to pack in the game after his birthday innings at the Oval in 1906, as he had promised.

On 28 May 1910, W.G and Charlie made their joint debut

for Eltham CC in a home match against Granville CC, another local club. W.G. was out leg before wicket for 3 as Eltham lost by 29 runs. Undaunted, W.G. played nine more games for Eltham in 1910, with a top score of 71. At the end of the season he felt pleased enough to send in his batting average in all games (27.13) to *Wisden Cricketers' Almanack*. 'Hoping this will enable you to make up a small paragraph,' he wrote in a note to *Wisden*'s statistician, the cricket historian Frederick Ashley-Cooper.

From now on, W.G.'s home from home in the summer became Eltham's ground at Chapel Farm, just behind St Andrew's Church on Court Road, where he and Agnes worshipped most Sundays. Eltham was not a front-rank cricket club, but its members took the game seriously, as their employment of Haywood as a professional indicated. It fell to three senior club members in particular to look after their illustrious recruit, handling him with just the right blend of tact and welcoming warmth. Eltham's captain Alfred Jackson, a rice trader in the City, kept in close touch on W.G.-related matters with the club's secretary Bryan Egerton and another senior committee member, Arthur Rammell, an insurance clerk.

Like Arrowsmith at Gloucestershire, they soon became familiar with W.G.'s habit of ignoring lines of authority when he saw a problem that demanded urgent action. 'You might inform Haywood he is to take orders from me,' W.G. wrote testily on one occasion to Egerton regarding some minor issue at Chapel Farm.

W.G. played about a dozen games a year for Eltham CC in 1911, 1912 and 1913, as well as other minor fixtures for MCC and invitation teams. All the while, he heard with depressing regularity of former cricketing friends and rivals who had not just stopped playing but had actually died. In February 1911 Billy Murdoch, on a visit to Australia, had just finished an agreeable lunch during the Melbourne Test match against South Africa when he suffered a fatal stroke. Murdoch's remains were brought back to his widow Jemima in England and buried in Kensal Rise cemetery in west London.

Three months later, E.M. died at Thornbury, his last years blighted by painful arthritis and too much drinking to relieve the pain. 'My dear Edgar,' W.G. wrote to E.M.'s son, 'We are very grieved to hear the sad news but it was not unexpected as John Dann & Blanche told us how bad he was.' E.M. had struggled through one last season for Thornbury in 1910, but as he confessed in a letter, 'it is as much as I can do to stand'.

W.G. and Agnes travelled to Downend for E.M.'s funeral, where they met up with W.G.'s only two surviving siblings, Alfred Grace and Blanche Dann. In Downend's crowded church, across the road from The Chestnuts, they all sang E.M.'s favourite hymn, 'Tell Me the Old, Old Story'. As with Fred's funeral more than thirty years earlier, Blanche's husband John led the service, and afterwards the various Graces repaired to the adjacent vicarage. Then Agnes and W.G. said their goodbyes and started the long journey back to Fairmount.

There were happier times with the grandchildren, Edgar, Bess, Gladys and 'Prim', who came often to Fairmount. W.G. taught them how to play croquet, bowls and clock golf on the back lawn, and of course cricket, which little girls were allowed to play, as Bessie had done.

'He was just very affectionate,' recalled Primrose Worthington, who said none of them saw 'Grandfather Grace' as anyone special. 'I can remember with my sister when we were very young, sitting one on each knee, plaiting his beard and tying it up with blue ribbons ... He must have been very long-suffering.'

In October 1913, ever the loyal clubman, W.G. agreed to help Eltham launch its latest recruitment drive. 'I appeal to all lovers of the grand old game to assist me by getting the younger generation and others to join the club,' he wrote to the *Eltham Times*. 'Those wishing to become members of the club should communicate with me, or to A.S. Jackson, Victoria Road, Eltham.'

By the following spring so many players had applied to join Eltham CC that the committee decided to put out two teams. W.G. became captain of the second eleven, composed mostly of

younger players, or the 'colts', as he inevitably called them. Grace
felt he owed it to the colts to play just one last season, so he could
pass on a little of his cricketing knowledge to them.

Soon to turn sixty-six, W.G. played nineteen times for Eltham
in the last peacetime summer of 1914. If he got injured, such as
the time he gashed his eyebrow against Goldsmith's College,
he carried on; he did not want to let down the side. 'For the
"slacker" at cricket the Doctor had no use,' *The Sportsman* would
soon observe. When Eltham were not playing, W.G. was ready
to help other cricket clubs at short notice. In May he agreed to
'get up' a side to play the Royal Army Ordnance Corps a month
later, when the Eton Ramblers pulled out.

The game in Woolwich, which began on 24 June, was the
reason why W.G. made his excuses to MCC and abandoned
its Lord's centary celebrations a day early. His appearance at
MCC's banquet at the Hotel Cecil was in fact the first time he
had attended a club dinner since 1898, his jubilee year. W.G. was
all for MCC as an institution, allowing his ghostwriter Porritt
to insert a pompous passage in his 1899 *Reminiscences* in praise
of the club's 'judicious conservatism' as the game's governing
body. Yet he was never that cricketing cliché, a 'tireless servant'
of MCC. For an assiduous clubman, the most striking aspect of
W.G.'s forty-six years as an MCC member was how he studiously
steered clear of committee work and internal politics at Lord's.
W.G. was more accurately seen as a tireless player for MCC,
appearing in his final game in 1913 against Old Charlton CC
in south-east London (he scored 18). For better and worse, he
remained married emotionally to Gloucestershire, even after his
painful divorce from the county of his 'affection'.

On 18 July, 'Dr W.G. Grace's XII' marked the captain's sixty-
sixth birthday by playing the boys of Eltham College at Chapel
Farm. Unusually, W.G. asked for a runner, because he was feeling
a bit lame. Grace scored only 1, giving young R.E. Rees, the
Eltham bowler, something to tell his children. The following
Saturday (25 July), W.G. travelled with his Eltham colts to nearby
Grove Park for what turned out to be his last-ever innings.

Eltham batted first and were in trouble when W.G. came to the wicket, with the score on 31 for five wickets. He took control of the situation, playing a calm, steady, unruffled game. 'W.G. batted admirably,' the *Eltham Times* reported. 'He got his runs all round the wicket, being especially strong on the off side.' As on so many earlier occasions, going right back to his 170 at Brighton in 1864, one shot in particular caught the correspondent's attention: W.G.'s distinctive shoulder-heavy backward cut, 'chopped' towards the boundary wherever it suited him. At the tea interval W.G. was 69 not out, and unable to run properly, probably because of his injured leg. Wanting to win, rather than limp to a century, he declared Eltham's innings closed. To his annoyance, Grove Park just held on for a draw, as Eltham's bowlers ran out of time.

Far away in Vienna, the Emperor Franz-Josef had just signed the orders for Austria's mobilisation against Serbia. Europe was going to war. W.G. played one last match for Eltham – a drawn game against Northbrook – but he did not bat. His heart was no longer in cricket, and he was appalled that the first-class season continued as the trains that passed the bottom of his garden in Mottingham carried young soldiers towards the battlefields of France.

By the end of August he could bear it no more. 'Sir,' he wrote to *The Sportsman*:

There are many cricketers who are already doing their duty, but there are many more who do not seem to realise that in all probability they will have to serve either at home or abroad before the war is brought to a conclusion. The fighting on the Continent is very severe, and will probably be prolonged. I think the time has arrived when the county cricket season should be closed, for it is not fitting at a time like the present that able-bodied men should play day after day and pleasure-seekers look on. There are so many who are young and able, and yet are hanging back. I should like to see all first-class cricketers of suitable age, etc, set a good example, and come to the help of their country without delay in its hour of need.

 Yours etc.,

 W.G. Grace

His letter had no impact on MCC, which failed to stop another round of county championship matches in late August and early September, days after the British Expeditionary Force suffered almost eight thousand casualties at the battle of Le Cateau. MCC just had time to squeeze in two final games of its own at the Scarborough Cricket Festival, as around thirteen thousand British soldiers were being killed at the First Battle of the Marne. Then the lights went out in the Lord's pavilion, more than a month after the rest of Europe.

32

SUNSET

W.G. detested the war and knew whom to blame. Whenever he met Arthur Rammell, the Eltham CC committee man, he 'felt too strongly about Germany to be able to express himself in measured terms'. Agnes and W.G. also feared for their two surviving children. On 28 August, the day after *The Sportsman* published W.G.'s letter, Edgar's battlecruiser HMS *New Zealand* was engaged in the Battle of Heligoland Bight off the north-west German coast. The thought that he might lose his third child as Jack Hearne was scoring a century for Middlesex against Kent at Lord's was more than W.G. could bear. At least Charlie was relatively safe. He had joined the Kent Fortress Engineers, and would spend most of the war maintaining telephones and other electrical equipment in the Medway and Thames Estuary districts.

Rhys Jones, the Rector of Mottingham at St Andrew's Church, saw W.G. regularly during the first months of the war: 'The tragedy of the war had opened his wide heart yet more widely,' Jones remembered, 'and many is the tale that our village lanes and gardens could tell of human conversations, in which rank and class were entirely forgotten, interesting bits of letters from his gallant Naval son read to interested listeners, and a listening ear offered, in return for what the person talked to might have to read or say about his own human folk here or over the seas.'

W.G. was not a coward, but nor was he a stiff upper-lipped Victorian. He could not contain his emotions about the war and the suffering it caused. Nobody took the slaughter 'more to heart', said Bernard Darwin, who saw W.G. – possibly for a discreet game of golf – as the death toll in France and Belgium mounted into tens of thousands: 'In addition to a father's anxieties, he had to bear the loss of so very many young friends – not only the boys he knew but their fathers who had once been boys to him. He could not endure the thought of them being, as he said over and over again, "mowed down".'

At Fairmount, W.G. passed the time as best he could. He looked after his carefully planted vegetable plots on the slopes beyond his abandoned cricket net and kept up correspondence with old acquaintances. The cricket historian Frederick Ashley-Cooper, too frail to enlist, was busy that winter at his home in Surrey with research on some games in the 1860s. W.G. tried to help. 'I have managed to get three of the matches all right, but the others have beaten me,' he replied just before Christmas to one of Ashley-Cooper's enquiries.

At Easter time, 1915, W.G. sent a dedication to go with a gift that he had bought for his little ones. 'To my grandchildren Edgar, Bess, Gladys & Prim,' he wrote, 'who I hope will always love books.' Once the Easter holiday was over, W.G. faced the prospect of a summer without cricket for the first time since his early boyhood. He fretted about the state of Eltham's Chapel Farm ground and often wandered over from Fairmount to make sure everything was in order. For a while, W.G. also regularly attended club committee meetings, and then it all got too much. The war 'preyed on his mind', Alfred Jackson recalled, and 'he seemed to grow more and more retiring, and we did not see much of him'.

In May, W.G. agreed to appear at a charity cricket match on

Whit Monday in Catford, three miles from Eltham, to raise money for the local Red Cross society. The game between Catford and the Army Service Corps was organised by the Lancashire and England cricketer Archie MacLaren and the former Kent player Alec Hearne, who thought W.G. had said he would play. Instead, W.G. turned up without his cricket bag, explaining to a reporter that since the war he had no appetite for sport.

'I can see him now coming through the gate and walking across the ground,' one of the players, Captain Percy Burke, recalled. 'No bag and in ordinary clothes. He must have seen our faces and he at once compromised by offering to stay all day and go round the ground with a collecting box.'

For the last time, W.G. stole the show. 'Great bursts of laughter' erupted from the crowd as he trudged round the boundary clutching his box, chatting and joking with spectators. Out on the playing field, Jack Hobbs was scoring a century. Hobbs, W.G.'s natural heir as the world's greatest batsman, was a modest man, unlikely to worry about being upstaged by the 'Old Man'.

On 18 July, W.G.'s sixty-seventh birthday, the Veteran Athletes Corps and the Fleet Street Company of the Athletes' Volunteer Force, en route to nearby Chislehurst, made a short detour along Mottingham Lane and lined up outside Fairmount. 'The Old Man came out, and Col. Tamplin, V.D., K.C., commanding, proffered a few words of congratulation, to which the doctor suitably responded. Then "Three Cheers for W.G." were given by the men with hearty good will, and the volunteers resumed their march.'

Four days later, W.G.'s brother-in-law John Dann collapsed and died at the vicarage in Downend, following an appendix operation. It was a mark of W.G.'s closeness to Dann and his widowed sister Blanche that he made the difficult wartime journey to Downend for the funeral. Agnes, who was also fond of Dann and Blanche, stayed at Fairmount, perhaps feeling she could not leave elderly Aunt Caroline and cousin Marian Coleman on their own.

*

On 9 October 1915 Grace suffered a cerebral haemorrhage at Fairmount, possibly while tending his vegetable patch. It was a mild stroke, causing him to slur his speech, and he was able to put himself to bed.

'The doctor is ill & may not do anything in the way of going through your proofs for a week at least from now,' Agnes wrote three days later to Frederick Ashley-Cooper, who had sent Grace some more material to check:

> He was taken ill on Saturday but read the first lot of proofs through & told me a lot of mistakes but they are not marked, & I am sure that I could not remember all, he would be very sorry for it to be published with such a number of errors. If you must have the proofs back before he can revise them, I must send them to you, but I am not allowed to bother him in any way.

On the night of 13 October, the Germans launched a wave of Zeppelin air raids across eastern England, with the arsenal at Woolwich, near Eltham, one of their main targets. This attack, and the coincidence of W.G.'s illness, formed the ingredients for a story told by the Surrey cricketer Henry Leveson Gower that, on a visit to W.G., he found him cowering in his bed from the Zeppelins. There was a good reason why the German newspapers did not pick up Leveson Gower's story to use as wartime propaganda, as was later rumoured. Leveson Gower (pronounced 'Loosen Gore') did not recount his tale publicly until 1953, when he published his memoirs. In his book Leveson Gower was vague about both the time of his visit and Grace's physical condition, describing him as 'not very well' rather than close to death. The only element in the story that rang true was W.G.'s justifiable fear of the Germans' new wonder weapon, which everyone shared.

W.G. languished in bed for ten days after his stroke, occasionally getting up to sit with Agnes, who kept an eye on him. Some time on Saturday, 23 October, W.G. clambered out of bed once

more to sit with Agnes. Ensconced in his armchair, he suffered
a heart attack, dying a few minutes later.

Alfred Gardiner, the editor of the London *Daily News*, was
standing on a country station railway platform, reading a paper to
catch up with the war, when a friend tapped him on the shoulder
and told him W.G. was dead:

> At the word I turned hastily to another column and found
> the news that had stirred him. And even in the midst of
> world-shaking events it stirred me too. For a brief moment
> I forgot the war and was back in that cheerful world where
> we used to be happy, where we greeted the rising sun with
> light hearts and saw its setting without fear. In that cheer-
> ful world I can hardly recall a time when a big man with
> a black beard was not my King ... I owe more undiluted
> happiness to him than to any man that ever lived. For he
> was the genial tyrant in a world that was all sunshine.

On a chilly, grey afternoon, W.G.'s gigantic coffin was transported by motor hearse from Fairmount to Elmers End cemetery,
where Bessie and Bertie were buried. In the dead of war, a crowd
of several thousand lined the road outside the cemetery and then
pressed through the gates as the hearse pulled up outside the
small funeral chapel. Blanche Dann, still grieving for her husband, travelled over from Downend. Charlie was there, but not
Edgar, whose cruiser HMS *Grafton* was engaged in the gathering
military disaster at Gallipoli.

Frizzy Bush came, 'representing the Gloucester club' and himself. Frank Townsend, W.G.'s other great Gloucestershire chum,
travelled the short journey from his home in Lambeth, where
he now worked as a private tutor. Ranji attended, his right eye
blinded from a recent shooting accident – not at the front, but on
a Yorkshire country estate. Lord Hawke, president of the MCC,
represented the club and read out telegrams of condolence from
Australia and New Zealand. Lord Harris, W.G.'s best and oldest

friend in high cricketing places, sat gaunt and erect in the chapel. The King, who did not attend, sent a message of sympathy to MCC, which the club passed on to Agnes.

Addressing the congregation, Rhys Jones, the rector of Mottingham, talked about the W.G. his parishioners got to know:

> We who lived so near him during the six years that he spent among us at Mottingham . . . shall always remember him as an almost ideal human neighbour, so kindly, so homely, so ready always to talk to anyone in a genial, simple way all his own. He steadfastly refused to identify himself with any of those narrow cliques which spoil parochial life so badly. He abhorred conventional class distinctions in his intercourse with humanity. Everyone to him was equally human; and he spoke to everyone, and dealt with everyone as such.

At the end of the service, there was a ghastly moment when the former Surrey batsman Bobby Abel, one of the pallbearers, stumbled and nearly dropped the coffin. The procession halted, Abel recovered, and they continued on to Bessie and Bertie's shared grave. Agnes, Charlie and Blanche watched as the pallbearers lowered W.G. into the pit. At the last moment, Frank Townsend leaned over the edge and shrieked, 'Goodbye, Gilly, Goodbye!'

33

FALSE MEMORIAL

The day after the funeral, Sir Home Gordon placed a notice in *The Sportsman* newspaper. Messrs Constable, the publishers, had invited him to write 'a lengthy memorial biography of Dr W.G. Grace', announced Gordon. Furthermore, Lord Hawke, as MCC president, had agreed to write the introduction. 'May I appeal, through your columns, to all who possess documents, anecdotes and reminiscences, to forward them as soon as possible to me at 2, Cheyne Walk, London S.W.' Gordon added: 'It is only through the general cooperation of his countless admirers that an adequate tribute can be compiled.'

Suave, debonair, carnation-wearing Gordon seemed an odd choice to produce what sounded like MCC's official biography of Grace. Gordon's latest book, *A Man's Road*, was a racy bodice-ripper, the hero of which, by artistic coincidence, also lived at Cheyne Walk. In Gordon's novel, the hero's shy, retiring wife fails to satisfy him in the way men need. In the real world, Gordon found himself 'utterly out of sympathy' with his childless wife Edith, who was considering whether to divorce him. Shortly after his advertisement in *The Sportsman* (also placed in *The Times*), Gordon decamped to his club in

Bournemouth with his latest girlfriend, while Edith consulted her lawyer.

MCC had always tolerated members with complicated private lives such as Gordon and – several decades earlier – Fitzgerald. Gordon's real offence in the eyes of the committee was his habit of writing pieces from time to time that criticised the club's stewardship of cricket. In 1900, the committee had formally rebuked Gordon for an 'objectionable article' he wrote containing 'inaccurate statements which were calculated to bring obloquy on the Executive'. Gordon apologised, explaining airily that he had been suffering from a 'disturbance'. Two years later, Gordon wrote an article for *The Sportsman* which the committee also found 'objectionable'. Gordon apologised again. And so it continued: in 1909 C.B. Fry complained to the MCC committee about an article by Gordon in *The Tatler* which Fry felt had defamed him.

Gordon's appeal for help with his biography of Grace was typically misleading. His project had not been authorised by MCC, as Gordon implied. His book was a purely private venture, which had occupied him for at least a year before W.G.'s death. Grace's funeral, which Gordon attended, looked to him like a commercial opportunity to boost sales by publishing an 'official' memorial biography with MCC's imprimatur. To that end, Gordon was counting on one extremely senior ally at Lord's to overcome any objections by the committee.

Martin Bladen Hawke, the 7th Baron Hawke of Towton, was the very model of the gentleman amateur. Unlike the older Lord Harris, Hawke was a mediocre batsman who in 936 first-class innings stretched over three decades scored only thirteen centuries. No matter: Hawke's title and considerable administrative energies delivered him the captaincy and then the presidency of Yorkshire CCC, and the presidency of MCC in 1914 – a position he held till 1918, because of the war. The still-unmarried Hawke was unique among MCC grandees in being a close friend of Gordon, as a fellow man about town. Gordon knew that Hawke's name on his book would give the biography an official MCC stamp, while Hawke was not averse to exploiting his name to earn a bit of extra money; in the late 1880s Hawke had been one of W.G.'s fellow directors on the board of the 'Magic Bat' company.

With Hawke behind him, Gordon had momentum. In the days following Grace's funeral it rapidly became clear that Gordon was well ahead of potential competitors in preparing a biography of Grace, especially given Gordon's claims to be acting on behalf of MCC.

'Buns' Thornton was one of the first of W.G.'s old acquaintances to respond to Gordon's advertisement, personally bringing his five cricketing scrapbooks round to Cheyne Walk. Ashley-Cooper also wanted to join Gordon's venture as the book's statistician, in return for a fee. Gordon replied on 29 October that he would of course be 'deeply honoured' to collaborate in future with Ashley-Cooper. However, 'in the present case I am reluctantly compelled to decline for two reasons. In confidence, the first is because I cannot afford to divide what little cash I shall get. The second is that there will not be space for statistics.'

Gordon continued: 'I expect there will be several books tried, but the scale on which my Memorial Biography is planned and the fact that the Committee of MCC (to whom it will be dedicated) will give it their hearty support, as well as my having promised contributions from the greatest of those who played with W.G., makes me believe this will be the book to tell posterity what he has been.'

Six days later, Gordon told Ashley-Cooper that he already had reminiscences of W.G. 'in hand' from Lord Harris and nine other cricketing dignitaries, 'as well as over 100 voluntary correspondents.' Hawke, meanwhile, had just hit a rather embarrassing obstacle that required the peer to make an urgent visit to Fairmount.

Agnes had heard about Gordon's project and sent a strong protest to Lord's. In the drawing room at Fairmount – possibly flanked by Aunt Caroline and Cousin Marian for support – an indignant Agnes showed Hawke a report by Gordon of a London County match in 1902. Gordon had accused W.G. of undermining 'the dignity of the game ... by thoughtlessly shouting to the fieldsman'. W.G. had been furious, and Agnes now told Hawke that MCC had to stop Gordon from bringing out his biography, which she felt was bound to insult her husband's memory. Like everyone else, Agnes thought MCC had commissioned Gordon to write the book and it is not clear whether Hawke told her the embarrassing truth. MCC had simply allowed Gordon to create the impression that his biography was somehow connected with the club.

According to Gordon, Hawke returned from Mottingham and 'peremptorily informed me that, as she [Agnes] wished it, of course I must abandon the book. Equally emphatic was my refusal, and this he communicated to her.'

On 13 December the committee considered 'correspondence' from Mrs Grace. 'It was decided that a letter drafted by the President should be sent ... and to reconsider the matter [of Gordon's request] if she withdraws her objection to the publication.' Three days later, Hawke took a deep breath and wrote to Agnes:

Dear Mrs Grace,

As promised last week I am now able to write you the result of the MCC meeting held this week.

They have asked me to say how thoroughly they enter into your feelings and how desirous they are to please you.

They have carefully considered the whole question of the Memorial Biography of your late Husband and feel that the Club may well accept some responsibility.

You must be well aware we are not in the Publishing Line having no machinery for that purpose.

We are, however, anxious to overcome your objection and, therefore, if you approve, would willingly take over the work which Sir Home Gordon has collected.

On the Title page no names of any Author will appear, only the statement that it is issued under the auspices of the President and Committee of MCC.

At the same time the Committee cannot avoid seeing the importance of what Sir Home Gordon has collected and that the arrangements he has made are invaluable.

They, therefore, propose in conjunction with myself and some one else to be nominated by the Committee to use his services as Co-Editor.

I am expressly desired to ask would the fact of his assisting in the manner above described be still displeasing to you.

A very large number of Cricketers, past and present, will furnish contributions and we hope you will nominate some one to write the special chapters on the private life of your Husband.

I may add Messrs Constable & Co will gladly give a cheque to the Cricketers Fund.

I shall indeed be glad to hear you approve of MCC producing the Biography and hope that all difficulties will have been surmounted ...

Hawke then suggested to Agnes that before replying she should show his letter to Charlie Townsend, now the Grace family's solicitor.

In his post-war autobiography, Hawke decided his exchanges with Agnes were irrelevant to capturing the essence of her character. 'As for Mrs Grace,' he wrote, 'I can only sum her up affectionately and respectfully with the words, "She is a dear".'

Agnes accepted Hawke's proposal, which the MCC committee rubber-stamped on 10 January. She now wrote Hawke a small masterpiece of command disguised by flattery.

Dear Lord Hawke,' Agnes began:

I thank you very much for your letter received this morning & for letting me know as quickly as was possible the decision of the MCC. I feel very grateful to you for all you have done in this matter & to the Committee of the MCC for they will gladly produce the Biography.

Have I your permission to tell any of our friends that 'Gilbert's biography will be produced under the auspices of the MCC & that we feel very gratified that it is to be so'.

Will there be a notice in the papers to this effect?

I am sorry to give you the trouble of writing yet another letter to me, but I should be sorry to make known anything amongst my friends before it should be done.

She added chattily: 'I have a day of quietude for the 4 elder grandchildren with their mother have gone to town to the Empire to see "Britain Prepared".'

On 13 January, Francis Lacey, MCC's secretary, drafted an agreement for Gordon to sign, based on the deal which Hawke had reached with Agnes:

Lord Hawke cannot get the support of Mrs Grace for Sir Home Gordon's biography. It would receive the support of the Grace family if the MCC brought out such a book. In order to meet this, if the MCC Committee will undertake the book, Sir Home is willing to hand over the whole material thus far prepared (a large amount) and he will continue to edit the volume in conjunction with Lord Hawke and a third member to be nominated by the Committee.

Lacey noted that MCC would have no financial liability for any losses, that the publisher would make a donation to the Cricketers' Benevolent Society charity, and that Gordon 'would look to the royalty he would receive on sales' for remuneration.

'I confirm this,' Gordon wrote and signed curtly at the end. Privately, he was seething. 'Naturally I was enchanted at this dignification of my memorial,' he recalled sarcastically, after Hawke and Agnes were dead.

Gordon gradually rallied, once it became clear that Hawke and Lord Harris, the third designated editor, would only exercise notional control over him. 'I reminded [Hawke] that it was my book after all, and it is superfluous to add that Lord Harris was as reasonable as he was helpful.' According to Gordon, Harris barely touched the manuscript. Gordon also changed his mind about using Ashley-Cooper's 'fine statistics'. 'I shall annex the lot, making it a chapter by you,' Gordon blithely informed Ashley-Cooper, without mentioning a research fee.

Gordon set to work on the text, writing the links between the anecdotes he selected. He excluded Alfred Pocock, 'a ridiculous personage', and decided not to approach the former Lancashire captain 'Monkey' Hornby for a contribution, even though Hornby had known W.G. well. Hornby 'cannot put 2 words together', Gordon confided to Ashley-Cooper.

There was much else to discard. Gordon claimed that more than four hundred people sent in material, which he then 'sifted . . . so that nothing in the volume should cause offence'. He also kept no notes of 'what seemed injudicious to put on record'. For her part, Agnes ruled out any discussion of W.G.'s private life, leaving readers to take Gordon's word that 'alike as son, as brother, as husband, and as father, in every relationship of family existence he [W.G.] was exemplary . . . The honoured privacy of his domesticity has nothing to do with the public career of the great sportsman.'

It is impossible to tell how many of W.G.'s former friends and fellow cricketers refused to contribute to the book, and how many Gordon omitted. But when the book was finally published in 1919, 'under the auspices of the Committee of MCC', knowledgeable readers could spot some notable absentees. Frank Townsend was missing, even though a photograph of Grace by Townsend's wife adorned the frontispiece. Frizzy Bush did not contribute, and nor did Fry or Ranji, with Ranji making a feeble excuse about being stranded in India. Gordon found space for three professionals – Dick Barlow of Lancashire, George Hirst of Yorkshire and Dick Lilley of Warwickshire – all of whom had been familiar with Grace. Otherwise the biography was an entirely amateur production.

Spofforth, stirring himself at his new home in Surrey,

submitted a story that was demonstrably untrue. 'The Demon' claimed to have bowled to Grace in the practice nets at Melbourne in December 1874, surprising W.G. with 'one of my very fastest' deliveries: 'Down went his off stump, and he called out in his quick fashion when not liking anything: "Where did that come from?" "Who bowled that?" But I slipped away, having done my job.'

As Spofforth knew, and shipping records prove, he was in Tasmania at the time, visiting his brother.

For his own amusement, Spofforth sunk Gordon's claim that the book would 'tell posterity what [W.G.] had been'. The true purpose of *The Memorial Biography of Dr W.G. Grace* was to stop posterity making further enquiries.

34

AFTERGLOW

The years went by. In July 1923, MCC opened the handsome, iron Grace Gates, set in pillars of Portland stone, at the main entrance to Lord's on St John's Wood Road. Grace's initials 'W.G.G.' were engraved in a wreath above an inscription:

TO THE MEMORY OF WILLIAM GILBERT GRACE THE GREAT CRICKETER: 1848–1915: THESE GATES WERE ERECTED: THE MCC AND OTHER FRIENDS AND ADMIRERS.

Agnes politely declined MCC's invitation to attend the ceremony and officially open the gates. 'While greatly appreciating the compliment paid her she does not feel equal to the task,' the *Western Daily Press* reported.

As time passed, there were fewer 'friends and admirers' with first-hand memories of the man. Frank Townsend had died in a south London hospital on Christmas Day 1920, following an operation. Frizzy Bush died in September 1924, leaving a vacancy for the post of Bristol's civic sword bearer. In the Surrey suburb of Long Ditton, Spofforth prowled about in his garden, satisfying his competitive urges by entering local horticultural shows. The greatest of all Grace's opponents died in June 1926 and was buried in deepest England, at the Brookwood cemetery near Woking.

By now, a procession of batsmen had passed or were approaching W.G.'s once-daunting landmark of 100 first-class centuries. The Surrey batsman Tom Hayward came first in 1913, followed after the war by Jack Hobbs (1923), the Hampshire professional Phil Mead (1927), Patsy Hendren of Middlesex (1928) and Frank Woolley of Kent (1929). Of this quintet, only Jack Hobbs, 'the Master', merited direct comparison with Grace as an authentic batting genius. The others were merely great batsmen who had profited, like Hobbs, from the improvement in batting surfaces since the 1870s and the increased volume of first-class matches.

Writing in 1924, Lord Hawke remained confident that Grace's status as the best batsman of all time would remain unchallenged. 'I do not hesitate to say that not only was he [Grace] the greatest that ever lived, but also the greatest that ever can be,' Hawke stated, 'because no future batsman will ever have to play on the bad wickets on which he made his mark and proved himself so immeasurably superior to all his contemporaries.'

In Australia, Hawke's prediction was about to be demolished by Don Bradman. During a career lasting from 1927 to 1949 (interrupted by the war), Bradman achieved such towering superiority over all other batsmen that his playing record still looks like a misprint. Bradman's Test match batting average of 99.94 was about forty runs per innings more than the next greatest Test batsmen of his era: the West Indian George Headley (60.83), and the English players Herbert Sutcliffe (60.73), Walter Hammond (58.45), and Len Hutton (56.67). Since Bradman's retirement in 1948, no Test batsman with a statistically meaningful record has come much closer to his record.

In the 1930s, there were occasional mutterings that Bradman might be human after all. On England's 'bodyline' tour of Australia in 1932–3, the terrifyingly fast Nottinghamshire bowler Harold Larwood, chiefly aided by his county team-mate

Bill Voce, reduced Bradman to a series average of 56.57 by deliberately targeting his body – or, as Larwood said, hitting Bradman 'smack on the arse'. Hedley Verity, the great pre-war Yorkshire and England left-arm spinner, took Bradman's wicket eight times in Test matches; when Verity bowled to Bradman on a turning pitch it looked like an equal contest.

Yet Bradman's overall record confounded Hawke's judgement that Grace would stand for ever as indisputably the greatest of all batsmen. If a time machine had transported Bradman at his absolute pre-war peak back to the terrible pitches of the 1860s and early 1870s, he would have found a way to match and possibly surpass W.G.'s titanic performances.

Suppose, then, that the same time machine now collected the younger Grace (not the 'Old Man') and deposited him on the placid, 'shirtfront' pitches of the inter-war period where Bradman piled up huge scores: what would have happened? In these benign batting conditions, it is hard to imagine W.G. *not* scoring double-, triple- and even quadruple-centuries. W.G. had the same limitless appetite for runs as Bradman, the same technical inventiveness and the same capacity to aim for previously inconceivable heights.

In its time and context, Grace's fifty first-class centuries by the age of twenty-seven was as astounding as Bradman's record-breaking performance six decades later. Yet W.G.'s achievement became ever harder to recognise, for two reasons. One was the avalanche of run-scoring that followed the improvement of pitches in the late nineteenth century. The other was the perception that the mid-Victorian round-arm bowlers against whom W.G. scored these centuries were not as good – and in particular, not as fast – as the greatest modern bowlers. Again, the context matters. Grace needed exceptionally quick reactions to deal with bowlers like Nottinghamshire's Jem Shaw, on surfaces where one ball might be a shooter and the next one fly past his head. As any modern batsman knows, the pace of the delivery in miles per hour is not the whole story.

For the sake of argument, one can also apply the same

perspective to Bradman. It is true that Bradman scored some of his 117 first-class centuries (in far fewer games than W.G.) against great bowlers. It is also true that he made a fair number of the runs for these centuries against mediocre bowlers on easy batting wickets. In the first Test at Brisbane in 1946, when Bradman scored 187, the main supporting bowlers for Alec Bedser and Doug Wright, both Test-class bowlers, were: Bill Voce, who at thirty-five was well past his best (he took no wickets); Bill Edrich, principally a batsman; and Norman Yardley, not even a front-rank county bowler. This is not to diminish Bradman's record, for it takes effort and will to score centuries against second-rate bowlers; but, like W.G., Bradman's run-making had a context.

Some observers did get Grace's measure, because they had seen him in his prime. The veteran Bristol cricket correspondent Henry Roslyn, who first watched W.G. batting in the late 1870s, identified Grace's 'ability to score from all kinds of bowling on all kinds of wickets' as the key to his greatness. 'Put him on a sun-baked sand-heap or on a stretch of ground which preparation had caused to crumble badly, and the chances were he would be equally difficult to dislodge.' W.G. was also unquestionably courageous. Roslyn remembered a match in August 1894 when Grace withstood the Surrey fast bowler Tom Richardson on a dire pitch at Cheltenham: 'The following day W.G. called me into the dressing room to see how he had been battered. Bruises extended from left knee to left shoulder, and there were other black marks about his body.'

Roslyn came nearer than any other writer to producing a cinematic image of some of Grace's signature batting strokes. One in particular stuck in Roslyn's memory: W.G.'s distinctive forcing shot off his legs:

His feet came together as he drew himself up and there was little space for the bat to swing; yet so much wrist power was employed that mid-on had little chance of stopping the ball, and long-on experienced considerable difficulty in saving a four: for W.G. had his position well in mind when making the stroke.

The picture is startlingly modern. Substitute the initials 'K.P.' for 'W.G.' and the image still holds good.

Roslyn's insights into Grace went largely unnoticed outside Gloucestershire. Instead, W.G. became swathed in a mist of 'golden age' nostalgia. In 1933 the cricket correspondent Archie Powell, Roslyn's rival on the *Western Daily Press*, produced his own recollections of Grace in a book-length series of articles for the *Bristol Evening World*. Unlike Roslyn, Powell did not even pretend to be objective. His pieces hailed a 'giant genius who has become a legend' without shedding much light on the man.

Bernard Darwin's slim biography of Grace, published in 1934, was original in two respects. Darwin had contacted Grace's son Edgar, who provided fresh details about the family's life at Thrissell House in the 1880s. A superb golf journalist, Darwin also used his memories of days out with W.G. at Walton Heath and other courses to sketch a vivid portrait of Grace at the end of his life. However, Darwin swallowed whole the prevailing snobbery about W.G.'s allegedly simple mind and boyish 'keenness'. Bradman, too, was rather keen.

As spectators poured each summer through the Grace Gates, Agnes guarded her privacy. In W.G.'s will, drawn up in 1910, Grace. had left her all his estate, which after death duties was valued at £6326. It was a tidy amount, but not a fortune for a woman who had no money of her own. In a sign of his concern about Charlie's prospects, W.G. included a proviso that if Agnes predeceased him, his youngest son would receive two-thirds of the estate, with one-third going to the more successful Edgar.

Agnes fell ill in 1926, preparing her own will in a Sussex hospital, with a doctor and nurse as witnesses. Increasingly frail, she spent her last years living with Charlie at his home in the Kent village of Hawkhurst. To some surprise, Charlie had married

Annie Hartnell, the daughter of a Gloucestershire doctor, and they now had two little grandchildren for 'Granny Grace'.

Agnes died at Hawkhurst, her death barely noticed by the press, in sharp contast to Martha Grace's passing almost half a century before. She was buried at Elmers End cemetery, next to W.G., Bertie and Bessie.

Two years later, Lord Harris finished lunch at Belmont, which he had repossessed after mending his finances in the City. Harris sat in an armchair in front of the fire, lit a cigarette and shortly afterwards collapsed and died. Harris's failings are easy to recognise today. He was autocratic, often pompous, and a rigid defender of the rights of cricketing gentlemen over players. Yet he was unique within the MCC hierarchy in treating the humbly born Grace purely on his merit as a cricketer. It had been enough to seal more than four decades of friendship.

Edgar Grace retired from the navy in 1934 with the rank of admiral and went into service for God. 'We could regard our lives as a Test match in which we were always batting, and in which it was no use complaining of bodyline tactics or sticky wickets,' Edgar told a Christian rally in July 1934. 'Victory was only to be gained by taking our bat and our courage in both hands.' In his firm, unbending fashion, Edgar was coping with his own sorrow. His eldest daughter Gladys, an amateur pilot, had been killed two years earlier in a failed flying stunt over Kent. In 1936, his wife Kitty died at their home near Portsmouth. Edgar's own innings was nearly over. Three months later, he died in his sleep while visiting his daughter Primrose ('Prim') and her naval husband in Devonport.

Charlie was now the only surviving member of the close family. Since 1925 he had been managing engineer of the Weald Electricity Supply Company, covering east Sussex and west Kent. Charlie was not, as his teachers at Clifton had thought, a hopeless dullard. Like his father, he had a practical mind, at its best when figuring out how things worked and how to repair them.

Charlie was also a decent cricketer, founding and captaining his company's team. On 6 June 1938, Charlie walked out to bat

for Weald Electricity CC in an away game against Sidley CC,
near Bexhill in east Sussex. His team's total stood on 285 for eight
wickets, and, as Charlie knew, the electricians had never made
300. Showing some of W.G.'s coolness, Charlie calmly scored 11
to take the total to 296, and then drove the ball to the boundary
to reach his team's record-breaking target. 'The crowd began to
cheer, but was silent almost immediately,' the *Gloucestershire Echo*
reported; for Charlie had collapsed on completing the shot. 'We
thought at first that he had just fainted from the excitement,'
a team-mate declared. 'It was a terrific shock when we found
he was dead.' Charlie's funeral took place three days later in
Hawkhurst Parish Church; he was only fifty-six.

Now there was no one left to tend W.G.'s grave at Elmers
End. War came, and in November 1943 the former Kent fast
bowler Bill Bradley was distressed while walking through the
cemetery to find the grave completely neglected. 'The cross surmounting the stone has been blown down by enemy action and
lies on the ground, and the grave is covered with long grass and
weeds,' Bradley wrote to the *Western Daily Press*. A local reader,
the appropriately named Edith Nettle, read Bradley's letter and
alerted her brother Harry, who lived in Elmers End. Harry did
his best, tidying up the grave, getting rid of all the grass and
long weeds, and leaning the heavy marble cross against W.G.'s
tombstone. 'I would have liked to have planted some tulip bulbs,
but they are not obtainable,' he reported back to the newspaper.

Peace came, and the weeds returned. On 18 July 1948, the
centenary of W.G.'s birth, the MCC grandee Sir Pelham Warner
opened the renamed Grace Gate at the Nevil Road entrance to
Ashley Down. Over lunch, Warner 'related many reminiscences
of his association with "W.G."'. In truth, Warner's acquaintance
with Grace had been slight. That evening, John Arlott presented
The Old Man, a semi-dramatised radio programme on the BBC
Home Service. Sadly, Arlott fell below his usual high standard,
content to draw the conventional, wildly inaccurate portrait
of W.G. as a man of 'pure country strain' whose cricket was
'instinctive'.

At Lord's, MCC had dedicated the annual match between the Gentlemen and the Players, starting on 14 July, to the memory of Grace. Fittingly, a partnership between Len Hutton and Denis Compton, the two greatest English batsmen of the 1940s, ensured an easy victory for the Players. It did not occur to the MCC committee that some kind of tribute at Elmers End might also be in order.

Only one wreath was laid on 18 July at W.G.'s half-ruined grave. Late in the afternoon, a passer-by stooped to read the card that had been left by W.G.'s broken tombstone. It said simply: 'In memory of the great cricketer, from all Australia'. The wreath had been sent by Don Bradman's 1948 Australian touring team, known ever after as the 'Invincibles' for their ruthless destruction of England. In W.G., they recognised a fellow spirit.

The respect paid by the Australians to W.G. marked a symbolic turning point. In the 1950s and 1960s the cricket world began to move towards a better understanding of Grace and his place in sporting history. The pioneers were two direct contemporaries, both admirers of Grace, who in every other respect were utterly different.

Neville Weston was a Worcestershire solicitor who lived all his life in his home town of Kidderminster. In the 1950s and 1960s, Weston spent much of his spare time assembling what he hoped would be the complete record of all Grace's 'minor' (i.e. non-first-class) matches. At first sight Weston's quest seemed pointless; who could be interested, for instance, in how many runs W.G. scored on 20 September 1879 against the Berkshire town of Newbury? Weston soldiered on, poring through Victorian newspapers and old club scorebooks, until in 1973 he finally published his work in a limited edition of fifty copies.

As Weston acknowledged, he fell short of his goal; even his exhaustive trawl had failed to capture all the minor fixtures that Grace had played. Yet Weston's pursuit of his Holy Grail had achieved something more important. Set forth in his book was an entirely different Grace from the Leviathan of 126 first-class centuries, the money-grubbing shamateur who fiddled his expenses, or the roguish 'Old Man' who refused to walk when given out. Here was a W.G. who loved cricket so much that he would play against anyone, anywhere: from the Bristol City and County Asylum in 1884 to a team called Egypt (actually a British Army team) which showed up at Crystal Palace in 1905.

Weston was about halfway through his labours in 1963 when a wandering, Trinidadian Marxist scholar ventured into W.G. territory. Cyril 'C.L.R.' James had seen a lot more of the world than Weston by the time he published *Beyond a Boundary*, often cited as the best cricket book ever written. Originally a Trotskyite, James had met the exiled (and soon to be assassinated) Russian revolutionary Leon Trotsky in Mexico in 1939. During the 1940s, James worked as a political agitator in the United States for the self-styled 'Johnson-Forest Tendency', a faction within the US Workers Party, which itself was a breakaway from the Socialist Workers Party. The US authorities ignored all these complications, deporting James as a straightforward communist in 1953.

James settled in Britain, where, to help fund his other writing, he took a job as a part-time cricket correspondent for the *Manchester Guardian*. As its title implied, *Beyond a Boundary* was about far more than cricket, drawing on James's eclectic background and wide reading, from the Greek classics to *Tom Brown's Schooldays*. James devoted most of the book to a series of reflections on the place of cricket and cricketers in the politics and culture of the Caribbean, written in alluring, rhetorical prose. However, the book's centrepiece was a three-part study of Grace under the imposing title 'W.G.: Pre-Eminent Victorian'. James deplored Grace's near-total absence from histories of nineteenth-century England and set out to establish his credentials as a major cultural and social figure.

According to James, the 'common people' in Victorian England needed 'organised sports and games' to divert them from the drudgery of factory and office life. Grace, the greatest sporting hero of the age, provided that essential diversion: 'Through

W.G. Grace, cricket, the most complete expression of popular life in pre-industrial England, was incorporated into the life of the nation. As far as any social activity can be the work of any one man, he did it.'

James's argument then unravelled, as he tried to reconcile the received view of Grace as a simple-minded son of the soil with his consciously Marxist perspective. For James, Grace 'was typical of an England that was being superseded. He was the yeoman, the country doctor, the squire, the England of yesterday'. Dependent on the existing literature about Grace, James could not see the W.G. who loved modern technology and lived happily in cities and suburbs for most of his adult life. As a result, he failed to grasp the forward-looking bent of Grace's mind and character.

Yet James had asked the right question – why was Grace so famous? – and because the rest of *Beyond a Boundary* was so brilliantly original, he forced other cricket writers to take W.G. seriously too. After James, no one could tackle Grace without considering the times in which he lived and his standing as a Victorian 'great man' on a level with Dickens, Livingstone and Darwin (Bernard's grandfather).

It was a measure of W.G.'s complexity that the basis for his fame proved remarkably difficult to pinpoint. The cricket historian Rowland Bowen, writing in 1970, suggested that Britain during the 1860s and 1870s found a heroic 'national figurehead' in Grace to compensate for the widowed Queen Victoria's retreat into mourning. Bowen's theory was a little far-fetched; there were plenty of Victorians, including Her Majesty, who found cricket baffling and dull. Eric Midwinter, in his 1981 biography, fixed more precisely than either Bowen or James that Grace's status as 'the most celebrated sportsman in the entire world' depended on the emergence of a new mass spectator audience for sport in Britain's industrial cities and towns.

In the late 1990s, the approach of the 150th anniversary of W.G.'s birth inspired three books which in different ways brought more of the real Grace back to life. Robert Low's biography rightly saw Grace as a modern figure while casting a sceptical journalist's eye over some of the myths about W.G., such as his supposed vocation for medicine. Simon Rae's substantial biography put the focus back on Grace's cricket, a bizarrely neglected subject since W.G.'s death. Rae recaptured the intensity of W.G.'s cricketing schedule, season after season, from Lord's and the Oval to English village greens and dusty Australian mining towns.

On 18 July 1998, the actual anniversary, the Association of Cricket Statisticians and Historians published the weightiest work ever compiled about Grace. Joe Webber's *The Chronicle of W.G.* was – as near as possible – the complete, 1102-page record of all the first-class and minor matches played by Grace across more than five decades. Webber made clear his debt to Weston, and enriched his feat of scholarship with numerous contemporary newspaper reports and long-forgotten ephemera, such as Conan Doyle's poem about bowling W.G. 'Behold the man' ('*Ecce homo*'), Eric Midwinter declared in his introduction to Webber's masterpiece. To be precise, *The Chronicle of W.G.* sets out the man's works; but it remains the indispensable source for measuring a man who lived for cricket.

These days, visitors to Downend find little trace of W.G. Downend House, his birthplace, still stands on North End Road, a drab, modest building now chopped up into offices. The Chestnuts was demolished several decades ago to make way for a shopping centre. In the village churchyard, visitors occasionally wander through the graveyard, trying to find the many members of Grace's family who are buried there. It is not easy. One soon spots the grave of Grace's sister Blanche and brother-in-law John Dann, lovingly restored by their great-grandson Bob Pigeon. Nearby, the tombstones of Grace's father and mother, his brothers E.M. and Fred, and his uncle Alfred Pocock are half-obscured beneath weeds.

On Stapleton Road, Thrissell House has vanished. Dispiritingly, the back garden where W.G. once laid out his practice net is now the car park for a leisure centre, a concept he would not have recognised; sport for W.G. was serious, hard work. Over in Clifton, one can still admire 15 Victoria Square, the grandest of all Grace's residences, and retrace his steps as he tramped up Lansdown Road to 'The Close', Clifton College's sports ground. It remains the most dramatic of all Grace's cricketing stages, the school's immense mock-Gothic architecture looming above the playing field.

At Ashley Down, Gloucestershire CCC's ground in northwest Bristol, the spirit of W.G. is everywhere. A new museum is planned, featuring a permanent exhibition devoted to the club's greatest and most unmanageable player. Stay a while and it is hard *not* to imagine W.G. celebrating his hundredth century on a chilly May morning, saluting Agnes and Bessie in the members' enclosure as E.M. trots out with a tray of champagne and glasses.

All vestiges of Grace's time in Sydenham have gone. On Lawrie Park Road, a modern apartment building stands on the site of W.G. and Agnes's home. A short walk to the bottom of the road brings the visitor to Crystal Palace Park, where the visitor initially struggles to locate the old London County CC ground; for there is no sign to commemorate W.G.'s association with the place. There is just an open stretch of parkland which, as W.G. realised, would make a perfect spot for a game of cricket.

At Elmers End, W.G.'s family grave has recovered from decades of neglect. A bed of synthetic grass ensures no weeds creep over the gravestone, while the Cricket Society has placed a stone tablet on top that commemorates 'W.G. Grace: Doctor and Cricketer'. W.G. might have smiled at this role reversal. In Mottingham, Fairmount is now a residential care home, greatly expanded, but still a place where W.G.'s memory is honoured in pictures hung around the corridors. Outside, the back lawn is invitingly flat – just the place for a cricket net – while, inside, one can imagine W.G. clutching the fine wooden banister as he and Agnes go upstairs to bed.

At St Andrew's Church on Court Road, wedding couples have for decades signed the marriage register in the vestry on W.G.'s old desk. Behind the church, Eltham's former cricket ground at Chapel Farm has disappeared. Once again, a shrine to W.G. is now the site of a leisure centre.

Since 1923, millions of cricket fans have streamed through the Grace Gates at Lord's, the most famous memorial to the great cricketer. It is a matter of opinion, but the gates have never really reminded me of Grace; they are, after all, just a set of handsome gates. Now Lord's has a more vivid tribute to W.G.

On big match days, many spectators head during the lunch interval to a small lawn behind the Warner Stand, to meet up with friends for a picnic. It is almost impossible, even after a few glasses of champagne, to ignore a larger-than-lifesize statue that has stood on the lawn since 1999. Created by the Australian sculptor Louis Laumen, the statue shows a huge Victorian batsman playing an on drive, one of the most difficult shots in cricket. He has no name plate and does not need one. The batsman's luxuriant beard, suspended above his technically perfect stroke, announces who he is.

AFTERWORD

In Search of W.G.

Anyone researching the most famous celebrity in late Victorian Britain soon notices W.G. Grace's absence from histories of the period. Sir Robert Ensor's classic study *England 1870–1914*, published in 1936, mentioned Grace only twice: on page 1 in parentheses, where he noted incorrectly that W.G. made his first-class debut in 1864 (it was 1865); and on page 165, where he observed vaguely that W.G. 'first made watching cricket a popular craze'.

Shunned by historians, W.G. became defined by his two ghostwritten memoirs, *Cricket* (1891) and *Cricketing Reminiscences and Personal Recollections* (1899), and by MCC's *The Memorial Biography of Dr W.G. Grace* (1919). All are often unreliable, as I explain in this book, but all are also unavoidable. Grace's memoirs are often the only source for his early life, and besides, W.G.'s sometimes comical inaccuracy about his childhood and youth casts an interesting light on his character. W.G. did not want to sit in his drawing room, droning on about his past. Quite reasonably, he much preferred playing cricket.

I decided early on that Grace's *Reminiscences* were largely untrustworthy, because of the traumatic circumstances in which the book was produced, immediately after the death of W.G.'s daughter Bessie, and the clear evidence that his ghostwriter Arthur Porritt wrote most of the manuscript. Conveniently, Porritt's rococo prose makes it easier to spot the occasional passages in *Reminiscences* where it is W.G. speaking, usually when an incident or memory makes him cross. I felt, for instance, that his withering comments about the performance of his bowlers at Melbourne in December 1873 were authentic, as were his remarks about the dreadful state of the pitch at the country town of Stawell a fortnight later.

There are many more such passages in the early chapters of *Cricket*, before W.G. got bored with the whole business of talking about himself. It helped that Methven Brownlee, the ghostwriter, was a friend of Grace, who felt relaxed in his company. Yet *Cricket* also needs to be treated with caution, because the manuscript draft (held by MCC) reveals the extent to which W.G. and Brownlee sanitised the less reputable aspects of Grace's character, such as his liking for a bet and a drink. By the time *Cricket* reaches the 1870s the book becomes a chore for everyone – W.G., Brownlee and the reader – which is a shame. It means few people bother to read the chapters buried at the back of *Cricket* that Grace certainly wrote, on batting, bowling and fielding.

MCC's *Memorial Biography* distorts Grace on two separate levels. As I describe in the book, the chief editor Sir Home Gordon was effectively handcuffed by MCC on Agnes Grace's orders and made to produce a 'memorial' that set in stone the authorised version of W.G.: bluff, genial, and 'boyish', a bit keen to win, but easy to forgive and not a man to hold grudges for long. Gordon achieved this effect by selective editing of a mass of anecdotes and recollections of Grace by his friends and fellow cricketers. Here lies the book's second challenge for a reader trying to find the 'real' W.G.

It is easy to be a spoilsport about the large number of anecdotes in the *Memorial Biography* that turn out to be embellished, incomplete or pure fiction. Fred Spofforth never bowled at W.G. in 1873 in the nets at Melbourne. W.G. probably did not save

Arthur Croome's life at Old Trafford in 1887. One has to pick through the rubble to find stories that are verifiable or at least seem genuine. Unlike Spofforth, most of the contributors to the *Memorial Biography* sincerely believed they were telling the truth. The problem is that many of them could not remember accurately events from the distant past, and in some cases, had not witnessed the incident in question.

There were, as well, a few former 'friends' of W.G. who exaggerated their familiarity with him, now that he was safely dead. The MCC grandee Pelham Warner was the outstanding example. In Grace's lifetime, the much younger Warner was not part of W.G.'s inner circle. Warner got his eye in with his contribution to the *Memorial Biography* (W.G. was 'awfully nice') and by 1928 had so many 'personal reminiscences' of Grace that he put together a radio programme to share his memories with the public.

I tried to follow two basic rules of good journalism when using anecdotes about Grace from the *Memorial Biography* or any other source. The story-teller needed to have been present at the scene recalled and, unlike Warner, have no interest in inflating their importance. This is why the book does not include any version of the often-told anecdote about Grace refusing to walk after being given out in a match, because the crowd had come to see him. The only first-hand account of the story which I found was told by the Surrey amateur Henry Leveson Gower almost half a century after the alleged incident; and Leveson Gower, like Warner, was not as close to Grace as he implied.

Unfortunately, some witnesses had an awkward way of forcing me to bend my rules. At first glance, the 'Golden Age' cricketer Charles Burgess 'C.B.' Fry looks like a must-avoid for any biographer of Grace. Fry was a self-promoter and fantasist, who graduated from claiming to have been offered the vacant throne of Albania after the First World War to a disastrous chapter in his 1939 memoirs about his top-level meetings with Hitler to discuss 'youth movements' (known in Britain as the Boy Scouts). On a more modest scale, Fry's story in the same autobiography about ending Grace's Test career at an 1899 selectors' meeting also bore the familiar 'C.B.' hallmarks. Fry was not in the room, literally, when W.G. announced his intention to drop himself; and Fry omitted to mention that, as a junior selector in a two-tier voting system, his opinion carried less weight on the matter.

Yet Fry was superbly qualified to comment on Grace in one specific area. Fry was a great batsman, who played often with and against W.G., and he knew exactly what he was talking about in analysing Grace's batting. In this context only, I felt it did not matter that Fry's recollection of specific matches was hazy (although I did spend a fruitless hour trying to find a match where Fry said they batted together at the Oval). Fry's acute observations on Grace's shot-making, which I use in the book, were clearly based on extensive first-hand knowledge.

It got harder to distinguish between true stories and false memories when it came to the many recollections of W.G. passed on by members of the public after his death. The anecdotes sent in by readers of the *Bristol Evening World* newspaper were particularly difficult to assess. Did W.G. really throw snowballs in the street at children while he was a doctor in Bristol? Probably, but readers told three different versions of this tale, one of which predated W.G.'s time as a Poor Law medical officer. Did he commandeer a boat to get across a flooded river to visit a sick patient? Possibly, but the story had W.G. crossing to the Stapleton Road side of the River Frome, where he lived.

In the end, I sometimes just went with my hunch that the story and the story-teller were credible. It is conceivable that 'E. Chappell', the self-effacing former district nurse, never received money from Grace to buy food for some poor people in his parish. I thought she was telling the truth.

The good news is that another, far richer source of contemporary material on Grace is now fully accessible. One does not have to depend on hoary anecdotes and unreliable recollections to get close to W.G.

Until about a decade ago. the only way to find out what the

Victorian press wrote about Grace was to visit public libraries
or the British Library's newspaper archive in Colindale, north
London, and wade through old editions. As one's hands got
blackened by old newsprint, the depressing thought would often
occur that one was only scratching the surface of a mountain of
elusive information. It was beyond human endurance to read
more than a fraction of the stories about W.G.'s 'doings' that the
Victorian press churned out.

The Colindale newspaper library shut for ever in 2014 for a
simple reason. Much of the British Library's immense newspaper archive is now digitised and available to read online, with
more being loaded at a rate of about 250,000 pages a month. In
Australia, the national library's equivalent digitisation programme
has so far put almost 16.5 million pages of nineteenth- and early-
twentieth-century newspapers and journals online.

Looking for W.G. in digitised newspapers is absurdly easy,
compared with the previous torture of visits to Colindale. Over
a period of two years, I searched more than fifty thousand separate British and Australian press articles containing Grace's
name, in the sense of reading headlines and scanning for words
or phrases in the body of the piece, such as 'money', 'Bessie' or
'Barton Regis Union'. Thanks to the *Whitstable Times and Herne
Bay Herald*, I learned that Grace stayed at the Fleur de Lys pub
on Canterbury's High Street during his great innings of 344 in
1876. I could not help noticing that W.G.'s great friend Lord
Harris booked in with his wife at the fancier Rose Hotel on The
Parade. Thanks to Bristol's *Western Daily Press*, I discovered that
W.G. requested a pay rise from £90 to £130 in 1884 from the
Barton Regis Poor Law union.

This sort of research can become distractingly addictive. I
wasted a couple of hours one evening trying to confirm whether
Grace had accepted an invitation to be an 'honorary steward'
with Oscar Wilde at a literary dinner. Sadly, W.G. seems to have
been detained at the Oval. Yet digitised newspapers yielded far
more significant information. A fleeting reference in another
article led me to the long-forgotten story of George Coppin's

almost successful bid to bring Grace to Australia in 1869. A search using the words 'Biddle', 'Grace' and 'money' took me to the bankruptcy of the main promoter of W.G.'s 1873–4 Australia tour, and from there to the story of Biddle's terrible last illness. In England, a close look at newspaper coverage of Grace's hundredth first-class century in 1895 revealed that initially there was not much press coverage of the story; certainly not enough to generate national interest in a testimonial for W.G.

Of course, Victorian journalists, like reporters today, could be – and often were – extremely biased. Yet to some extent, nineteenth-century newspapers could not help correcting their own bias, because in the absence of radio or television, they also functioned as a public information service. As I describe in the book, in February 1874 a host of Australian cricket pundits condemned W.G. for telling his batsmen to get out in a game at Sydney in order to have time to bowl out the opposition. Newspaper readers could then turn to the detailed match report, which showed that the Sydney crowd cheered Grace and his team for going all out for victory.

The sheer quantity of accessible stories in Victorian newspapers also works as a reality check on a researcher's own prejudices. For a long period, I felt that Australian press allegations about Grace's disdainful treatment of the professionals on this 1873–4 tour were unfair. Then I came across the March 1874 letter in Melbourne's *The Age* that Grace dictated to his distant relative, the stenographer William Day. In the letter, Grace heaped scorn on the professionals' pretensions to equality with the gentlemen amateurs, as if they had ideas above their station. So there it was: Grace was a snob and I was wrong. There, too, was the start of a more complicated story about why a man who could be so dislikeable could eventually be so loved.

In setting out to answer this question, and many others about W.G., I owe a debt to previous writers. Three fine biographies of Grace by Eric Midwinter (1981), Robert Low (1997) and Simon Rae (1998) finally paid W.G. the courtesy of treating him as a serious historical figure. I gained much as well from four books about some of W.G.'s greatest contemporary rivals. *The Demon Spofforth* (1990), by the Australian historian Richard Cashman, captured the full, Mephistophelian glory of the greatest and cleverest early fast bowler. *'Give me Arthur'*, Peter Wynne-Thomas's biography of Arthur Shrewsbury, brought back to life the lugubrious, obsessive Nottinghamshire professional who supplanted Grace in the late 1880s as the world's best batsman. *'Stoddy': England's Finest Sportsman* (1970, updated 2015), by David Frith, described the dazzling rise and poignant fall of Andrew Stoddart who, like Shrewsbury, eventually committed suicide. *Ranji: A Genius Rich and Strange* (1990), Simon Wilde's biography of Ranjitsinhji, used original archive sources to expose the Indian prince-cricketer's full complexity and duplicity. I also learned much from *W.G.'s Birthday Party* (1998, republished 2010), David Kynaston's vivid reconstruction of Grace's jubilee match at Lord's in 1998.

In following some of the same paths as these writers, I soon confronted a surprising obstacle. Cricket's leading clubs and administrators talk a good game about preserving the sport's heritage, while often neglecting the material in their care. There are shining exceptions, such as Melbourne CC and Cricket NSW in Australia, and Nottinghamshire CCC, Gloucestershire CCC and Sussex CCC in England. Around the counties, there are also many dedicated volunteers at groups like the Yorkshire Cricket Foundation, who preserve their club's heritage and keep it alive for the next generation of fans.

Yet overall, the impression left after making enquiries at some English county clubs is that, as institutions, they do not see preserving their history and records as a priority. It was perhaps bad luck that I contacted Lancashire CCC while the club was still completing its overhaul of Old Trafford to bring the ground up to international Test match standards. It still seemed surprising that one of English cricket's richest county clubs, with a history dating back to the mid-nineteenth century, did not employ a professional archivist at the time of my enquiry.

Any club that locks up its past loses part of its identity. At Lancashire – to take only one example – Monkey Hornby, the club's dominant Victorian amateur, and Arthur Appleby, its best early bowler, are as much a part of the county's history as Clive Lloyd, Mike Atherton and Jimmy Anderson. Encouragingly, the situation at Old Trafford has improved since I contacted the club in 2014. By 2015 a new room had been provided for the library and volunteers had begun assembling an online catalogue of Lancashire's extensive collection. Meanwhile, there is a simple solution for a county that lacks the means or the will to manage its archive. Surrey CCC has transferred all its historic records to the county council's publicly funded archive in Woking. At the Surrey History Centre, a mixed staff of professionals and volunteers look after what remains of the club's sadly depleted material, following an earlier clear-out of old papers at the Oval.

The situation at Lord's is more complicated. As I make clear in the acknowledgements, this book would not have been possible without unrestricted access to the world's largest cricket archive and library, and the generous help and advice of the present staff there. But they, in turn, are working in impossible conditions. The sad truth is that MCC has been a poor guardian of the material in its care for most of its history, going all the way back to the club's foundation in 1787.

As I describe in the book, Grace was fed up more than a century ago at MCC losing his gift of a pair of batting pads that had belonged to the famous early Kent cricketer Alfred Mynn. A biographer of W.G. has other frustrations at Lord's, none of them the fault of the present team. It is astonishing, for instance, that MCC has mislaid the original of a photograph of W.G. batting for Eltham in 1914, possibly for the last time in his life. The library and archive staff are now engaged in a heroic effort to catalogue the material in the collection, a long overdue task that should have been performed before Alfred Mynn's pads went missing. But they have a problem.

The main store room for all MCC's historic records and rare books is barely the size of a small kitchen. Put another way, it is about a third the size of MCC's newly refurbished ticket office, directly across the corridor. Into this tiny space, MCC has crammed everything from the club's minute books, accounts and correspondence, dating back to the mid-nineteenth century. Shelf room still has to be found for MCC's many other treasures, ranging from the complete set of cricket scrapbooks of John Loraine Baldwin, one of the founders of I Zingari, to the increasingly demented correspondence of Arthur Haygarth, a Victorian cricket chronicler driven mad by MCC's failure to continue publishing his multi-volume *Scores and Biographies*. For lack of any alternative, some of this material is packed in cardboard boxes, awaiting shelf space that does not exist.

As this book was published, MCC began demolishing the old Warner Stand to make way for a new one, at a projected cost of about £21 million. For a fraction of this budget, MCC could find an additional room – say, the size of the Lord's ticket office – to store its peerless collection. This does not seem too much to ask.

NOTES

PREFACE

ix *'If we do not get some fine weather'* W.G. Grace to Bryan Egerton, 29 March 1914 (Eltham CC Collection).

ix *'The Hockey ground must not be wider than 50 yds'* Ibid., 2 April 1914 (Eltham CC Collection).

x *'Very little mercy indeed should be shown to defaulters'* W.G. Grace, 'Cricket Clubs: Their Formation and Management', in G. Andrew Hutchinson (ed.), *Outdoor Games and Recreations: A Popular Encylopaedia for Boys* (1892), p. 36.

x *'I notice you have Bexley down to play'* Grace to Egerton, 15 February, 7 March, 25 March, 29 March 1914 (Eltham CC Collection).

x *'The best way to tackle the old man'* Alfred Jackson to Bryan Egerton, undated note (Eltham CC Collection).

x *'like "a wind blowing out of the past"'* Newspaper report of Lessness Park CC v Eltham CC, 17 August 1912 (Eltham CC Collection).

xi *'THE CHAMPION BATSMAN OF THE WORLD'* Philadelphia Inquirer, 18 September 1872.

xi *Well-wishers 'rushed' the decks* South Australian Register (Adelaide), 10 November 1891, p. 7.

xi *'medicinal stimulant'* Advertisement in *Horsham Times* (Victoria), 8 March 1892, p. 2.

xi *'rustic'* ... *'of pure country strain'* Bernard Darwin, *W.G. Grace* (1934), p. 101; John Arlott, *The Old Man*, BBC Home Service, 18 July 1948, BBC Sound Archive.

xii *must have been 'instinctive'* ... *thought W.G. 'simple-minded'* Arlott, *The Old Man*; Darwin, *W.G. Grace*, p. 101.

xii *'a simple, almost puerile mind'* Tony Lewis, *Double Century: The Story of MCC and Cricket* (1987), p. 116.

xii *'When you block, infuse a little power into what you do'* W.G. Grace, 'Cricket, and How to Excel in it' in Hutchinson (ed.), *Outdoor Games and Recreations: A Popular Encyclopaedia for Boys*, p. 22.

xiv *'Great scores at cricket'* W.G. Grace, 'How to Score', in A.G. Steel and the Hon. R.H. Lyttelton (eds), *The Badminton Library of Sports and Pastimes, Vol. 10: Cricket* (1888), p. 301.

xiv *'a gentleman in the best sense of the word'* Anthony Trollope (ed.), *British Sports and Pastimes* (1868), p. 5. As a post office employee, Trollope hardly qualified as a gentleman himself.

xvii *one had to add up all the hundreds* Irving Rosenwater, 'W.G. Grace, A Leviathan was He', *Journal of the Cricket Society*, Autumn 1997, pp. 1–2.

xvii *he came from out of the West Country* Neville Cardus, 'W.G. Grace', in H.J. Massingham and Hugh Massingham (eds), *The Great Victorians* (1932), p. 229.

xviii *that was just the start of the menu* Cheltenham Chronicle, 27 August 1878, p. 5.

xix *so he is not eating and drinking alone* Ibid., p. 102.

xix *'It will be a jolly match, do try and come'* W.G. Grace to Dick Bell, 25 May 1914 (Eltham CC Collection).

1 BECOMING W.G.

1 *board at Ridgway House school* Grace's first biographer Methven Brownlee mistakenly wrote that Grace attended 'Rudgway' House school, possibly because he misheard Grace and then confused the name with the Gloucestershire village of Rudgway. W. Methven Brownlee, *W.G. Grace* (1887), p. 20.

1 *Herr Adelbert Bertelheim* Bath Chronicle and Weekly Gazette, 22 January 1857, p. 8; England census, 1861.

1 *about the same as a Gloucestershire plumber or bricklayer* Bath Chronicle and Weekly Gazette, 21 January 1858, p. 8; R. Dudley Baxter, *National Income: The United Kingdom* (1868), p. 42.

2 *'Patience I found to be my greatest friend'* W.G. Grace, *Cricket* (1891), p. 110.

2 *'I had to work as hard at learning cricket'* Ibid., pp. 73, 75, 90.

2 *'a steady working lad'* Brownlee, *W.G. Grace*, p. 20.

2 *his testimony was not objective* Ibid., p. 21.

3 *'soon made my mark as a real good rider'* Lord Harris, 'Reminiscences of 4th Lord Harris', Harris Family Papers, Vol. II, pp. 10–11, 12, 19 (Belmont House, Throwley, Faversham, Kent).

3 *'no one ever had a more unanalytic brain'* Lord Hawke, Lord Harris and Sir Home Gordon (eds), *The Memorial Biography of Dr W.G. Grace* (1919), p. 142.

3 *'By instinct or genius'* Ibid., pp. 100, 101.

3 *remained in service as a butler* Contrary to later suggestions, there is no

evidence that the elder Henry and Elizabeth Grace were estranged. Two of their four children were born after Elizabeth opened her dame school and Henry Grace named her as his sole beneficiary in the will he drew up a year before his death in 1820. The allegation that the couple lived apart because the marriage had broken down came from a court case brought by an impostor in 1853 who claimed to be the legitimate heir to the Smyth family fortune. The case collapsed after three days. See Henry Grace, Will, 20 June 1820, *England & Wales, Prerogative Court of Canterbury Wills, 1384–1858*. Thomas Provis, calling himself Richard Smyth, *Report on the Most Extraordinary Trial of Smyth v Smyth and Others* (Bristol, 1853), pp. 7–8.

4 *'It was a small scattered village'* Grace, *Cricket*, p. 62.

4 *Dr Grace received an annual salary of about £80* The salary was raised to £90 in 1871. *Gloucestershire Chronicle*, 30 December 1871, p. 8.

5 *'My father had to make his way in life'* Grace, *Cricket*, p. 62.

5 *took over his debts in return for interest payments* Bristol Mirror, 27 November, 4 December 1847 (W.T. Sanigar Collection, Bristol Record Office).

5 *a strange kite-powered carriage* George Pocock, A Treatise on the Aeropleustic Art, or Navigation in the Air, by Means of Kites or Buoyant Sails (1851).

5 *to ride around the village lanes when the wind was up* W.G. Grace, interview in *Strand Magazine*, Vol. X, July–December 1895. Grace incorrectly thought the charvolant was invented by Alfred Pocock.

5 *'Mr Chick', who was fed up with Alfred's constant absences* Heber Mardon, *Landmarks in the History of a Bristol Firm 1824–1904* (1918), p. 27.

6 *now settled in Worcestershire* In 1852 Gilbert had sold his Dickensian-sounding Goodenough House school to another teacher, who immediately sued, accusing him of inflating the number of pupils and lying about the length of the lease. Gilbert countersued for reasons that are obscure, and, like *Jarndyce* v *Jarndyce* in *Bleak House*, the litigants eventually got buried beneath scrolls of Chancery Court parchment and withdrew to count their costs. *Frank Howard* v *George Mowbray Gilbert*, 1852 (National Archives, Cause Number, C14/1331/H33).

6 *'a block of black lead'* London Gazette, 21 October 1864, p. 4982.

7 *left about £400 in government bonds to her daughter* Elizabeth Grace, Will, 14 July 1847, *England & Wales, Prerogative Court of Canterbury Wills, 1384–1858*. I am indebted to research by Elizabeth Grace's descendant Bob Pigeon for information in this will.

7 *the proud owner of Cock-a-Hoop* Morning Post (London), obituary of Henry Mills Grace, 1 January 1872, p. 6.

7 *Raglan's long journey home to Badminton* Darwin, *W.G. Grace*, p. 134. Grace told this story to his second son Edgar, who passed it on to Darwin.

8 *'Understand now and for good, you boys'* Grace, *Cricket*, p. 68.

8 *'a good mind to keep it out of their allowance'* W.G. Grace, *Cricket* (1891), Manuscript version, Vol. 1, Folio 5, p. 1 (MCC Archive). Grace's use of

the plural 'their' is indirect evidence that Alfred Pocock may already have been dependent to some degree on the Graces in 1853.

8 'To say that the Bristol XI were laughed at' Grace, Cricket, p. 70.

9 'as long as they obtained their price' Ibid., p. 36.

9 'much hospitality' The Rev. James Pycroft, The Cricket Field (1862), p. 19.

9 'the principles of the national game' Ibid., p. 19.

10 'something to boast of for a lifetime' Grace, Cricket, p. 37.

10 lost by 149 runs W.G. Grace, Cricketing Reminiscences and Personal Recollections (1899), p. 4.

10 'No-one could look on for a quarter of an hour' Bath Chronicle and Weekly Gazette, 29 June 1854, p. 3.

10 impossible to determine how much, if any profit Henry and his partners made Bristol Mercury, 1 July 1854, p. 6.

10 talk of a third fixture Bath Chronicle and Weekly Gazette, 12 June 1856, p. 3.

11 Downend House, Gilbert's first home Grace's sister Annie told the local antiquarian, the Rev. Emlyn Jones, that Grace was born a few doors along Downend's North Street at Clematis House. Rev A. Emlyn Jones, Our Parish. Mangotsfield, including Downend. A Brief Account of its Origin and History (1899), p. 168.

11 the Graces' leasehold was due to expire 'at Ladyday' Bristol Mirror, 3 March 1849, p. 1.

11 in the nearby village of Kingswood In October 1850 a house and adjoining surgery in Kingswood were put on the market, 'all in the occupation of Mr Henry Grace, surgeon, at the low annual rent of £45'. Bristol Mercury, 1 October 1850 (W.T. Sanigar Collection, Bristol Record Office).

11 The forgotten interlude in Kingswood Grace, Reminiscences, p. 7; Grace, Cricket, p. 70.

12 'a most compact English home' Emlyn Jones, Our Parish. Mangotsfield, including Downend, p. 168.

12 a reasonable legacy to pass on to Martha Henry Mills Grace, Probate, Bristol, 31 January 1872.

12 did not leave much cash in the bank Morning Post, 1 January 1872, p. 6.

12 provide Martha with a little more money Western Daily Press, 6 January 1872, p. 6.

12 using a stump as his bat Don Bradman, Farewell to Cricket (1950), p. 10.

12 whenever it is hit into an adjacent quarry Grace, Cricket, p. 74.

13 'or more if time allowed' Ibid., p. 73.

13 sometimes used a broom-handle instead of a bat Grace, Reminiscences, p. 7.

13 'To my uncle great credit is due for teaching me' Grace, Cricket, p. 72.

2 THE E.M. PROBLEM

14 'born in the atmosphere of cricket' Grace, Reminiscences, p. 1.

14 'That was the extent of their efforts' Grace, Cricket, p. 71.

15 *'he always plays with a straight bat'* Arlott, *The Old Man*.

15 *responsible for W.G.'s cricketing 'tuition'* Hawke, Harris and Gordon (eds), *The Memorial Biography of Dr W.G. Grace*, p. 25.

15 *tribute to Grace on the centenary of W.G.'s birth* Richard Daft, *Kings of Cricket* (1893), p. 107; Arlott, *The Old Man*.

15 *a typical skilled labourer or craftsman could expect to earn* Dudley Baxter, *National Income*, p. 64.

16 *would have needed some close family or educational tie to one of these counties* At a push E.M. could have claimed to be eligible for Middlesex, having attended George Mowbray Gilbert's Goodenough House prep school in Ealing, west London.

17 *'Not one of them is satisfied unless she has her Roger'* Philip Norman to Frederick Ashley-Cooper, 25 December 1913 (F.S. Ashley-Cooper Correspondence, MCC Archive).

17 *'found it impossible to get up an eleven'* MCC Committee Minutes, 27 July 1857 (MCC Archive).

17 *'a very nice young fellow with nothing to do'* Sir Spencer Ponsonby-Fane to Frederick Ashley-Cooper, 30 July 1913 (F.S. Ashley-Cooper Correspondence).

17 *Senior MCC members like the Grimstons and the Ponsonbys* Sir Spencer lengthened his surname from Ponsonby to Ponsonby-Fane in 1875 when he added his mother's maiden name of Fane on inheriting her estates in Somerset. His brother Frederick was plain Ponsonby until he became the 6th Earl of Bessborough in 1880. To avoid confusion, I have referred to the brothers collectively as the Ponsonbys.

18 *'I question if it be worth the trouble to try'* Grace, *Cricket*, p. 97.

18 *'penetrating into the interior life upstairs'* R.A. Fitzgerald 'R.A.F.G. Scrapbook', frontispiece (MCC Archive).

18 *'the "Beau Sabreur" of the cricket field'* Harris, 'Reminiscences of 4th Lord Harris', Vol. II, p. 28.

19 *his tendency to get in a muddle about events in the distant past* I have used the account in the manuscript of his 1891 memoirs *Cricket* as the most plausible. In the published version of *Cricket*, Grace said his father approached Sir Spencer Ponsonby (as he then was) and offered E.M. as a replacement. In this account Ponsonby only said that he would 'try to arrange' for E.M. to play for MCC against Kent. In his 1899 *Reminiscences* Grace said Fitzgerald 'told my father he was one man short, and asked him to let E.M. play'. See Grace, *Cricket*, Manuscript version, Vol. 1, Folio 4, p. 12; *Cricket*, p. 56; *Reminiscences*, p. 11.

19 *'perhaps the most remarkable player the game has produced'* Wisden *Cricketers' Almanack* (1912), p. 168.

19 *'Good-lengths, half-volleys, and long-hops'* Grace, *Cricket*, p. 58.

20 *'emergency' replacement for MCC Kentish Gazette*, 19 August 1862, p. 6.

21 *more embarrassing to have E.M. outside MCC than inside* The game was

between Gentlemen of Kent and Gentlemen of MCC, denoting its all-amateur status. When MCC used professionals to strengthen its team, it played as MCC and Ground.

3 THE RULEBREAKER

23 *offer of 'a very good player'* Grace, *Cricket*, p. 87.

23 *would have looked stupid if he had tried to drop Gilbert* Grace, *Reminiscences*, p. 15.

23 *'Nothing pleased him so much as watching a correct style of play'* Grace, *Cricket*, p. 64.

24 *'I had to work as hard at learning cricket'* Ibid., p. 73.

24 *'clumsy and laborious'* Hawke, Harris and Gordon (eds), *The Memorial Biography of Dr W.G. Grace*, p. 35.

24 *'with a stamp of the right foot'* Ibid., pp. 139–40.

24 *'There were no fireworks or extravagances'* C.B. Fry, *Life Worth Living: Some Phases of an Englishman* (1939), p. 214.

25 *spectators hemmed around the boundary* Judy Middleton, http://portslade-history.blogspot.co.uk/2012/07/brunswick-cricket-ground.html. I am grateful to Roger Packham for further information about the Royal Brunswick Ground.

25 *directly behind the bowler's arm* Grace later recalled this problem when batting at the Royal Brunswick Ground. Grace, 'How to Score', p. 307.

25 *his weight firmly on the back foot* Grace later described standing with the weight on both legs as a 'grave mistake' because it encouraged a tendency to move the back foot when defending, 'which is opposed to all good play'. Grace, *Cricket*, p. 227.

25 *hit off successive deliveries by Napper* Grace, *Reminiscences*, p. 16.

25 *gave the teenager a second bat to commemorate Gilbert's innings* Brighton *Gazette*, 21 July 1864, p. 7.

26 *give W.G.'s performance more than a passing mention* Sussex *Advertiser*, 20 July 1864, p. 4; *Cheltenham Chronicle*, 26 July 1864, p. 2; *Bath Chronicle and Weekly Gazette*, 21 July 1864, p. 8.

26 *travelled all the way home by train for a village game* The fixture was the annual game between the Graces' West Gloucestershire CC and Knole Park.

26 *'an indignant but dignified reply'* MCC Committee Minutes, 4 March 1864.

26 *one of the best medium-pace bowlers in England* In MCC's classification system the presence of Hearne and another professional, Thomas Nixon, to strengthen the team meant it was not a full all-amateur MCC team, but MCC & Ground.

27 *at Croxteth Hall, the earl's stately home* The Earl of Sefton was MCC President in 1862. In 1869 Cecilia Molyneaux married Viscount Downe, MCC President in 1872. Cecilia features in all three of Fitzgerald's scrapbooks held at Lord's. See R.A. Fitzgerald, 'I Zingari Scrapbook',

'R.A.F.G. Scrapbook' and 'Quidnunc Cricket Club 1861 Scrapbook' (MCC Archive).

27 *playing for the Gloucestershire village of Hanham* Western Daily Press, 4 August 1864, p. 4.

27 *potentially fatal bout of pneumonia* According to his ghostwriter Arthur Porritt, Grace was convinced that he had lost the use of one lung as a result of his teenage bout of pneumonia. Porritt was not a reliable witness and he may have exaggerated Grace's recollection. Arthur Porritt, *The Best I Remember* (1922), p. 34.

28 *promised not to 'commit fornication'* 'Indenture, Edward Mills Grace, 16 September 1857, Apprentice to Henry Mills Grace of Downend, near Bristol' (Royal College of General Practitioners Archives, London).

28 *a brief spell at Bristol Medical School* The school's records show that Henry, Alfred and E.M. respectively registered as students in 1855, 1860 and 1862. G. Parker, *Schola Medicinae Bristol: Its History, Lecturers and Alumni 1833–1933* (1933), pp. 41–2.

28 *W.G. was making a point about the need to concentrate* See Hawke, Harris and Gordon (eds), *The Memorial Biography of Dr W.G. Grace*, p. 257.

28 *'always love books'* Item 2269 in MCC Photograph Album, series 2078–2388 (MCC Archive).

28 *delivering a lecture on public health in 1870* Henry Grace, 'A Lecture on Health and its Preservation. Delivered before the Young Men's Christian Association at Kingswood', 21 January 1870, frontispiece image (Wellcome Library, London).

29 *'I hope specialists will not take exception'* Grace, *Cricket*, Manuscript version, Vol. II, Folio 12, p. 2.

29 *'for I was 6 feet in height and over 11 stone'* Ibid.

29 *'play together in a friendly manner'* MCC Committee Minutes, 21 May 1866.

30 *'trusting to the ground to do the rest'* Hawke, Harris and Gordon (eds), *The Memorial Biography of Dr W.G. Grace*, p. 67. The Eton and Oxford amateur Richard Mitchell, who did not play in this game, later said Grace was picked for his bowling. This seems wrong, given that Grace batted number three in the order; A.W. Pullin ('Old Ebor'), *Talks with Old English Cricketers* (1900), p. 174.

30 *players' walk-out at the Oval in 1862* 'The Eleven Left the Ground [Field], Willsher Throwing the Ball Indignantly on the Ground', *Evening Standard* (London), 27 August 1862, p. 3.

31 *'What was I doing in the way of bowling?'* Grace, *Cricket*, p. 75.

31 *'Take stock of your enemy and endeavour to outwit him'* Grace, 'Cricket, and How to Excel in It', p. 22.

31 *a well-disguised slower delivery* 'I bowled faster than I do at present now and then putting in a slower one, which often deceived the batsman.' Grace, *Cricket*, p. 121.

31 *some 'wretchedly bad' batting* The Era (London), 25 June 1865, p. 5.

32 *and for some reason the Dean of Norwich* Kentish Gazette, 15 August 1865, p. 3.

32 *another drops her parasol and cries, 'Oh save me!'* R.A. Fitzgerald, 'I Zingari Scrapbook'.

32 *scoring 80 for J.J. Smith's Twelve* E.M. was invited to Canterbury, but had a miserable week, scoring 0 and 5 for South v North and 0 and 26 for MCC v Kent.

32 *'Miss Blanche, in her early days'* Brownlee, *W.G. Grace*, p. 18.

32 *'There cometh a time to us all'* Ibid., p. 128.

33 *because of his squeaky voice* Simon Rae, *W.G. Grace* (1998), p. 128.

33 *'Oh! that I may spend every succeeding one with you'* Henry Grace to Leanne Pocock, 21 June 1857 (Gill Watts Private Collection).

33 *'I really thought that Alice'* E.M. Grace to Alfred Grace, February 1864 (n.d.), extract in *Thornbury and District Museum Research Group*, Paper No. 125, July 2013.

34 *'a very black and sooty end it seemed!'* Grace, *Cricket*, p. 117.

34 *Grace had ventured into dangerous territory* Ibid. Grace wrote about 'the honour of leadership' against 'an eleven of world-wide fame'.

34 *'That idea I determined to test'* Grace, *Cricket*, Manuscript version, Vol. II, Folio 12, p. 12.

35 *credited E.M. with pioneering this approach* Grace, *Cricket*, p. 116.

35 *'with him the stroke was perfectly safe'* H.E. Roslyn, 'My Hero', *Bristol Evening Post*, 9 March 1939 (Roger Gibbons Private Collection).

35 *'"Why didn't they catch it, then?"'* Ibid.

35 *'the shouting which followed at the end of the innings'* Grace, *Cricket*, p. 114.

36 *'A diary would have been invaluable'* Grace, *Cricket*, Manuscript version, Vol. II, Folio 12, p. 12.

36 *'bowling in a very wild manner'* The Rev. James Pycroft, 'Chats on the Cricket Field' in J.R. Webber, *The Chronicle of W.G.* (1998), p. 55.

36 *'He ran from the wicket to the pavilion'* Ibid., p. 54.

36 *'evidence this week of the weakness of the Surrey bowling'* Bradford Observer, 2 August 1866, p. 8.

36 *to compete in a quarter-mile hurdle race at Crystal Palace Park* Grace, *Cricket*, p. 114.

37 *W.G. had won the 200 yards hurdles and the quarter-of-a-mile flat race* Western Daily Press, 11 June 1866, p. 3.

37 *a crowd of around ten thousand turning up on the day* The Citizen (Gloucester), 20 July 1898, p. 3; *The Sportsman*, 4 August 1866, p. 6.

37 *astonished that Walker let him leave the Oval* W.G. Grace, *The History of a Hundred Centuries* (1895), p. 12.

37 *only one hurdler – himself – finishing the course* The Citizen, 20 July 1898, p. 3.

37 *W.G. returned to the Oval to appear for the Gentlemen of the South* The

regional selection the result of another northern professional boycott of southern games.

37 *'long-hops off the wicket I pulled to square-leg or long-on'* Grace, *Cricket*, p. 116.

37 *'the perfection of batting'* *Sporting Life,* 17 October 1866, p. 4.

4 JOINING THE CLUB

38 *'Matches are nowadays becoming speculative'* Ibid., p. 9.

38 *'gentlemen cricketers of England to assert their position'* R.A. Fitzgerald, writing as 'Quid', *Jerks in from Short Leg* (1866), p. 136.

39 *during the same period USE played a total of 63 fixtures* Grace also played in a professional game for Bishop's Stortford in Hertfordshire as a 'given man' lent to the opposition by the All-England Eleven.

39 *to about 1100 members in 1869* MCC Account Book, 1867–78 (MCC Archive).

39 *a senior courtier in the royal household* Ponsonby was Comptroller of the Lord Chamberlain's Office from 1862 until 1901.

40 *'my amusements were much restricted'* Harris, 'Reminiscences of 4th Lord Harris', Vol. II, p. 6.

40 *one possible host was the Oxford cricket Blue Edmund Carter* Hawke, Harris and Gordon (eds), *The Memorial Biography of Dr W.G. Grace*, p. 37. Carter said that he tried to persuade Grace to come to Oxford as an undergraduate but W.G. explained that his father would not spare him the time from his medical studies. If true, Grace's remark was a damning comment on the quality of medical education at Oxford compared with his father's surgery at The Chestnuts. It seems more likely that Grace never went to Oxford or Cambridge because he came from the wrong social background and his father would not have been able to afford the college fees.

40 *Strangers One Mile Handicap organised by Merton Bell's Life in London, and Sporting Chronicle,* 24 November 1866, p. 6.

41 *failed to turn up for the race* In his *Reminiscences* Grace could not remember clearly when he had joined MCC. He inaccurately stated that he made his MCC debut on 14 May 1869 (it was 13 May), adding that 'I had sometime previously been elected a member'. He was elected exactly a week before his debut, on 6 May 1869. Grace, *Reminiscences*, p. 33.

41 *sprained his ankle while training for an athletics meeting* Western Daily Press, 28 May 1867, p. 3.

41 *MCC paid him his expenses for all three fixtures* MCC Account Book 1867–78, 20 July 1867. The games were England v Middlesex CCC, North of the Thames v South of the Thames and Gentlemen v Players.

41 *financial pressure Grace must have felt to play professional cricket* The MCC committee certainly treated W.G. as some kind of special case when it came to authorising expenses. Between 1867 and 1874, when the entries cease, W.G.'s expenses are the only ones recorded in the club's minutes

and accounts, apart from brief references to claims by E.M. and his younger brother Fred.

41 *about £1 16s* Dudley Baxter, *National Income*, p. 42.

41 *at least £3, even travelling third-class Western Daily Press*, 15 June 1867, p. 2; *Gloucester Journal*, 29 June 1867, p. 5.

41 *potentially fatal disease in the 1860s* C.J. Duncan, S.R. Duncan, and S. Scott, 'The Dynamics of Scarlet Fever Epidemics in England and Wales in the 19th Century', Abstract, in *Epidemiology & Infection*, December 1996, pp. 493–9: http://www.ncbi.nlm.nih.gov/pmc/articles/PMC2271647/

42 *he had not scored enough runs earlier in the summer* Grace, *Cricket*, p. 121.

42 *failing again when he batted Standard* (London), 27 August 1867, p. 6.

42 *a grace-and-favour cottage owned by MCC on Elm Tree Road* The committee allowed Fitzgerald to instal a gate at the bottom of the garden at Aucuba Lodge which gave him a private entrance to Lord's. The gate was located close to where the present statue of W.G. Grace now stands. MCC Committee Minutes, 16 April 1867.

42 *'receive the profits arising from the use of such stand'* Ibid., 12 December 1866.

42 *'subject to such terms as may be Sanctioned by the Committee'* Ibid.

43 *MCC could forcibly purchase the grandstand* Ibid., 28 January 1867. The committee also ruled that only MCC members could invest in the grandstand.

43 *'the wishes of the Committee & interests of the Club'* Ibid., 29 July 1867.

43 *noting her weight (9 stone 10 lbs) in one of his cricketing scrapbooks* Fitzgerald, 'I Zingari Scrapbook'.

43 *his very own IZ marriage licence* Ibid. The licence was signed by Baldwin.

44 *between Viscount and Viscountess Dupplin* Ibid.

44 *'Mrs Fitz as seen [on] A Windy Day at Brighton'* Ibid.

44 *Strangers' Handicap Hurdles at Lincoln College's annual athletics meeting Pall Mall Gazette*, 21 February 1868, p. 9.

44 *Strangers' Quarter Mile Race Jackson's Oxford Journal*, 21 March 1868, p. 5.

44 *several other USE regulars at Lord's* USE somehow lost to the railwaymen by 30 runs, suggesting that not even Grace could take the game seriously.

45 *'especially bumpy' The Sportsman*, 13 June 1868, p. 8.

45 *'covered with rough grass wetted and rolled down'* Frederick Gale, letter to *Bell's Life in London, and Sporting Chronicle*, in Webber, *The Chronicle of W.G.*, p. 70.

46 *'Mr Gilbert Grace was in terrific hitting form' Standard*, 30 June 1868, p. 7.

46 *'A magnificent batsman, with defensive and hitting powers second to none' John Lillywhite's Cricketers' Companion for 1868*, p. 140.

46 *as Robert Winder has shown* Robert Winder, *The Little Wonder: The Remarkable History of Wisden* (2013), pp. 37–8.

46 *'a batting feat as wonderful as it is unparalleled' Wisden Cricketers' Almanack* (1869), p. 100.

46 *'for the present'* MCC Committee Minutes, 29 June 1868.

46 *St Michael's Hill, a short walk from the city centre* Bristol Medical School, 'Register of Entries, 1845–74', DM.727, Winter Session 1868–9 (Special Collections, University of Bristol Library).

46 *earning £378 from premium-priced ticket sales in 1868* Lord's Grand Stand Company, Accounts, 1867, 1868 (MCC Archive).

47 *'right into the middle of it'* Morning Post, 19 April 1869, p. 6.

48 *'held the Stand for the short space of two years'* MCC Committee Minutes, 5 May 1869.

48 *'a Tipperary tenant, who took'* Ibid.

48 *peace between the two factions superficially restored* The grandstand was bought by the club in September 1869 for £1703 7s 8d. Lord's Grand Stand Company, Accounts, 1869.

48 *'the kind feeling expressed towards him by the members'* MCC Committee Minutes, 5 May 1869.

48 *'W.G. Grace of Downend' was finally elected a member* MCC Members Book, 6 May 1869.

48 *E.M. had 'retired' his membership* MCC Members' Subscription Book, 1869–73 (MCC Archive). E.M. played one more minor game for MCC at Cheltenham in 1871.

5 THE AGENT FROM MELBOURNE

49 *more than half the stories that mentioned him* http://www.britishnewspaper-archive.co.uk/ Accessed 25 February 2015.

49 *'the most wonderful series of large first-class innings ever played'* Wisden Cricketers' Almanack (1870), p. 20.

49 *series of centuries went as follows Jackson's Oxford Journal*, 22 May 1869, p. 5; *Exeter Flying Post*, 7 July 1869, p. 8; *Nottinghamshire Guardian*, 9 July 1869, p. 7; *Sheffield and Rotherham Independent*, 19 July 1869, p. 4; *Leeds Times*, 31 July 1869, p. 8; *Chelmsford Chronicle*, 13 August 1869, p. 8.

50 *'He knew exactly where every ball he hit would go'* Webber, *The Chronicle of W.G.*, p. 88.

51 *'Mr Coppin is a good businessman'* Sally O'Neill, 'Coppin, George Selth (1819–1906)', in *Australian Dictionary of Biography*, Vol. 3 (1969).

51 *learned in October 1868 about W.G.'s 134 not out* Goulburn Herald and Chronicle, 10 October 1868, p. 7, from a syndicated *Pall Mall Gazette* story.

51 *and again in 1866–7* Frank Tyson, *The History of the Richmond Cricket Club* (Richmond CC, 1987), p. 30.

51 *come to Australia in the winter of 1869–70* Ballarat Star (Victoria), 26 July 1869, p. 2.

52 *did not reach Shoosmith via the mailboat until 9 August* Shoosmith letter to Coppin, 13 August 1869, quoted in *The Australasian*, 2 October 1869, p. 12.

52 *Grace had so far played no openly professional cricket that summer* Grace played

one game for USE in late August in Swindon against another Great
Western Railway Twenty-Two.

52 *Royal Fountain Hotel on St Margaret's Street Kentish Gazette*, 10 August
1869, p. 5.

53 *this modest rate in other fixtures* MCC Committee Minutes, 24 May 1869.

53 *gold rush that peaked in the mid-1850s* I am grateful to the Reeses descendant Keith Rees for this information.

53 *tales of a 'golden land'* F.S. Ashley-Cooper, *Edward Mills Grace* (1916), p. 84.

53 *'had spoken to several gentlemen about the trip'* Ibid.

53 *'to speak first to Mr V.E. Walker'* Shoosmith letter to Coppin, 13 August
1869, quoted in *The Australasian*, 2 October 1869, p. 12.

53 *colossally rich from his family's north London brewing fortune* When he died
Walker left 'personal effects' valued at almost £1.6 million in the money
of the day. Vyell Edward Walker, Probate, London, 20 March 1906.

54 *'without whom no team would be complete'* The Australasian, 2 October
1869, p. 12.

54 *'ventilate the matter'* Ibid.

54 *it was too late in the season to recruit any amateurs* Shoosmith letter to unidentified Melbourne correspondent, 9 September 1869, quoted in *The
Australasian*, 30 October 1869, p. 12.

54 *in time for the start of the 1870 first-class cricket season* Ibid. Burrup clearly
had in mind the Surrey player William Caffyn, who went to Australia on
Parr's 1863–4 tour and did not return until 1871. I am grateful to Peter
Wynne-Thomas for this information.

54 *deposit their tour fees in a London bank before departure* Burrup also wanted the
players to return from Australia by the shorter 'overland' route through
the Red Sea and then by land and Nile riverboat to the Mediterranean
port of Alexandria, rather than round the Cape of Good Hope.

54 *forcing Shoosmith to wire several northern professionals* Shoosmith claimed
he had 'positively engaged' the Yorkshire players Tom Emmett,
Joseph Rowbotham, George Atkinson and John Smith, and the
Nottinghamshire players Alfred Shaw and William Oscroft.

54 *W.G. would head a party of twelve cricketers* Bath Chronicle and Weekly
Gazette, 9 September 1869, p. 3.

55 *could easily have overcome W.G.'s 'objection'* The Australasian, 30 October
1869, p. 12.

55 *'renowned champion walker'* The Argus (Melbourne), 27 October 1869, p. 5.

55 *the 'rather silent' member for East Melbourne* Sally O'Neill,'Coppin, George
Selth (1819–1906)', in *Australian Dictionary of Biography*, Vol. 3 (1969).

6 SUPREMACY

56 *nicknamed Tibbits 'Slasher'* G. Munro Smith, *A History of the Bristol Royal
Infirmary* (1917), p. 361.

56 'the operator may well be congratulated'. 'Quot Homines Tot Sententiae, Edward Rudway, Compound Comminuted Fracture of Scull [sic], Trephined, Mr Tibbits' (Bristol Record Office (no date), BRO 35893/34/a). Based on Tibbits' notes, the operation probably took place in either July 1868 or July 1869.

56 'every disease which could be caused or fostered' Munro Smith, A History of the Bristol Royal Infirmary, p. 351.

56 campaign in the 1870s to clean up the infirmary Ibid., p. 361. Tibbits would die suddenly in November 1878 from an 'attack of paralysis' before his clean-up campaign was completed.

57 'had difficulty in accepting the germ theory of disease' Royal College of Surgeons, Plarr's Lives of the Fellows Online, 'Marsh, Frederick Howard (1839–1915)'. Marsh's ignorance did not prevent him from later becoming Master of Downing College, Cambridge.

57 when he made his first-class debut in 1865 Hawke, Harris and Gordon (eds), The Memorial Biography of Dr W.G. Grace, pp. 35–6.

57 W.G. possibly then shaved the whole thing off Ibid., p. 36.

58 the parched, cracked surface Nottinghamshire Guardian, 17 June 1870, p. 7.

58 failed to fend off his short deliveries Ibid.

58 presenting the bruised Daft with a souvenir bat Ibid.

58 the exceptionally accurate medium-pacer Alfred Shaw Grace, Cricket, p. 371.

59 whether Walker had broken the rules Law XXXII only covered the use of substitute fielders, not batsmen. In a note the MCC committee reminded cricketers that the use of substitutes should be 'carried out in a spirit of fairness and mutual concession'. Wisden Cricketers' Almanack (1871), p. 15.

59 'an act of chivalry' Grace, Reminiscences, p. 113.

59 Daft was still holding firm Nottinghamshire Guardian, 17 June 1870, p. 7.

59 full schedule of lucrative games at Lord's This was only the second first-class game at Lord's between MCC and Nottinghamshire since George Parr had begun organising northern boycotts of southern fixtures in the early 1860s. Parr did not play in either the 1869 or 1870 games (and retired in 1870) but this background soured the atmosphere of both games, as the partisan Nottinghamshire Guardian's reporting makes plain.

60 shied down Grace's wicket Nottinghamshire Guardian, 17 June 1870, p. 7.

60 making his score 117 Ibid.

61 'Summers reeled backwards senseless' Ibid.

61 'and then fell all of a heap' Pullin ('Old Ebor'), Talks with Old English Cricketers, p. 275.

61 appeared to be simultaneous Ibid., p. 246.

61 'scarcely able to drag his limbs after him' Nottinghamshire Guardian, 17 June 1870, p. 7.

61 'the bowler was taken off after that over' Pullin ('Old Ebor'), Talks with Old English Cricketers, p. 275

61 drinking 'herb beer' as a potion Nottinghamshire Guardian, 24 June 1870, p. 6.

62 *'impossible for it to get up in that way from the ordinary turf'* Ibid., p. 246.

62 *picking gravel out of the Lord's pitch* Grace, *Reminiscences*, p. 23.

62 *'cut short a career full of promise'* MCC Committee Minutes, 20 June, 25 July 1870.

62 *became known as 'Summers' match'* In 1869 Robert Grimston, one of the most conservative MCC committee members, had proposed that the ground should be rolled every morning from 8 to 11. But the description of the pitch in June 1870 suggests MCC had yet to take any concerted action to improve the playing surface. MCC Committee Minutes, 7 June 1869.

62 *barely remembered even by him* Grace referred in passing to his 117 in his 1891 memoirs and not at all in his 1899 *Reminiscences*, where he pointedly recalled the 'dangerous' condition of the Lord's pitch. See *Cricket*, p. 130; *Reminiscences*, p. 108.

62 *a run of form that prompted Morning Post*, 18 July 1870, p. 2; *Nottinghamshire Guardian*, 22 July 1870, p. 7; *Sporting Life*, 30 July 1870, p. 3; *The Era*, 7 August 1870, p. 4.

63 *annual subscription rate of £3 per head* MCC Account Book, 1867–78.

63 *'which had for 14 years been paid by the club'* MCC Committee Minutes, 5 May 1884. The entry in the MCC secretary Henry Perkins' scrawled handwriting appears to use 's-ion' as an abbreviation for 'subscription'.

63 *a total of £27 8s in expenses* Ibid., 16 May, 6 June, 20 June, 4 July 1870.

7 THE CANADIAN GAMBLE

64 *winter and summer sessions if he wished* Bristol Medical School, 'Register of Entries, 1845–74', DM.727.

64 *category that did not exist in the school's prospectus* Munro Smith, *A History of the Bristol Royal Infirmary*, p. 339; Prospectus of the Bristol Royal Infirmary. Session 1869–70, July 1869 (Bristol Record Office, BRO 35893/28/p).

64 *the one which, after cricket, gave him the most pleasure* The Citizen, 7 December 1898, p. 3.

65 *'as some slight acknowledgement of his services'* Bristol Mercury, 18 February 1871, p. 10.

65 *pick up Grace's travel, bed and board costs* The match in question was Twenty-Two of Melton Mowbray v All-England Eleven, 13–15 June 1872, in which Grace played as a lent or 'given' man for the home team. W.G. Grace to Thomas Wright, undated letter, probably May 1872, item 2259 in MCC Photograph Album, series 2078–2388.

65 *two new sets of turnstiles* MCC Account Book, 1872.

65 *'sent cracking down for six to the armoury wall or the Pavilion'* The Graphic (London), 20 May 1871, p. 18.

66 *'Mr W.G. Grace, in vulgar parlance, is "at it again"'* The Australasian, 8 July 1871, p. 10.

66 *poised for 'another brilliant season' The Graphic*, 20 May 1871, p. 18.

66 *Here are the highlights Liverpool Mercury*, 27 May 1871, p. 6; *Sheffield and Rotherham Independent*, 30 May 1871, p. 8; *Cambridge Independent Press*, 3 June 1871, p. 8; *Illawarra Mercury* (New South Wales), 24 October 1871, p. 4; *The Era*, 23 July 1871, p. 13; *The Australasian*, 30 September 1871, p. 12; *The Graphic*, 5 August 1871, p. 22; *Whitstable Times and Herne Bay Herald*, 19 August 1871, p. 2; *Morning Post*, 17 August 1871, p. 6; *Sheffield Daily Telegraph*, 24 August 1871, p. 4.

67 *'this gentleman dwarfs all who have preceded him' Sydney Mail*, 27 January 1872, p. 109.

67 *'a very fair muster of spectators' Sheffield and Rotherham Independent*, 19 March 1872, p. 3. Grace occasionally played football for Wanderers, a public school old boys' side run by his friend Charles Alcock, secretary of both the Football Association and Surrey CCC.

67 *'Lawn tennis will never rank among our great games' Epsom and Ewell History Explorer*, 'Spencer William Gore (1850–1906)', at http://www.epsomandewell historyexplorer.org.uk/Gore.html. Gore spoke with authority, as the nephew of the cricketing Ponsonby brothers and an occasional player for Surrey CCC.

68 *received the summary report in time for breakfast on Wednesday Huddersfield Chronicle*, 31 December 1873, p. 2.

68 *'My readers I have no doubt will be relieved too' Grace, Cricket*, Manuscript version, Vol. II, Folio 20, p. 11.

68 *staked huge sums on the outcome of prize matches* Derek Birley, *A Social History of English Cricket* (1999), pp. 30–1.

69 *'laid me £30 to £20'* Harris, 'Reminiscences of 4th Lord Harris', Vol. II, p. 40.

69 *Oxford won, and so did Harris* Harris conveniently forgot his wager with Thornton in his published memoirs, where he condemned the widespread gambling on cricket in the first half of the nineteenth century. 'Cricket then needed the cleansing fires, and has passed through them and emerged refined, the scum and the dross scraped and cleared away,' he wrote. Lord Harris, *A Few Short Runs* (1921), p. 268.

69 *where individual batsmen took on fielding teams* Single-wicket competitions involved one or two batsmen taking on a fielding team, each of whom also had a turn at batting as the players rotated. In 1871 MCC rules stated that 'no bets upon any match is [*sic*] payable unless it be played out or given up.' *Wisden Cricketers' Almanack* (1871), p. 15.

69 *attending the annual races at Bath in May The Australasian*, 8 July 1871, p. 10.

69 *'bet W.G. Grace half a crown on my runs against his'* Pullin ('Old Ebor'), *Talks with Old English Cricketers*, p. 242.

69 *to take up a coaching job at Uppingham School in Rutland* The German Chancellor Otto von Bismarck was responsible for Stephenson's retirement. During the winter Stephenson was chief huntsman to the exiled

Duc d'Aulnay, the Orleanist pretender to the French throne. Prussia's defeat of France in 1870 and the collapse of the Bonapartist Second Empire prompted the duke to return to Paris. With no off-season employment, Stephenson decided to take the all-year job at Uppingham.

70 *he gave W.G. a gold ring* Grace, *Cricket*, p. 135.

70 *publisher of the Cricketers' Companion that bore his name* Like a 'murder of crows', there ought to be a 'confusion of Lillywhites'. John Lillywhite was the cousin of James Lillywhite Jr., the Sussex bowler, and the brother of James Lillywhite Sr., also of Sussex and later the cricket coach at Cheltenham College. There were other cricketing Lillywhites, including several with the initial 'J', who do not feature in this book.

70 *'and want of five minutes practice did it'* Grace, 'How to Score', p. 307.

70 *keep all of Lillywhite's £2* Grace, *Cricket*, pp. 135–6.

70 *giving W.G. an incentive to score a century* Grace, *Cricket*, Manuscript version, Vol. II, Folio 14, pp. 9–10.

71 *'through my nose and into [the] corner of my eye'* Thomas Patteson, *The Reminiscences of T.C. Patteson*, unpublished manuscript (Archives of Ontario, Toronto).

72 *against Surrey at Clifton, starting on 17 August* Between 1870 and 1873 W.G. was Gloucestershire CCC's secretary. In practice E.M. did the job, taking official charge from 1874.

72 *'The immense attendance of spectators'* Yorkshire Post, 22 August 1871, p. 8.

73 *'Lacrosse, I was informed'* Colonel Wallace, 'Reminiscences of Canadian Cricket' in John E. Hall and R.O. McCullough, *Sixty Years of Canadian Cricket* (1895), p. 121.

8 THE BIDDING WAR

74 *'It is a treat to see Mr W.G. Grace running after the hounds'* Bath Chronicle and Weekly Gazette, 21 December 1871, p. 7.

74 *provide Martha with some of the income* Morning Post, 1 January 1872, p. 6.

75 *'Pray let me know the latest news on the subject'* R.A. Fitzgerald, 'North America Tour Notebook': 'Notebook of R.A. Fitzgerald XII's Tour of North America in 1872' (MCC Archive).

75 *'crossing the water with their cricket-bags'* Fitzgerald, *Wickets in the West*, p. 10.

75 *W.G. was the indispensable* 'sine qua non' Melbourne Cricket Club Minutes, 16 May 1872, p. 17 (Melbourne Cricket Club Archives, A9.4).

76 *'there was a good chance of making a handsome profit'* Ibid.

76 *captured Wardill's charming, reckless character* Gideon Haigh, 'The Hero and the Ham', in *Game for Anything: Writings on Cricket* (2004), pp. 93–106.

76 *'Large meeting enthusiastic unanimous all your propositions'* Fitzgerald, 'North America Tour Notebook'.

77 *'Why should a humble cricketer as I'* Harris, 'Reminiscences of 4th Lord Harris', Vol. II, p. 27. Harris was correct that this was the first officially

amateur cricket tour of North America. However, there had been two earlier professional tours, in 1859 and 1868.

77 *'the initiative was not taken by the MCC'* Bell's Life in London, and Sporting Chronicle, 8 June 1872, reprinted in *Wisden Cricketers' Almanack* (1872), pp. 91–2.

77 *'really an MCC venture'* Lord Harris and F.S. Ashley-Cooper, *Lord's and the MCC* (1914), p. 158.

77 *calling his party 'R.A. Fitzgerald's XII'* After the tour Fitzgerald admitted that 'the Committee of the MCC sanctioned the undertaking, and eventually authorized the Secretary to distinguish on their behalf any cases of individual or public merit which might arise during the tour'. R.A. Fitzgerald, 'The English Twelve in America', in *John Lillywhite's Cricketers' Companion for 1873*, p. 25.

77 *tour to Australia in the English winter of 1872–3* The Australasian, 14 June 1873, p. 13.

77 *fortnight of 'considerable negotiation' with Grace* Land and Water (London), 16 November 1872, published in *The Australasian*, 25 January 1873, p. 12.

78 *all communication between Shoosmith and Melbourne was at least six weeks out of date* The Melbourne clubs must therefore have sent Shoosmith instructions by mailboat before the 16 May meeting at Scott's Hotel.

78 *'a large sum to give for a match in Sydney'* Newcastle Chronicle (New South Wales), 29 June 1872, p. 7.

78 *as well as five or six top professionals* The Australasian, 29 June 1872, p. 13.

79 *increased the sum to £117,000* Figures calculated using the purchasing power converter on the website www.measuringworth.com.

80 *'refer the matter back to my Australian friends'* Land and Water, 16 November 1872, reprinted in *The Australasian*, 25 January 1873, p. 12.

80 *'true to the tryst'* Fitzgerald, *Wickets in the West*, p. 11.

80 *'so the matter dropped'* Land and Water, 23 November 1872, reprinted in *The Australasian*, 25 January 1873, p. 12.

81 *a fee of 880 Canadian dollars on top of his amateur expenses* Fitzgerald, 'North America Tour Notebook'. The C$880 fee included the absurdly high sum of C$130 for the return trip from the player's home to the port of Liverpool.

81 *'amply returned by the great success that attended his play'* Ibid.

81 *the player whose financial 'circumstances' were most stretched* Arthur Appleby, the outstanding bowler on the tour, was the well-off son of a Lancashire mill owner.

82 *'The recipients of the information here are considerably be-fogged'* Bendigo Advertiser (Victoria), 21 August 1872, p. 2.

82 *latest news of W.G.'s batting feats* Leeds Times, 6 July 1872, p. 8; *Morning Post*, 5 July 1872, p. 3; *Sheffield Daily Telegraph*, 9 July 1872, p. 6; *Daily News* (London), 27 July 1872, p. 6; *Sheffield and Rotherham Independent*, 31 July 1872, p. 2.

82 *'sparkling operetta'* Sheffield Daily Telegraph, 30 July 1872, p. 7.

82 *'one of the pleasantest experiences of my life'* Grace, *Reminiscences*, p. 37.

9 'X IS FOR EXPENSES'

83 *washed down by champagne and Madeira* Fitzgerald, 'North America Tour Notebook'.

83 *They were, as follows, with their first-class teams* All ages at the time of departure for Canada, 8 August 1872. Edgar Lubbock played three times for Kent in 1871. Pickering played five first-class matches for Oxford University, MCC and Sussex between 1873 and 1875. Rose played seven first-class matches for MCC and representative sides between 1867 and 1871.

84 *'my mother dying when I was quite a baby'* Harris, 'Reminiscences of 4th Lord Harris', Vol. I, p. 11.

84 *'carried it about with me for months afterwards'* Ibid., p. 1.

85 *he and Agnes became engaged in 1872, at least informally* Brownlee, *W.G. Grace*, p. 128.

85 *'X the Expenses in Gold to be Paid In'* Fitzgerald, 'North America Tour Notebook'. Fitzgerald's poem and Patteson's tour balance sheet confused the normally meticulous Victorian cricket chronicler Arthur Haygarth. He mistakenly wrote that 'for each match each gentleman cricketer received from their opponents 600 dollars in gold' as expenses. In fact the Canadian clubs raised $600 each to cover the entire cost of hosting matches, including expenses for Fitzgerald's team. Haygarth also incorrectly stated that the St George's Cricket Club of New York provided financial guarantees for the tour. Arthur Haygarth, *Scores and Biographies* (1879), Vol. XII, p. 562.

85 *the Canadians agreeing to pay for the hotel* Fitzgerald, 'North America Tour 78'.

86 *the club's rules banned members from discussing politics and religion* Constitution, Rules and Regulations of the Stadacona Club (1868), p. 3. See http://archive. org/ stream/cihm_18651#page/n3/mode/2up.

87 *it dislocated Walter Hadow's finger* Fitzgerald, *Wickets in the West*, p. 38.

87 *Grace would pull in the crowds* Patteson's tour balance sheet, in Fitzgerald, 'North America Tour Notebook'.

87 *a Toronto entrepreneur and politician with multiple business interests* See 'Cumberland, Frederic William', in *Dictionary of Canadian Biography*, Vol. XI, 1881–90 at: http://www.biographi.ca/en/bio/cumberland_frederic_ william_ 11E.html.

87 *'which the Americans call "cock-tails"'* Grace, *Reminiscences*, p. 42.

87 *just in case readers had missed his previous reference* Fitzgerald, *Wickets in the West*, p. 110. Fitzgerald devoted much of the rest of the chapter to praising the investment opportunities in Canada.

88 *complained with his team-mates to anyone who would listen* Grace, *Reminiscences*, p. 42.

88 *clutched his groin and caught it* Fitzgerald, *Wickets in the West*, p. 50.

88 *'I hope to see as good wherever I go'* Ibid., p. 52.

89 *once or twice, quite moving* Grace's speeches at the Sports Club in London in July 1898 and at his farewell dinner hosted by the Clifton Beagles club in November 1898 provide ample evidence that he was not tongue-tied in public. See Chapter 29.

89 *he hoped to see as good wherever he went* Fitzgerald, *Wickets in the West*, p. 171.

89 *writing 'spoony' letters home to their girlfriends* Unidentified US newspaper article in Fitzgerald, 'North America Tour Notebook'.

89 *'was especially noticeable for the skill and agility of his movements'* Undated Canadian newspaper article in Fitzgerald, 'North America Tour Notebook'.

89 *so they could spend a little more time with him. He agreed* Fitzgerald, *Wickets in the West*, p. 136.

89 *to see what cricket's enfeebled 'Leviathan' could do* Undated Canadian newspaper article in Fitzgerald, 'North America Tour Notebook'.

90 *the worst half-century of his life, giving six chances* Ibid. In his *Reminiscences*, Grace recalled being 'in good form', illustrating why his memoirs were often untrustworthy. Grace, *Reminiscences*, p. 45.

90 *opening a crate of champagne* Fitzgerald, *Wickets in the West*, p. 88.

90 *'about one-fifth of the actual expenses incurred and paid by myself or Colonel Maude'* Figure from Patteson's tour balance sheet in Fitzgerald, 'North America Tour Notebook'.

91 *holding his sun-hat in one hand* Grace, *Reminiscences*, pp. 51–2.

91 *kept the photograph on his mantelpiece as a fond souvenir* Ibid.

91 *had sent him $1800 to cover the team's expenses for an American leg of the tour* Patteson appears to have still been finalising the US tour arrangements after the start of the Canada tour. See Patteson's tour balance sheet, in Fitzgerald, 'North America Tour Notebook'.

91 *'Be sure to keep the boys straight until the match is over'* Letter from G. Haddison to Fitzgerald, 16 September 1872, in Fitzgerald, 'North America Tour Notebook'.

10 SHOWDOWN IN PHILADELPHIA

92 *'You are disgusted in your delight'* Fitzgerald, *Wickets in the West*, p. 231.

92 *'he can lose his money to his heart's will'* Ibid., pp. 233–4.

93 *'In baseball all is lightning'* Quoted in 'Henry Chadwick', National Baseball Hall of Fame, http://baseballhall.org/hof/chadwick-henry. Chadwick went on to become baseball's greatest early writer, while Elysian Fields remained a major baseball venue through the 1860s.

93 'by their smart fielding and accurate throwing' W.G. Grace to Land and Water, in Sheffield Evening Telegraph, 25 March 1889, p. 2.

93 an aerial distance of 117 yards Bradford Observer, 31 August 1869, p. 4.

93 'beautiful thrower' Hawke, Harris and Gordon (eds), The Memorial Biography of Dr W.G. Grace, p. 34.

93 'The Monkey (A.N. Hornby) & I arranged one day' Lord Harris, 'Reminiscences of 4th Lord Harris', Vol. II, pp. 29–30.

94 'simply magnificent' Grace, Reminiscences, p. 54.

95 he hoped to see as good wherever he went Fitzgerald, Wickets in the West, p. 224.

95 'The visitors were too much fatigued' The Philadelphia Inquirer, 21 September 1872.

96 'a very fair lot' M.H. Spielmann, questionnaire submitted to W.G. Grace, 1884 (F.S. Ashley-Cooper Correspondence, MCC Archive).

96 'Philadelphia expects every man' The Philadelphia Inquirer, 21 September 1872.

96 In the weeks before the game the promoters had spent Charles E. Cadwalader and others, Official Report of the International Cricket Fêtes at Philadelphia in 1868 and 1872, including Balance Sheets (1873), p. 9.

96 'the CHAMPION BATSMAN OF THE WORLD', was coming to town The Philadelphia Inquirer, 18 September 1872.

96 'than has been bestowed on them' Ibid.

97 to catch a peek of the game Undated newspaper article in Fitzgerald, 'North America Tour Notebook'.

98 'kept up a wonderfully good length' Grace, Reminiscences, p. 56.

98 'threw up their hats and danced for joy' Chronicle (Pennsylvania), 23 September 1872.

98 'wild roar that greeted my downfall on this occasion' Grace, Reminiscences, p. 56.

99 wounds sustained during the American Civil War Meade died of pneumonia in November 1872.

99 'the defeat of the Americans in one [English] innings' Chronicle (Pennsylvania), 24 September 1872.

99 the quality of the home side's fielding Fitzgerald, Wickets in the West, pp. 253–4.

99 for an evening's gala performance Fitzgerald, 'North America Tour Notebook'.

100 not with General Meade but with W.G. The banquet cost $900 in total, with the Union League contributing $600 from guests' subscriptions and the Philadelphian cricket clubs paying $300. Cadwalader and others, Official Report of the International Cricket Fêtes at Philadelphia in 1868 and 1872, including Balance Sheets, p. 9.

100 'Then came the tug of war' Grace, Reminiscences, p. 57.

100 towards the largely undefended boundary Match description from The Philadelphia Inquirer, 25 September 1872; Chronicle (Pennsylvania), 25 September 1872.

100 'not a very promising start' Grace, *Reminiscences*, p. 57.

100 'in unbroken monotony' Ibid.

101 'slowest pace at which I ever remember scoring' Ibid., p. 58.

101 'never remember a team or a crowd of spectators more excited' Ibid., p. 59.

101 so tense he could hardly speak Fitzgerald, *Wickets in the West*, p. 257.

101 'wild rush of thousands across the ground to the pavilion' The Philadelphia *Inquirer*, 25 September 1872.

101 run up $403 in 'entertainment' expenses during their stay The city's four cricket clubs still booked a profit of $1500 from the fixture, despite the English team's runaway spending. Cadwalader and others, *Official Report of the International Cricket Fêtes at Philadelphia in 1868 and 1872, including Balance Sheets*, p. 9.

102 'fair and young nymphs' Fitzgerald, *Wickets in the West*, p. 282.

102 'less than a quarter of an hour after the demand' Ibid., p. 283.

102 excused himself from the start of the game Ibid., p. 282.

102 'not in the best of health' Grace, *Reminiscences*, p. 60.

102 'a sight never to be forgotten' Ibid., p. 63.

102 'weak tea and indifferent coffee' Ibid.

103 'by that gentleman from his own funds' Fitzgerald, 'North America Tour Notebook'.

103 set to work on Wickets in the West The book would flop and Fitzgerald had to repay his publisher £101 6s 11d for unsold copies. He paid the money 'with a heavy sigh but proud to add my name to the long list of Calamitous Authors'. Fitzgerald, 'North America Tour Notebook'.

103 Dr Frederick Brittan, another member of the faculty Munro Smith, *A History of the Bristol Royal Infirmary*, p. 339.

103 offering no public explanation The *Australasian*, 31 August 1872, p. 13.

11 THE MELBOURNE SPECULATOR

104 You Yang granite ridges in the distance The *Argus*, 13 January 1875, p. 2.

104 in 1854 at the age of twenty-seven Ibid., 13 December 1854, p. 4.

104 different from Hennessy's battle-axe motif Ibid., 21 July 1869, p. 5.

105 manager stole £207 from the accounts Ibid., 23 June 1870, p. 7.

105 hunting for treasure that did not exist Bendigo *Advertiser*, 22 March 1873, p. 3.

105 'to improve the play of the colonial cricketers' The *Argus*, 17 December 1873, p. 5.

105 withdrew their institutional backing from the tour project Land and Water, 16 November 1872, in The *Australasian*, 25 January 1873, p. 12. The clubs also reclaimed their £1600 advance to Shoosmith.

105 Biddle never publicly named them After the tour one of Grace's team wrote anonymously that they had 'fallen into the hands of twelve speculators, all of whom were in business of some sort or another, and, I am sorry to say, knew really nothing of cricket'. *John Lillywhite's Cricketers' Companion*

for 1875, p. 25. It is not clear whether there really were twelve, and in one respect the charge was unfair. Biddle, Josh Pickersgill, William Runting and Charles Croaker were prominent figures in Melbourne cricket who knew a lot about the game.

105 *Runting . . . joined Biddle's private consortium* Croaker spoke on behalf of the promoters at a meeting to discuss the tour at Scott's Hotel, 9 December 1873. Melbourne Cricket Club Committee Minutes, 9 December 1873, p. 99. For Pickersgill, see letter by F.J. Hickling, *The Argus*, 28 January 1874, p. 6. For Runting, see *The Empire* (Sydney), 27 January 1874, p. 3.

106 *decided to cancel the fixture Bell's Life in London, and Sporting Chronicle*, 3 May 1873. E.M. Grace sent his brother's letter to *Bell's* in response to an earlier letter to the journal from Davy about the fixture dispute.

106 *had real authority over him* The theory that Grace's eldest brother Henry filled this paternal role is based partly on Henry's protest to the South Wales captain John Lloyd in 1864, when Lloyd wanted to drop Grace; and partly on Grace's year in Kingswood in 1877–8, when he spent time assisting Henry in his surgery. I have found no other evidence to support the theory.

107 *'advance considerably upon his original terms' The Argus*, 16 June 1873, p. 4.

107 *'coming out at the end of the year' Sydney Morning Herald*, 18 June 1873, p. 5.

107 *one of his staggering bursts of form Bradford Observer*, 27 June 1873, p. 4; *Leeds Times*, 5 July 1873, p. 8; *Standard*, 19 July 1873, p. 6.

108 *'with but a slight modification' The Mercury* (Hobart), 22 July 1873, p. 3.

108 *demanding further negotiations The Australasian*, 26 July 1873, p. 11.

108 *Gentlemen to Canada Touring Team against a weak MCC Fifteen South Australian Register*, 2 August 1873, p. 6.

108 *'Electrifying' Sheffield and Rotherham Independent*, 25 July 1873, p. 4.

108 *'free from all expense whatever' Melbourne Cricket Club Minutes*, 29 July 1873, p. 61.

108 *found his terms 'rather tight' Bendigo Advertiser*, 29 July 1873, p. 2.

108 *'would have been willing to come' The Age* (Melbourne), 18 March 1874, p. 2.

109 *'not likely to be afforded again in Australia for many years' The Australasian*, 9 August 1873, p. 11; *The Empire*, 20 August 1873, p. 3; *Adelaide Observer*, 23 August 1873, p. 10.

109 *scoring 160 not out for Gloucestershire against Surrey Western Daily Press*, 28 August 1873, p. 4.

109 *negotiating terms with five of them in Inverness and Aberdeen* Fred Grace and Gilbert may have signed similar contracts to those signed by the professionals. Fred Grace's name appears on a scribbled list of names on the back of James Lillywhite's contract, after those of the seven professionals, including Lillywhite, who joined the tour. 'Articles of Agreement Between W.G. Grace and the English Cricket Team that Went to Australia in September 1873' (National Library of Australia, MS 214).

109 *in a private room set aside by one of their hosts* Northampton Mercury, 20 September 1873, p. 3.

109 *They were:* All ages at the time of departure for Australia, 23 October 1873. Cricket teams are those first-class counties with which individuals were most associated during their careers.

110 *and second-class passage there and back* 'Articles of Agreement Between W.G. Grace and the English Cricket Team that Went to Australia in September 1873'.

110 *they could earn more money by staying at home* Grace fudged this point in his memoirs, making it sound as if Alfred Shaw (Nottinghamshire), Tom Emmett (Yorkshire), George Pinder (Yorkshire) and Ted Pooley (Surrey) were merely 'unavailable'. Grace, *Reminiscences*, p. 65.

111 *'get them to "stand in"'* Pullin ('Old Ebor'), *Talks with Old English Cricketers*, p. 162.

111 *'a gross of photos of myself and [Richard] Daft'* Ibid., p. 162.

111 *a task he completed in early October* Sheffield Daily Telegraph, 10 October 1873, p. 3.

111 *'compromise my position as an amateur'* Ibid., p. 243.

12 AGNES

112 *acquiring a royal warrant in the late 1820s* I am indebted to the art historian Kathy Tidman and Professor Michael Twyman for information about William Day Sr. and Jr. and the history of lithography. See Kathy Tidman, *Art for the Victorian Household* (1998).

112 *proudly showing off his latest productions* Illustrated London News, 3 May 1856, p. 486.

112 *the Days would eventually have fifteen children* F. Colebrook, 'A Fine Old Lithographer', *The Modern Lithographer*, September 1906, pp. 535–7.

113 *for 'fomenting war' against his empire* Standard, 28 February 1861, p. 5.

113 *Day was declared bankrupt* London Gazette, 17 March 1868, p. 1756.

113 *living about three miles north-east of Lord's in Islington* The Days' various addresses are recorded in the Board of Trade's list of dissolved companies. See Files of Dissolved Companies, Day and Son Ltd (National Archives, BT/31/1030/1717C).

113 *at meetings in the capital* In November 1866, for instance, Grace competed for London Athletic Club in a quarter-mile handicap race at a meeting in West Brompton. *Bell's Life in London, and Sporting Chronicle*, 3 November 1866, p. 7.

113 *Hawke's patronising description* Lord Hawke, *Recollections and Reminiscences* (1924), p. 119.

114 *'I never would have done as well as I had, even in cricket'* Bristol Mercury, 7 February 1896, p. 3.

114 *'another howl for Mr W.G.'* The account came from Grace's friend and

fellow dinner guest Charles Alcock, the secretary of Surrey CCC, writing as 'Incog.', '1873–1874 Australian Tour Scrapbook' (Michael Grace Private Collection).

114 *SS Mirzapore steamed out of Southampton* Grace, *Reminiscences*, p. 66.

115 *manager for the United South of England Eleven* Founded in 1872, *James Lillywhite's Cricketers' Annual* was known as the 'Red Lilly' after its cover, to distinguish it from the 'Green Lilly', *John Lillywhite's Cricketers' Companion*. James's annual was edited by the sports journalist and administrator Charles Alcock, one of the well-wishers who waved the team goodbye at Southampton.

115 *Each time Biddle had refused The Argus*, 14 March 1874, p. 9.

115 *'this wretched second-class business'* Ibid., p. 7.

115 *He was a vivid writer* Southerton passed on his writing talent to his son Sydney, who became editor of *Wisden*.

115 *while his younger team-mates went chasing women* James Southerton, 'Diary of 1873–1874 Australia Tour, Book "C"', unpublished manuscript, pp. 8–9 (Nottinghamshire CCC Archive).

116 *'He is a damn bad captain'* Ibid., 'Book "B"', p. 33.

116 *W.G. then organised a practice session* Grace, *Reminiscences*, p. 68.

116 *'and some good English beer was eagerly called for at 1s 6d per quart'* *Sporting Life*, 18 February 1874 (Michael Grace Private Collection). The long delay in publication was because Southerton had to send his reports home by the mailboat, which on average took at least six weeks to reach England.

116 *affirmed their 'greatest respect and esteem' for Klemm The Argus*, 4 December 1873, p. 6. For Biddle's management of Klemm's affairs, see *South Australian Register*, 15 April 1875, p. 5.

13 HUMILIATION IN MELBOURNE

118 *one of the best-connected businessmen in Melbourne* Geoffrey Blainey, 'McArthur, David Charteris (1808–87)', *Australian Dictionary of Biography*, Vol. 5 (1974).

118 *Old White Hart Hotel at the corner of Bourke and Spring streets* *Sporting Life*, 18 February 1874 (Michael Grace Private Collection).

119 *'Of course being newly married'* Ibid.

119 *'fiasco which the whole affair has turned out to be'* *Bendigo Advertiser*, 17 January 1874, p. 2.

119 *'more satisfactory had it been done voluntarily'* *Sporting Life*, 18 February 1874 (Michael Grace Private Collection).

120 *sounded like some of the players were not trying The Age*, 16 December 1873, p. 2.

120 *'they will be easily beaten by the Victorian eighteen'* Ibid., 19 December 1873, p. 2.

120 *the first three-day match of the tour The Australasian*, 27 December 1873, p. 11.

120 *'Obviously our men were not up to their standard'* Grace, *Reminiscences*, pp. 72–3.

120 *'a thrill of exultation through our borders'* The Argus, 29 December 1873, p. 5.

121 *'and faintly in far off South Yarra'* Ibid., p. 5.

121 *type who might enter prizefights (which he did)* Obituary of Harry Boyle by 'Felix' (Tom Horan), *The Australasian*, 23 November 1907.

121 *Boyle's first four-ball over* Until the late 1880s an 'over' in cricket represented four balls in England and Australia. Subsequently, the number of balls in an over generally varied between the cricket-playing countries until the late 1970s, when all the major Test match nations agreed to play six-ball overs.

121 *despite 'some very hard hits'* The Argus, 29 December 1873, p. 5.

122 *'bound to play the strict game without conceding a single point'* Ibid., 30 December 1873, p. 5.

122 *invented an illness in order to avoid going into work* Ibid.

122 *'magnificent lift' over the fielders to the boundary* Ibid.

123 *'conspicuous in the centre of every scrimmage'* Obituary of J.A. Bush in *112 Daily Press*, 23 September 1924, p. 5.

123 *'the most feared man on the field because of his mighty frame and great pace'* 'James Arthur Bush', *Clifton Rugby Football Club History*: http://www.cliftonrfchistory.co.uk/internationals/england/bush/bush.htm.

123 *'in the face of the field'* The Argus, 30 December 1873, p. 5.

123 *'hoped a return match would be played on the same ground'* Ibid.

124 *'the Victorians might have had the same thing to contend with'* Ibid.

14 THE TOUR FROM HELL

125 *'Grace stepped out to the slows'* The Argus, 2 January 1874, p. 5.

125 *'a perfect scorcher'* The Age, 3 January 1874, p. 3.

125 *the poor quality of the English bowlers* Ibid., 5 January 1874, p. 2.

125 *'they are able to hit bowling so fearlessly'* Southerton, 'Diary of 1873–1874 Australia Tour, Book "B"', p. 3.

126 *more than £300 for the right to host the game* The promoters in Warrnambool, for example, paid £330. *The Argus*, 28 January 1874, p. 6.

126 *open up negotiations with Biddle* The Age, 5 January 1874, p. 2.

126 *'although the precise date is not fixed'* Ibid., 6 January 1874, p. 2.

126 *'dependant on the engagements of the Eleven at Sydney'* Ibid., 5 January 1874, p. 2.

126 *catch the train to Melbourne* Ibid., 5 January 1874, p. 2, 6 January 1874, p. 2. Grace later recalled incorrectly that he stayed in Ballarat on Sunday, witnessing a dust storm. The storm in fact took place in Melbourne. Grace, *Reminiscences*, p. 74. *The Argus*, 5 January 1874, p. 4.

127 *the club wanted a rematch against Grace's team* The Argus, 5 January 1874, p. 2, 6 January 1874, p. 2.

127 *in a road accident after a visit to a gold mine* The Age, 6 January 1874, p. 2.

128 *'the Graces and Gilbert shot some'* Southerton, 'Diary of 1873–1874 Australia Tour, Book "B"', p. 6.

128 *slaughter of the 'lively and entertaining' Australian parrot* Grace, Reminiscences, p. 75.

128 *'no bath in the House, rooms very small'* Southerton, 'Diary of 1873–1874 Australia Tour, Book "B"', p. 7.

128 *'telegraph you the number killed, in place of number of runs'* The Age, 9 January 1874, p. 2.

128 *'One slow ball actually stuck in the dust'* Grace, Reminiscences, p. 77.

128 *leaving the jaundice-stricken Boult in bed at Cherry's* Boult was ill for most of the rest of the tour and his health may have been permanently damaged. He retired from cricket soon after his return to England and died in 1881 at the age of twenty-nine.

128 *an exhibition game for a total group fee of £25 against some of the Twenty-Two* Southerton, 'Diary of 1873–1874 Australia Tour, Book "B"', pp. 9–10.

129 *Southerton spotted 'sore shoulders'* Ibid., p. 12.

129 *the ever-available B.B. Cooper, now due to play for Warrnambool* Ibid., pp. 12–14.

129 *'we are cut up into three pieces this time, infernal rot, not to be all together'* Ibid., p. 16.

129 *'by mutual consent, both parties ensuring to themselves greater freedom thereby'* The Mercury, 2 February 1874, p. 3.

129 *Warrnambool's 'sodden' pitch was almost as bad as Stawell's dust-track* Grace, Reminiscences, p. 80.

130 *'I thereupon lost the last idea I had nurtured, viz., witnessing a pleasant match'* The Argus, 23 January 1874, p. 7.

130 *'damned paper fellows'* South Australian Register, 27 January 1874, p. 5, reporting story in Hamilton Spectator (Ontario).

130 *because the game had finished a day early* The Argus, 23 January 1874, p. 7.

130 *Warrnambool wanted a rebate on the £330 they had paid Biddle* Ibid., 28 January 1874, p. 6.

130 *'be careful not to get in front of the animal or he may be ripped up'* Grace, Reminiscences, p. 82.

130 *The game 'resolved itself into skittles, no-one caring how or what was done'* Southerton, 'Diary of 1873–1874 Australia Tour, Book "B"', p. 20.

131 *'speak of them as anything but Gentlemen'* Ibid., p. 21.

131 *'Did you ever hear of anything so contemptible?'* Portland Guardian and Normanby General Advertiser (Victoria), 23 January 1874, p. 2.

131 *he still missed the bigger point* The Age, 18 March 1874, p. 2.

15 THE SPIRIT OF CRICKET

132 *Frederic Rees, who ran the Pembroke Hotel in St Kilda, just south of Melbourne*
I am grateful to research by the Rees family in Australia for this information. In his 1899 memoirs Grace referred to Agnes staying with 'friends',
a description that covered his Rees relatives, who had emigrated to
Victoria. Grace, *Reminiscences*, p. 83.

132 *W.G. took some more potshots at seagulls* Southerton, 'Diary of 1873–1874
Australia Tour, Book "B"', p. 25.

133 *the 'cold collation [was] very good, with the usual accompaniments of Cham,
Hock & C.'* Ibid., p. 29.

133 *'nearly all say they would not go back to live there'* Ibid., pp. 29–30.

133 *'let the excitement culminate in the afternoon'* The Empire, 27 January 1874, p. 3.

133 *'a scuffle' broke out between Runting and Grace* Southerton, 'Diary of
1873–1874 Australia Tour, Book "B"', p. 35.

133 *'the combatants were separated by the spectators'* Bendigo Advertiser, 27
January 1874, p. 2.

133 *'A slight misunderstanding only, not worth noticing!'* Ibid.

134 *'The rules are all that is wanted, but might be made plainer for the umpires'*
Spielmann, questionnaire submitted to W.G. Grace.

134 *'all for the rigour of the game'* Hawke, Harris and Gordon (eds), *The
Memorial Biography of Dr W.G. Grace*, p. 257.

134 *when rainstorms flooded Maitland's ground up the coast* Bathurst was origi-
nally outbid by Maitland, which agreed to pay £450 for a fixture against
Grace's team. *Maitland Mercury and Hunter River General Advertiser* (New
South Wales), 10 January 1874, p. 3.

134 *'There was not much enthusiasm or excitement'* Sydney Morning Herald, 3
February 1874, p. 3.

135 *'and so Mrs Grace lost her bet'* Grace, *Reminiscences*, p. 88.

135 *'We wanted to show these NSW people that we could play a bit'* Southerton,
'Diary of 1873–1874 Australia Tour, Book "B"', p. 49.

136 *The state of the game was as follows:* Based on scorecard in *Sydney Morning
Herald*, 7 February 1874, p. 7.

136 *under intense pressure from Grace and probably his own team-mates* Sydney
Morning Herald, 7 February 1874, p. 7.

137 *the English, including W.G., had placed bets on a win* The Empire, 9 February
1874, p. 3.

137 *in no hurry to resume play* Ibid. The newspaper also thought Boult's
decisions against the NSW/Victoria batsmen Gibson (run out) and Dave
Gregory (leg before wicket) were 'very doubtful indeed'.

137 *and ordered them to hurry up and get out* Ibid.; *Sydney Morning Herald*, 9
February 1874, p. 2.

137 *'one of the worst decisions ever given in cricket'* Evening News (Sydney), 9
February 1874, p. 3.

138 *'which the cricketing public hoped to witness from first to last'* Sydney Morning *Herald*, 9 February 1874, p. 2.

138 *'spoil the speculation of those who cared more for what they had on the result than for cricket itself'* Sydney Mail, 14 February 1874, p. 214.

138 *'where encouragement would have come with a better grace'* The Empire, 9 February 1874, p. 3.

138 *'submit themselves to public inspection and applause'* Sydney Morning Herald, 9 February 1874, p. 2.

139 *'a pretty general move was made for the city'* Evening News (Sydney), 9 February 1874, p. 3. W.G. may have used underhand means to win the game but in the long term he helped get rid of one of cricket's most ridiculous rules. From 1890 MCC allowed declarations on the last day of county championship games, with declarations at any time eventually permitted in 1957.

139 *'see the game played in a courteous and manly spirit'* The Australasian, 14 February 1874, p. 14.

139 *'a good shower and plunge bath'* Southerton, 'Diary of 1873–1874 Australia Tour, Book "B"', p. 29.

139 *filed a lawsuit against the local promoters for unpaid bills* The Mercury, 24 April 1874, p. 2.

139 *'You acted in a damned ungentlemanly way'* Bendigo Advertiser, 14 February 1874, p. 2.

140 *probably because they were unhappy with their fees* Ibid., 18 February 1874, p. 2.

140 *Biddle's 'preposterous' admission charges* The Argus, 20 February 1874, p. 6; Bendigo Advertiser, 21 February 1874, p. 2. Pickersgill probably lost more money from this low attendance than any other consortium member. He paid £42 10s at auction for three concession booths to sell food and drink during the game. *Bendigo Advertiser*, 16 February 1874, p. 2.

140 *'There is no other cricketer in the world who could accomplish that feat'* The Argus, 23 February 1874, p. 6.

141 *Boyle's word had to be 'accepted'* Ibid., 14 March 1874, p. 7.

141 *'a means of transit more suitable to his merits and desserts'* The Argus, 16 March 1874, p. 6. When Lillywhite led a professional team to Australia in 1876–7, he insisted on first-class return passages for all the players.

141 *may also have owed W.G. and the other amateurs part of their fees* Southerton wrote that the professionals handed Grace their account on 16 March and were paid 'our promised parcel [of] cash' on 17 March. Southerton, 'Diary of 1873–1874 Australia Tour, Book "C"', pp. 31, p. 35.

142 *more than a hundred miles west of Adelaide* Grace was certainly in contact with SACA's secretary, the confusingly named Yorke Sparks, by 11 March. Chris Harte, *SACA: The History of the South Australian Cricket Association* (1990), p. 42.

142 *'everything in his power to make their stay in Australia a pleasant one'* The Argus, 16 March 1874, p. 6.

142 *Grace began by accusing Southerton of 'a deliberate error'* The Age, 18 March 1874, p. 2.

143 *'to the detriment of their pockets at the least'* Ibid.

144 *held up as proof of his deceitful, money-grasping character* See, for instance, Bernard Whimpress's carefully researched study of Grace's visit to Kadina: Bernard Whimpress, *W.G. Grace at Kadina: Champion Cricketer or Scoundrel?* (1984).

144 *catch a coach to Yorke Peninsula in time for the start of the match* Southerton, 'Diary of 1873–1874 Australia Tour, Book "C"', pp. 36–7, 40–2.

144 *hired a professional to teach them the rudiments of the game* He was Tom Wills (1835–80), more famous today as a pioneer of Australian rules football. Wills, who had played for Ballarat against Grace's team, was at the start of his own slide into alcoholism. He committed suicide in 1880 while apparently suffering from delirium tremens.

145 *'present something like a "show" against the English Champions'* Wallaroo Times and Mining Journal (South Australia), 4 March 1874, p. 2.

145 *appalling pitch was partly due to dry weather* Ibid., 25 March 1874, p. 3.

146 *if the game against Twenty-Two of South Australia went ahead* Southerton, 'Diary of 1873–1874 Australia Tour, Book "C"', p. 48.

146 *advertised his expertise as a 'commercial broker'* The Argus, 11 June 1874, p. 3.

146 *with Biddle's house in St Kilda as collateral* Geelong Advertiser (Victoria), 21 December 1874, p. 3.

146 *Biddle's cherished croquet ground* The Argus, 13 January 1875, p. 2.

146 *brooded on his disastrous business career and the suicide of his friend Richard Wardill* Telegraph and St Kilda, Prahran and South Yarra Guardian (Victoria), 3 April 1875, p. 3; *South Australian Register*, 15 April 1875, p. 5, quoting *Ballarat Star*.

146 *'genial, frank and manly straightforwardness'* Telegraph and St Kilda, Prahran and South Yarra Guardian, 3 April 1875, p. 3.

16 HARD TIMES

147 *into the neighbouring fields* Western Daily Press, 22 May 1874, p. 3. Thornbury beat Clifton, who batted first, when Thornbury's total passed 112. As was common in nineteenth-century club cricket, Thornbury then batted on. E.M., Fred and Alfred Grace all played in this game, as did Grace's brother-in-law John Dann and his uncle Alfred Pocock.

147 *caught the train from Bristol to Paddington* Grace's first match of the season at Lord's, for South v North, started on 25 May.

148 *the Princes' shady business dealings* The Era, 13 February 1859, p. 14.

148 *with three of her children for a social engagement* Morning Post, 25 July 1874, p. 3. In contrast to her husband, there is no evidence that Princess Alexandra had any interest in cricket, although the game had just been introduced to Denmark by English railway engineers.

149 'and the Players' appeals were mainly met with NOT OUT' Wisden Cricketers' Almanack (1875), pp. 118–19.

149 more ambiguous than Wisden's report made it sound In 1950 the MCC grandee and cricket journalist Pelham Warner removed the quotation remarks around 'palpably baulked' to make the incident sound even more like a matter of fact, rather than opinion. P.F. Warner, Gentlemen v Players 1806–1949 (1950), p. 148.

149 accused Grace of deliberate obstruction James Lillywhite's Cricketers' Annual for 1875, p. 62. James Lillywhite merely lent his name to the publication, which was edited by Grace's friend Charles Alcock, the secretary of Surrey CCC.

149 suggesting the obstruction could have been accidental Morning Post, 25 July 1874, p. 3.

149 criticised the standard of umpiring at Prince's John Lillywhite's Cricketers' Companion for 1875, pp. 8, p. 101. John Lillywhite died in October 1874, so this was the first issue edited by his sons.

150 'That, however, does not make him a professional' The Age, 18 March 1874, p. 2.

150 'of the term amateur, as distinct from professional' MCC Committee Minutes, 6 May 1874.

150 a precise description of Grace's status on Fitzgerald's tour of North America Sheffield and Rotherham Independent, 16 May 1874, p. 6, reprinting article in Nottingham Express.

151 did excellent business at the gate when Grace played Ibid.

151 the club's annual fixture against Kent at Canterbury MCC Account Book 1867–78, 8 June 1874. MCC Committee Minutes, 17 August 1874.

151 remembered as 'well-qualified' British Medical Journal, 6 April 1929, p. 666.

152 Far from being unpolitical John Major, More than a Game (London, 2007), pp. 333, 348.

152 'I need hardly point out' E.M. Grace, letter to west Gloucestershire voters, undated (Michael Grace Private Collection).

152 'that gentleman would have retired much earlier than he had' Bristol Times and Mirror, 19 February 1875 (Michael Grace Private Collection).

153 'desperately unhappy proportions' Hermione Hobhouse (ed.), Survey of London, Vol XLII, Southern Kensington, Kensington Square to Earls Court (1986), p. 316.

153 Liberal MP for Gloucestershire West Fitzhardinge recalled his discussion with Kingscote during a meeting in February 1877 at Berkeley Castle to discuss a testimonial fund for Grace. Western Daily Press, 8 February 1877, p. 5.

154 his hundred at Clifton was Grace's fiftieth first-class century There is an unresolved debate among cricket statisticians and historians about whether W.G.'s 152 in 1873 for Fitzgerald's touring team to Canada against an MCC Fifteen counted as first class. If not, Grace's 119 at Clifton was his

forty-ninth first-class century. After an internal debate, *Wisden* would decide in 1982 in favour of the conventional opinion that the Clifton hundred was his fiftieth. *Wisden's* ruling is based on an absurdity, as research by the Association of Cricket Statisticians has shown. Grace's 152 in 1873 is the only score in this game which is acknowledged as first class. See Winder, *The Little Wonder*, p. 295.

154 *just ten years after his first-class debut in 1865* Grace's games for South Wales CC in 1864 against Gents of Surrey, Gents of Sussex and MCC & Ground are not generally regarded as first class.

155 *'I felt as fit as I ever felt in my life'* Grace, *Cricket*, p. 148.

155 *'Avoid late dinners and many courses. Take simple, wholesome food'* Grace, 'Cricket, and How to Excel in It', p. 28.

155 *'while we entertained the poor sea-sick passengers to a feast of stout and oysters'* Grace, *Reminiscences*, pp. 91–2.

155 *he weighed about 15 stone by the mid-1870s* Grace, *Cricket*, p. 148.

156 *'when more scientific professors of the art of trundling have failed to bring about such a desirable result'* John Lillywhite's *Cricketers' Companion for 1875*, p. 78.

156 *'Bowl a bit with your head'* Grace, 'Cricket, and How to Excel in It', p. 22.

156 *'it requires the utmost ingenuity to beat them'* Bristol *Mercury*, 24 May 1886, p. 3, quoting interview by Spofforth in *Umpire* magazine.

157 *'and the ball would roll out of his hand'* H.E. Roslyn, 'Memories of Gloucestershire Cricket', unpublished manuscript compiled by W.L.A. Coleman from series of thirty-five articles in *Bristol Evening Post,* 9 March–9 November 1939, p. 20.

157 *'he cannot believe that this baby-looking bowling is really the great man's'* Steel and Lyttelton (eds), *The Badminton Library of Sports and Pastimes, Vol 10: Cricket*, p. 173.

158 *and turned to see Bush 'neatly' remove the bails* Western *Daily Press*, 16 August 1875, p. 3.

158 *speared through the neck by one of the shafts from the unhinged donkey cart* The accident was reported in several newspapers. See *Lancaster Gazette*, 28 August 1875, p. 3.

17 SHOWTIME: AUGUST 1876

159 *'Mr Grace intends at the end of the season to bring his cricketing career to a close'* Western *Daily Press*, 15 July 1875, p. 3.

159 *W.G. would only play occasionally in 1876 because of his commitment to medicine* Bradford Daily *Telegraph*, 27 August 1875, p. 4.

159 *rest 'for some months from all work that might in any way press upon his mental faculties'* MCC Committee Minutes, 10 December 1875.

160 *'was too affected to read my own death warrant'* Fitzgerald, 'R.A.F.G. Scrapbook'.

160 *while providing him with additional clerical assistance* MCC Committee Minutes, 10 December 1875.

160 *'Like Byron I know not where my Pen will guide me'* Fitzgerald, 'Quidnunc Cricket Club 1861 Scrapbook', p. 85. Like Fitzgerald, Byron went to Harrow School. Despite his club foot, Byron played for Harrow against Eton in 1805 at the first Lord's ground in Dorset Square, Marylebone, scoring 11 and 7.

160 *'"Perkino", short of stature, with the ugliest and scraggiest of beards'* Hawke, *Recollections and Reminiscences*, pp. 262–3.

160 *Sydney Pardon, Wisden's editor, alluded tactfully to Perkins' 'foibles'* Wisden *Cricketers' Almanack* (1917), p. 269.

160 *'Increase of years and increase of weight may account for it'* Grace, *Cricket*, p. 148.

161 *he 'even' observed 'a little care in my food'* Grace, *Cricket*, Manuscript version, Vol. 1, Folio 7, p. 9.

161 *Mr Mortlock felt it 'inadvisable' to dismiss W.G. so early in the game* Bob Lincoln, *Reminiscences of Sport in Grimsby* (1912), p. 116. Lincoln was one of the Twenty-Two and recalled the team's disappointment that the USE did not include most of its regular players.

161 *W.G. announced with jovial menace that he would like to celebrate with a record score* Ibid., p. 116.

161 *'The public, undoubtedly, were tired of seeing him at the wickets and stayed away.'* Ibid., p. 1.

162 *Grace's quadruple-century became fact* Ibid., p. 117.

162 *W.G. scored 50 centuries in 207 first-class matches, or about one in every four fixtures* All statistics and averages calculated from Grace's scores on Cricket Archive: http://cricketarchive.com/Players/0/43/statistics_lists. html.

162 *against a strong bowling attack led by Alfred Shaw* United North of England were in effect a combined Yorkshire and Nottinghamshire side.

162 *with 'the fair sex predominating'* Whitstable Times and Herne Bay Herald, 12 August 1876, p. 2.

163 *about the grass that the MCC secretary imagined was sprouting through his skin* Manor House Asylum. Archives and manuscripts MSS.5725, p. 234 (Wellcome Library, London).

163 *Grace walked out to open MCC's second innings with the Surrey amateur Alfred Lucas* Whitstable Times and Herne Bay Herald, 12 August 1876, p. 2.

164 *Finally he took guard; W.G. was ready* Roslyn, 'Memories of Gloucestershire Cricket', pp. 20, 78–9. Like many cricketers, W.G. would still be wearing brown cricket boots in the late 1880s, when he posed for Archibald Stuart-Wortley's portrait. By the end of his cricket career he always wore white boots. Grace's nephew Edgar described in almost identical detail Grace's unchanging routine when at the start of an innings; Dr E.M. Grace, 'Notes for Speech to the Society of Thornbury Folk', 10 March 1972 (Michael Grace Private Collection).

164 *he would throw away his wicket and the match by taking undue risks* Grace, *Cricket*, p. 149. Grace said more vaguely in his second autobiography that he 'meant to get home as soon as possible'. Grace, *Reminiscences*, p. 148.

164 *'I made up my mind to play a fast game'* Grace, 'How to Score', p. 307.

164 *W.G. unleashed 'hitting almost unexampled in its brilliant severity'* Wisden *Cricketers' Almanack* (1877), p. 85.

165 *'the extraordinarily brilliant batting of Mr Grace'* Daily News, 14 August 1876, p. 3.

165 *twenty-one-year-old Percy Crutchley, just down from Cambridge* Grace may have used Crutchley as a so-called 'nightwatchman' to protect better batsmen from losing their wickets. This would explain Crutchley's promotion from number twelve in MCC's first innings, when he scored 0 not out, to number six in the second innings.

165 *St Lawrence Ground grew to become another full house* Daily News, 14 August 1876, p. 3.

165 *Grace found the handle on his replacement bat too thin* Grace, *Cricket*, Manuscript version, Vol. II, Folio 15, p. 13. It is possible that Grace used three bats during his innings. The Surrey amateur Charles Clarke, playing for MCC, remembered helping Grace replace a broken bat on Friday evening. However, Grace did not mention this episode in his memoirs. See Hawke, Harris and Gordon (eds), *The Memorial Biography of Dr W.G. Grace*, p. 212.

165 *'the fun and their outing spoiled for want of a little attention of that kind'* Grace, *Cricket*, Manuscript version, Vol. II, Folio 15, p. 13.

166 *'relief came pretty often from the Officers' Tent in the form of Champagne and Seltzer'* Ibid., p. 13; Grace, *Cricket*, pp. 149–50.

166 *'That air and W.G.'s batting on that afternoon are forever linked in memory'* Quoted in Webber, *The Chronicle of W.G.*, p. 88.

166 *dining out on the day he batted with W.G.* Crutchley eventually became a gentleman farmer in Berkshire. He died in 1940 at the age of eighty-five.

166 *W.G. hit him for two successive fours* Daily News, 14 August 1876, p. 3.

167 *'when the clock struck the players left the ground to groans and hisses'* Webber, *The Chronicle of W.G.*, p. 235.

167 *'and a tiny MCC cap surmounting an enormous head'* Cheltenham Chronicle, 30 October 1915, p. 7.

168 *confounding W.G.'s fixed belief that his friend was too lazy to score runs* H.E. Roslyn, 'The Inventor of the Off Theory', *Bristol Evening Post*, 13 April 1939 (Roger Gibbons Private Collection).

168 *'The well known secretary of the Marylebone Cricket Club' has a 'highly nervous temperament'* Manor House Asylum. Archives and manuscripts MSS.5725, p. 234.

168 *'With Insanity, the Demon Spider weaves but one web'* Fitzgerald, 'Quidnunc Cricket Club 1861 Scrapbook'.

18 THE FUND THAT FLOPPED

169 'dirty and noisy' 'the time has arrived for presenting such testimonial' Manor
House Asylum. Archives and manuscripts MSS.5725, p. 234; MCC
Committee Minutes, 11 December 1876.

169 'If so, will you kindly inform me what plan you would advise' Henry Perkins
to Lord Fitzhardinge, 16 December 1876, in Western Daily Press, 8
February 1877, p. 5.

169 and MCC's incoming president for 1877 Western Daily Press, 8 February
1877, p. 5.

169 Gloucestershire were 'likely to be more keen' than any other county Ibid.

170 'He had not heard his brother intended playing this year' Ibid.

170 soon be installed as 'a county surgeon and perhaps an officer of health in the fair
vale of Berkeley' Cheltenham Chronicle, 27 February 1877, p. 2.

170 the practice's potential value could be far higher Anne Digby, Making a Medical
Living: Doctors and Patients in the English Market for Medicine, 1720–1911
(1994), p. 143.

170 a testimonial committee composed of 'influential persons from all parts of the
country' Western Daily Press, 8 February 1877, p. 5.

170 W.G. 'intended to follow his profession after this season' MCC Committee
Minutes, 21 May 1877.

171 builders were erecting the mansion blocks that would soon encircle the venue
First-class cricket ended at Prince's in 1878 because the ground became
too small. The brothers closed this second Prince's Club in the mid-
1880s. A third Prince's Club on the same site was established in the early
1900s, after the brothers' deaths, with an ice skating rink that W.G., a
keen skater, enjoyed visiting.

171 'Which she did, very carefully, very gravely' Brownlee, W.G. Grace, p. 94.

171 with the club contributing 100 guineas MCC Committee Minutes, 11 June
1877.

172 and his presidency was confirmed Ibid., 2 July 1877.

172 W.G. and his team-mates would play a novelty game using broomsticks as bats
Western Daily Press, 4 August 1877, p. 4.

172 the injury turned out to be minor Hastings and St Leonard's Observer, 15
September 1877, p. 7. Much later one of Grace's shooting partners, the
amateur cricketer Charles Francis, left an implausible account of how
Fred Grace, also present, had 'saved' his brother's eye. Francis failed
to explain how Grace could be nearly blinded and then on top batting
form within the space of a week. See Hawke, Harris and Gordon (eds),
The Memorial Biography of Dr W.G. Grace, p. 347. I am grateful to Mark
Crudgington of the gunmakers George Gibbs Ltd for clarifying this
incident.

172 decided to shelve the whole project till the following spring MCC Committee
Minutes, 3 October 1877.

172 *'in order to give those who have not already subscribed an opportunity of doing so' Western Daily Press*, 16 November 1877, p. 5.

172 *where his eldest brother Henry had his medical practice* Brownlee, *W.G. Grace*, p. 129.

172 *as Henry Grace's assistant* Rae, *W.G. Grace* (1998), p. 222.

173 *for whom their father had worked as a medical officer* Barton Regis Union. Statement of Accounts, half-year ended September 1881, p. 16 (Bristol Record Office, BRO 22936/130).

174 *'a head like an almanac, he was always dodging you' Yorkshire Evening Post*, 4 February 1899, p. 3.

174 *Spofforth bowled 'judgmatically'* Lord Harris, interview in *Kentish Observer*, undated cutting, July 1886, Harris Family Papers (Belmont House, Throwley, Faversham, Kent).

174 *he caught and bowled Flowers, the last MCC batsman* My description of the match is based on the detailed report in the *Standard*, 28 May 1878, p. 6.

174 *Billy Murdoch to stand right up to the wicket Edinburgh Evening News*, 28 May 1878, p. 4.

174 *His first delivery 'evidently puzzled' Grace* Some accounts suggest Grace gave a catch to Murdoch, the wicketkeeper, who dropped it. However, the *Standard*, which carried the most detailed report of the game, does not mention this incident. *Standard*, 28 May 1878, p. 6.

175 *'rather a slow one that came across from the leg, clean bowled him'* Ibid.

175 *He took six wickets for 3 runs* Boyle's natural heir was perhaps Terry Alderman (1956–), the Australian medium-pacer who tormented English batsmen, and Graham Gooch especially, on two tours of England in 1981 and 1989.

175 *Agnes gave birth at Kingswood to a daughter, Bessie* Contemporary newspaper notices confirm that Bessie was born in Kingswood, not London, as was later suggested. See *Standard*, 1 June 1878, p. 1.

175 *brought Midwinter back with him for the Gloucestershire game* Grace, *Reminiscences*, p. 160.

176 *the Australians were a 'lot of sneaks' The Australasian*, 10 August 1878, p. 13. This version was written by Horan, who was playing at Lord's.

176 *stop whingeing about their treatment by the Australian press The Argus*, 16 March 1874, p. 6.

176 *the promise of a 'hearty welcome' when the Australians came to Clifton The Mercury*, 24 September 1874, p. 2.

177 *'which has been before the public for two seasons' Bristol Mercury*, 8 October 1878, p. 5.

177 *quietly postponed W.G.'s award for a second year running* MCC Committee Minutes, 14 November 1878.

177 *In future, 'no cricketer who takes more than his expenses' Western Daily Press*, 5 November 1878, p. 7, and other newspapers.

177 *'One well-known cricketer in particular' John Lillywhite's Cricketers'*

Companion for 1879, pp. 7–8. *Lillywhite's* implication that MCC paid Grace such high expenses that he pocketed a large profit was almost certainly wrong. By 1878 MCC had ceased itemising Grace's expenses, but an internal investigation in 1878 found that the club's annual bill for *all* expenses claimed by amateurs came to less than £50. MCC Committee Minutes, 29 July 1878.

177 *and £15 for W.G* Leeds Times, 11 January 1879, p. 8, and other newspapers. It was customary for the host county to pay the visitors' expenses. Surrey CCC queried E.M.'s total claim for the whole Gloucestershire team of £102 10s and referred it to Gloucestershire's committee, which ordered E.M. to reduce it by £20. The special meeting of county club members in January 1879 ostensibly concerned whether to strip E.M. of his power to vote in committee.

178 *'even when a little boy [I] could recollect it'* Leeds Times, 11 January 1879, p. 8.

178 *higher than the rate for Gloucestershire's other amateurs* Ibid.

178 *'He has become a very well-paid amateur'* Leicester Chronicle, 18 January 1879, p. 10.

178 *under Dr William Allchin, a far more capable surgery tutor* Allchin was knighted and later became Physician Extraordinary to the King. He would die in 1912, remembered as 'an author of distinction who ... took an extreme interest in the academic side of his work'. *Yorkshire Post*, 12 February 1912, p. 8.

178 *W.G. had been 'treated with an amount of indulgence'* Standard, 12 April 1879, p. 6.

178 *Alfred Shaw, whose recent benefit game at Lord's* MCC Committee Minutes, 2 June 1879.

179 *'that the original fixture, viz over & under 30, must be adhered to'* Ibid., 19 May 1879.

179 *and contactable at Lord's for any late contributions* Bristol Mercury, 16 June 1879, p. 6.

179 *'to gladly join in hearty good wishes for his [W.G.'s] future welfare'* Ibid.

179 *does not progress so successfully as could be desired* York Herald, 28 June 1879, p. 8. Other newspapers carried similar comment e.g. *Sunderland Daily Echo and Shipping Gazette*, 28 June 1879, p. 3.

180 *'a business-like speech' 'Mr Grace was old enough and strong enough'* Sheffield Daily Telegraph, 24 July 1879, p. 6; *Leeds Times*, 26 July 1879, p. 7. Different versions of Fitzhardinge's comment appeared in the press.

181 *Gloucestershire and MCC's combined funds: £1458* Ibid.

181 *another game spoiled by rain* Leeds Times, 26 July 1879, p. 7. Shaw did not get another benefit match.

181 *no sign of the promised album* The album was not mentioned by the press or by Grace in his memoirs when he described the testimonial ceremony and receiving the clock.

181 *Dr William . . . Day resigned*, Day retired into private practice following a pay dispute with the Barton Regis Union. *Bristol Mercury*, 8 March 1879, p. 6.

19 DOCTOR AT LARGE

182 *'Unfortunately, they do not all pay'* W.G. Grace, letter to Mr Stone, 12 April 1880 (Wellcome Library, London. MS.8746).

183 *area containing almost twenty-five thousand people* Barton Regis Union, Statement of Accounts, half-year ended September 1881, p. 14.

183 *David Bernard, the husband of W.G.'s sister Alice* David Bernard was originally a teacher at Ridgway House school, where he taught Grace in the early 1860s. He then retrained as a doctor, attending Bristol Medical School. Bernard's grandson Richard Bernard, also a doctor, played for Gloucestershire from 1956 to 1961.

183 *in order to qualify for a meal of bread and gruel* Barton Regis Union. Statement of Accounts, half-year ended September 1881, p. 25.

183 *paid David Bernard £40 a year more than him* Ibid., p. 14.

184 *'begin to build up a competing practice Digby'* *Making a Medical Living*, p. 50.

184 *'and how many had been attended by his assistant'* Ibid.

184 *charged the club £36 in expenses to cover Elliot's wages* Grace's annual 'expense' for hiring a locum in the summer was originally set by Gloucestershire CCC at £20. In 1882 the club agreed to raise this sum to the oddly precise figure of £36 15s. Gloucestershire CCC Committee Minutes, 27 October 1882 (Gloucestershire CCC Archive).

184 *W.G. would be away from his surgery playing cricket* Western Daily Press, 3 May 1884, p. 7.

184 *'on no future occasion will it be allowed'* Ibid.

185 *'the real reason I shall not play much away from home next season'* Spielmann, questionnaire submitted to W.G. Grace. Spielmann wrote up Grace's answers to give the impression he had interviewed him face to face, which was not true. See *Pall Mall Gazette*, 3 October 1884, pp. 1–2.

185 *for a rent of £22 a year* Western Daily Press, 26 September 1882, p. 1.

186 *settled down with the family for the rest of their lives* Darwin, *W.G. Grace*, p. 133.

186 *estate valued at almost £14,500 in the money of the time* John Rodick Nicholls, Will, 24 February 1885, proved at Bristol Probate Office, 30 May 1889. Unlike most of the Graces, Nicholls paid great attention to his financial affairs throughout his life. In 1835 he sued his father Samuel over a disputed inheritance, and in 1856 he published a long, intensively researched open letter to the directors of the Equitable Life Assurance Society, accusing them of mismanaging the mutual fund's interest rates. See *Nicholls v Nicholls*, 1835 (UK Public Record Office, NA C 13/1538/23). John Rodick Nicholls, 'Second Letter to the Directors

of the Equitable Life Assurance Society. On the Inequalities of the Existing System', 1856 (Archive of the Equitable Life Assurance Society at Institute and Faculty of Actuaries Library, London, EL/5/1/6).

186 *where the Nicholls lived* Thrissell Cottage was different from Thrissell Lodge, a separate property next door at 55 Stapleton Road, which Grace never occupied. Details of Thrissell House and Thrissell Cottage from 'Conveyance of Thrissell House and Thrissell Cottage and Thrissell Lodge Numbers 55 and 57 in Stapleton Road, Bristol', 21 December 1887 (Bristol Record Office, BRO 40126/D/18-24); 'Sale Particulars of Estate of Joseph Hennessy, Deceased', Auction 6 October 1887 (Bristol Record Office, BRO 33349).

187 *'the cook eventually put protective bars across the kitchen window'* Brownlee, *W.G. Grace*, p. 131.

187 *ties with two village clubs* Grace's association with Downend Cricket Club did not begin until 1893, when the club was founded.

187 *W.G. had captained Stapleton Sporting Life*, 3 April 1867, p. 4. Unfortunately for Stapleton, this was the season when W.G. got injured and then went down with scarlet fever.

187 *watch his team in a game against Clifton Western Daily Press*, 15 May 1882, p. 6.

188 *and tincture of digitalis for fevers* Barton Regis Union, Statement of Accounts, half-year ended March 1882, p. 15. Barton Regis Union, Annual Book, May 1897, p. 45 (Bristol Record Office, BRO 10900).

188 *W.G.'s patients spoke 'most highly of him' Western Daily Press*, 3 May 1884, p. 3.

189 *'loss of consciousness from falling blood pressure'* Ibid., 21 February 1882, p. 3.

189 *suffered an 'apoplectic seizure'* Ibid.

189 *spent most of his money on alcohol* Ibid., 12 February 1883, p. 7.

190 *despatched them to Bristol Royal Infirmary* Ibid., 22 February 1886, p. 2.

190 *best letter would win a small cash prize* 'Letters Remembering W.G. Grace Sent by Readers to *Bristol Evening World*, Published 18 November 1933–1 January 1934' (Roger Gibbons Private Collection).

191 *'I shall never forget his kindness'* Letter from E. Chappell, 11 December 1933, in 'Letters Remembering W.G. Grace Sent by Readers to *Bristol Evening World*, Published 18 November 1933–1 January 1934'.

191 *'children's business to hand out the oranges and apples'* Darwin, *W.G. Grace*, p. 132.

192 *fetched a needle and thread to stitch it up* Hawke, Harris and Gordon (eds), *The Memorial Biography of Dr W.G. Grace*, p. 226. Croome was a journalist who may have allowed his desire to tell a good story get ahead of the facts.

192 *'not a dangerous one' Manchester Courier*, 23 July 1887, p. 3.

192 *Kelsey then left Bristol Mercury*, 30 May 1884, p. 3.

192 *sensing that Kelsey was mentally disturbed* Ibid.

193 *'the doctor was always ready to oblige'* *Western Daily Press*, 30 November 1938, p. 7.

20 FIRST TEST

194 *'They have no-one to blame but themselves'* *Evening News* (Sydney), 5 June 1880, p. 7.

195 *leaked the letter to the* Daily Telegraph *Daily Telegraph*, 31 March 1879.

195 *had settled the first-class fixture list for the season Australian Town and Country Journal* (Sydney), 22 May 1880, p. 35.

195 *'who play as professionals and who as amateurs'* *Evening News* (Sydney), 5 June 1880, p. 7.

195 *'decision of the umpire is final, whether right or wrong'* Ibid.

195 *Fred ... had appeared as a guest professional for local clubs* At Manchester and Harrogate the Australians won so quickly that the two sides then played a 'fill–up' game to entertain spectators.

197 *should organise a fixture between an England XI, captained by him, and the Australians* MCC Committee Minutes, 5 July 1880.

197 *'This may have been due in part to my artfulness'* Hawke, Harris and Gordon (eds), *The Memorial Biography of Dr W.G. Grace*, pp. 130–1.

197 *in return for £105 in compensation Sheffield and Rotherham Independent*, 27 November 1880, p. 14.

198 *'if the Surrey Club ask you, which they are sure to do'* Lord Harris to A.G. Steel, 20 August 1880, Harris Family Papers, Vol. II, p. 6a; 4pp (Belmont House, Throwley, Faversham, Kent).

198 *having been captain of the 79–80 eleven to Australia* Ibid.

198 *batting order for the first innings* Ages are at the time of the Test match, 6–8 September 1880. List is according to the batting order in the first innings. All the players were amateurs apart from Barnes, Shaw and Morley, the three Nottinghamshire professionals.

199 *stoutly defended against attack Sydney Morning Herald*, 23 October 1880, p. 6.

199 *coveted position was again stormed and taken possession of* Ibid.

199 *'than in any other part of the kingdom'* *Yorkshire Post*, 15 March 1880, p. 3.

199 *label soon attached to all England v Australia cricket fixtures* For instance, the *Derby Daily Telegraph* referred to the game as a 'test match'. *Derby Daily Telegraph*, 9 September 1880, p. 2.

200 *pulled a ball from 'Joey' Palmer for a boundary Standard*, 7 September 1880, p. 3.

200 *'which only missed his leg stump by a shave'* *The Australasian*, 23 October 1880, p. 12.

200 *cut Palmer 'grandly' for four Standard*, 7 September 1880, p. 3.

200 *Lucas scored 55 in elegant, 'Cantab' style* Ibid.

200 *cut two balls to the boundary* Ibid.

200 *'this was the only big hit for several overs'* Ibid.

201 *Alexander 'jumped in and got to the ball, but failed to hold it'* The Australasian, 23 October 1880, p. 12.

201 *'took Mr Grace's off stump a couple of inches below the bail'* Standard, 7 September 1880, p. 3.

201 *'applause for a splendidly played 152'* The Australasian, 23 October 1880, p. 12.

201 *attacking finale that reinforced England's dominant position* Almost forty years later Sir Home Gordon, the main editor of the MCC's memorial biography of Grace, still did not grasp why W.G. took so much care at the start of his innings. Gordon wrote: 'Anxiety to do himself justice made him over-cautious at the start.' Hawke, Harris and Gordon (eds) *The Memorial Biography of Dr W.G. Grace*, p. 146.

201 *'and was very treacherous'* The Australasian, 23 October 1880, p. 12.

202 *until a client failed to pay a large bill* At his insolvency hearing, the court estimated that Murdoch had liabilities of £775 2s and personal assets of just £10. *Australian Town and Country Journal*, 3 January 1880, p. 13.

202 *Murdoch and Bonnor continue the Australian innings in overcast weather* Sydney Morning Herald, 25 October 1880, p. 6.

202 *'Murdoch could make nothing of his bowling'* Ibid.

203 *'and then seemed for a few minutes in a faint'* Ibid.

203 *carrying a jug of water and a glass on a tray* Ibid.

203 *as Australia's score crept up* Ibid.

203 *'spectators fairly stood on their legs and yelled with delight'* The Australasian, 23 October 1880, p. 12.

203 *'again Lord Harris and Dr Grace had a consultation'* Standard, 9 September 1880, p. 3.

204 *'and the excitement something terrible'* The Australasian, 23 October 1880, p. 12.

204 *when he realised he was too ill* Bristol Mercury, 24 September 1880, p. 3.

205 *on Monday, Henry returned to Bristol, leaving Gilbert at the hotel* Ibid.

205 *carrying yet another telegram* Ibid.

205 *the Victorian fascination with untimely death* Bath Chronicle and Weekly Gazette, 30 September 1880, p. 7.

21 ULTIMATE TEST

206 *too ill to cause Ettie any more trouble* UK Census, 1881.

206 *Victorian euphemism for tertiary syphilis* Robert Allan Fitzgerald, Death Certificate, 31 October 1881. Fitzgerald's widow Ettie soon remarried and had three more children. She died in 1925 at the age of seventy-nine.

206 *largely due to his exertions* Daily News, 4 May 1882, p. 2.

206 *played a Test match at Lord's* Since September 1881 the committee had been negotiating with the Australians about sharing gate money for tour

fixtures at Lord's. Originally, the committee agreed to host two matches, but reduced this to one match after deciding the Australians' terms were too high. MCC Committee Minutes, 19 September 1881, 6 March 1882.

207 *Perkins had let the opportunity slip* In 1886, largely at Lord Harris's prompting, an MCC subcommittee investigated 'the positions and duties of the paid officers and servants' of the club. Harris may have been trying to build a case to sack Perkins, with the subcommittee's report noting pointedly: 'We consider the general business of the Club is now of so extensive a nature as to require the constant and active personal supervision of the Secretary throughout the year.' Perkins kept his job and continued to commute to Lord's from his home in Hertfordshire.

207 *Mephistopheles, the collector of damned souls* Sam Jones, 'Unpublished Memoir of 1882 Australia Tour', 1935 (Cricket NSW Archives).

207 *the side read as follows* Ages are at the time of the Test match, 28–29 August 1882. The professionals in the side were Barlow, Ulyett, Read, Barnes and Peate.

208 *attempt to stop the Lancashire captain selecting these bowlers* Harris, 'Reminiscences of 4th Lord Harris', Vol. III, p. 5.

208 *the most influential selector* The other selectors were the retired Surrey amateur Frederick Burbidge, Teddy Walker and his brother Donny. None of them had Harris's authority as a recent England captain.

208 *'where shall we be without Palmer?'* South Australian Register, 18 October 1882, p. 3.

209 *get at the English on the rain-damaged pitch* Sam Jones letter to B.H. Kent, 27 May 1947 (F.S. Ashley-Cooper Correspondence).

209 *sawdust to keep his footing on the damp grass* Pall Mall Gazette, 30 August 1882, p. 4.

210 *'bank of spectators 60 or 70 feet deep'* Standard, 30 August 1882, p. 3.

210 *then Jones was definitely out* At the end of his life Spofforth fabricated a story that Grace's deception of Jones was made worse by W.G. feinting to throw the ball back to the bowler. Spofforth's version was obviously untrue, since he identified Peate, not Steel, as the bowler. *Western Daily Press*, 18 August 1926, p. 5. In 1956 Hugh Massie's son Jack added further confusion by reporting that his father remembered Jones, not Murdoch, hitting the ball for two runs. All contemporary newspapers confirm that Murdoch was the batsman. R.J.A. Massie, letter to E.A. 'Chappie' Dwyer, 30 October 1956 (F.S. Ashley-Cooper Correspondence).

210 *'purely within his rights, and it was the strict game'* Sydney Morning Herald, 21 October 1882, p. 8.

210 *if he repeated his absent-minded error?* In modern Test cricket the incident brings to mind Tony Greig's 'run out' of the West Indies batsman Alvin Kallicharran at Port-of-Spain in February 1974. Greig threw down Kallicharran's stumps after the batsman had left his ground, thinking

play was over for the day. After much overnight negotiation Kallicharran was reinstated.

211 *'thank the champion for teaching him something'* Wisden Cricketers' Almanack (1883), p. 272.

211 *'cricket, but dirty'* South Australian Register, 18 October 1882, p. 3

211 *moaning to each other about the 'Jones affair'* Ibid.

211 *'This will lose you the match'* R.J.A. Massie, letter, 8 September 1956 (F.S. Ashley-Cooper Correspondence).

211 *'an entertaining raconteur of "tall stories"'* Christopher Morris, 'Spofforth, Frederick Robert (1853–1926)', in *Australian Dictionary of Biography*, Vol. 6 (1976).

212 *where he died a few minutes later* Standard, 1 September 1882, p. 2.

212 *all of which W.G. calmly defended* Morning Post, 30 August 1882, p. 3.

213 *knew the significance of the moment* Alick Bannerman was the younger brother of Charles, who scored the first-ever Test century in the first-ever Test match at Melbourne in March 1877. *South Australian Register*, 18 October 1882, p. 3.

213 *70 for six* Ibid.

213 *'seemed to go round the ground'* Border Watch (South Australia), 21 October 1882, p. 2.

213 *tipped by some pundits to become the next W.G. Grace* York Herald, 15 July 1882, p. 15. Charles Studd had five brothers who also played first-class cricket. Two of them, George ('G.B.') and Kynaston ('J.E.K.') were regarded as almost as good as Charles.

214 *smash the delivery to the boundary* Jones, 'Unpublished Memoir of 1882 Tour'.

214 *had not even faced a ball* England needed seven runs to tie with Australia (the margin of defeat) and eight runs to win.

215 *'crush Spoff to his manly breast & chest'* Jones, 'Unpublished Memoir of 1882 Tour'.

215 *waved to the cheering crowd below* South Australian Register, 18 October 1882, p. 3.

215 *'waved their handkerchiefs to us'* The Argus, 20 October 1882, p. 9

215 *a revealingly patronising remark* The Australasian, 21 October 1882, p. 6 (Supplement). The writer was Tom Horan, one of the team and the best of the early Australian cricketer-journalists.

22 THE 'OLD MAN'

217 *'I wanted to win souls for the Lord'* Norman P. Grubb, *C.T. Studd: Cricketer and Pioneer* (1933), p. 33. Studd spent the rest of his life as a missionary, in China, India and the Belgian Congo. In 1903 he would come out of retirement to play for Gentlemen of India against the touring Oxford University Authentics at the Polo Ground in Delhi.

217 *Arthur Shrewsbury was a bundle of neuroses* This is vividly captured by his biographer, Peter Wynne-Thomas, in *'Give me Arthur'* (1985).

218 *'bend over it to recover his breath'* Roslyn, 'Memories of Gloucestershire Cricket', p. 17.

218 *'Grand Old Cricketer'* Bury and Norwich Post, 29 May 1888, p. 5.

218 *to select him for a Test match at the Oval* Spofforth was convinced he would be unplayable on the rain-damaged Oval pitch and would bowl England out for under 50 runs. Richard Cashman, *The 'Demon' Spofforth* (1990), p. 211.

218 *'observing a little care in my food'* Grace, *Cricket*, Manuscript version, Vol. 1, Folio 7, p. 9.

218 *seeing W.G. in the flesh for the first time since his 1873–4 tour* Reprinted in *The Citizen*, 21 January 1892, p. 3.

218 *'You have a bit of that cold beef, like I'm going to'* F.B. 'Freddie' Wilson, *Sporting Pie* (1922), p. 102.

219 *'all through lunch his eyes were never still'* Ibid., p. 102.

219 *'the advantages of abstinence from alcoholic drinks'* Bath Chronicle and Weekly Gazette, 13 January 1887, p. 3.

219 *'was a teetotaller'* Bury and Norwich Post, 26 April 1887, p. 5.

219 *'has more to do with nervousness and small scores than moderate drinking'* Grace, *Cricket*, p. 90.

219 *'when the innings is over a little wine or spirits is undoubtedly useful'* Grace, *Cricket*, Manuscript version, Vol. 1, Folio 7, p. 9.

220 *'than a liqueur glass of Kummel on a bunker on a golf course'* Lord George Scott, 'The Cricket of W.G. Grace', *National Review*, Vol. 109, No. 654, August 1937, pp. 229–31.

220 *during a banquet in Bristol in his honour in 1895* R.C. Robertson-Glasgow, *46 Not Out* (1954), pp. 130–1.

221 *'awfully surprised at your joint telegram'* W.G. Grace to J.W. Arrowsmith, undated letter (Gloucestershire CCC Archive).

222 *Lost: 62* Figures include matches against visiting Australian teams.

223 *Grace alternated with Page's second-string bowling* Walter Gilbert and Frank Townsend also bowled more occasionally.

223 *who seemed to have forgotten Woof* Western Daily Press, 25 April 1885, p. 3.

223 *young players 'were never much use at first'* Ibid.

224 *on the part of the Gloucestershire Colts than in former years* The Citizen, 19 May 1885, p. 4.

224 *explaining to the crowd what had happened* Manchester Courier, 26 July 1884, p. 3. Other newspapers suggested that Grace or Hornby received the news of Martha's death after Grace began batting. This version is contradicted by the *Courier*'s more detailed report.

225 *meagre estate was put in the hands of a local creditor* Rose Rachel Gilbert, Probate, Worcester Probate Office, 11 June 1879.

225 *a daughter of one of the Lillywhite cricket clan* Sarah Lillywhite's father James

Lillywhite Sr., who died in 1882, was a brother of John Lillywhite, who founded the *Cricketers' Companion*, and a cousin of James Lillywhite Jr., the Sussex bowler.

225 *'a present of £24 on account of his having been injured'* Gloucestershire CCC Committee Minutes, 7 October 1884.

225 *if he played in all the county's matches during the summer* Ibid., 8 January 1886.

225 *'quietly conveyed' in a cab to the police station* The Citizen, 7 June 1886, p. 4. Gilbert subsequently confessed to stealing a half-sovereign from another player's clothes.

226 *next match between Gloucestershire and Sussex* Morning Post, 5 June 1886, p. 3.

226 *as a late replacement for Gilbert* Margrett scored 14 and 0, did not bowl and never played for the county again.

226 *'if they would forgive him he would go to Australia'* Daily British Colonist (Canada), 1 July 1886, reprinted from *The Times*.

226 *no question of Gilbert beginning a completely new life* Ibid. *The Times* was in turn reprinting from the Gloucestershire newspapers.

226 *'don't blame the bat if you don't'* Arthur Shrewsbury to W.R. Gilbert, 10 March 1897, in 'Letters of Arthur Shrewsbury', transcribed by Peter Wynne-Thomas (Nottinghamshire CCC Archive).

23 W.G. INC.

228 *'severest shock that it had yet received'* Sir Robert Ensor, *England 1870–1914* (1936), p. 111.

228 *'& everything was excellent'* Harris, 'Reminiscences of 4th Lord Harris', Vol. III, p. 2.

229 *'one half-sovereign, three half-crowns and four pennies'* Letter from T.P.R. Renwick, 20 December 1933, in 'Letters Remembering W.G. Grace Sent by Readers to *Bristol Evening World*, Published 18 November 1933–1 January 1934'.

229 *the newsagent was a 'red-hot Liberal'* Letter from Albert E. Bole, 18 November 1933, in 'Letters Remembering W.G. Grace Sent by Readers to *Bristol Evening World*, Published 18 November 1933–1 January 1934'.

229 *needed additional support from her brothers to make ends meet* UK Census, 1891. Fanny would die intestate in 1900, and appears to have left no assets.

229 *'collector of debts'* Pocock had a habit of playing jokes at census time; in 1861 he popped up twice in the returns, once at his sister Jemima's house in Bristol and again at The Chestnuts.

229 *as the auction notice described him* 'Sale Particulars of Estate of Joseph Hennessy, Deceased', Auction 6 October 1887.

229 *more of a nuisance as a landlord than Hennessy* 'Conveyance of Thrissell

House and Thrissell Cottage and Thrissell Lodge Numbers 55 and 57 in Stapleton Road, Bristol', 21 December 1887.

230 *He held a life insurance policy with Equitable Life* M.E. Ogborn, *Equitable Assurances: The Story of Life Assurance in the Experience of the Equitable Life Assurance Society, 1762–1962* (1962), p. 251. The policy number is not indicated. I am grateful to David Raymont at the Institute and Faculty of Actuaries Library for this information.

230 *Ancient Order of Druids and the Loyal Order of Ancient Shepherds Bristol Mercury,* 11 November 1885, p. 3; 28 March 1887, p. 6.

230 *Ashley Down, on the northern outskirts of Bristol* Gloucestershire CCC Committee Minutes, 15 February 1888.

230 *'but no other fault could be found with it' Western Daily Press,* 9 June 1888, p. 3.

231 *'tried their hands at baseball with much success' Morning Post,* 16 March 1889, p. 3.

231 *would never be able to deliver a curve ball Sheffield Evening Telegraph,* 25 March 1889, p. 2.

231 *'by some of his friends'* Grace to Arrowsmith, letter 26 May 1889.

232 *'to the delight of the crowd surrounding them'* Obituary of Mabel Tansley, 1973 (Michael Grace Private Collection).

233 *turned on his heels, laughing* Letter from Edward E. Bankin, in 'Letters Remembering W.G. Grace Sent by Readers to *Bristol Evening World,* published 18 November 1933–1 January 1934'.

233 *obliterated by the new craze for lawn tennis Western Daily Press,* 23 June 1884, p. 1.

233 *Cricket, A Table Game did not catch on Taunton Courier and Western Advertiser,* 12 November 1902, p. 8.

233 *'Magic Bat'* Advertisement in the *Standard,* 2 November 1888, p. 1.

234 *'wishing some to be made and sent on to him' Cheltenham Chronicle,* 27 December 1890, p. 6. Sadly, Woof and Grace appear to have fallen out over Gloucestershire's refusal to give Woof a benefit. Woof said Grace was annoyed when the bowler became cricket coach at Cheltenham College, which meant he could only play for the county in the school's summer holidays. Pullin ('Old Ebor'), *Talks with Old English Cricketers,* p. 331.

234 *declining an invitation to stay the night* W.G. Grace to M.H. Spielmann, 15 September 1884 (F.S. Ashley-Cooper Correspondence)

234 *had no desire to drag Agnes into the public eye* Spielmann, questionnaire submitted to W.G. Grace.

234 *wholesome Christian values among the working class Sheffield Daily Telegraph,* 5 August 1880, p. 8. Grace also wrote pieces for *Boy's Own* about 'the formation and management of cricket clubs' and 'the Cricket Bat'. *Derby Mercury,* 14 September 1881, p. 6, 27 June 1883, p. 6.

235 *a disagreeable and annoying interruption* Grace, 'How to Score', pp. 301, 307.

235 *the batsmen cannot be parted* Hutchinson (ed.), *Outdoor Games and Recreations*, p. 14.

236 *Dunlop, Mackie & Co., a local wine merchant Aberdeen Journal*, 10 July 1903, p. 4, England and Wales Marriage Index.

236 *and other local doctors* Brownlee, *W.G. Grace*, p. 134.

236 *heard W.G.'s school as 'Rudgway'* Ibid., p. 20.

236 *was also his first cousin* Ibid., p. 128.

236 *from W.G.'s diary on his voyage to Australia in 1873* Ibid., pp. 18, 66.

237 *Brownlee acting as ghostwriter and Arrowsmith as publisher Pall Mall Gazette*, 7 December 1889, p. 6.

237 *'I wanted Brownlee to let me off, but he cannot'* W.G. Grace to 'Wood' (unidentified), 13 March 1890 (Clifton College Archives).

237 *a keen amateur cricket statistician* Obituary of Charles Pratt Green, *Berrow's Worcester Journal*, 7 December 1940, p. 4.

237 *'a small size will spoil the whole thing'* W.G. Grace to Henry Perkins, 14 October 1888, in MCC Photograph Album, series 1905-2077.

237 *commission a portrait of its most famous member* MCC Committee Minutes, 13 July, 16 July 1888.

238 *'reputation as England's foremost cricketer' Bristol Mercury*, 18 July 1888, p. 8.

238 *may have been earmarked to pay Grace* MCC Committee Minutes, 21 July 1890.

238 *used it as the background for his canvas* Ibid., 10 December 1888.

238 *'I cannot then wait to give you a sitting'* W.G. Grace to A. Stuart-Wortley, copy of undated letter, 1889.

238 *possibly another fee for his subject* MCC Committee Minutes, 21 July 1890.

238 *sold these high-quality prints on the open market Western Daily Press*, 15 September 1890, p. 5.

239 *By then, sadly, W.G. was even fatter* Harry Furniss cartoon of Grace, 'Ready for Bowling' in Harry Furniss, E.J. Milliken and E.B.V. Christian, *How's That?* (1896), p. 49. Unlike Stuart-Wortley's picture, Furniss's sketch does not show Grace's distinctive cocked front left foot, which may have appeared a split second later.

239 *bought the twenty-six extracts 'at considerable cost' Sydney Morning Herald*, 3 May 1890, p. 10.

239 *'the most popular history of our national game ever written' Nottingham Evening Post*, 12 April 1890, p. 2.

239 *Arrowsmith withheld £25 to cover the publisher's 'expenses'* J.W. Arrowsmith Ltd, 'Register of Royalties 1884–1918', 16 April 1891 (Bristol Record Office, BRO 40145/P/l).

239 *with a cover price of 6 shillings Daily News*, 8 April 1891, p. 4.

239 *snapped up most of this first edition run immediately Bristol Mercury*, 14 April 1891, p. 8.

240 *instructed a shooting chum in a one-line note* W.G. Grace to Mr Blundell, October 1890 (F.S. Ashley-Cooper Correspondence).

240 *'Ye Salmone from ye loved River offe ye Severne'* Menu card, 5 May 1891 (Roger Gibbons Private Collection).

240 *spin off three chapters* I am grateful to Roger Gibbons of Gloucestershire CCC on whose research this information is based. Brownlee referred to this issue in a later letter to the Reverend R.S. Holmes, a cricket historian and compiler. See W.M. Brownlee to R.S. Holmes, 12 February 1893 (F.S. Ashley-Cooper Correspondence).

240 *'about eight yards is the best distance to be from each other in backing up'* Grace, *Cricket*, p. 253.

240 *and even unintentionally comic* Rae, *W.G. Grace*, p. 338.

241 *'or at least sponge rubbers for the heels'* Sir Donald Bradman, *The Art of Cricket* (1958), pp. 14, 15.

241 *'it must be done nicely or not at all'* Grace to Arrowsmith, first letter, 31 August 1891.

241 *'better not at present proceed any further in the matter'* Grace to Arrowsmith, second letter, 31 August 1891.

241 *'whether it is customary or not'* Grace to Arrowsmith, undated note, September 1891.

241 *'although on business matters we do not agree'* Grace to Arrowsmith, 1 October 1891.

24 THE MAJOR AND THE EARL

243 *for the following (English) winter* Augustus Robinson wrote to a local promoter regarding the hire of Melbourne CC's ground for a fixture against James Lillywhite Jr.'s proposed all-professional English team: 'Referring to my letter of 17th inst, I would add that if Mr Grace's Eleven do not come out, the committee will be happy to treat with you, with reference to letting the ground to Lillywhite's eleven.' Lillywhite's tour went ahead, while Grace spent the winter studying medicine in London. Augustus Robinson to Mr J.N.[?] Bennett, 20 May 1876, Melbourne CC Letter Book, A1.2, p. 283.

243 *tour of Australia and New Zealand in 1886–7* Manchester Evening News, 29 April 1886, p. 3.

243 *where Wardill was also secretary* Nottingham Evening Post, 24 June 1886, p. 3.

243 *Wardill put his own plans on hold* Grace suggested acting as an arbitrator between the two rival tours, but, according to Shrewsbury and Shaw, Ben Wardill rejected his proposal.

244 *a man whose word was his bond* Louis R. Cranfield, 'Wardill, Benjamin Johnston (1842–1917)' in *Australian Dictionary of Biography*, Vol. 6 (1976).

244 *'every day of the voyage, almost!'* Ben Wardill to W.G. Grace, 3 February 1887, Melbourne CC Letter Book, A1.6, p. 373.

244 *'especially when he finds your team is coming'* Ben Wardill to George Vernon, 4 February 1887, Melbourne CC Letter Book, A1.6, p. 373.

245 'a dead loss of more than this amount' Ben Wardill to W.G. Grace, 16 May 1887, Melbourne CC Letter Book, A1 6, p. 465.

245 and no admission charge for spectators Manchester Courier, 19 May 1884, p. 3.

245 Shrewsbury estimated in his covering note Arthur Shrewsbury, 27 February 1891, proposed tour budget for Lord Sheffield, in Wynne-Thomas, 'Give me Arthur', p. 108.

246 'the water was said to contain some thirty potenders' Manchester Evening News, 16 May 1890, p. 2.

246 Bessie and Charlie to come on the trip as well No direct evidence has materialised to confirm that Sheffield paid Grace £3000. The source for this figure is Arthur Shrewsbury. In January 1892 Shrewsbury wrote to Alfred Shaw: 'If he hadn't taken Grace out, Lord Sheffield would have been £3000 better off at the end of the Tour, and also had a better team.' Arthur Shrewsbury to Alfred Shaw, 20 January 1892, 'Letters of Arthur Shrewsbury', transcribed by Peter Wynne-Thomas. Lord Sheffield, who died in 1909, left instructions in his will for his solicitors Dawson, Bennett & Co. to 'take charge' of all his 'letters and papers of every description' and 'deal with them in accordance with the wishes I have already made known to them'. It appears likely that Dawson, Bennett & Co. destroyed Sheffield's papers, which are not held by the successor firm.

246 his latest load-bearing injury Lord Sheffield to Aubrey Harcourt, 15 July 1891 (Correspondence and papers of Aubrey Harcourt, 1866–1903, Bodleian Libraries, University of Oxford, MS. Eng. e. 3803, Folios 78–127).

247 'from October next to May 1892' Western Daily Press, 29 August 1891, p. 3.

247 'desire to uphold the honour of England in the colonies. (Laughter.)' Ibid. Rumsey and W.G. went back a long way. The major was a member of Gloucestershire CCC and in his cricketing days had played with and against W.G. in minor matches in the Bristol area. In May 1882 it was Rumsey (Clifton) who had caught Grace (Bedminster), while W.G. was stricken with mumps.

248 lined up for the passengers Sheffield Evening Telegraph, 13 October 1891, p. 3; Sussex Agricultural Express, 30 October 1891, p. 7.

248 to take the needle-and-cigar race Bristol Mercury, 26 October 1891, p. 3.

248 'keen delight' of the umpire (W.G. Grace) The girls still lost by 8 runs. Sheffield Evening Telegraph, 16 December 1891, p. 3, quoting article in The Sportsman.

248 'for the treatment of vomiting, alcoholism [and] fevers' Advertisement in Horsham Times, 8 March 1892, p. 2.

25 A TOUR TOO FAR

249 Lord Sheffield's tour party Ages correct at time of departure from England, 2 October 1891.

250 *ninth best batsman in the tour party* Abel, Bean, Stoddart, Read, Peel, Lohmann, MacGregor and Radcliffe all had better batting averages than Grace in 1891.

250 *beset by constant money worries* See David Frith, *'Stoddy: England's Finest Sportsman'* (first published as *'My Dear Victorious Stod'* in 1970, updated 2015), pp. 11–12.

251 *led by the Surrey amateur Walter Read* Murdoch thus became one of the few players to have appeared for both Australia and England in Test matches.

252 *'one of his vast, carpet bag-like hands'* The Citizen, 21 January 1892, p. 3.

252 *'scarcely worth while commencing'* The Argus, 28 November 1891, p. 5.

252 *'Grace ignored it and went on batting'* Ibid.

252 *'The umpires are all bad and some are unfair as well'* W.G. Grace to William Rees, 25 December 1891 (Rosemary Marryatt Private Collection, courtesy of Lakes District Museum, New Zealand).

253 *'Shaw being appointed umpire in place of Cotter'* Evening News (Sydney), 5 December 1891, p. 6.

253 *marched off the field in a huff* Rick Smith and Ron Williams, *W.G. Down Under: Grace in Australia, 1873–74 and 1891–92* (1994), p. 103.

253 *'tossed many a time, and sometimes heavily'* The Argus, 2 January 1892, p. 7.

253 *'found after close inspection that he had won'* The Australasian, 2 January 1892, p. 18.

253 *'hardly tell the head from the tail'* Ibid., 9 January 1892, p. 16. The reporter was Tom Horan, who had played in the great 1882 Oval Test match.

254 *that evening at the Oriental Hotel* The Argus, 2 January 1892, p. 7.

254 *he refused to talk to the same reporters* South Bourke and Mornington Journal (Victoria), 6 January 1892, p. 2.

254 *at the Melbourne Athletic Club* The Argus, 4 January 1892, p. 3.

255 *'a sound policy under the circumstances'* Ibid., 6 January 1892, p. 6.

255 *'very indignant at the action of the ungracious Grace'* Barrier Miner (Broken Hill), 7 January 1892, p. 4.

255 *'he will see a whole display of Pain's fireworks free of charge'* Windsor and Richmond Gazette (New South Wales), 16 January 1892, p. 6.

256 *'injury having been received in a former match'* Sydney Morning Herald, 30 January 1892, p. 10.

256 *'Jack, you can have a man to run for Moses'* The Mercury, 6 February 1892, p. 4.

256 *'within his rights in declining any substitute for him'* Sydney Morning Herald, 1 February 1892, p. 6.

257 *'W.G. returned to the pavilion with a heavier step than usual'* The Referee (Sydney), 3 February 1892, p. 8.

257 *acted like a 'genuine sportsman'* The Mercury, 6 February 1892, p. 4.

257 *'of the letter referred to'* Evening News (Sydney), 4 February 1892, p. 5.

258 *'you all deserve I don't know what'* Ben Wardill to W.G. Grace, 16 February 1892, Melbourne CC Letter Book, A1-9, p. 588.

258 'lady correspondent' in Sydney reported Daily Telegraph (Tasmania), 19
     February 1892, p. 3. The Hay Standard and Advertiser (New South Wales),
     9 March 1892, p. 2 (Supplement).

259 '"his team had better go home at once"' The Referee, 2 March 1892, p. 4.

259 'necessary on the statements therein made' New South Wales Cricket
     Association Committee Minutes, 2 March 1892 (Cricket NSW Archives).

259 'nor did I think him a cheat' Evening News (Sydney), 19 March 1892, p. 3.

259 'decision of the umpire on the occasion referred to' New South Wales Cricket
     Association Committee Minutes, 18 March 1892.

260 'to enable the Comtee to thoroughly investigate the matter' Ibid.

260 'and two others were waiting to have one' The Advertiser (Adelaide), 24
     March 1892, p. 5.

260 surviving some early nerves and 'streaky' shots Ibid., 25 March 1892, p. 6.

260 'the champion found it difficult to make a passage to the reserve' South
     Australian Register, 28 March 1892, p. 6.

260 'I am sorry to say he is not a good umpire' The Argus, 30 April 1892, p. 7.

26 CLIFTON MAN

261 'I failed to get anything out of him about the tour' Western Daily Press, 13
     July 1934, p. 3.

261 betrayed his boredom when writing about the past W.G. Grace, 'Australian
     Notes', The Cricket Field, 28 May 1892, pp. 57–8.

261 eighteen thousand copies sold by early 1893 W. Methven Brownlee to R.S.
     Holmes, 12 February 1893, 'Letters (Misc) 19th and 20th Century'
     (MCC Archive).

261 selling the book to British expatriates in Paris Ibid.

262 suggests W.G. received some compensation Western Daily Press, 14 September
     1892, p. 3. The report incorrectly identified James Farmer as 'Mr W.
     Farmer'.

262 Messrs Lewis and Sons, a local estate agent Clifton Chronicle, 22 February
     1893, list of Clifton residents.

263 'might just as well elect one of them. (Laughter)' Western Daily Press, 4
     February 1893, p. 7.

263 Farmer gave him a year's notice to quit James Farmer to W.G. Grace, 21
     March 1894, in 'Conveyance of Thrissell House and Thrissell Cottage
     and Thrissell Lodge Numbers 55 and 57 in Stapleton Road', 21
     December 1887.

263 back and forth from 15 Victoria Square Barton Regis Union, Annual Book,
     May 1897, p. 45.

263 Rosa was too unwell to give evidence Western Daily Press, 1 December 1894,
     p. 6. The husband, Fred Gannaway, was sentenced to twelve months hard
     labour although 'several of the jurors thought the girl ought to be blamed
     for being too passive, but they did not think she consented'.

263 *for his personal autograph collection* Swindon Advertiser and North Wilts Chronicle, 1 December 1894, p. 9.

264 *'He promises to be a very good cricketer'* Pall Mall Gazette, 3 October 1884, p. 2.

264 *in a village game against Twenty-Four of Bedminster* Northern Daily Mail (Hartlepool), 2 May 1888, p. 3.

264 *'Come on, lazybones!'* Letter from J.W.S. Toms, 18 November 1933, in 'Letters Remembering W.G. Grace Sent by Readers to *Bristol Evening World*, published 18 November 1933–1 January 1934'.

264 *journey back to Bristol with his father yet to come* Sheffield Daily Telegraph, 17 April 1893, p. 8. Toms incorrectly remembered Bertie coming second.

265 *photograph that would appear in a magazine article about the school* Ludgate Monthly, Vol. VI, No. 1, pp. 61–70, November 1893 (Clifton College Archives).

265 *prep school he attended next to the college with his younger brother Edgar* Bath Chronicle and Weekly Gazette, 13 October 1887, p. 5. Clifton College Fees Ledger, 1888 (Clifton College Archives).

265 *'the making of a Senior Wrangler in him'* Manchester Courier, 30 November 1888, p. 5.

265 *a teacher 'complains of maths'* W.G. Grace Jr., School Record Sheet, 1893 (Clifton College Archives).

265 *HMS Britannia, stationed at Dartmouth* Commander E.P. Statham, R.N., *The Story of the 'Britannia': The Training Ship for Naval Cadets* (1904), p. 206.

266 *did not expect to see him again for several years* W.G. Grace to William Rees, 25 December 1891.

266 *having returned to Bristol on sick leave* Liverpool Echo, 24 June 1893, p. 3.

266 *'not as bright as his brothers'* E.M. Grace, 'Notes for Speech to the Society of Thornbury Folk', 10 March 1972.

266 *someone who could supply references for the institution* Advertisement in the *Standard*, 2 May 1896, p. 9.

266 *Charlie's conduct was 'good'* C.B. Grace, School Record Sheet, 1896 (Clifton College Archives).

267 *'revelling in her inherited prowess'* Huddersfield Chronicle, 16 September 1893, p. 2, quoting article in *Woman*.

267 *Miss Fyffe's XI and Mrs Baker's XI* 'Manuscript Volume of Sports Teams and Fixtures from the 1890s', Clifton High School Archives.

267 *'now 17 her cricket days are over'* Pall Mall Gazette, 14 June 1895, p. 2. W.G. was not quite right. Bessie would persuade her old-fashioned father to let her play in one last cricket match in 1896 for Clifton Old Girls against the school.

268 *'the playing members of the Club are of my opinion'* Gloucestershire CCC Committee Minutes, 9 December 1892, 26 January 1893, 5 September 1893, 31 October 1893.

268 *dropping one or more of them from the side* Ibid., 31 October 1893.

268 *decamped in the spring to the Devon seaside town of Barnstaple* Bristol Mercury, 21 January 1893, p. 1.

268 *'gift of 100 guineas . . . as a slight acknowledgement'* Gloucestershire CCC Committee Minutes, 26 January 1893.

269 *'Even home supporters despaired of his ever regaining form'* Gilbert Jessop, 'W.G.: 1848–1915', undated article, Eltham CC Collection.

27 THE NATIONAL TREASURE

270 *sent 'right over the track'* Bristol Mercury, 18 May 1895, p. 3.

271 *to bring up his landmark century* Ibid.

271 *must have thought: Why not?* The Bristol cricket correspondent H.E. Roslyn said a friend took the empty jeroboam as a souvenir. When the friend died his family threw it away. Roslyn, 'Memories of Gloucestershire Cricket', p. 17.

271 *by the Somerset professional Edwin Tyler* Bristol Mercury, 18 May 1895, p. 3.

272 *in his latest incarnation as Hampstead CC's captain* Yorkshire Post and Leeds Intelligencer, 20 May 1895, p. 5.

272 *'the hero of yesterday's play'* See, for instance, *Exeter and Plymouth Gazette*, 18 May 1895, p. 4; *Evening Telegraph* (Dundee), 18 May 1895, p. 3.

272 *in the last line of the story* Daily News, 18 May 1895, p. 5.

272 *'third three-figure innings this year, and his 101st in first-class cricket'* Nottingham Evening Post, 25 May 1895, p. 3.

272 *'a four-wheeler cab which took him to the station'* Wisden Cricketers' Almanack (1949), p. 101.

273 *'the Editor must respectfully decline to take charge of this subscription'* Roslyn, 'Memories of Gloucestershire Cricket', pp. 17–18.

273 *'in recognition of his cricket achievements'* Gloucester Citizen, 1 June 1895, p. 3.

273 *press the county's plan on the MCC committee* Derby Daily Telegraph, 31 May 1895, p. 4.

274 *Knollys wrote to Grace on Saturday, 1 June* The letter was published in numerous newspapers. See, for instance, *Morning Post*, 3 June 1895, p. 2.

274 *postponed any decision about W.G.'s testimonial until the following week* MCC Committee Minutes, 3 June 1895.

274 *not 'see their way to undertaking the organisation of such a fund'* Bristol Mercury, 7 June 1895, p. 8.

274 *to lobby the committee again* Ibid.

274 *receiving agency for any further contributions from the public* Ibid.

274 *thought had come to him while watching W.G. at Lord's* Essex County Chronicle (Chelmsford), 25 October 1907, p. 5.

275 *'willing to undertake the direction & management'* MCC Committee Minutes, 10 June 1895.

275 'under the authority of the Marylebone Cricket Club' Ibid., 17 June 1895. See also circular letter from Henry Perkins to provincial newspapers, e.g. *Hull Daily Mail*, 14 June 1895, p. 3.

275 earned on average about £70 per year Arthur L. Bowley, *Wages in the United Kingdom in the Nineteenth Century* (1900), p. 133.

276 'bowed his acknowledgements from a window in the pavilion' *Morning Post*, 24 June 1895, p. 2.

276 convincing visual evidence of Grace's dynamic batting style Harry Furniss, 'A Century of Grace', in Furniss, Milliken and Christian, *How's That?*, pp. 45–94.

276 'an enormous expanse of white shirt' Roslyn, 'Memories of Gloucestershire Cricket', p. 18.

277 report of his speech in the Bristol press next morning made clear *Western Daily Press*, 25 June 1895, p. 3.

277 'in the front of a great amusement, year after year' Ibid.

277 'The Nestor of the Bat' *Western Daily Press*, 1 July 1895, p. 7.

278 also sent 1 guinea apiece *The Era*, 29 June 1895, p. 15.

278 'delighted to add to the Grace Fund' *Leeds Times*, 15 June 1895, p. 8.

279 'silliness of the actors' attempts at wit and humour' *Manchester Courier*, 29 June 1895, p. 14.

279 Rosebery lost the election anyway *Yorkshire Evening Post*, 15 June 1895, p. 2; *The Citizen*, 14 June 1895, p. 4; *Hampshire Advertiser*, 15 June 1895, p. 2.

279 'first position among Practical Furriers in the Provinces' *Sheffield Evening Telegraph*, 14 September 1895, p. 3.

280 'sustaining the Empire' *Daily Telegraph* testimonial fund announcement, reprinted in *Evening Telegraph* (Dundee), 8 June 1895, p. 3.

280 Le Sage's description of the grossly overweight W.G. *Western Daily Press*, 19 August 1895, p. 3.

28 HANGING ON

281 'I never would have done as well as I had, even in cricket' *Bristol Mercury*, 7 February 1896, p. 3.

282 a pair (0 and 0) in the Varsity match at Lord's He graduated as 'Senior Optime', the second class in the Mathematical Tripos. Information from Clifton College.

282 because he was not 'of British extraction' Ranji's biographer Simon Wilde has shown that Lord Harris, an active Tory peer and the lead MCC selector, may have reacted to pressure from the Conservative government to pick purely 'British' players. An explanatory letter by Henry Perkins to Ranji made clear that MCC's position had nothing to do with cricket. 'It must not be supposed that your merits as a cricketer are not fully recognised,' Perkins wrote, 'but the Committee think it advisable to play in this match cricketers of purely British extraction.' See Simon

Wilde, *Ranji: A Genius Rich and Strange* (1990), p. 64; MCC Committee Minutes, 15 June 1896.

283 'Alas, poor W.G.!' *Yorkshire Post*, 28 July 1896, p. 10; *Yorkshire Evening Post*, 28 July 1896, p. 3.

283 *he had also withdrawn his protest* In the same letter Lohmann also thanked the Surrey public for contributing so generously to his benefit match the previous week. Lohmann revealed his true feelings about Surrey CCC in a private letter two months later, when he accused the committee of colluding with other county clubs to hold down professionals' pay. *Sheffield Daily Telegraph*, 13 August 1896, p. 9; George Lohmann to R.S. Holmes, 13 October 1896, 'Letters (Misc) 19th and 20th Century'.

283 *'one farthing for playing in a match at the Oval' Standard*, 11 August 1896, p. 11.

283 *'which it is well known will be paid to Mr W.G. Grace' Derby Daily Telegraph*, 10 August 1896, p. 2.

283 *'outweighs a hundredfold every other consideration' Wisden Cricketers' Almanack* (1897), plix.

284 *'and I cannot possibly get away' York Herald*, 30 September 1896, p. 5.

284 *to pay off betting debts* Sir Home Gordon, *Background of Cricket* (1939), p. 333.

284 *'a sovereign or two to satiate his optimism'* Gilbert Jessop, *A Cricketer's Log* (1922), p. 47.

284 *£9000 to MCC and Gloucestershire to invest on his behalf* MCC Committee Minutes, 6 March 1896, 'Report of the Grace Fund Sub-committee'; *Bristol Mercury*, 7 February 1896, p. 3.

285 *large garden to lay out a practice cricket area* Ashley Grange would be demolished in the late 1930s to make way for a building development. *Gloucestershire Echo*, 23 December 1936, p. 3.

285 *overhanging branch that got in the way of his net Bristol Times and Mirror*, 12 May 1928, in 'Looking Back. Forty Years of County Cricket', p. 90.

285 *failed to persuade Ranji to bring a side* Dublin University CC Committee Minutes, 24 May 1897 (Trinity College, Dublin Archives, TCD MUN CLUB CRICKET/4). Grace was paid £110 to bring Gloucestershire's team, who almost certainly shared this money. TCD MUN CLUB DUCAC/16. I am grateful to Ellen O'Flaherty of Trinity College, Dublin's library for this information.

286 *'it worried him to death'* Major W. Troup, *Sporting Memories: My Life as Gloucestershire County Cricketer, Rugby and Hockey Player, and Member of Indian Police Service* (1924), p. 84.

286 *'ludicrous in the extreme'* Chris Massie, Letter recalling Essex v Gloucestershire at Leyton, 7–9 July 1898, undated press cutting (Michael Grace Private Collection).

287 *about exactly when or where it happened* This was the source of another questionable story about Grace. The young amateur C.B. Fry thought

the incident occurred during the Australians' match against Lord Sheffield's XI in May 1896, in which they both played. Lord Harris thought Jones 'grazed' Grace's beard in the Test match at Lord's in June 1896. Fry, *Life Worth Living*, pp. 205–6.

287 *through the slip area to the boundary* Arlott, *The Old Man*.

287 *'running was reduced to the minimum'* Chris Massie, Letter recalling Essex v Gloucestershire at Leyton, 7–9 July 1898.

288 *five-ball overs* From 1889 to 1899, five-ball overs were the rule in English first-class cricket. In 1900, the modern six-ball over was introduced.

288 *'could he distinctly heard in the pavilion'* Jessop, *A Cricketer's Log*, pp. 40–1.

289 *'Surely you're not going, Doc?'* A.A. Thomson, *Cricket My Happiness* (1954), p. 57.

289 *'Is that out, Mr Grace?'* Essex County Chronicle, 15 July 1898, p. 2.

289 *'one of the classic apocryphal stories'* Ibid.

289 *'morally gained the victory'* Ibid.

289 *his fiftieth birthday jubilee match* 'Looking Back. Forty Years of County Cricket', pp. 9–10.

289 *W.G's 'birthday party'* David Kynaston, *W.G.'s Birthday Party* (1998, republished 2010).

290 *'braved the asphyxiating dangers of the underground'* Pall Mall Gazette, 18 July 1898, p. 10.

290 *completely exhausted the Essex bowler* Arlott, *The Old Man*. Contrary to subsequent accounts, there is no evidence that Kortright and Grace were not on speaking terms at the start of the match.

290 *Balfour, was exactly the same age* In fact Balfour was born a week later than Grace on 25 July 1848.

290 *I feel them.' ('Cheers.')* The Citizen, 20 July 1898, p. 3.

290 *had also hurt his heel* Standard, 21 July 1898, p. 6.

291 *Schofield Haigh, who ran back and caught it* Arlott, *The Old Man*.

291 *'greatest cricketer of this or any other age'* Standard, 21 July 1898, p. 6.

29 BESSIE

292 *'about twice the rent we ought to give'* W.G. Grace letter to A.J. Webbe, 7 October 1898, posted on Robert Saunders Autographs Ltd: http://autographs.co.uk/about-us.html, accessed 26 November 2013.

292 *takeover of his parish by the neighbouring Bristol Poor Law Union* David Large, 'Bristol and the New Poor Law', Historical Association, Bristol Branch, 1995, p. 18; The Citizen, 26 September 1898, p. 4.

293 *retirement from Gloucestershire an obvious 'deduction'* Sunderland Echo and Shipping Gazette, 12 October 1898, p. 3.

293 *'he hoped to have more before he gave up Gloucestershire cricket'* The Citizen, 7 December 1898, p. 3.

293 *'very dull and feeble'* C.B. Grace, School Record Sheet, 1898.

293 *'to the popular London suburb'* York Herald, 9 February 1899, p. 4.

294 *'one which nobody could forget'* The Citizen, 21 December 1898, p. 3.

294 *'a hearty "God-speed" to the adventurous aeronauts'* Ibid.

294 *dangers of unclean water piped from London* London County Council, 'Typhoid Fever Epidemic in Maidstone and the London Water Supply', Special Joint Sub-committee of Public Health and Water Committees, 1898 (London Metropolitan Archives, LCC/MIN-107).

294 *thought Bessie had only suffered a mild attack* Western Daily Press, 7 February 1899, p. 5.

295 *'on such a dreadful day'* W.G. Grace to E.C. Sewell, 19 March 1899 (Roger Gibbons Private Collection, copy of original held by Roger Mann Collection).

295 *'carefully following the game and keeping score'* Western Daily Press, 7 February 1899, p. 5.

295 *'accompanied her father when he went out after the Clifton Beagles'* Bristol Mercury, 7 February 1899, p. 8.

295 *'came away with scarcely sufficient material for a paragraph'* Porritt, *The Best I Remember*, p. 32.

296 *planning to publish the first extracts in May* Ibid., p. 34. Sheffield and Rotherham Independent, 31 March 1899, p. 4, on the sale of serialisation rights. The first extracts began appearing in the press at the end of April. See, for instance, *Dundee Courier*, 24 April 1899, p. 4.

296 *'Often I left his house in absolute despair'* Porritt, *The Best I Remember*, p. 32.

296 *removal of 'inimical', a word he never used* Ibid., p. 33.

296 *'of which we had already had a surfeit'* Grace, *Reminiscences*, p. 86.

296 *'leading Gloucestershire to a few victories in the season'* W.G. Grace to C.O.H. Sewell, 19 April 1899 (Roger Gibbons Private Collection, copy of original held by Roger Mann Collection).

296 *strict orders about the team's composition* Troup, *Sporting Memories*, p. 93. Troup mistakenly thought his conversation with Grace occurred after a later game at Lord's, but it is clear from the context that the exchange took place at Blackheath.

297 *were distracting to batsmen* Yorkshire Evening Post, 16 May 1899, p. 4.

297 *W.G. wanted to avoid Bristol* The Gloucestershire County Ground Company noted Grace's disapproval of the adverts at its annual meeting on 15 May. *Western Daily Press*, 16 May 1899, p. 7.

297 *Agnes was so distressed by Bessie's death* Fry, *Life Worth Living*, p. 216.

297 *'exactly what matches he intends playing in'* Western Daily Press, 3 June 1899, p. 8.

298 *at Nottingham, starting on 1 June* Standard, 20 May 1899, p. 3.

298 *'for sentimental reasons alone'* Sheffield Daily Telegraph, 22 May 1899, p. 8.

298 *'yours truly, W.G. Grace'* A.G. Powell, 'An Ultimatum to the Doctor', *Bristol Evening World*, 30 December 1933 (Roger Gibbons Private

Collection). There is a continuing mystery about what happened to the most famous letter that W.G. ever wrote. It was first published in 1933 by the Bristol cricket journalist Archie Powell, who said the letter was the only document in Grace's 'familiar handwriting' in Gloucestershire CCC's records. The letter has since vanished, suggesting it was either thrown away or passed into the hands of a private collector with no right to the document.

299 *Grace's designated successor* The county of London was created by the Local Government Act of 1888. By coincidence one of the main promoters of the new administrative county was John Lloyd, captain of the South Wales Cricket Club in 1864 when Grace scored 170 against the Gentlemen of Sussex. Lloyd later moved to London to practise law.

299 *underline the word* contempt *'a hundred times'* Troup, *Sporting Memories*, p. 94.

299 *'more graceful act on his part to do so voluntarily'* *Yorkshire Evening Post*, 30 May 1899, p. 2, from the *Yorkshire Post*. The newspaper also suggested that Ranji, who was out of form, be picked on the basis of reputation.

299 *a crowd of about thirteen thousand* *Standard*, 3 June 1899, p. 2.

299 *'never dared called W.G. for a second run to the long field'* Fry, *Life Worth Living*, pp. 207–8.

300 *'when he stopped a simple hit'* *Sheffield and Rotherham Independent*, 3 June 1899, p. 10.

300 *reluctantly accepted his resignation* *Western Daily Press*, 3 June 1899, p. 8.

300 *'voluntarily withdraw from the remaining matches'* *Yorkshire Evening Post*, 5 June 1899, p. 3.

300 *'no longer a source of strength'* *Morning Post*, 5 June 1899, p. 2.

300 *over Hawke and Bainbridge's objections* Fry, *Life Worth Living*, pp. 206–7.

301 *'the necessity of giving way to younger and more active men'* *Derby Daily Telegraph*, 12 June 1899, p. 2.

301 *'the less you have to say to them the better for you'* W.G. Grace to C.O.H. Sewell, 12 July 1899.

301 *The committee would not hear of it* Troup, *Sporting Memories*, p. 94.

301 *Kittie Slaughter, a local Clifton girl* *Hampshire Telegraph*, 26 August 1899, p. 4.

30 THE PALACE YEARS

303 *from a 4500-pipe 'Great Organ' to livestock auctions* 'Open Again, 1854', article on Crystal Palace Foundation website, http://www.crystalpalace-found ation.org.uk/history

303 *'the Dutch W.G.'* Posthuma first caught Grace's eye when he played for a visiting Netherlands team against London County in 1901.

304 *'or they might be destroyed'* W.G. Grace to Lord Harris, 20 August 1900 (F.S. Ashley-Cooper Correspondence).

304 *'I dare say I shall find a few more slips'* W.G. Grace to F.S. Ashley-Cooper,
8 January 1903 (F.S. Ashley-Cooper Correspondence).

304 *'cannot accept your kind invitation to dine afterwards'* W.G. Grace to F.R.
Spofforth, 24 July 1901, in Cashman, *The 'Demon' Spofforth*, p. 219.

304 *'took no other wicket in the innings'* Hawke, Harris and Gordon (eds), *The
Memorial Biography of Dr W.G. Grace*, p. 310.

304 *'His great shoulders curved to a hunch'* Webber, *The Chronicle of W.G.*, p.
674.

305 *'had my bails off in a twinkling'* Arthur Conan Doyle, *Memories and
Adventures and Western Wanderings* (1924), pp. 200–1.

305 *navigated an airship above the park Shields Daily Gazette*, 17 July 1902, p. 2.

305 *'because I was slow in the field'* Hawke, Harris and Gordon (eds), *The
Memorial Biography of Dr W.G. Grace*, p. 308.

306 *'"Bring four more bottles"'* Albert E. Lawton, 'My W.G.' unpublished
manuscript, 1947, pp. 14–15 (MCC Archive).

306 *for the National Society for the Prevention of Cruelty to Children Western
Daily Press*, 30 May 1902, p. 7.

306 *'Hoping you and Harry will be able to work it'* W.G. Grace to J.W.
Arrowsmith, 4 November 1902. Source unknown.

306 *'showing old pals over a new home'* Roslyn, 'Memories of Gloucestershire
Cricket', p. 18.

306 *'solely concerned with the present and the future'* Ibid.

307 *'and anyone who you think might like to know'* W.G. Grace to J.W.
Arrowsmith, 27 June 1903 (Bristol Record Office, BRO 42069/GCC/62).

307 *that only added to their agony Birmingham Daily Mail*, 3 March 1905, p. 4.

307 *'from what he felt to be his duty'* Memorial service for W.G. Grace, Jr., 5
March 1905, 'Text of Sermon by Rev. F.S. Horan, Chaplain, at Royal
Naval College, Osborne' (Michael Grace Private Collection).

307 *'in connection with the summer game' Birmingham Daily Mail*, 3 March
1905, p. 4.

307 *'he did it with his might'* Memorial service for W.G. Grace, Jr., 5 March
1905.

308 *'We know what it is to lose those that are dear to us'* W.G. Grace to J.W.
Arrowsmith, 6 July 1907, Records of J.W. Arrowsmith Ltd, 'Production
and Sales – Letters from Authors' (Bristol Record Office, BRO
40145/P/19–32).

308 *'for which we all have a sneaking kindness'* Colebrook, 'A Fine Old
Lithographer', pp. 535–7.

308 *winning a prize in 1903 as the club's best batsman Sheffield Daily Telegraph*,
3 December 1903, p. 12.

308 *Edgar, Alice, Gladys and Primrose ('Prim')* A fifth child, John, was born
in 1911.

309 *Walter Lees, John Gunn and Albert Trott* The Surrey and England player
Ernest Hayes, who also bowled in this match, was primarily a batsman.

309 *'chop away from the wicket many balls that almost bowled him'* The Citizen, 19 July 1906, p. 3, quoting *Sporting Life.*

309 *using one signature shot in particular* Sheffield Evening Telegraph, 18 July 1906, p. 4.

309 *'with nothing more than a flick'* Ibid.

309 *'tremendously cheered' by the crowd of around six thousand* Ibid.

309 *'something like 20 per cent of the runs he really deserved were lost'* The Citizen, 19 July 1906, p. 3, quoting *Sporting Life.*

310 *as manager of the company's cricket and bowls clubs* Agreement between W.G. Grace and Crystal Palace Company, 4 August 1906 (London Metropolitan Archives, CPT/049/B).

310 *a completely different sport: bowls* Geoff Barnett, 'Do You Know What W.G. Grace Did for Bowls?' (2011) Tring Bowls Club, www.tringbowls. co.uk.

310 *London County Bowling Club (Captain: W.G. Grace)* Evening News (Portsmouth), 31 May 1901, p. 4.

311 *'We must catch the 7.35 back'* W.G. Grace to A.T. Barton, 14 May 1905, 16 September 1906 (Berkshire Record Office).

311 *'loud greetings to some friend playing another hole'* Darwin, *W.G. Grace,* p. 123.

312 *same back-of-the-hand action as for a leg-break (left to right)* Bosanquet was the father of the future television newscaster Reginald Bosanquet, who did not inherit his father's cricketing talent.

312 *'much greater physical strain than is any other kind of bowling'* W.G. Grace, *W.G.'s Little Book* (1909), p. 29.

312 *bowl the 'bosie' (after 'Bosanquet') with tremendous accuracy* Grimmett was originally from New Zealand, which was not yet a Test match–playing country.

313 *'and gaps mean singles and twos to an observant and good batsman'* Grace, *W.G.'s Little Book,* p. 34.

313 *'were not what might be called popular editions'* Ibid., preface.

31 CLOSE OF PLAY

314 *finally collapsed and went bankrupt* Manchester Courier, 25 June 1909, p. 18.

314 *a short-term lease for £110 per year* Copy of counterpart lease between Thomas Bond of Fairmount, Mottingham, Licensed Victualler, and W.G. Grace, Physician and Surgeon, 29 September 1909 (Eltham CC Collection).

314 *'get as much interest as I can with a fair amount of safety'* W.G. Grace to Lord Harris, 10 November 1910, Harris Family Papers, Vol. 4, p. 43.

315 *less than half the approximately £6000 he had returned after his testimonial* Board of Stamps, Legacy Duty Office and Successors, Selected Death Duty Accounts, 'Grace, William Gilbert' (National Archives, IR59/459).

315 *rather than riskier short-term equities* Ibid.

316 *from their mounted glass boxes in the hall* Valuation of W.G. Grace's estate, Board of Stamps, Legacy Duty Office and Successors, Selected Death Duty Accounts, 'Grace, William Gilbert'.

317 *in a locked case in the morning room* Richard Beaumont, *Purdey's: The Guns and the Family* (1984), p. 75.

317 *lent W.G. another weapon to satisfy his shooting needs* Ibid.

317 *'running about 2 and a half hours'* W.G. Grace to Mr Blundell, undated note (F.S. Ashley-Cooper Correspondence).

317 *'implored the huntsman to take no notice of him'* E.M. Grace, 'Notes for Speech to the Society of Thornbury Folk', 10 March 1872.

317 *practise his golf shots in a field by the road* Hawke, Harris and Gordon (eds), *The Memorial Biography of Dr W.G. Grace*, pp. 330–1.

318 *'with an air so pretty and gracious'* Darwin, *W.G. Grace*, p. 118.

318 *'to whom he liked to wave his hand'* Ibid., p. 102.

318 *the oldest and keenest member of the club* Bristol *Evening World*, 20 December 1933, 'Letters Remembering W.G. Grace Sent by Readers to *Bristol Evening World*, published 18 November 1933–1 January 1934'.

318 *to pack in the game* I am grateful to research by the Eltham local historian John King and information from Eltham CC's chairman David Jones regarding the Norths' connection with the club.

319 *'Hoping this will enable you to make up a small paragraph'* W.G. Grace to F.S. Ashley-Cooper, 12 October 1910 (F.S. Ashley-Cooper Correspondence).

319 *when he suffered a fatal stroke* The Referee, 22 February 1911, p. 12.

320 *'John Dann & Blanche told us how bad he was'* W.G. Grace to Edgar Grace, 20 May 1911 (Michael Grace Private Collection).

320 *'it is as much as I can do to stand'* E.M. Grace to Fred Weaver, April 1910 (Roger Gibbons Private Collection).

320 *E.M.'s favourite hymn* Theodore Robinson to Edgar Grace, 12 January 1944 (Michael Grace Private Collection).

320 *'He must have been very long-suffering'* Cliff Morgan radio interview with Primrose Worthington, BBC *Sport on Four*, 25 November 1995.

320 *'or to A.S. Jackson, Victoria Road, Eltham'* Eltham Times, 31 October 1913, quoted in John King, 'Manuscript Article on Grace's Association with Eltham CC', p. 17 (Eltham CC Collection).

321 *'the Doctor had no use'* The Sportsman, 29 October 1915, in Pelham Warner Scrapbook, 1915 (MCC Archive).

321 *'judicious conservatism'* as the game's governing body Grace, *Reminiscences*, p. 27.

322 *'being especially strong on the off side'* Eltham Times, 31 July 1914.

322 *'chopped' towards the boundary wherever it suited him* King, 'Manuscript Article on Grace's Association with Eltham CC', p. 26.

323 *'Yours etc., W.G. Grace'* The Sportsman, 27 August 1914.

32 SUNSET

324 *'felt too strongly about Germany' Weekly Dispatch*, 24 October 1915, in Pelham Warner Scrapbook, 1915.

324 *in the Medway and Thames Estuary districts Kent & Sussex Courier*, 15 January 1915, p. 5. Obituary of Major Charles Butler Grace in *Journal of the Institution of Electrical Engineers*, Vol. 83, Issue 504, December 1938, pp. 891–2.

325 *'his own human folk here or over the seas'* E. Rhys Jones, funeral address for W.G. Grace, 27 October 1915 (Eltham CC Collection).

325 *'"mowed down"'* Darwin, *W.G. Grace*, p. 138.

325 *'but the others have beaten me'* W.G. Grace to F.S. Ashley-Cooper, 20 December 1914 (F.S. Ashley-Cooper Correspondence).

325 *'who I hope will always love books'* Item 2269 in MCC Photograph Album, series 2078–2388.

325 *'and we did not see much of him' Weekly Dispatch*, 24 October 1915, in Pelham Warner Scrapbook, 1915.

326 *who thought W.G. had said he would play* King, 'Manuscript Article on Grace's Association with Eltham CC', p. 33.

326 *since the war he had no appetite for sport Daily Mail*, 25 May 1915, in Pelham Warner Scrapbook, 1915.

326 *'and go round the ground with a collecting box'* G. Neville Weston, *W.G. Grace, The Great Cricketer: A Statistical Record of His Performances in Minor Cricket* (1973), pp. 152–3.

326 *'and the volunteers resumed their march' Nottingham Evening Post*, 19 July 1915, p. 2.

327 *'but I am not allowed to bother him in any way'* Agnes Grace to F.S. Ashley-Cooper, 12 October 1915 (F.S. Ashley-Cooper Correspondence).

327 *did not recount his tale publicly until 1953, when he published his memoirs* H.D.G. Leveson-Gower, *On and Off the Field* (1953), pp. 228–9.

327 *describing him as 'not very well' rather than close to death* Ibid., p. 229.

328 *suffered a heart attack, dying a few minutes later* William Gilbert Grace, Death Certificate, registered 25 October 1915, Bromley Registration District.

328 *genial tyrant in a world that was all sunshine* A.G. Gardiner, writing as Alpha of the Plough, *Pebbles on the Shore* (1916), pp. 27, 29.

328 *travelled over from Downend* Details of funeral from *Daily Telegraph*, 27 October 1915, in Pelham Warner Scrapbook, 1915; *Western Daily Press*, 27 October 1915, p. 10; Rhys Jones, funeral address for W.G. Grace, 27 October 1915.

329 *'Goodbye, Gilly, Goodbye!'* E.M. Grace, 'Notes for Speech to Society of Thornbury Folk, 10 March 1972'.

33 FALSE MEMORIAL

330 *adequate tribute can be compiled The Sportsman*, 27 October 1915, Pelham Warner Scrapbook, 1915.

331 *while Edith consulted her lawyer* In 1926 Gordon's girlfriend Gertrude Dellow committed suicide a few months after he left her. At the inquest Gordon testified that he had ended the relationship because of her addiction to alcohol and drugs. He was cleared of any responsibility for her death. *Sunday Post* (Lanarkshire), 28 February 1926, p. 4; *Gloucestershire Echo*, 26 February 1926, p. 6.

331 *suffering from a 'disturbance'* MCC Committee Minutes, 18, 25 June 1900.

331 *Gordon apologised again* Ibid., 2 June 1902.

331 *which Fry felt had defamed him* Ibid., 8 November 1909.

331 *as a fellow man about town* Gordon later claimed that when Hawke finally married at the age of fifty-five in 1916, the MCC president used Gordon's office or home as a base to write all his thank-you letters for wedding presents. Gordon, *Background of Cricket*, p. 135.

332 *bringing his five cricketing scrapbooks round to Cheyne Walk* Irving Rosenwater, 'Sir Home Gordon, Bart. An Affectionate Retrospect' (2000), p. 12.

332 *'there will not be space for statistics'* Sir Home Gordon to F.S. Ashley-Cooper, 29 October 1915.

332 *'the book to tell posterity what he has been'* Ibid.

332 *'as well as over 100 voluntary correspondents'* Ibid., 4 November 1915.

332 *sent a strong protest to Lord's* MCC Committee Minutes, 8 November 1915.

333 *'and this he communicated to her'* Gordon, *Background of Cricket*, p. 334.

333 *'objection to the publication'* MCC Committee Minutes, 13 December 1915.

333 *and now the Grace family's solicitor* Lord Hawke to Agnes Grace, 16 December 1915, 'Letters (Misc) 19th and 20th Century'.

334 *'"She is a dear"'* Hawke, *Recollections and Reminiscences*, p. 119. Gordon persuaded Hawke to write his memoirs William & Northcote, the publisher where Gordon worked. Ibid. p. 1.

334 *rubber-stamped on 10 January* MCC Committee Minutes, 10 January 1916.

335 *'to see "Britain Prepared"'* Agnes Grace to Lord Hawke, 11 January 1916, 'Letters (Misc) 19th and 20th Century'. Agnes wrote a third letter to Hawke, which was read to the committee on 7 February. This letter has not been located in the MCC Archive.

335 *signed curtly at the end* MCC agreement with Sir Home Gordon, 13 January 1916, 'Letters (Misc) 19th and 20th Century'.

335 *after Hawke and Agnes were dead* Gordon, *Background of Cricket*, p. 335.

336 *Harris barely touched the manuscript* Ibid.

336 *'I shall annex the lot, making it a chapter by you'* Home Gordon to F.S. Ashley-Cooper, 2 April 1916 (F.S. Ashley-Cooper Correspondence).

336 *'cannot put 2 words together'* Ibid., undated.

336 *'what seemed injudicious to put on record'* Gordon, *Background of Cricket*, p. 333.

336 *'the public career of the great sportsman'* Hawke, Harris and Gordon (eds), *The Memorial Biography of Dr W.G. Grace*, p. vi.

337 *in Tasmania at the time, visiting his brother* Ibid., p. 104. The Australian cricket historian Ric Finlay first noticed the evidence from shipping lists that Spofforth may have been in Tasmania. See *The Argus*, 14 January 1874, p. 4.

34 AFTERGLOW

338 *'she does not feel equal to the task'* *Western Daily Press*, 4 May 1922, p. 7.

338 *on Christmas Day 1920, following an operation* Ibid., 31 December 1920, p. 3.

338 *vacancy for the post of Bristol's civic sword bearer* Ibid., 23 September 1924, p. 5.

339 *at the Brookwood cemetery near Woking* Spofforth left £169, 268 9s 6d in 'personal effects'. Probate, London, 6 July 1926.

339 *'immeasurably superior to all his contemporaries'* Hawke, *Recollections and Reminiscences*, p. 119.

339 *and Len Hutton (56.67)* I have only chosen those batsmen who are generally accepted as 'great'. There is plenty of room for debate about other candidates for this elite grouping, such as the underrated pre-war Lancashire and England batsman Eddie Paynter (59.23).

340 *hitting Bradman 'smack on the arse'* Duncan Hamilton, *Harold Larwood* (2009), p. 20.

341 *'he would be equally difficult to dislodge'* H. E. Roslyn, 'W.G. My Idol', *Bristol Times and Mirror*, 5 May 1928, in 'Looking Back. Forty Years of County Cricket', p. 87.

341 *'black marks about his body'* Ibid., 5 May 1928.

342 *'his position well in mind when making the stroke'* Ibid.

342 *without shedding much light on the man* A.G. (Archie) Powell, 'The Life of W.G. Grace', a series of articles originally published in the *Bristol Evening World*, 13 November 1933–2 January 1934 (Roger Gibbons Private Collection).

342 *allegedly simple mind and boyish 'keenness'* *The Citizen*, 5 May 1934, p. 11.

342 *not a fortune for a woman who had no money of her own* William Gilbert Grace, Last Will and Testament, 24 November 1910, Probate Registry.

342 *with a doctor and nurse as witnesses* Agnes Nicholls Grace, Will, 21 January 1926.

343 *lit a cigarette and shortly afterwards collapsed and died* Sheffield *Evening Telegraph*, 24 March 1932, p. 6.

343 *Edgar told a Christian rally in July 1934* Untitled newspaper cutting, July 1934 (Michael Grace Private Collection).

343 *in a failed flying stunt over Kent* Nottingham *Evening Post*, 21 July 1930, p. 1. Gladys's sister Primrose witnessed the accident, which occurred over Maidstone while Gladys and her flying partner attempted a second 'loop the loop'.

343 *and her naval husband in Devonport* Western *Morning News*, 20 March 1937, p. 6.

344 *'a terrific shock when we found he was dead'* Gloucestershire *Echo*, 7 June 1938, p. 5.

344 *'the grave is covered with long grass and weeds'* Western *Daily Press*, 24 November 1943, p. 3.

344 *'but they are not obtainable'* Ibid., 17 December 1943, p. 3.

344 *Warner's acquaintance with Grace had been slight* Ibid., 15 July 1948, p. 4.

344 *a man of 'pure country strain' whose cricket was 'instinctive'* Arlott, *The Old Man.*

345 *In memory of the great cricketer, from all Australia'* Western *Morning News*, 19 July 1948, p. 3.

345 *a limited edition of fifty copies* Weston, *W.G. Grace, The Great Cricketer.*

347 *'As far as any social activity can be the work of any one man, he did it'* C.L.R. James, *Beyond a Boundary* (1963), p. 169.

347 *'the yeoman, the country doctor, the squire, the England of yesterday'* Ibid., p. 176.

347 *Queen Victoria's retreat into mourning* Rowland Bowen, *Cricket: A History of its Growth and Development Throughout the World* (1970), p. 111.

347 *new mass spectator audience for sport in Britain's industrial cities and towns* Eric Midwinter, *W.G. Grace: His Life and Times* (1981), p. 3.

348 *such as his supposed vocation for medicine* Robert Low, *W.G.: A Life of W.G. Grace* (1997), pp. 3, 8.

348 *played by Grace across more than five decades* Webber, *The Chronicle of W.G.*, p. 674.

W.G. GRACE:
CAREER STATISTICS

First-Class Career, Batting, Bowling and Fielding

TEST CAREER BATTING AND FIELDING (1880–99)

	M	I	NO	Runs	HS	Ave	100	50	Ct
England	22	36	2	1098	170	32.29	2	5	39

TEST CAREER BOWLING (1880–99)

	Balls	Mdns	Runs	Wkts	BB	Ave	5wI	10wM	SRate	Econ
England	666	65	236	9	2-12	26.22	0	0	74.00	2.12

FIRST-CLASS CAREER BATTING AND FIELDING (1865–1908)

	M	I	NO	Runs	HS	Ave	100	50	Ct	St
Overall	870	1478	104	54211	344	39.45	124	251	876	5

FIRST-CLASS CAREER BOWLING (1865–1908)

	Balls	Mdns	Runs	Wkts	BB	Ave	5wI	10wM	SRate	Econ
Overall	124833	11170	50980	2809	10–49	18.14	240	64	44.44	2.45

SEASON BY SEASON FIRST-CLASS BATTING

Season		Matches	Inns	Not Out	Runs	HS	Ave	100	50	Ct	St
1865	(England)	5	8	1	189	48	27.00	0	0	5	
1866	(England)	8	13	2	581	224*	52.81	2	1	9	
1867	(England)	4	6	1	154	75	30.80	0	1	4	
1868	(England)	7	11	2	588	134*	65.33	3	2	5	
1869	(England)	15	24	1	1320	180	57.39	6	3	12	
1870	(England)	21	38	5	1808	215	54.78	5	9	19	
1871	(England)	25	39	4	2739	268	78.25	10	9	32	3
1872	(England)	20	29	3	1485	170*	57.11	6	6	27	
1873	(England)	20	32	7	1805	192*	72.20	6	8	29	
1874	(England)	21	32	0	1664	179	52.00	8	2	35	
1875	(England)	26	48	2	1498	152	32.56	3	5	40	
1876	(England)	26	46	4	2622	344	62.42	7	10	46	
1877	(England)	24	40	3	1474	261	39.83	2	9	37	
1878	(England)	24	42	2	1151	116	28.77	1	5	42	
1879	(England)	18	28	3	880	123	35.20	2	5	23	
1880	(England)	16	27	3	951	152	39.62	2	5	17	
1881	(England)	13	22	1	792	182	37.71	2	4	20	
1882	(England)	22	37	0	975	88	26.35	0	8	22	
1883	(England)	22	41	2	1352	112	34.66	1	9	35	1
1884	(England)	26	45	5	1361	116*	34.02	3	6	30	
1885	(England)	25	42	3	1688	221*	43.28	4	10	31	
1886	(England)	33	55	3	1846	170	35.50	4	9	36	
1887	(England)	24	46	8	2062	183*	54.26	6	8	21	1
1888	(England)	33	59	1	1886	215	32.51	4	7	34	
1889	(England)	24	45	2	1396	154	32.46	3	7	22	
1890	(England)	30	55	3	1476	109*	28.38	1	9	31	
1891	(England)	24	40	1	771	72*	19.76	0	5	19	
1891–2	(Australia)	8	11	1	448	159*	44.80	1	2	17	
1892	(England)	21	37	3	1055	99	31.02	0	8	14	
1893	(England)	28	50	5	1609	128	35.75	1	11	21	
1894	(England)	27	45	1	1293	196	29.38	3	5	18	
1895	(England)	29	48	2	2346	288	51.00	9	5	31	
1896	(England)	30	54	4	2135	301	42.70	4	11	18	
1897	(England)	25	41	2	1532	131	39.28	4	7	15	
1898	(England)	26	41	5	1513	168	42.02	3	8	20	

Season		Matches	Inns	Not Out	Runs	HS	Ave	100	50	Ct	St
1899	(England)	13	23	1	515	78	23.40	0	3	7	
1900	(England)	19	31	1	1277	126	42.56	3	8	6	
1901	(England)	19	32	1	1007	132	32.48	1	7	7	
1902	(England)	22	35	3	1187	131	37.09	2	7	6	
1903	(England)	16	27	1	593	150	22.80	1	1	5	
1904	(England)	15	26	1	637	166	25.48	1	3	2	
1905	(England)	9	13	0	250	71	19.23	0	1	2	
1906	(England)	5	10	1	241	74	26.77	0	2	4	
1907	(England)	1	2	0	19	16	9.50	0	0	0	
1908	(England)	1	2	0	40	25	20.00	0	0	0	

TEST MATCH BATTING AND FIELDING

Season		Matches	Inns	Not Out	Runs	HS	Ave	100	50	Ct	St
1880	(England)	1	2	1	161	152	161.00	1	0	1	
1882	(England)	1	2	0	36	32	18.00	0	0	4	
1884	(England)	3	4	0	72	31	18.00	0	0	5	
1886	(England)	3	4	0	200	170	50.00	1	0	8	
1888	(England)	3	4	0	73	38	18.25	0	0	8	
1890	(England)	2	4	1	91	75★	30.33	0	1	1	
1891–2	(Australia)	3	5	0	164	58	32.80	0	2	9	
1893	(England)	2	3	0	153	68	51.00	0	1	2	
1896	(England)	3	6	0	119	66	19.83	0	1	0	
1899	(England)	1	2	0	29	28	14.50	0	0	1	

Number of First-Class Centuries: 124
(Association of Cricket Statisticians and Historians)

Or:
126★
(*Wisden Cricketers' Almanack*)

★Includes:
July 1873: 152 for Gentlemen to Canada Touring Team v MCC Fifteen
August 1879: 113 for Gloucestershire v Somerset

This book believes that the ACSH number is more accurate, since neither the MCC Fifteen nor Somerset (in 1879) was a first-class side. However, most lists of Grace's first-class centuries follow *Wisden's* figure of 126, which is the reference point used below.

SEASON BY SEASON FIRST-CLASS BOWLING

Season		Balls	Mdns	Runs	Wkts	BB	Ave	5wI	10wM
1865	(England)	626	64	268	20	8-40	13.40	2	1
1866	(England)	1269	123	483	31	7-51	15.58	3	0
1867	(England)	799	96	293	39	8-25	7.51	5	2
1868	(England)	1308	116	639	44	7-23	14.52	5	3
1869	(England)	3141	356	1189	73	6-10	16.28	7	1
1870	(England)	1817	173	785	50	6-24	15.70	4	0
1871	(England)	3084	282	1345	79	7-67	17.02	5	2
1872	(England)	1670	166	678	56	8-33	12.10	7	3
1873	(England)	2225	201	1093	75	10-92	14.57	5	1
1874	(England)	4084	378	1758	139	7-18	12.64	16	9
1875	(England)	6765	684	2473	191	9-48	12.94	22	8
1876	(England)	6313	650	2457	130	8-69	18.90	12	2
1877	(England)	7170	788	2293	179	9-55	12.81	17	7
1878	(England)	6610	733	2208	153	8-23	14.43	13	6
1879	(England)	4242	442	1414	105	8-81	13.46	13	1
1880	(England)	4062	432	1479	84	7-65	17.60	9	3
1881	(England)	2047	194	879	45	7-30	19.53	3	0
1882	(England)	3405	273	1752	101	8-31	17.34	8	2
1883	(England)	4417	395	2077	94	7-92	22.09	9	4
1884	(England)	4149	448	1762	82	6-72	21.48	5	0
1885	(England)	5738	662	2199	117	9-20	18.79	8	2
1886	(England)	6102	648	2439	122	10-49	19.99	10	1
1887	(England)	5098	526	2082	97	7-53	21.46	7	1
1888	(England)	4390	503	1691	93	6-74	18.18	6	0
1889	(England)	2318	146	1020	44	8-37	23.18	2	1
1890	(England)	3048	212	1182	61	6-68	19.37	3	0
1891	(England)	2364	146	973	58	7-38	16.77	5	1
1891–2	(Australia)	390	21	134	5	3-64	26.80	0	0
1892	(England)	2128	131	958	31	5-51	30.90	2	0
1893	(England)	1705	95	854	22	4-95	38.81	0	0
1894	(England)	1507	69	732	29	6-82	25.24	1	0
1895	(England)	900	44	527	16	5-87	32.93	1	0
1896	(England)	2818	158	1249	52	7-59	24.01	3	1
1897	(England)	2971	181	1242	56	6-36	22.17	4	0

Season		Balls	Mdns	Runs	Wkts	BB	Ave	5wI	10wM
1898	(England)	2368	157	915	36	7-44	25.41	3	1
1899	(England)	1220	66	482	20	5-86	24.10	1	0
1900	(England)	1759	54	969	32	5-66	30.28	3	0
1901	(England)	2755	128	1111	51	7-30	21.78	5	1
1902	(England)	2917	150	1074	46	5-29	23.34	4	0
1903	(England)	798	18	479	10	6-102	47.90	1	0
1904	(England)	1308	36	687	21	6-78	32.71	1	0
1905	(England)	510	7	383	7	4-121	54.71	0	0
1906	(England)	506	18	268	13	4-71	20.61	0	0
1908	(England)	12	0	5	0				

TEST MATCH BOWLING

Season		Balls	Mdns	Runs	Wkts	BB	Ave	5wI	10wM
1880	(England)	117	10	68	3	2-66	22.66	0	0
1884	(England)	168	28	38	3	1-2	12.66	0	0
1886	(England)	40	3	22	1	1-21	22.00	0	0
1890	(England)	70	10	12	2	2-12	6.00	0	0
1891–2	(Australia)	96	2	34	0				
1896	(England)	65	4	25	0				
1899	(England)	110	8	37	0				

ACKNOWLEDGEMENTS

My greatest pleasure in writing this book has been meeting W.G. and Agnes's descendants, who keep alive the memory of the Graces and the interconnected clan of Pococks, Days, Pigeons, Reeses and Gilberts.

I wish to thank Bob Pigeon in particular for sharing his own research on his ancestors and answering endless questions over more than two years. He became my indispensable first call for all Grace family enquiries. I am extremely grateful as well to Mike Grace, who made available his extensive private collection on two visits; Gill Watts, who showed me E.M.'s old home in Thornbury and shared her own family papers; Dinah Bernard, who made available the collection compiled by her late husband Richard Bernard; and Simon Awdry, who sifted through a trove of Grace family photographs. Thanks as well to Charles Kidd, Peter Ward and Robin Gilbert for help with other Grace enquiries.

In Australia, Keith Rees kindly shared his own and his family's detailed research on their ancestors and provided much information about the Reeses whom W.G. met on his 1873–4 tour. In New Zealand, Rosemary Marryatt told me about her ancestor Alfred Pocock's 'world tour' from 1867 to 1870, a story unknown in the cricket world. I thank her also for permission to use a particularly grumpy letter by W.G.

At Trent Bridge, Peter Wynne-Thomas, Nottinghamshire CCC's archivist, made available James Southerton's diary of Grace's 1873–4 tour and then became the man who saved me from many factual mistakes about W.G. and his cricketing times. I cannot thank him enough; any remaining errors are of course my own. I am equally indebted to Roger Gibbons, executive board member and honorary archivist at Gloucestershire CCC, who shared his own and the club's archive material, answered countless questions about W.G.'s volatile relationship with Gloucestershire's committee, and solved the mystery of why W.G. got so angry with his publisher in 1891.

In south-east London, Eltham CC's chairman David Jones kindly lent me the club's material on W.G., allowing me to piece together the poignant story of Grace's final cricketing years. Very many thanks. I am grateful as well to the local Eltham historian John King, whose original research on Grace's matches for Eltham CC was an essential reference point.

Many thanks to Elizabeth Sedgwick, who helped in so many ways as a researcher, reality check for my wilder theories about Grace, and reader of early drafts of this book. In Bristol, Mike Pascoe provided essential local historical knowledge, becoming my guide to nineteenth-century Bristol.

Two friends in Canada and the United States pursued W.G. from Quebec's *Basse-Ville* to the Union League in Philadelphia. Thank you so much, Rod Mickleburgh and Jennifer Lin.

Robert Winder spent two years going back and forth with me about W.G. My own thoughts were better as a result. In cricket jargon, Robert executed his skills set advice-wise and took my research to the next level. In plain English, he played a blinder.

Other friends saw drafts at various stages and helped immeasurably with the writing. Many thanks to Conrad Williams, who knew how to tell a story; Mark Redhead, who saw the importance of jeopardy; Simon Garfield, who brought it back to the beard; and Ross Biddecombe, who cut to the chase. Thanks as well to Lawrence Booth, *Wisden*'s editor, who commissioned me to write an article on W.G. for the 2015 edition.

My research began and ended at Lord's, and I am tremendously grateful for the help given by Neil Robinson, MCC's library and research manager, and Robert Curphey, MCC's archivist, and all the museum, library and collection team under Adam Chadwick. At Belmont House, Lord Harris's country home in Kent, Margaret Woodall alerted me to Harris's remarkable unpublished 'Reminiscences', W.G.'s request for financial advice from 'my dear George' and much else besides. Thank you. Dr C.S. Knighton of Clifton College Archives produced Bertie and Charlie Grace's terrifyingly fierce school reports, a letter from Grace complaining about his ghostwriter and other gems, as well as answering my questions about The Close, where Grace delivered many of his greatest performances. Sarah Cuthill at Clifton High School found Bessie Grace's academic reports and details of her cricket career. Anne Bradley confirmed that Edgar Grace attended Bristol Grammar School before he joined the Navy.

In Australia, Patricia Downs, Melbourne Cricket Club's archivist, was constantly helpful during two years of enquiries about the club's extensive material relating to Grace's two tours there. Thanks to her, I was able to trawl through committee minutes, letter books and other records and see the Australian side of the story. I am grateful as well to David Studham, Melbourne CC's librarian, for his expert advice.

In Sydney, Colin Clowes, honorary research librarian at Cricket NSW, provided much archive material and kindly agreed to read all the draft 'Australian' chapters in this book, correcting errors and pointing out details I had missed. I am extremely grateful to Colin and to Bob Brenner, honorary librarian at Cricket NSW, who also read the chapters. As with my 'English' research, I am to blame for any remaining errors.

I also wish to thank many people and organisations for help with different enquiries and requests. In no particular batting order: the Bristol Record Office, which helped find material on Grace's career in Bristol as a medical student and doctor; Michael Richardson and Hannah Lowery at the University of

Bristol Library's Special Collections department for the Bristol Medical School's student register; Sharon Messenger, archivist at the Royal College of General Practitioners in London, for the college's material on E.M. and W.G. I thank as well Dr Bill Reith of the RCGP for answering my questions about nineteenth-century medical examinations in England and Scotland; Professor Anne Digby, historian of medicine at Oxford Brookes University, for kindly reading my chapter on Grace's time as a doctor in Bristol; Joe Lynn and Kathleen Burns at the C. Christopher Morris Cricket Library and Collection at Haverford College, Pennsylvania, for material on Grace's visit to Philadelphia; Theresa Altieri at Philadelphia's Union League for details of the banquet for the English cricketers in 1872; Ellen O'Flaherty at the archives of Trinity College, Dublin for the committee minutes of Dublin University CC; Elaine Milsom, archivist at Badminton House, Gloucestershire, for help with enquiries about the 8th Duke of Beaufort; Jayne Ringrose, honorary archivist at Pembroke College, Cambridge, for information about Bertie Grace's academic career; the Surrey History Centre in Woking for Surrey CCC committee minutes and correspondence; David Frith, cricket historian and collector, for a letter by Grace and much helpful advice on Victorian and Edwardian cricketers; Les Summerfield and David Allen for their hospitality and help when showing me around Thornbury CC. I am sad that David Allen, Gloucestershire CCC and England, died before I completed this book. I am grateful to Bob Laverton and his son Tony for help with my enquiries about Grace's appearances for W.H. Laverton's XI; Riet Saward, for showing me around Fairmount, W.G.'s last home in Mottingham; Kathy Tidman, for sharing her research on William Day and Day & Son, and Professor Michael Twyman, for answering my questions about nineteenth-century lithography; my friends Xanthe Mosley, Jenny Hall and Mark Smale-Adams, for helping me understand why Harry Furniss's cartoon of W.G. taking guard is better than Stuart-Wortley's portrait; Louis Laumen, for information about his fine sculpture of W.G. at Lord's; Duncan

Simpson and Nick Stevenson, for putting me straight about the googly and the merits (or otherwise) of Grace's statue's on drive; David Robertson, honorary archivist at Kent CCC, for help with questions about Grace's triple-century at Canterbury in 1876; Howard Milton, Mike Kelleher and Pat Harlow at Gravesend CC for confirming the location of a photograph of Grace; Rob Boddie, honorary archivist at Sussex CCC, for help with questions about Grace at Hove; Judy Middleton, for her research on the Royal Brunswick Ground and Nicholas Sharp, for sharing his material about James Lillywhite Jr.; Roger Packham, for information on Lord Sheffield, and Malcolm Lill at Sheffield Park, for information about the cricket ground; Andrew Hignell, archivist at Glamorgan CCC, for information about the history of South Wales CC and its enterprising captain John Lloyd; Chris Goldie, chairman of Richmond CC, for information about the club's early history and Old Deer Park, where W.G. once fell in the water (in a steeplechase); Ron Reiffel of Richmond CC, Victoria, Australia, for making enquiries about George Shoosmith; David Wrede in Melbourne, for pursuing the Shoosmith trail; Laura Appleton in New South Wales, for kindly checking her records of the 1892 game between Lord Sheffield's XI and Nepean District; Mark Grogan of the Ballarat Cricket Association, for information about the Eastern Oval; Alex de la Mar of the Netherlands Cricket Board, for information about Carst Posthuma; Brian Sanderson and Mick Pope of the Yorkshire Cricket Foundation, for information about the price of admission at Bramall Lane in the 1870s; Jerry Rudman, archivist at Uppingham School, for clarifying that Grace played against the town, not the school, in 1871; Stephen Forge, archivist at Oundle School, for information about Bertie Grace's time as a teacher at the school; Chris Ridler of the collectors' website http://www.wisdens.org/ for unravelling the tangled history of the various Lillywhites' cricket companions and almanacks.

I am grateful to the many people at the following cricket clubs who helped with information about fixtures against Grace's United South of England XI. In particular: Murrough

MacDevitt, Leinster CC; Alistair Bolingroke and Ian Gilbertson, Rochdale CC; Howard Smith, Aberdeenshire CC; Alan McKenna, Northumberland CCC; Alan Lockwood, Grantham CC; Ricky Gunn, Southgate CC; Simon Hoadley and Chris Westcott, Eastbourne CC; Peter Hood, Melton Mowbray CC; Stephen Cranston, Inverness CC; Dave Carter, Carlton CC; Tom Law, Bootle CC; Julia Gault, Mitcham CC; Peter Hall, Sefton Park CC.

Thanks, as well, to the following people who answered miscellaneous enquiries or sent stories and information about W.G.: Geoff Barnett of Tring Bowls Club, for his fine article on Grace's bowls career; Tony Quinn, for a story by James Agate about Grace; Mike Hudd, for information about John Dann; David Raymont at the Institute of Actuaries Library for material about John Nicholls; Katie Jarman of St Bartholomew's Hospital Archives; Estela Dukan at the Royal College of Physicians of Edinburgh; Pippa Mole and Nicky Valentine at James Purdey & Sons Ltd; Mark Crudgington of George Gibbs Ltd, Marlborough, for information about guns and shooting; Dr Michael Whitfield, for information about Grace's residence in Victoria Square, Clifton; RoseMary Musgrave of the Clifton and Hotwells Improvement Society; Richard Scantlebury, for valiantly checking old addresses in Bristol; Rick Glanvill, historian of Chelsea F.C., for information about the London Athletic Club's association with Stamford Bridge; Martin Codd of Penningtons Manches LLP law firm, for checking whether its archives contained any of Lord Sheffield's papers; Felix Pryor, for information about letters by Grace sold at auction; John Porter, Group Archivist at Prudential plc, for investigating whether W.G. ever worked for the company as a medical 'referee'; June Ellner at Aberdeen University's library, for confirming Fred Grace's attendance at the medical school; Cooper Harding, curator of Thirsk Museum, for information on a letter by Grace that the museum holds; Craig Mowat of the Royal Navy's press office, for information about Edgar Grace's naval career; Nick Hindley, for explaining the meaning of 'syncope'; Amethyst

Byrne of Grimsby Central Library, for Bob Lincoln's account of W.G.'s faked quadruple-century at Grimsby in 1876.

I am grateful to the Trustees of the Harris (Belmont) Charity for permission to quote from the memoirs, correspondence and other papers of the 4th Lord Harris. I am indebted to the Association of Cricket Statisticians and Historians and the Cricket Archive website (http://cricketarchive.com) for the statistics on W.G. Grace's career.

Every effort has been made to trace copyright holders in all material in this book. The publisher regrets any oversight and will be pleased to rectify any omissions in future editions.

At Little, Brown, Richard Beswick, my editor, saw that there was more to W.G. than 126 first-class centuries and was tremendously supportive throughout the research and writing; and Iain Hunt, my copy editor, improved the prose, spotted the errors, filled the gaps, and in the nicest way, made sure that I kept to deadlines (more or less). Very many thanks to both. Many thanks as well to Stephen Dumughn and Emily Burns for marketing and publicising the book; and to Stephanie Cohen for kindly photocopying several entire drafts.

My agent Jane Turnbull put on her pads for W.G. and scored a triple-century. Very many thanks. My parents Angela Crum Ewing and Brian Tomlinson kindly read my manuscript and corrected many mistakes I would never have seen. This book is dedicated to them. Lastly, my partner Tess Poole and our daughter Hannah put up with the presence of a large bearded cricketer in our house for over two years. I could not have written this book without them.

BIBLIOGRAPHY

ARCHIVES

Belmont House Archive, Throwley, Faversham, Kent
Lord Harris, 'Reminiscences of 4th Lord Harris', Unpublished manuscript, 4 vols, Harris Family Papers

Berkshire Record Office
Correspondence from W.G. Grace to A.T. Barton, 1905, 1906

Bodleian Libraries, University of Oxford
Correspondence and papers of Aubrey Harcourt, 1866–1903, letters from Lord Sheffield, MS. Eng. e. 3803, Folios 78–127

University of Bristol Library, Special Collections
Bristol Medical School, 'Register of Entries, 1845–74', DM.7.27, Winter Session 1868–9

Bristol Record Office
Principal sources:
J.W. Arrowsmith Ltd, 'Production and Sales – Letters from Authors', BRO 40145/P/19–32
J.W. Arrowsmith Ltd, 'Register of Royalties 1884–1918', 16 April 1891, BRO 40145/P/1
Barton Regis Union, Statement of Accounts, 1881, 1882, 1884, 1889, BRO 22936/130
Barton Regis Union, Annual Book, May 1897, BRO 10900
Prospectus of the Bristol Royal Infirmary, Session 1869–70, July 1869, BRO 35893/28/p

'Quot Homines Tot Sententiae, Edward Rudway, Compound Comminuted Fracture of Scull [*sic*], Trephined, Mr Tibbits', BRO 35893/34/a

'Conveyance of Thrissell House and Thrissell Cottage and Thrissell Lodge Numbers 55 and 57 in Stapleton Road, Bristol, 21 December 1887', BRO 40126/D/18-24

'Sale Particulars of Estate of Joseph Hennessy, Deceased', Auction 6 October 1887, BRO 33349

Clifton College Archives, Bristol

Article on school, *Ludgate Monthly*, Vol. VI, No. 1, pp. 61–70, November 1893

Clifton College Fees Ledger, 1888

W.G. Grace Jr., School Record Sheet, 1893

C.B. Grace, School Record Sheet, 1896

Clifton High School Archives, Bristol

'Manuscript Volume of Sports Teams and Fixtures from the 1890s'

Cricket New South Wales Archives

New South Wales Cricket Association Committee Minutes, February/March 1892

Sam Jones, 'Unpublished Memoir of 1882 Australia Tour', 1935

Eltham Cricket Club Collection

Miscellaneous letters by W.G. Grace and other club correspondence

John King, 'Manuscript Article on Grace's Association with Eltham CC'

E. Rhys Jones, funeral address for W.G. Grace, 27 October 1915

Gloucestershire County Cricket Club Archive

Principal sources:

Gloucestershire CCC Committee Minutes Book 1881–93

W.G. Grace to J.W. Arrowsmith, miscellaneous letters, 1891

London Metropolitan Archives

Agreement between W.G. Grace and Crystal Palace Company, 4 August 1906

London County Council, 'Typhoid Fever Epidemic in Maidstone and the London Water Supply', Special Joint Sub-committee of Public Health and Water Committees', 1898, LCC/MIN-107

Marylebone Cricket Club Archive, Lord's
Principal sources:
F.S. Ashley-Cooper Correspondence
R.A. Fitzgerald, 'I Zingari Scrapbook'
R.A. Fitzgerald, 'North America Tour Notebook': 'Notebook of R.A. Fitzgerald XII's Tour of North America in 1872'
R.A. Fitzgerald, 'Quidnunc Cricket Club 1861 Scrapbook'
R.A. Fitzgerald, 'R.A.F.G. Scrapbook'
W.G. Grace, *Cricket* (1891), Manuscript version, 3 vols
Albert E. Lawton, 'My W.G.', unpublished manuscript, 1947
Lord's Grand Stand Company, Accounts, 1867–9
MCC Committee Minutes, 1857–1923
MCC Accounts, Members' Ledger, Subscription Books (miscellaneous dates)

Melbourne Cricket Club Archives
Melbourne CC Committee Minutes, 1872–91 (miscellaneous dates)
Melbourne CC Letter Books, 1876–92 (miscellaneous dates)

National Archives, Kew
Board of Stamps, Legacy Duty Office and Successors, Selected Death Duty Accounts, 'Grace, William Gilbert', National Archives, IR 59/459
Files of Dissolved Companies, Day and Son Ltd, BT/31/1030/1717C
Frank Howard v *George Mowbray Gilbert*, 1852, Cause Number, C14/1331/ H33
Nicholls v *Nicholls*, 1835, UK Public Record Office, NA C 13/1538/23

National Library of Australia
Copy of James Lillywhite's draft contract, September 1873

Nottinghamshire County Cricket Club
James Southerton, 'Diary of 1873–1874 Australia Tour', unpublished manuscript
'Letters of Arthur Shrewsbury', transcribed by Peter Wynne-Thomas

Archives of Ontario, Toronto
Thomas Patteson, *The Reminiscences of T.C. Patteson*, unpublished manuscript

Royal College of General Practitioners Archives, London
'Indenture, Edward Mills Grace, 16 September 1857, Apprentice to Henry Mills Grace of Downend, near Bristol'

Thornbury and District Museum, Gloucestershire
E.M. Grace to Alfred Grace, February 1864 (n.d.), extract in *Thornbury and District Museum Research Group*, Paper No. 125, July 2013

Trinity College, Dublin Archives
Dublin University CC Committee Minutes, 1875, 1876, 1897

Wellcome Library, London
W.G. Grace, letter to Mr Stone, 12 April 1880
Manor House Asylum. Archives and manuscripts MSS.5725

PRIVATE COLLECTIONS

Roger Gibbons Private Collection, Gloucestershire
Principal sources:
'Letters Remembering W.G. Grace Sent by Readers to *Bristol Evening World*, Published 18 November 1933–1 January 1934'
A.D. (Archie) Powell, 'The Life of W.G. Grace', series of articles in *Bristol Evening World*, 13 November 1933–2 January 1934
H.E. Roslyn, 'Looking Back. Forty Years of County Cricket', series of articles in the *Bristol Times and Mirror*, 5 May–25 August 1928
H.E. Roslyn, 'Memories of Gloucestershire Cricket', unpublished manuscript compiled by W.L.A. Coleman from series of thirty-five articles in *Bristol Evening Post,* 9 March–9 November 1939

David Frith Collection, Surrey
Michael Grace Private Collection, Monmouthshire
Rosemary Marryatt Private Collection, Lakes District Museum, New Zealand
Bob Pigeon Private Collection, Cheshire
Rees Family Collection, Victoria, Australia
Gill Watts Private Collection, Gloucestershire

NEWSPAPERS AND JOURNALS

Great Britain (1848–1948)
Aberdeen Journal
Bath Chronicle and Weekly Gazette
Bell's Life in London and Sporting Chronicle
Berrow's Worcester Journal
Birmingham Daily Mail
Bradford Observer

Brighton Gazette
Bristol Mercury
Bristol Mirror
Bury and Norwich Post
Cambridge Independent Press
Chelmsford Chronicle (later, Essex County Chronicle)
Cheltenham Chronicle
The Citizen (Gloucester)
Clifton Chronicle and Directory (Bristol)
Daily News (London)
Daily Telegraph
Derby Daily Telegraph
Derby Mercury
Edinburgh Evening News
The Era (London)
Exeter Flying Post
Exeter and Plymouth Gazette
Evening News (Portsmouth)
Evening Standard (London)
Evening Telegraph (Dundee)
Gloucestershire Chronicle
Gloucestershire Echo
Grantham Journal (Lincolnshire)
The Graphic (London)
Hampshire Telegraph and Naval Chronicle
Hastings and St Leonard's Observer
Huddersfield Chronicle
Jackson's Oxford Journal
Kent and Sussex Courier
Kentish Gazette
Illustrated London News
Lancaster Gazette
Leeds Times
Leicester Chronicle and Leicestershire Mercury
Liverpool Echo
Liverpool Mercury
London Gazette
Manchester Courier and Lancashire General Advertiser
Manchester Evening News and Daily Advertiser
Morning Post (London)
Northampton Mercury
Northern Daily Mail (Hartlepool)

Nottingham Evening Post
Nottinghamshire Guardian
Pall Mall Gazette (London)
Sheffield Daily Telegraph
Sheffield and Rotherham Independent
Shields Daily Gazette (South Shields)
Sporting Life
The Sportsman (London)
Standard (London)
Sunday Post (Lanarkshire)
Sunderland Daily Echo and Shipping Gazette
Sussex Advertiser
Sussex Agricultural Express
Swindon Advertiser and North Wilts Chronicle
Taunton Courier and Western Advertiser
Western Daily Press (Bristol)
Western Morning News (Plymouth)
Whitstable Times and Herne Bay Herald
York Herald
Yorkshire Evening Post
Yorkshire Post and Leeds Intelligencer

Australia (1848–1915)

New South Wales

Australian Town and Country Journal (Sydney)
Barrier Miner (Broken Hill)
The Empire (Sydney)
Evening News (Sydney)
Goulburn Herald and Chronicle
Hay Standard and Advertiser
Illawarra Mercury (Wollongong)
Newcastle Chronicle
The Referee (Sydney)
Sydney Mail
Sydney Morning Herald
Windsor and Richmond Gazette

South Australia

Adelaide Observer
Border Watch (Mount Gambier)
South Australian Register (Adelaide)
Wallaroo Times and Mining Journal

Tasmania
Daily Telegraph (Launceston)
The Mercury (Hobart)

Victoria
The Age (Melbourne)
The Argus (Melbourne)
The Australasian (Melbourne)
Ballarat Star
Bendigo Advertiser
Geelong Advertiser
Portland Guardian and Normanby General Advertiser
South Bourke and Mornington Journal
Telegraph and St Kilda, Prahran and South Yarra Guardian

United States (1872)

The Chronicle (Pennsylvania)
Philadelphia Inquirer

Canada (1872, 1886)

Daily British Colonist
Miscellaneous Canadian newspaper cuttings in R.A. Fitzgerald's 'North
    America Tour Notebook: 'Notebook of R.A. Fitzgerald XII's Tour of
    North America in 1872' (MCC Archive)

ARTICLES

Geoff Barnett, 'Do You Know What W.G. Grace Did for Bowls?' (2011),
    Tring Bowls Club, www.tringbowls.co.uk
Geoffrey Blainey, 'McArthur, David Charteris (1808–87)' in *Australian
    Dictionary of Biography*, Vol. 5 (1974)
Robert Brooke, 'The Tragedy of W. R. Gilbert', *The Cricket Statistician*,
    No. 37 (March 1982), pp. 10–13
Neville Cardus, 'W.G. Grace', in H.J. Massingham and Hugh Massingham
    (eds), *The Great Victorians* (1932)
F. Colebrook, 'A Fine Old Lithographer', *The Modern Lithographer*,
    September 1906, pp. 535–7
Louis R. Cranfield, 'Wardill, Benjamin Johnston (1842–1917)' in
    Australian Dictionary of Biography, Vol. 6 (1976)
Anonymous, Obituary of Alphonso Cumberbatch, *British Medical Journal*,
    6 April 1929, p. 666

'Cumberland, Frederic William', in *Dictionary of Canadian Biography*, Vol. XI, 1881–90

C.J. Duncan, S.R. Duncan and S. Scott, 'The Dynamics of Scarlet Fever Epidemics in England and Wales in the 19th Century', *Epidemiology & Infection*, December 1996, pp. 493–9

R.A. Fitzgerald, 'The English Twelve in America', *John Lillywhite's Cricketers' Companion*, 1873, pp. 25–42

Obituary of Major Charles Butler Grace, *Journal of the Institution of Electrical Engineers*, Vol. 83, Issue 504, December 1938, pp. 891–2

W.G. Grace, 'How to Score', in A.G. Steel and the Hon. R.H. Lyttelton (eds), *The Badminton Library of Sports and Pastimes*, Vol. 10: *Cricket* (1888), pp. 300–14

W.G. Grace, 'Cricket, and How to Excel in it', in G. Andrew Hutchinson (ed.), *Outdoor Games and Recreations: A Popular Encyclopaedia for Boys* (1892), pp. 1–30

W.G. Grace, 'Cricket Clubs: Their Formation and Management', in G. Andrew Hutchinson (ed.), *Outdoor Games and Recreations: A Popular Encylopaedia for Boys* (1892), pp. 34–8

W.G. Grace, 'Australian Notes', *The Cricket Field*, 28 May 1892, pp. 57–8

W.G. Grace, interview in *Strand Magazine*, Vol. X, July–December 1895 (Supplement)

Gideon Haigh, 'The Hero and the Ham', in *Game for Anything: Writings on Cricket* (2004), pp. 93–106.

David Large, 'Bristol and the New Poor Law', *Historical Association*, Bristol Branch, 1995

Derek Lodge, *W.G. Grace: His Record Innings by Innings*, Famous Cricketer Series No. 15, Nottingham, pp. 98–9

Christopher Morris, 'Spofforth, Frederick Robert (1853–1926)', in *Australian Dictionary of Biography,* Vol. 6 (1976)

Sally O'Neill, 'Coppin, George Selth (1819–1906)', in *Australian Dictionary of Biography,* Vol. 3 (1969)

Irving Rosenwater, 'Sir Home Gordon, Bart. An Affectionate Retrospect' (2000)

Irving Rosenwater, 'W.G. Grace, A Leviathan was He', *Journal of the Cricket Society*, Autumn 1997, pp. 1–2

Royal College of Surgeons, *Plarr's Lives of the Fellows Online*, 'Marsh, Frederick Howard (1839–1915)'

Lord George Scott, 'The Cricket of W.G. Grace', *National Review*, Vol. 109, No. 654, August 1937, pp. 229–31

P.J. Toghill, 'Dr W.G. Grace: Medical Truant', *Journal of the Royal College of Physicians*, January–February 1997, pp. 35–9

RADIO BROADCASTS

John Arlott, *The Old Man*, BBC Home Service, 18 July 1948, British Library Sound Archive

Cliff Morgan radio interview with Primrose Worthington, BBC *Sport on Four*, 25 November 1995

WEBSITES

http://cricketarchive.com/
http://www.espncricinfo.com/
http://home.ancestry.co.uk/ (UK Census, Probate, Marriage and Death Records)

BOOKS

David Rayvern Allen (ed.), *Cricket with Grace: An Illustrated Anthology of W.G.* (London, 1990)

John Arlott, *Vintage Summer: 1947* (London, 1967)

F.S. Ashley-Cooper, *Edward Mills Grace* (London, 1916)

Alf Batchelder, *Pavilions in the Park: A History of the Melbourne Cricket Club and its Ground* (Melbourne, 2005)

Clifford Bax, *W.G. Grace* (London, 1952)

Richard Beaumont, *Purdey's: The Guns and the Family* (Newton Abbot, 1984)

Derek Birley, *A Social History of English Cricket* (London, 1999)

Rowland Bowen, *Cricket: A History of its Growth and Development Throughout the World* (London, 1970)

Arthur L. Bowley, *Wages in the United Kingdom in the Nineteenth Century* (Cambridge, 1900)

Donald Bradfield, *The Lansdown Story: A History of Lansdown Cricket Club* (Bath, 1971)

Don Bradman, *Farewell to Cricket* (London, 1950)

Sir Donald Bradman, *The Art of Cricket* (London, 1958)

W. Methven Brownlee, *W.G. Grace* (London, 1887)

Charles E. Cadwalader and others, *Official Report of the International Cricket Fêtes at Philadelphia in 1868 and 1872, including balance sheets* (Philadelphia, 1873)

Richard Cashman, *The 'Demon' Spofforth* (Randwick, New South Wales, 1990)

Arthur Conan Doyle, *Memories and Adventures and Western Wanderings* (London, 1924)

Richard Daft, *Kings of Cricket* (Bristol, 1893)

Anne Digby, *Making a Medical Living: Doctors and Patients in the English Market for Medicine, 1720–1911* (Cambridge, 1994)

R. Dudley Baxter, *National Income: The United Kingdom* (London, 1868)

Sir Robert Ensor, *England 1870–1914* (Oxford, 1936)

R.A. Fitzgerald, writing as 'Quid', *Jerks in from Short Leg* (London, 1866)

R.A. Fitzgerald, *Wickets in the West* (London, 1873)

David Frith, *'Stoddy': England's Finest Sportsman* (first published as *'My Dear Victorious Stod'*, 1970, updated 2015)

C.B. Fry, *Life Worth Living: Some Phases of an Englishman* (London, 1939)

Harry Furniss, E.J. Milliken and E.B.V. Christian, *A Century of Grace* (Bristol, 1896)

A.G. Gardiner, writing as Alpha of the Plough, *Pebbles on the Shore* (London, 1916)

Sir Home Gordon, *Background of Cricket* (London, 1939)

W.G. Grace, *Cricket* (Bristol, 1891)

W.G. Grace, *Cricketing Reminiscences and Personal Recollections* (London, 1899)

W.G. Grace, *The History of a Hundred Centuries* (London, 1895)

W.G. Grace, *W.G.'s Little Book* (London, 1909)

Norman P. Grubb, *C.T. Studd: Cricketer and Pioneer* (London, 1933)

John E. Hall and R. O. McCullough, *Sixty Years of Canadian Cricket* (Toronto, 1895)

Lord Harris, *A Few Short Runs* (London, 1921)

Lord Harris and F.S. Ashley-Cooper, *Lord's and the MCC* (London, 1914)

Chris Harte, *SACA: The History of the South Australian Cricket Association* (Adelaide, 1990)

Lord Hawke, *Recollections and Reminiscences* (London, 1924)

Lord Hawke, Lord Harris and Sir Home Gordon (eds), *The Memorial Biography of Dr W.G. Grace* (London, 1919)

Arthur Haygarth, *Scores and Biographies,* Vol. XII (Marylebone Cricket Club, 1879)

Hermione Hobhouse (ed.), *Survey of London, Vol XLII, Southern Kensington, Kensington Square to Earls Court* (London, 1986)

C.L.R. James, *Beyond a Boundary* (London, 1963)

Gilbert Jessop, *A Cricketer's Log* (London, 1922)

The Rev. A. Emlyn Jones, *Our Parish. Mangotsfield, including Downend. A Brief Account of its Origin and History* (Bristol, 1899)

Peris Jones, *Gentlemen and Players* (Downend Local History Society, 1989)

David Kynaston, *W.G.'s Birthday Party* (London, 1998, republished 2010)

John Lazenby, *The Strangers Who Came Home: The First Australian Cricket Tour of England* (London, 2015)

H.D.G. Leveson Gower, *On and Off the Field* (London, 1953)

Tony Lewis, *Double Century: The Story of MCC and Cricket* (London, 1987)

James Lillywhite's Cricketers' Annual (London, 1872–1900)

John Lillywhite's Cricketers' Companion (London, 1865–85)

Bob Lincoln, *Reminiscences of Sport in Grimsby* (Grimsby, 1912)

Robert Low, *W.G.: A Life of W.G. Grace* (London, 1997)

Alfred Lubbock, *Memories of Eton and Etonians* (London, 1899)

John Major, *More than a Game: The Story of Cricket's Early Years* (London, 2007)

Heber Mardon, *Landmarks in the History of a Bristol Firm 1824–1904* (Bristol, 1918)

Eric Midwinter, *W.G. Grace – His Life and Times* (London, 1981)

G. Munro Smith, *A History of the Bristol Royal Infirmary* (1917)

Roger Packham, *Cricket in the Park: The Life and Times of Lord Sheffield 1832–1909* (London, 1909)

G. Parker, *Schola Medicinae Bristol: Its History, Lecturers and Alumni 1833–1933* (Bristol, 1933)

Grahame Parker, *Gloucestershire Road: A History of Gloucestershire County Cricket Club* (London, 1983)

George Pocock, *A Treatise on the Aeropleustic Art, or Navigation in the Air, By Means of Kites or Buoyant Sails* (London, 1851)

Jack Pollard, *The Formative Years of Australian Cricket 1803–93* (New South Wales, 1987)

Jack Pollard, *The Turbulent Years of Australian Cricket 1893–1917* (New South Wales, 1987)

Arthur Porritt, *The Best I Remember* (London, 1922)

A.G. Powell and S. Canynge Caple, *The Graces: E.M., W.G. and G.F.* (London, 1948)

Thomas Provis, calling himself Richard Smyth, *Report on the Most Extraordinary Trial of Smyth v Smyth and others* (Bristol, 1853)

A.W. Pullin ('Old Ebor'), *Talks with Old English Cricketers* (London, 1900)

A.W. Pullin (ed.), *Alfred Shaw, Cricketer: His Career and Reminiscences* (London, 1902)

The Rev. James Pycroft, *The Cricket Field* (London, fourth edition, 1862)

Simon Rae, *W.G. Grace* (London, 1998)

R.C. Robertson-Glasgow, *46 Not Out* (London, 1954)

Charles Sale, *Korty: The Legend Explained* (Hornchurch, 1986)

Keith A.P. Sandiford, *Cricket and the Victorians* (Aldershot, 1994)

E.H.D. Sewell, *Overthrows* (London, 1946)

Rick Smith and Ron Williams, *W.G. Down Under: Grace in Australia, 1873–74 and 1891–92* (Tasmania, 1994)

Stadacona Club, *Constitution, Rules and Regulations of the Stadacona Club* (Quebec, 1868)

Commander E.P. Statham, R.N., *The Story of the 'Britannia': The Training Ship for Naval Cadets* (London, 1904)

A.A. Thomson, *Cricket My Happiness* (London, 1954)

A.A. Thomson, *The Great Cricketer* (London, 1957)

Kathy Tidman, *Art for the Victorian Household* (www.onlineoriginals.com, 1998)

Anthony Trollope (ed.), *British Sports and Pastimes* (London, 1868)

Major W. Troup, *Sporting Memories. My Life as Gloucestershire County Cricketer, Rugby and Hockey Player, and Member of Indian Police Service* (London, 1924)

Frank Tyson, *The History of the Richmond Cricket Club* (Richmond C.C., 1987)

Wray Vamplew, *Pay Up and Play the Game: Professional Sport in Britain, 1875–1914* (Cambridge, 1988)

F.G. Warne, *Dr W.G. Grace, the King of Cricket* (Bristol, 1899)

P.F. Warner, *Gentlemen v Players 1806–1949* (London, 1950)

J.R. Webber, *The Chronicle of W.G.* (West Bridgford, 1998)

G. Neville Weston, *W.G. Grace, The Great Cricketer: A Statistical Record of His Performances in Minor Cricket* (Wymondham, Norfolk, 1973)

Bernard Whimpress, *W.G. Grace at Kadina: Champion Cricketer or Scoundrel?* (Australia, 1984)

Simon Wilde, *Ranji: A Genius Rich and Strange* (London, 1990)

F.B. 'Freddie' Wilson, *Sporting Pie* (London, 1922)

Robert Winder, *The Little Wonder: The Remarkable History of Wisden* (London, 2013)

Wisden Cricketers' Almanack , 1864–1916

Acton Wye, *Dr W.G. Grace* (London, 1901)

Peter Wynne-Thomas, *'Give me Arthur': A Biography of Arthur Shrewsbury* (London, 1985)

INDEX